The Register of
The Fife Fallen in the Great War
1914–1919
Volume I

Kirkcaldy and Dysart Fallen

D1438579

Edüard Klak and Janet Klak

Additional material by
Scott Birrell
Sheila Campbell
Ella Dickson
Stuart Matthewson

Front cover: *Kirkcaldy War Memorial*
Rear cover: *Dysart War Memorial*

© E. Klak 2002

ISBN 0 9544946 0 1

Financed by
Awards for All

Published by
Fife Military History Society
23 Station Road
Thornton
Fife KY1 4AX
Tel: 01592 775844

Printed by
Cordfall Ltd
G21 2QA

Introduction

The Register of the Great War Fallen of Fife. Volume 1: Kirkcaldy and Dysart Fallen, is the first in a series of volumes recording the names of those men and women of Fife who gave their lives in the First World War. Each volume will contain the names on war memorials in the towns and villages in Fife.

Our special thanks go to Scott Birrell and Ella Dickson for their work on this project, and to Stuart Matthewson for providing access to his archives.

The excellent resources of the Local Studies Department of the Central Library, Kirkcaldy provided many of the sources used in the compilation of this book. The compilers wish to thank Sheila Campbell for her unstinting encouragement and support.

The compilers especially wish to thank Mr. Tom Smyth, Regimental Archivist, The Black Watch Museum, Balhousie Castle, Perth who has patiently provided much valued help and information during the years of this project.

Mr. Roger Strugnell, Archivist for Messrs Forbo-Nairn & Co. Ltd., Kirkcaldy, provided a copy of *Michael Nairn & Coy Ltd.'s Roll of Honour*. This is a list of all employees of the company who served during the Great War.

We are particularly indebted to Mr. Tom Manson and Mr. A.B. Wehrle, representatives of two local families, who provided us with much detailed information about their relatives who were killed in action.

The compilers also acknowledge the help of those, too numerous to mention individually, who have provided information for the book.

Finally, Fife Military History Society is grateful for the financial support and patience of **Awards for All** who have made the publication of this volume possible.

How to use this book

This book lists the men of Kirkcaldy and Dysart who gave their lives in the First World War and whose names appear on the Kirkcaldy and Dysart civic war memorials. Many who served in that war do not, for a variety of reasons, appear on any official war memorials. The details of these servicemen, who have been identified as having links with Fife, will appear in the final volume of the series.

The aim of the book is to show researchers sources of information available on each fallen serviceman, not to provide a comprehensive biography. Basic information of name, rank, number, regiment, date of death and place of burial or commemoration are provided, where known, in order to identify the individual. This is followed by a list of sources. The user should always refer to the original sources listed in each entry, where more information will be found.

Newspaper entries for individuals are very often inaccurate. *Soldiers Died in the Great War* and the *Commonwealth War Graves Commission* also have some factual errors. Wherever possible information has been verified from more than one source. If it has not proved feasible to identify the correct information, conflicting details may be cited. Researchers should look at the sources given and make their own decision as to which is the correct data.

The initial newspaper entry for an individual is not necessarily the first time that person has been mentioned in the newspaper. Due to lack of space, we have had to limit entries to intimation of death and subsequent information. Information on an individual will not appear in this publication until after death has been confirmed.

Sources include *In Memoriam* entries up to and including 1919. Entries may continue after this date, but, with few exceptions, newspaper sources are not cited after this date.

Names: Many people were wrongly named in the newspapers and some are also wrongly cited on war memorials. Names are given as they appear on the War Memorial, with reference made to variations of spelling etc in *Further Information*.

In a number of cases, spelling has not been consistent throughout the sources cited. Mc and Mac were used indiscriminately, as was Millar/Miller. The researcher should check under all variations of spelling of a name.

Regiments and Service Numbers: During the period of the Great War, the British Army continued to use the regimental numbering system. In effect, every regiment had its own numbers. Consequently, it is possible that many of the fallen had the same regimental number. Army numbers were only introduced much later.

For a variety of reasons there were frequent transfers of men between regiments, with corresponding changes of regimental number. Where these changes have been verified they have been included.

Addresses: Addresses should be taken as a guide only. In some database entries more than one address has been given for an individual. The addresses given may be the address of the serviceman at the time of his death, the address of his next of kin at the time of his death, the address of his next of kin at the time the Commonwealth War Graves registers were compiled or an address from an *In Memoriam* entry. When house number varies, all variations are shown.

Cause of Death: Missing in Action (MIA), Killed in Action (KIA), Died of Wounds (DOW) are self-explanatory. *Died* usually means died as a result of an accident, illness or disease. *Died at Home* means died in the United Kingdom, not necessarily at the serviceman's home address.

Place of Death: Place of death is assumed to be the country in which the fallen serviceman is commemorated. Only in cases where there is a discrepancy between the reported theatre of war and the commemoration of the death will the entry under *Further Information* include the country of death.

Date of Death: Dates of death have not always been the same in all sources. Where possible the date accepted is that given in more than one source.

Ages: Ages have not always been compatible in all sources. Where possible the age given has been verified in more than one source.

Memorial: This is usually either a gravestone in a local cemetery or churchyard or inclusion on a roll of honour in a local church, school or workplace. (Photo) after the location of a gravestone indicates the compilers have a photograph of the gravestone. Contact them for further details.

‡ on an entry indicates the compilers have a photograph of the Commonwealth War Grave for that individual serviceman. Contact them for further information.

War Memorials: Individuals may be commemorated on more than one war memorial.

Relationships: Where members of the same family have been killed, the relationship is given in *Further Information*. Details will only be included if the relationship has been cited in a source. No assumption of relationship will be made based on address and surname.

Abbreviations: Please refer to the list of abbreviations on the following page.

Finally, this is not an exhaustive list of sources of information on First World War casualties for Fife. New sources appear all the time and some older sources are now out of print. Sadly, some memorials have disappeared as factories close down, schools and churches are demolished and so on. For example, we have been unable to obtain some regimental histories and rolls of honour. Nor have we included details of records held in the Public Record Office.

Most of the sources listed may be found in the Local Studies Department of Central Library, War Memorial Grounds, Kirkcaldy. If travelling from a distance to consult these sources, it is advisable to telephone in advance and book a microfilm reader or computer. The telephone number of the Reading Room of Kirkcaldy Central Library is 01592 412879.

Surname[1] Forenames[2] Decoration[3] Rank[4]

Number[5] Unit[6]

Further information[7] Date died[8] Age[9]

Address[10]

Local Memorials[11]

War Memorial[12]

Commonwealth War Graves Commission

Memorial[13] Commonwealth War Graves

photograph[14] *Soldiers Died*[15]

Sources[16]

Dunsire[1], Robert Anderson[2], VC[3]: Lance Corporal[4] (18274[5] Royal Scots [13th][6]); . Brother-in-law of Ralph Pitt[7]; DOW 30.01.16[8], 24 years[9]; 107/210 Denbeath, Methil/Commercial Street, Kirkcaldy[10]; E.U. Congregational Church Memorial Plaque. Buckhaven Higher Grade School War Memorial[11]; Kirkcaldy War Memorial. Methil War Memorial[12]; Mazingarbe Communal Cemetery, Pas de Calais, France. Grave 18[13]; ‡[14]; *Soldiers Died* Part 6[15]; *FA* 20.11.15; *FA* 27.11.15 (2 entries); *FA* 04.12.15; *FA* 11.12.15; *FA* 08.01.16; *FA* 15.01.16; *FA* 22.01.16; *FA* 12.02.16 (2 entries); *FFP* 12.02.16; *FA* (BMD) 19.02.16; *FFP* 05.08.16; *FA* 26.08.16; *FFP* 02.09.16; *FFP* 09.09.16; *FFP* 16.09.16; *FA* 30.09.16; *FA* (Service List) 04.11.16; *FA* (Service List) 16.12.16; *FA* (BMD) 02.03.17; *FA* (BMD) 02.02.18; *FA* (FRoH) 16.11.18; *FA* 21.12.18; *FFP* (BMD) 25.01.19[16]

Abbreviations

A & S Hldrs	Argyll & Sutherland Highlanders
AIF	Australian Imperial Forces
AM	Air Mechanic
Amb	Ambulance
Att'd	Attached
Batt'y	Battery
Bde	Brigade
BMD	Births, Marriages, Deaths & In Memoriam column in local newspapers
Bn	Battalion
BQMS	Battalion Quarter Master Sergeant
CasList	Casualty List as printed in local newspapers
CBoR	Canadian Books of Remembrance
CCS	Casualty Clearing Station
CEF	Canadian Expeditionary Forces
Coy	Company
CQMS	Company Quarter Master Sergeant
CSM	Company Sergeant Major
CWGC	Commonwealth War Graves Commission. Taken either from printed registers or the CWGC web site
DCM	Distinguished Conduct Medal
Div	Division
DOW	Died of wounds
DSO	Distinguished Service Order
F & F Yeo	Fife and Forfar Yeomanry
FA	*Fifeshire Advertiser*
FFP	*Fife Free Press*
FGCM	Field General Court Martial
Fld	Field
FRoH	Final Roll of Honour
HCB	Highland Cyclist Battalion
Hldrs	Highlanders
HLI	Highland Light Infantry
KHS	Kirkcaldy High School
KIA	Killed in Action
KOSB	Kings Own Scottish Borderers
Mem	Memorial
MIA	Missing in Action
MID	Mentioned in Despatches
MM	Military Medal
MSM	Meritorious Service Medal
MT	Motor Transport
NZEF	New Zealand Expeditionary Forces
PoW	Prisoner of War
PPCLI	Princess Patricia's Canadian Light Infantry
RAMC	Royal Army Medical Corps
RASC	Royal Army Service Corps
RAVC	Royal Army Veterinary Corps
RDC	Royal Defence Corps
Regt	Regiment
Res	Reserve
RFA	Royal Field Artillery
RGA	Royal Garrison Artillery
RNAS	Royal Naval Air Service
RM	Royal Marine
RND	Royal Naval Division
RNVR	Royal Naval Volunteer Reserve
RoH	Roll of Honour
SAEF	South African Expeditionary Forces
SRO	Scottish Record Office
Sp	Special
StAC	*St Andrews Citizen*
USEF	United States Expeditionary Force
VC	Victoria Cross

Useful Web Sites

www.awm.gov.au	Australian War Memorial
www.archives.ca	Canadian Archive
www.collections.ic.gc.ca/books	Canadian Books of Remembrance
www.cwgc.org.uk	Commonwealth War Graves Commission
www.iwm.org.uk	Imperial War Museum
www.nas.gov.uk	National Archive of Scotland
www.pro.gov.uk	Public Record office

List of Sources

Source	Abbreviation
Records held in the Scottish Record Office	Army Returns
www.awm.gov.au	Australian War Memorial web site
Canadian Books of Remembrance	*CBoR*
Official List of Casualties to the Members of the Canadian Expeditionary Force (Issued with Militia Orders). Government Printing Bureau, Ottawa	CEF Official List of Casualties
Blindfold and Alone: British Military Executions in the Great War. Cathryn Corns & John Hughes-Wilson. ISBN 0304353973	Corns & Hughes-Wilson
Court Journal	Newspaper
Vol. 1: Officers Who Died in the Service of the British, Indian and East African Regiments and Corps 1914-1919. S.D. & D.B. Jarvis. ISBN 1873058268	*Cross of Sacrifice* (5 vols)
Vol. 2: Officers Who Died in the Service of the Royal Navy, Royal Naval Reserve, Royal Naval Volunteer Reserve, Royal Marines, Royal Naval Air Service and Royal Air Force 1914-1919. S.D. & D.B. Jarvis. ISBN 1873058314	
Vol. 3: Officers Who Died in the Service of British Commonwealth and Colonial Navies, Regiments and Corps and Air Forces 1914–1919. S.D & D.B. Jarvis. ISBN 1873058365	
Vol. 4: Non-Commissioned Officers, Men and Women of the United Kingdom, Commonwealth and Empire Who Died in the Service of the Royal Navy, Royal Marines, Royal Naval Air Service, Royal Flying Corps and the Royal Air Force 1914–1921 Including the Commonwealth Navies and Air Forces. S.D. & D.B. Jarvis. ISBN 1897632975	
Vol. 5: The Officers, Men and Women of the Merchant Navy and Mercantile Fleet Auxiliary 1914–1919. S.D. & D.B. Jarvis. ISBN 1897632037	
Commonwealth War Graves Commission Registers & www.cwgc.org.uk	CWGC
Daily Telegraph – newspaper	
Despatch – newspaper	
The Dinna Forget Book of the 7th Black Watch. Pictorial supplement to the *Dundee Advertiser.* 1917	*Dinna Forget*
Dundee Advertiser – newspaper	
Evening News – newspaper	
Fifeshire Advertiser – newspaper	*FA*
Fife Free Press – newspaper	*FFP*
The Jutland Roll of Honour. Compiled from Official Admiralty Sources in the Public Record Office by Stuart Tamblin. 1998 Electronic format	*Jutland RoH*

Source	Abbreviation
Memorial Parchment given to families of those killed in the Great War	Kirkcaldy Council Memorial Scroll
Kirkcaldy War Memorial. Souvenir of the Opening Ceremony, Saturday, 27th June, 1925. Supplement to the *Fifeshire Advertiser*, Saturday, 13th June, 1925	Kirkcaldy War Memorial
The Sixth Gordons in France & Flanders (with the 7th and 51st Divisions). Captain D. MacKenzie. 1921	MacKenzie
The 5th Battalion The Cameronians (Scottish Rifles) T.F. 1914–1919. Edited by Major David Martin. 1936	Martin
Muster Roll of the Manse 1914–1919. Final edition. [Earlier editions entitled Muster Roll of the Sons of the Manse]	MRoM
The Great War, 1914–1918. New Zealand Expeditionary Force Roll of Honour. 1999. First published 1923	NZEF RoH
The Fife and Forfar Yeomanry and 14th (F. & F. Yeo) Battn. R. H. 1914–1919. Major D. D. Ogilvie. 1921	Ogilvie
A Pictorial History of Fife Constabulary. 1999	*Pictorial History of Fife Constabulary*
Shot at Dawn:Executions in World War One by authority of the British Army Act. New & revised edition. Julian Putkowski and Julian Sykes. ISBN 0850522951	Putkowski & Sykes
The Roll of Honour Royal Flying Corps and Royal Air Force for the Great War 1914–1918. H. J. Williamson. ISBN 1897632207	RFC/RAF RoH
With Full and Grateful Hearts: A Register of Royal Marine Deaths 1914–1919. Royal Marines Historical Society. 1991	RMD
Roll of Honour for Dunnikier Colliery, Kirkcaldy	RoH Dunnikier Colliery
Scotsman – newspaper	
Soldiers Died in the Great War 1914–18 [In 80 parts]. HMSO 1921. Now issued on cd-rom	*Soldiers Died*
National Archives of Scotland, HM General Register House, Edinburgh	SRO
St Andrews Citizen – newspaper	*StAC*
Courts Martial & Executions WO71 and WO93. Stuart Tamblin, 1998. Electronic format	Tamblin
The 2nd Battalion Highland Light Infantry in the Great War. Major A.D. Telfer-Smollett et al. n.d.	Telfer-Smollett
History of the 16th Battalion (The Canadian Scottish) Canadian Expeditionary Force in the Great War, 1914–1919. H.M. Urquhart. 1932	Urquhart
Kirkcaldy and District War Album 1914–15; Kirkcaldy and District War Album 1915; Kirkcaldy and District War Album 1915–16. Published by the *Fifeshire Advertiser*, Kirkcaldy	War Album
A History of the Black Watch [Royal Highlanders] in the Great War 1914–1918. 3 vols. Edited by Major-General A. G. Wauchope, C.B. 1925	Wauchope

Church and School Memorials

The following lists the locations of war memorials. Most of the church war memorials are in buildings closed except for services. Please contact the local minister or session clerk before travelling to view the memorial.

To view school war memorials, please contact the head teacher of the school for permission to enter the school before travelling to view the memorial.

Abbotshall Parish Church Memorial Plaque, Abbotshall Parish Church, Abbotshall Road, Kirkcaldy

Barony Church Plaque, Barony Church, Normand Road, Dysart. This plaque is on an exterior wall.

Bethelfield Church Plaque, Linktown Church, Nicol Street, Kirkcaldy

Dunnikier Church Roll of Honour, Pathhead Parish Church, Harriet Street, Kirkcaldy

E. U. Congregational Church Memorial Plaque, E.U. Congregational Church, Mid Street, Kirkcaldy

Forth RGA Plaque, Territorial Hall, Hunter Street, Kirkcaldy. This plaque is on an exterior wall.

Gallatown Church Roll of Honour, Viewforth Parish Church, Viewforth Street, Kirkcaldy

Invertiel Parish Church Memorial Tablet, Linktown Church, Nicol Street, Kirkcaldy

Kirkcaldy High School War Memorial, Kirkcaldy High School, Dunnikier Way, Kirkcaldy

Old Parish Church Memorial Panels, Old Parish Church, Kirk Wynd, Kirkcaldy

Pathhead Baptist Church War Memorial, Pathhead Baptist Church, Anderson Street, Kirkcaldy

Pathhead Parish Church Memorial Plaques and Windows, Pathhead Parish Church, Harriet Street, Kirkcaldy

Police Memorial Plaque, Police Station, St Brycedale Avenue, Kirkcaldy

Raith Church Memorial Plaque, Linktown Church, Nicol Street, Kirkcaldy

Sinclairtown Parish Church War Memorial Chair, Viewforth Parish Church, Viewforth Street, Kirkcaldy

St Andrew's Church Memorial Plaque, St Andrew's Parish Church, Victoria Road, Kirkcaldy

St Brycedale Church Plaque, St Bryce Church, St Brycedale Avenue, Kirkcaldy

St Columba's Church Memorial Plaque, St Peter's Church, Townsend Place, Kirkcaldy

St Michael's Church Memorial Plaque, St Peter's Church, Townsend Place, Kirkcaldy

St Peter's Church Memorial Plaque, St Peter's Church, Townsend Place, Kirkcaldy

St Serf's Church Lectern and Memorial Plaque, St Serf's Church, Dysart

Union Church Plaque, Bennochy Cemetery, Kirkcaldy

West End Congregational Church Memorial Plaque, West End Congregational Church, Whytehouse Avenue, Kirkcaldy

Whytescauseway Baptist Church Memorial Plaque, Whytescauseway, Kirkcaldy

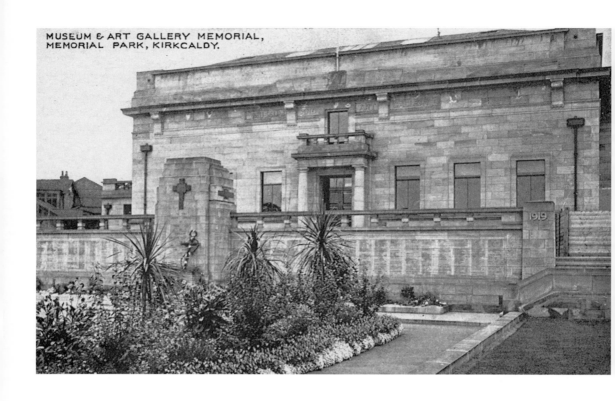

MUSEUM & ART GALLERY MEMORIAL,
MEMORIAL PARK, KIRKCALDY.

Lance Corporal John F. **Affleck** went to
France in February 1915 and was killed
in action in April 1915, aged 26. In his brief
time in France he had some hairsbreadth
escapes, the worst being when a bullet
passed through his cap badge.

Kirkcaldy War Memorial

Adams, William Henry: Private (44093 KOSB [7/8th] "D" Coy. Formerly 2256 HCB); Brother-in-law of Thomas Ferguson and William Thain; KIA, 19.08.17, 36 years; 15 Hill Street, Kirkcaldy; Tyne Cot Memorial, Zonnebeke, West Vlaanderen, Belgium. Panels 66-68; Kirkcaldy War Memorial; *Soldiers Died* Part 30; *FA* 15.09.17; *FA* (BMD) 15.09.17; *FFP* 15.09.17; *FFP* (BMD) 15.09.17; *FFP* (CasList) 29.09.17; *FA* 13.10.17; *FFP* (RoH) 13.10.17; *FA* 26.04.19

Adamson, Alfred James: Signaller (S/20444 A & S Hldrs [1/5th]); Lost at sea from HMT *Aragon*; 30.12.17, 21 years; Myrtle Cottage, 118 Dunnikier Road, Kirkcaldy; St Peter's Church Memorial Plaque; Chatby Memorial, Egypt; Kirkcaldy War Memorial; *FA* 09.02.18; *Soldiers Died* Part 70; *FA* 02.02.18; *FFP* (RoH) 02.02.18; *FFP* (BMD) 02.02.18; *FA* 09.02.18 (2 entries); *FA* (BMD) 09.02.18; *FA* (RoH) 16.02.18; *FFP* (RoH) 16.02.18; *FA* (FRoH) 07.12.18; *FFP* (BMD) 28.12.18

Adamson, James Stark: Private (S/17688 Cameron Hldrs [7th]); Shot for Cowardice by Sentence FGCM, Arras. Last man shot for this offence in Great War; 23.11.17, 30 years; 234 Links Street, Kirkcaldy; St Nicolas British Cemetery, Arras, Pas de Calais, France. Grave II.C.18; Kirkcaldy War Memorial; *FA* 16.09.16; *FA* 08.12.17; *Soldiers Died* Part 66; *FA* 08.12.17; *FA* (BMD) 08.12.17; *FA* (RoH) 15.12.17; *FFP* 15.12.17; *FFP* (RoH) 15.12.17; *FFP* (BMD) 23.11.18 (3 entries); *FA* (FRoH) 07.12.18; Putkowski & Sykes p221; Corns & Hughes-Wilson; SRO - Vol 116/AF p265; Tamblin

Adamson, Thomas: Private (44077 KOSB [7/8th]. Formerly 2078 HCB); KIA, 29.05.18, 33 years; 16 Patterson Street, Kirkcaldy; Pathhead Parish Church Memorial Plaques & Windows; Arras Memorial, Pas de Calais, France. Bay 6; Kirkcaldy War Memorial; *Soldiers Died* Part 30; *FFP* (CasList) 22.06.18; *FFP* (BMD) 22.06.18; *FA* (RoH) 13.07.18; *FA* (FRoH) 14.12.18; *FFP* 21.06.24

Affleck, John F.: Lance Corporal (69 A & S Hldrs [1st]); KIA, 24.04.15, 26 years; 51 Overton Road, Kirkcaldy; Ypres (Menin Gate) Memorial, Ieper, West Vlaanderen, Belgium. Panels 42 & 44; Kirkcaldy War Memorial; *Soldiers Died* Part 70; War Album 15; *FA* 29.05.15; *FFP* (CasList) 05.06.15; *FFP* 05.08.16 Roll of the Brave; *FA* (FRoH) 16.11.18

Aitken, James: Private (7661 Cameron Hldrs [2nd]); DOW whilst a PoW at Baghtche. Cousin of Driver James Smith; 03.09.16; 6 Hill Street, Kirkcaldy; Baghdad (North Gate) War Cemetery, Iraq. Grave XXI.A.8; Kirkcaldy War Memorial; *FA* 14.08.15; *FA* 28.04.17; *Soldiers Died* Part 66; *FA* 17.06.16; *FA* 28.04.17; *FFP* 05.05.17; *FA* (RoH) 19.05.17; *FFP* (RoH) 19.05.17; *FFP* (RoH) 06.04.18; *FA* 13.04.18; *FA* (FRoH) 30.11.18

Aitken, William Neil: Private (351676 Royal Scots [9th]); Brother-in-law of George F. Marshall; MIA, 23.04.17; 3/9 Whytehouse Mansions, Kirkcaldy; Roeux British Cemetery, Pas de Calais, France. Grave D.21; Kirkcaldy War Memorial; *Soldiers Died* Part 6; *FA* 02.06.17; *FFP* 09.06.17; *FFP* 16.06.17; *FFP* (BMD) 16.06.17; *FFP* (CasList) 30.06.17; *FA* 14.07.17; *FFP* 14.07.17; *FA* 06.10.17; *FFP* 06.10.17; *FFP* (BMD) 28.09.18; *FA* (FRoH) 07.12.18

Alexander, David: Lance Corporal (13115 KOSB [7th] "D" Coy, 13th Platoon); Brother of George Alexander & James Alexander & brother-in-law of Robert Manson; KIA, 11.05.16, 18 years; 229 St Clair Street, Kirkcaldy; Vermelles British Cemetery, Pas de Calais, France. Grave IV.E.15; Kirkcaldy War Memorial; *FA* 18.03.16; *FA* 27.05.16; *Soldiers Died* Part 30; *FA* 05.06.15; *FA* 27.05.16; *FA* (BMD) 27.05.16; *FFP* 27.05.16; *FA* (RoH) 17.06.16; *FFP* (RoH) 17.06.16; *FA* 15.07.16; *FFP* 05.08.16 Roll of the Brave; *FA* (Service List) 25.11.16; *FA* (Service List) 02.12.16; *FA* (BMD) 12.05.17; *FFP* 24.08.18; *FA* 31.08.18; *FA* (FRoH) 23.11.18; Mr T. Manson

Alexander, George: Sergeant (3/2689 Black Watch [1st]); Brother of David Alexander & James Alexander & brother-in-law of Robert Manson; MIA Ypres, 29.10.14, 37 years; 2 Rossend Terrace, Nether Street, Kirkcaldy; Ypres (Menin Gate) Memorial, Ieper, West Vlaanderen, Belgium. Panel 37; Kirkcaldy War Memorial; War Album 14/15; *FA* 18.03.16; *Soldiers Died* Part 46; War Album 14/15; *FA* 28.11.14; *Dundee Advertiser* 06.02.15; *FA* 13.02.15; *FFP* 13.02.15; *FA* (CasList) 20.02.15; *FA* 05.06.15; *FA* 12.06.15; *FFP* 22.01.16; *FA* 29.01.16 (2 entries); *Scotsman* 29.01.16; *FA* 27.05.16; *FFP* 27.05.16; *FA* 15.07.16; *FFP* 05.08.16 Roll of the Brave; *FFP* (BMD) 21.10.16; *FA* (Service List) 30.12.16; *FA* 31.08.18; *FA* (FRoH) 16.11.18; RoH Dunnikier Colliery; Wauchope Vol 1; Mr. T. Manson

Alexander, James: Sapper (446937 Royal Engineers [215th AT Coy]); Brother of William Alexander & Samuel Alexander; KIA, 30.03.18; 26 Lorne Street, Kirkcaldy; Gallatown Church Roll of Honour; Pozieres Memorial, Somme, France. Panels 10-13; Kirkcaldy War Memorial; *FFP* 27.04.18; *Soldiers Died* Part 4; *FFP* (RoH) 27.04.18; *FFP* (BMD) 27.04.18; *FA* (RoH) 18.05.18; *FFP* (RoH) 18.05.18; *FA* (FRoH) 14.12.18

Alexander, James Philp: Private (628950; CEF; Canadian Infantry [29th] 2nd Div 6th Bde. [British Columbia Regt] [Tobin's Tigers]); Brother of George Alexander & David Alexander & brother-in-law of Robert Manson; KIA, 09.08.18, 36 years; 208 Links Street, Kirkcaldy; St Columba's Church Memorial Plaque; Rosieres Communal Cemetery Extension, Somme, France. Grave I.A.5; Kirkcaldy War Memorial; *FA* 18.03.16; *CBoR* Page 358; *FA* 05.06.15; *FFP* 24.08.18; *FFP* (BMD) 24.08.18; *FA* 31.08.18; *FA* (BMD) 31.08.18; *FA* (RoH) 14.09.18; *FFP* (RoH) 14.09.18; *FA* (FRoH) 14.12.18; Mr. T. Manson

Alexander, Samuel: Private (44070 KOSB [2nd]. Formerly 1940 HCB); Brother of James Alexander & William Alexander. In *FA* Service List as Anderson; KIA, 03.09.16, 27 years; 113 Commercial Street, Kirkcaldy; Gallatown Church Roll of Honour; Thiepval Memorial, Somme, France. Pier & Face 4A & 4D; Kirkcaldy War Memorial; *Soldiers Died* Part 30; *FA* 14.10.16; *FA* (RoH) 14.10.16; *FFP* 14.10.16; *FFP* (RoH) 14.10.16; *FFP* (BMD) 14.10.16; *FFP* (CasList) 28.10.16; *FA* (Service List) 04.11.16; *FA* (Service List) 16.12.16; *FA* 30.12.16; *FFP* 30.12.16; *FFP* (RoH) 30.12.16; *FFP* (BMD) 01.09.17; *FFP* (RoH) 27.04.18; *FFP* (BMD) 31.08.18; *FA* (FRoH) 23.11.18

Alexander, Thomas: Private; RDC; Not identified on CWGC web site; Kirkcaldy War Memorial

Alexander, William: Lance Corporal (219123; CEF; Canadian Infantry [78th] 4th Div 12th Bde. [Manitoba Regt]); Brother of James Alexander & Samuel Alexander; KIA, 19.11.16, 31 years; 26 Lorne Street, Kirkcaldy; Gallatown Church Roll of Honour; Vimy Memorial, Pas de Calais, France; Kirkcaldy War Memorial; *CBoR* Page 46; *FA* 30.12.16; *FFP* 30.12.16; *FA* (RoH) 13.01.17; *FFP* (RoH) 13.01.17; *FFP* (BMD) 17.11.17; *FFP* (RoH) 27.04.18; *FA* (FRoH) 30.11.18

Allan, Thomas: Sergeant (72840 Royal Fusiliers [City of London Regt] [7th]. Formerly 3470 RASC); KIA, 05.04.18, 28 years; 2 Watt Street, Dysart/Duddingston, Edinburgh; Arras Memorial, Pas de Calais, France. Bay 3; Kirkcaldy War Memorial; *Soldiers Died* Part 12; *FA* 22.06.18; *FA* 12.07.19; *FA* (BMD) 12.07.19; *FA* 26.07.19

Allan, William Morton: Private (20318 Cheshire Regt [15th] Bantam Bn); DOW, 25.07.16, 21 years; 9 Maryhall Street, Kirkcaldy; Corbie Communal Cemetery Extension, Somme, France. Grave 1.F.30; Kirkcaldy War Memorial; *FA* 19.08.16; *FFP* 19.08.16; *Soldiers Died* Part 27; *FA* 12.08.16; *FA* (BMD) 12.08.16; *FFP* 12.08.16; *FFP* (BMD) 12.08.16; *FA* (BMD) 19.08.16; *FFP* 19.08.16; *FA* 26.08.16; *FFP* (CasList) 09.09.16; *FA* (RoH) 16.09.16; *FFP* (RoH) 16.09.16; *FA* (Service List) 25.11.16; *FFP* (RoH) 30.12.16; *FFP* (BMD) 27.07.18; *FA* (FRoH) 23.11.18

Allan, William Smart: Private (1631 A & S Hldrs [12th]); In *Soldiers Died* Part 70 as George Allan; KIA Balkans, 10.12.16, 32 years; 66 Overton Road, Kirkcaldy; Karasouli Military Cemetery, Greece. Grave F.1393; Kirkcaldy War Memorial; *Soldiers Died* Part 70; *FA* 20.01.17 (2 entries); *FFP* 20.01.17; *FA* (RoH) 17.02.17; *FFP* (RoH) 17.02.17; *FA* (FRoH) 30.11.18

Anderson, Alexander: Private (22783 Royal Scots [12th]); KIA, 04.07.16, 20 years; 5 Buchanan Street/241 Overton Road, Kirkcaldy; Thiepval Memorial, Somme, France. Pier & Face 6D & 7D; Kirkcaldy War Memorial; *Soldiers Died* Part 6; *FFP* 12.08.16; *FA* (CasList) 19.08.16; *FFP* 19.08.16; *FFP* (CasList) 02.09.16; *FA* (RoH) 16.09.16; *FFP* (RoH) 16.09.16; *FA* (Service List) 04.11.16; *FA* (Service List) 30.12.16; *FFP* (RoH) 30.12.16; *FA* (FRoH) 23.11.18

Anderson, Andrew: Private (S/40528 Black Watch [8th] "D" Coy); KIA, 20.10.16, 36 years; 7 Den Road, Kirkcaldy; Old Parish Church Memorial Panel; Thiepval Memorial, Somme, France. Pier & Face 10A; Kirkcaldy War Memorial; *FFP* 30.12.16; *Soldiers Died* Part 46; *FFP* 28.10.16; *FA* 11.11.16; *FFP* 11.11.16; *FFP* (BMD) 11.11.16; *FA* (RoH) 18.11.16; *FA* (BMD) 18.11.16; *FFP* (RoH) 18.11.16; *FA* (CasList) 25.11.16; *FFP* (CasList) 25.11.16; *FFP* (RoH) 30.12.16; *FFP* (BMD) 20.10.17; *FA* (FRoH) 23.11.18; Wauchope Vol 3

Anderson, David: Private (S/11316 Seaforth Hldrs [1st]); Died Persian Gulf, 08.09.16, 17 years; Cowstrandburn, Carnock; Amara War Cemetery, Iraq. Grave III.B.9; Kirkcaldy War Memorial; *Soldiers Died* Part 64; *FFP* (CasList) 14.10.16

Anderson, George: Private (241890 Royal Warwickshire Regt [2/6th]. Formerly 1855 HCB); MIA, 10.09.16, 21 years; 74 Alexandra Street, Kirkcaldy; Loos Memorial, Pas de Calais, France. Panels 22-25; Kirkcaldy War Memorial; *FA* 30.09.16; *Soldiers Died* Part 11; *FA* 23.09.16; *FA* (RoH) 14.10.16; *FFP* (RoH) 14.10.16; *FFP* (RoH) 18.11.16; *FA* (Service List) 25.11.16; *FFP* (RoH) 30.12.16; *FA* 02.06.17; *FFP* 02.06.17; *FFP* (BMD) 02.06.17; *FA* 09.06.17; *FA* (BMD) 09.06.17; *FA* (RoH) 16.06.17; *FFP* (RoH) 16.06.17; *FFP* (BMD) 15.09.17; *FFP* (BMD) 14.09.18; *FA* (FRoH) 23.11.18; *FA* (FRoH) 30.11.18

Anderson, James: Private (791 Black Watch [2nd]); KIA Battle of Neuve Chapelle, 11.03.15, 28 years; 9 Fourth Street, Bowhill; Le Touret Memorial, Pas de Calais, France. Panels 24-26; Kirkcaldy War Memorial. Dysart War Memorial. Auchterderran War Memorial; *Soldiers Died* Part 46; *FA* 27.03.15; *FA* 03.04.15; Wauchope Vol 1

Anderson, James: Sapper (45161 Royal Engineers [89th Fld Coy]); KIA, 22.03.17, 32 years; 166 Overton Road, Kirkcaldy; Gravestone in Dysart Cemetery; Beaurains Road Cemetery, Beaurains, Pas de Calais, France. Grave C.19; Kirkcaldy War Memorial; *Soldiers Died* Part 4; *FA* 31.03.17; *FFP* 31.03.17; *FA* (RoH) 14.04.17; *FFP* (BMD) 23.03.18; *FA* (FRoH) 30.11.18; RoH Dunnikier Colliery

Anderson, John: Corporal (350329 Black Watch [1/7th]. Formerly 1382 HCB)*;* KIA Cambrai, 24.10.18, 38 years; 147 Ramsay Road, Kirkcaldy; Raith Church Memorial Plaque; Thiant Communal Cemetery, Nord, France. Grave A.8; Kirkcaldy War Memorial; *FFP* 07.12.18; *FFP* 04.01.19; *Soldiers Died* Part 46; *FFP* (BMD) 23.11.18; *FA* 07.12.18; *FFP* 07.12.18; *FA* (FRoH) 14.12.18; *FFP* (RoH) 14.12.18; *FFP* 04.01.19; *FFP* (BMD) 23.10.20; Wauchope Vol 2

Anderson, John: Private (9246 Machine Gun Corps [277th Coy]. Formerly 93042 RFA); Shoeing Smith. Died of pneumonia, 63rd General Hospital, Salonika, 25.09.18, 29 years; 13 Dunnikier Row, Kirkcaldy; Kirechkoi-Hortakoi Military Cemetery, Greece; Kirkcaldy War Memorial; *Soldiers Died* Part 75; *FA* 12.10.18; *FA* (BMD) 12.10.18; *FFP* 12.10.18; *FFP* (BMD) 12.10.18; *FA* 19.10.18; *FA* (RoH) 19.10.18; *FA* (FRoH) 14.12.18; *FA* (BMD) 27.09.19

Anderson, Robert: Sergeant (344046 RGA [118th Siege Batt'y] [Forth]); KIA France, 05.07.18, 30 years; 96 Meldrum Road, Kirkcaldy; Forth RGA Plaque. St Andrew's Church Memorial Plaque; Grootebeek British Cemetery, Poperinge, West Vlaanderen, Belgium. Grave F.6; Kirkcaldy War Memorial; *Soldiers Died* Part 3; *FA* 27.07.18; *FFP* 27.07.18; *FA* 03.08.18; *FA* (BMD) 03.08.18; *FFP* 03.08.18; *FFP* (BMD) 03.08.18; *FA* (RoH) 14.09.18; *FFP* (RoH) 14.09.18; *FA* (FRoH) 14.12.18

Anderson, Robert: 2nd Lieutenant (Royal Scots [2nd]); DOW 43rd CCS, 22.03.18, 24 years; Inchview, Lady Nairn Avenue, Kirkcaldy; Gravestone in Dysart Cemetery. Kirkcaldy High School War Memorial; Bac-du-Sud British Cemetery, Bailleulval, Pas de Calais, France. Grave I.A.24; Kirkcaldy War Memorial; *Officers Died*; *Cross of Sacrifice Vol 1*; *FA* 06.04.18; *FFP* (RoH) 06.04.18; *FFP* (BMD) 06.04.18; *FA* (RoH) 13.04.18; *FA* (FRoH) 07.12.18

Anderson, Thomas: Lance Corporal (3/2199 Black Watch [1st] "C" Coy); MIA, 29.10.14, 21 years; 11 Maryhall Street, Kirkcaldy; Ypres (Menin Gate) Memorial, Ieper, West Vlaanderen, Belgium. Panel 37; Kirkcaldy War Memorial; *FA* 29.07.16; *FA* 14.10.16; *FFP* 21.10.16; *Soldiers Died* Part 46; *FA* 14.10.16; *FA* (BMD) 14.10.16; *FFP* 14.10.16; *FFP* (BMD) 14.10.16; *FA* (BMD) 21.10.16; *FFP* 21.10.16; *FA* (RoH) 18.11.16; *FFP* (RoH) 18.11.16; *FA* (Service List) 25.11.16; *FFP* (RoH) 30.12.16; *FFP* (BMD) 27.10.17; *FA* (FRoH) 23.11.18; Wauchope Vol 1

Appleby, David: Corporal (S/3663 Black Watch [8th]); Brother of Patrick Appleby; KIA, 19.10.16; Gow Square, Glasswork Street, Kirkcaldy/Lochgelly; Thiepval Memorial, Somme, France. Pier & Face 10A; Kirkcaldy War Memorial. Lochgelly War Memorial; *FFP* 02.06.17; *Soldiers Died* Part 46; *FA* (CasList) 25.11.16; *FFP* 26.05.17; *FA* 02.06.17; *FA* (RoH) 16.06.17; *FFP* (RoH) 16.06.17; *FA* (FRoH) 30.11.18; Wauchope Vol 3

Appleby, Patrick: Private (292499 Gordon Hldrs [7th]); Brother of David Appleby; KIA, 23.04.17, 28 years; Gow Square, Glasswork Street, Kirkcaldy; Brown's Copse Cemetery, Roeux, Pas de Calais, France. Grave II.F.6; Kirkcaldy War Memorial; *FFP* 02.06.17; *Soldiers Died* Part 65; *FFP* 26.05.17; *FA* 02.06.17; *FA* (CasList) 02.06.17; *FFP* (CasList) 02.06.17; *FA* (RoH) 16.06.17; *FFP* (RoH) 16.06.17; *FA* (FRoH) 30.11.18

Arnot, William: Private (2260 Royal Scots [9th]); DOW 13th Stationary Hospital, Boulogne as a result of wounds suffered near Ypres, 16.05.15, 21 years; 114 High Street, Kirkcaldy; Gravestone in Bennochy Cemetery. Bethelfield Church Plaque; Boulogne Eastern Cemetery, Pas de Calais, France. Grave VII.D.20; Kirkcaldy War Memorial; *Soldiers Died* Part 6; War Album 15; *FA* 15.05.15; *FA* 22.05.15; *FA* (BMD) 22.05.15; *FFP* (CasList) 05.06.15; *FFP* 05.08.16 Roll of the Brave; *FA* (Service List) 28.10.16; *FA* (Service List) 09.12.16; *FA* (FRoH) 16.11.18

Arnott, George: Private (S/22185 Cameron Hldrs [6th]); KIA, 14.07.16, 27 years; 73 Glebe Park, Kirkcaldy; St Andrew's Church Memorial Plaque; Loos Memorial, Pas de Calais, France. Panels 119-124; Kirkcaldy War Memorial; *Soldiers Died* Part 66; *FA* 09.09.16; *FA* (BMD) 09.09.16; *FFP* (BMD) 09.09.16; *FA* (CasList) 16.09.16; *FA* (RoH) 16.09.16; *FFP* (CasList) 16.09.16; *FFP* (RoH) 16.09.16; *FA* (Service List) 25.11.16; *FFP* (RoH) 30.12.16; *FA* (FRoH) 23.11.18

Arnott, George: Private (S/9191 Gordon Hldrs [10th]); KIA by a German mine while on sentry duty, 11.02.16; 236 St Clair Street, Kirkcaldy; Loos Memorial, Pas de Calais, France. Panels 115-119; *FFP* 18.03.16; Kirkcaldy War Memorial; *Soldiers Died* Part 65; *FA* 26.02.16; *FFP* 26.02.16; *FFP* 18.03.16; *FFP* 05.08.16 Roll of the Brave; *FA* (FRoH) 23.11.18

Arnott, John: Private (292128 Black Watch [9th] "A" Coy); DOW No 19 CCS, 17.12.17, 20 years; 50 Salisbury Street, Kirkcaldy/Russel Place, Strathmiglo; Old Parish Church Memorial Panel; Duisans British Cemetery, Etrun, Pas de Calais, France. Grave V.D.47; Kirkcaldy War Memorial; *Soldiers Died* Part 46; *FFP* (BMD) 05.01.18; *FA* (CasList) 14.09.18; *FFP* (RoH) 14.09.18; *FA* (FRoH) 14.12.18; Wauchope Vol 3

Baillie, James: Lance Corporal (290770 Black Watch [7th] [Lewis Gun Section]); DOW German Field Hospital. Originally buried in Tomb 392, Bouchain Cemetery, 30.03.18, 23 years; 6/8 Buchanan Street, Kirkcaldy; Gravestone in Bennochy Cemetery; Cabaret-Rouge British Cemetery, Souchez, Pas de Calais, France. Grave XVI.F.11; Kirkcaldy War Memorial; *Soldiers Died* Part 46; *FFP* (RoH) 20.04.18; *FA* 27.04.18; *FFP* 03.08.18; *FA* 10.08.18; *FFP* (BMD) 10.08.18; *FA* (BMD) 17.08.18; *FA* (RoH) 14.09.18; *FFP* (RoH) 14.09.18; *FA* (FRoH) 14.12.18; Wauchope Vol 2

Baillie, James: Sergeant (451153; CEF; Canadian Infantry [58th] 3rd Div 9th Bde. [Central Ontario Regt]); KIA, 20.09.16, 36 years; 39 Nicol Street, Kirkcaldy; Vimy Memorial, Pas de Calais, France; Kirkcaldy War Memorial; *CBoR* Page 49; *FA* 04.11.16; *FFP* 04.11.16; *FA* (Service List) 18.11.16; *FA* (RoH) 18.11.16; *FFP* (RoH) 18.11.16; *FFP* (RoH) 30.12.16; *FA* (FRoH) 30.11.18

Baillie, Peter Robert: Private (2025 Black Watch [9th]); KIA, 10.04.17, 22 years; Fergus Wynd, Kirkcaldy; Arras Memorial, Pas de Calais, France. Bay 6; Kirkcaldy War Memorial; *Soldiers Died* Part 46; *FA* 12.05.17; *FA* (BMD) 12.05.17; *FFP* 12.05.17; *FFP* (BMD) 12.05.17; *FA* (RoH) 19.05.17; *FFP* (CasList) 19.05.17; *FFP* (RoH) 19.05.17; *FA* (FRoH) 30.11.18; Wauchope Vol 3

Bain, Alexander: Private (S/10327 Black Watch [1st]. Formerly 6175 Res Cavalry Regt [5th]); DOW, 08.09.16; Heilly Station Cemetery, Mericourt-L'Abbe, Somme, France. Grave IV.A.72; Kirkcaldy War Memorial; *Soldiers Died* Part 46; Wauchope Vol 1

Bain, David: Gunner (158863 RGA [346th Siege Batt'y]); KIA, 09.07.18, 31 years; 47 East March Street, Kirkcaldy; Gravestone in Dysart Cemetery. Barony Church Plaque; Tannay British Cemetery, Thiennes, Nord, France. Grave 3.G.5; Kirkcaldy War Memorial; *Soldiers Died* Part 3; *FFP* 20.07.18; *FA* 27.07.18; *FA* (RoH) 14.09.18; *FFP* (RoH) 14.09.18; *FA* (FRoH) 14.12.18

Bain, George: Private (S/9793 Gordon Hldrs [9th]); Brother-in-law of George Latto; KIA, 21.04.17, 23 years; 20 Buchanan Street, Kirkcaldy/Stenhouse Street, Cowdenbeath; Wancourt British Cemetery, Pas de Calais, France. Grave IV.C.4; *FA* 12.05.17; Kirkcaldy War Memorial; *Soldiers Died* Part 65; *FA* (BMD) 05.05.17; *FFP* 05.05.17; *FFP* (BMD) 05.05.17; *FA* (RoH) 19.05.17; *FFP* (RoH) 19.05.17; *FFP* (CasList) 26.05.17; *FFP* (BMD) 20.04.18; *FA* (FRoH) 30.11.18

Bain, Jerry: 3rd Engineer (Merchant Navy; Wireless Operator); 31.05.17; Tower Hill Memorial, London; Kirkcaldy War Memorial; *Cross of Sacrifice Vol 5*

Bain, John: Private (5332 Cameron Hldrs [1st]); On CWGC as 6332; KIA, 25.09.14; Ann Place, 34 Links Street, Kirkcaldy; La Ferte-Sous-Jouarre Memorial, Seine-et-Marne, France; War Album 14/15; *FFP* 14.11.14; Kirkcaldy War Memorial; *Soldiers Died* Part 66; War Album 14/15; *FA* 31.10.14; *FFP* 31.10.14; *FA* (CasList) 21.11.14; *FA* 02.01.15; *FA* (CasList) 20.02.15; *FFP* 05.08.16 Roll of the Brave; *FA* (Service List) 02.12.16; *FA* (FRoH) 16.11.18

Bain, John: Lance Corporal (74170; CEF; Canadian Infantry [28th] 2nd Div 6th Bde. [Saskatchewan Regt]); KIA, 06.06.16; Ypres (Menin Gate) Memorial, Ieper, West-Vlaanderen, Belgium. Panels 18, 26 & 28; Kirkcaldy War Memorial; *CBoR Page 49*

Baird, James: Corporal (S/15201 Gordon Hldrs [1st]. Formerly 25465 RAMC); KIA, 07.05.17, 33 years; 15 West Fergus Place, Kirkcaldy; Old Parish Church Memorial Panel; Feuchy Chapel British Cemetery, Wancourt, Pas de Calais, France. Grave I.D.19; Kirkcaldy War Memorial; *Soldiers Died* Part 65; *FA* 26.05.17; *FA* (BMD) 26.05.17; *FFP* 26.05.17; *FFP* (BMD) 26.05.17; *FA* (RoH) 16.06.17; *FFP* (CasList) 16.06.17; *FFP* (RoH) 16.06.17; *FA* (FRoH) 30.11.18

Bald, Robert: Lance Corporal (44044 KOSB [2nd]. Formerly 1165 HCB); KIA, 03.09.16, 21 years; 1 Aitken Street, Kirkcaldy/Priory Cottage, North Queensferry; La Neuville British Cemetery, Corbie, Somme, France. Grave II.B.37; Kirkcaldy War Memorial. North Queensferry War Memorial. Inverkeithing War Memorial; *FA* 07.10.16; *Soldiers Died* Part 30; *FA* 16.09.16; *FA* 30.09.16; *FFP* 07.10.16; *FA* (RoH) 14.10.16; *FFP* (RoH) 14.10.16; *FFP* (CasList) 16.12.16; *FFP* (RoH) 30.12.16; *FA* (Service List) 17.03.17; *FA* (FRoH) 23.11.18

Bald, Thomas: Private (3/2602 Black Watch [7th]); KIA, 26.03.18; Mill Street, Kirkcaldy; Arras Memorial, Pas de Calais, France. Bay 6; Kirkcaldy War Memorial; *FA* 18.08.17; *Soldiers Died* Part 46; *FA* 25.05.18; Wauchope Vol 2

Balfour, David: Private (303222 A & S Hldrs [1/7th]); Brother of James Balfour; KIA, 21.11.17, 28 years; 23 Smeaton Road, Kirkcaldy/27 South Overgate, Kinghorn; Anneux British Cemetery, Nord, France. Grave II.E.9; Kirkcaldy War Memorial; *Soldiers Died* Part 70; *FA* 08.12.17; *FFP* 08.12.17; *FFP* (BMD) 08.12.17; *FA* 15.12.17; *FA* (RoH) 15.12.17; *FA* (BMD) 15.12.17; *FFP* (RoH) 15.12.17; *FFP* 27.07.18; *FA* 03.08.18; *FFP* (BMD) 23.11.18; Corns & Hughes-Wilson

Balfour, George: Private (2751 Black Watch [1/7th]); Cousin of Robert Saunders; KIA, 30.07.16, 23 years; 113 Sutherland Street/Links Street, Kirkcaldy; Gallatown Church Roll of Honour; Serre Road Cemetery No. 2, Somme, France. Grave V.G.24; Kirkcaldy War Memorial; ‡; *FA* 05.02.16; *FA* 12.08.16; *FA* 19.08.16; *Soldiers Died* Part 46; *FA* 12.08.16 (4 entries); *FFP* 12.08.16; *FA* 19.08.16 (2 entries); *FA* (BMD) 19.08.16; *FFP* 26.08.16; *FA* (CasList) 09.09.16; *FFP* (CasList) 09.09.16; *FA* (RoH) 16.09.16; *FFP* (RoH) 16.09.16; *FFP* (RoH) 30.12.16; *FA* (Service List) 03.03.17; *FFP* (BMD) 27.07.18; *FA* (FRoH) 23.11.18; Wauchope Vol 2

Balfour, James: Private (S/2701 Gordon Hldrs [8/10th]); Brother of David Balfour; MIA, 26.08.17, 24 years; 23 Smeaton Road, Kirkcaldy; Bethelfield Church Plaque; Dochy Farm New British Cemetery, Zonnebeke, West Vlaanderen, Belgium. Grave II.E.1; Kirkcaldy War Memorial; *Soldiers Died* Part 65; *FFP* 08.12.17; *FFP* 27.07.18; *FFP* (BMD) 27.07.18; *FA* 03.08.18; *FA* (RoH) 14.09.18; *FFP* (BMD) 23.11.18; *FA* (FRoH) 14.12.18

Balfour, James: Lance Sergeant (587 Seaforth Hldrs [1st]); KIA, 09.05.15; Le Touret Memorial, Pas de Calais, France. Panels 38-39; Kirkcaldy War Memorial; *Soldiers Died* Part 64; *FFP* (BMD) 31.07.15

Ballingall, Daniel: Private (S/19713 A & S Hldrs [11th]); MIA, 22.08.17, 25 years; 13 Pratt Street, Kirkcaldy; Pathhead Parish Church Memorial Plaques & Windows; Tyne Cot Memorial, Zonnebeke, West Vlaanderen, Belgium. Panels 141-143 & 162; Kirkcaldy War Memorial; *FFP* 10.08.18; *Soldiers Died* Part 70; *FA* 29.09.17; *FFP* 27.07.18; *FA* 03.08.18; *FFP* 10.08.18; *FA* (RoH) 14.09.18; *FFP* (RoH) 14.09.18; *FA* (FRoH) 14.12.18

Ballingall, William: Private (27759 KOSB [7/8th]. Formerly 2674 F & F Yeo); KIA, 09.04.17; Arras Memorial, Pas de Calais, France. Bay 6; Kirkcaldy War Memorial; *Soldiers Died* Part 30; *FA* (CasList) 02.06.17

Barbour, Andrew: Private (2278 Black Watch [2nd]); KIA, 09.05.15, 22 years; 6 Gas Wynd, Kirkcaldy; Pont-du-Hem Military Cemetery, La Gorgue, Nord, France. Grave V.L.22; Kirkcaldy War Memorial; War Album 15; *FA* 05.06.15; *Soldiers Died* Part 46; War Album 15; *FA* 22.05.15; *Scotsman* 22.05.15; *FA* 29.05.15; *Scotsman* 31.05.15; *FA* 05.06.15; *FFP* (CasList) 05.06.15; *FFP* (BMD) 13.05.16; *FFP* 05.08.16 Roll of the Brave; *FA* (Service List) 04.11.16; *FA* (Service List) 23.12.16; *FFP* (BMD) 12.05.17; *FFP* (BMD) 11.05.18; *FA* (FRoH) 16.11.18; Wauchope Vol 1

Barn, John D.: Private (S/21378 Black Watch [8th]); KIA, 23.03.18, 19 years; Pozieres Memorial, Somme, France. Panels 49-50; Kirkcaldy War Memorial; *Soldiers Died* Part 46; *FA* (BMD) 04.05.18; *FFP* (BMD) 04.05.18; Wauchope Vol 3

Barnet, Henry Morton: 2nd Lieutenant (Kings Royal Rifle Corps [1st]); Brother of J.H. Barnet; DOW whilst a PoW, Ohrdruf, Saxony. Buried Ohrdruf Military Cemetery. 24.03.18, 27 years; Meadowbank, West Albert Road, Kirkcaldy; Gravestone in Bennochy Cemetery. St Andrew's Church Memorial Plaque. Kirkcaldy High School War Memorial; Niederzwehren Cemetery, Germany. Grave IV.E.12; Kirkcaldy War Memorial; *FFP* 15.06.18; *Officers Died*; *Cross of Sacrifice Vol 1*; *FFP* (RoH) 06.04.18; *FA* 13.04.18; *FA* 08.06.18; *FA* (BMD) 08.06.18; *FFP* 08.06.18; *FFP* (BMD) 08.06.18; *FA* 15.06.18; *FA* (RoH) 15.06.18; *FFP* 15.06.18; *FFP* (RoH) 15.06.18; *FA* 13.07.18; *Scotsman* 14.08.18; *FA* 17.08.18; *FFP* 17.08.18; *FA* (FRoH) 14.12.18; *FA* (KHS RoH) 29.03.19

Barnet, James Howieson: 2nd Lieutenant (Black Watch [4th]); Brother of H. M. Barnet; KIA, 01.08.18, 23 years; Meadowbank, West Albert Road, Kirkcaldy; Gravestone in Bennochy Cemetery. St Andrew's Church Memorial Plaque. Kirkcaldy High School War Memorial; Raperie British Cemetery, Villemontoire, Aisne, France. Grave III.E.5; Kirkcaldy War Memorial; *Officers Died*; *Cross of Sacrifice Vol 1*; *Scotsman* 13.08.18; *Scotsman* 14.08.18; *FA* 17.08.18; *FA* (BMD) 17.08.18; *FFP* 17.08.18; *FFP* (BMD) 17.08.18; *FA* 24.08.18; *FFP* 24.08.18; *Court Journal* 31.08.18; *FA* (RoH) 14.09.18; *FA* (FRoH) 14.12.18; *FFP* 08.02.19; *FA* (KHS RoH) 29.03.19; *FA* (KHS RoH) 19.07.19; Wauchope Vol 2

Barrie, George Falls: Private (307828 Royal Tank Corps [13th]. Formerly KOSB & 2236 RAMC); DOW whilst a PoW at Fortress Hospital, Köln, Germany, 30.05.18, 28 years; 21 Forth Avenue, Kirkcaldy. Formerly Markinch; Abbotshall Parish Church Memorial Plaque; Cologne Southern Cemetery, Germany. Grave VIII.C.12; Kirkcaldy War Memorial; *Soldiers Died* Part 75; *FFP* 17.08.18; *FFP* (BMD) 17.08.18; *FA* 24.08.18; *FA* 19.11.21

Barrons, George: Private (859741; CEF; Canadian Infantry [43rd] 3rd Div 9th Bde. [Manitoba Regt] [Cameron Hldrs of Canada]); KIA, 26.05.17, 29 years; 2 Forth Avenue North, Kirkcaldy; Gravestone in Abbotshall Churchyard. Abbotshall Parish Church Memorial Plaque; La Chaudiere Military Cemetery, Vimy, Pas de Calais, France. Grave IV.D.17; Kirkcaldy War Memorial; *CBoR* Page 197; *FA* 16.06.17; *FA* (BMD) 16.06.17; *FFP* 16.06.17; *FA* 14.07.17; *FFP* 14.07.17; *FA* (FRoH) 07.12.18; *FA* 19.11.21

Bartholomew, Thomas Wilson: Private (859284; CEF; Canadian Infantry [43rd] 3rd Div 9th Bde. [Manitoba Regt] [Cameron Hldrs of Canada]); KIA Vimy Ridge, 13.03.17, 31 years; Clonliffe, Milton Terrace, Pratt Street, Kirkcaldy; Gravestone in Abbotshall Churchyard; Ecoivres Military Cemetery, Mont-St Eloi, Pas de Calais, France. Grave IV.F.13; Kirkcaldy War Memorial; *CBoR* Page 197; *FA* 31.03.17; *FA* (BMD) 31.03.17; *FFP* 31.03.17; *FFP* (BMD) 31.03.17; *FA* (RoH) 14.04.17; *FA* (FRoH) 30.11.18

Bathie, George: Guardsman (3137 Scots Guards [2nd]); KIA France, 18.12.14, 32 years; Burleigh Street/22 Mitchell Street, Kirkcaldy. Subsequently Bowhill; Ploegsteert Memorial, Comines-Warneton, Hainaut, Belgium. Panel 1; Kirkcaldy War Memorial. Auchterderran War Memorial; *FFP* 13.02.15; *Soldiers Died* Part 5; *FA* 13.02.15; *FFP* 13.02.15; *FA* (CasList) 20.02.15; *FFP* (BMD) 18.12.15; *FFP* 05.08.16 Roll of the Brave; *FFP* (BMD) 16.12.16

Baxter, David S.: Private (36810 RAMC [13th Fld Amb]); DOW No 1 Canadian Hospital, 14.10.16; 20 Rosslyn Street, Kirkcaldy; Etaples Military Cemetery, Pas de Calais, France. Grave VII.E.5; Kirkcaldy War Memorial; *Soldiers Died* Part 79; *FA* 28.10.16; *FA* (BMD) 28.10.16; *FFP* 28.10.16; *FFP* (BMD) 28.10.16; *FFP* (CasList) 11.11.16; *FA* (RoH) 18.11.16; *FFP* (RoH) 18.11.16; *FA* (Service List) 09.12.16; *FFP* (RoH) 30.12.16; *FFP* (BMD) 12.10.18; *FA* (FRoH) 30.11.18

Baxter, Robert: Private (24993 Royal Scots (5/6th]); KIA,11.08.18, 33 years; 2 Malcolm's Wynd, Kirkcaldy; Bouchoir New British Cemetery, Somme, France. Grave III.A.14; Kirkcaldy War Memorial; *Soldiers Died* Part 6; *FA* 07.09.18; *FFP* (BMD) 07.09.18; *FA* (RoH) 14.09.18; *FFP* 14.09.18; *FFP* (RoH) 14.09.18; *FA* (FRoH) 14.12.18

Baxter, William: Private (S/15989 A & S Hldrs [14th]); DOW Maritz, whilst a PoW, 26.03.18, 29 years; 1 Gas Wynd, Kirkcaldy; Raith Church Memorial Plaque; Tournai Communal Cemetery, Belgium. Allied Extension Grave V.M.10; Kirkcaldy War Memorial; *Soldiers Died* Part 70; *FA* 06.04.18; *FA* 13.04.18; *FA* (BMD) 13.04.18; *FFP* (BMD) 13.04.18; *FA* 24.08.18; *FA* 14.09.18; *FA* (RoH) 14.09.18; *FFP* (RoH) 14.09.18; *FA* (FRoH) 14.12.18

Beaton, William: Lance Sergeant (16765 KOSB [6th]); KIA Somme, 17.07.16, 29 years; 82 Balfour Street, Kirkcaldy; Pathhead Parish Church Memorial Plaques & Windows; Thiepval Memorial, Somme, France. Pier & Face 4A & 4D; Kirkcaldy War Memorial; *FA* 19.08.16; *FFP* 19.08.16; *Soldiers Died* Part 30; *FA* 12.08.16; *FFP* 12.08.16; *FFP* 19.08.16; *FFP* (BMD) 19.08.16; *FA* (BMD) 26.08.16; *FA* (CasList) 02.09.16; *FFP* (CasList) 02.09.16; *FA* (RoH) 16.09.16; *FFP* (RoH) 16.09.16; *FA* (Service List) 18.11.16; *FFP* (RoH) 30.12.16; *FFP* (BMD) 21.07.17; *FA* (BMD) 18.08.17; *FFP* (BMD) 20.07.18; *FA* (FRoH) 23.11.18

Beatson, Beaumont Crowther Oswald: 2nd Lieutenant (Black Watch [7th]. Formerly Royal Scots); KIA, 23.04.17, 22 years; Townsend Place, Kirkcaldy; Gravestone in Bennochy Cemetery. Kirkcaldy High School War Memorial. St Peter's Church Memorial Plaque; Brown's Copse Cemetery, Roeux, Pas de Calais, France. Grave II.H.23; Kirkcaldy War Memorial; *FA* 05.05.17; *FFP* 05.05.17; *Officers Died*; *Cross of Sacrifice Vol 1*; *Scotsman* 02.05.17; *FA* 05.05.17; *FFP* 05.05.17; *FA* (RoH) 19.05.17; *FFP* (RoH) 19.05.17; *FA* 14.07.17 (KHS War Honours); *FA* (FRoH) 30.11.17; *FA* (KHS RoH) 29.03.19; Wauchope Vol 2

Beattie, John: Private (202384 Black Watch (4/5th] [Lewis Gun Team]); KIA, 31.07.17, 33 years; 60 Sutherland Street, Kirkcaldy; New Irish Farm Cemetery, Ieper, West Vlaanderen, Belgium. Grave XXIII.C.19; Kirkcaldy War Memorial; *Soldiers Died* Part 46; *FFP* (CasList) 18.08.17; *FA* 25.08.17; *FA* 01.09.17; *FFP* (CasList) 08.09.17; *FA* 15.09.17; *FFP* (RoH) 15.09.17; *FFP* (BMD) 03.08.18; Wauchope Vol 2

Begg, Andrew Currie: Captain & Adjutant (Black Watch [1/7th]); KIA High Wood, 30.07.16, 36 years; 68 Milton Road, Kirkcaldy; Abbotshall Parish Church Memorial Plaque and personal plaque. Kirkcaldy High School War Memorial; Serre Road Cemetery No. 2, Somme, France. Grave V.G.9; Kirkcaldy War Memorial; ‡; *FA* 12.08.16; *FFP* 12.08.16; *Officers Died*; *Cross of Sacrifice Vol 1*; *FA* 12.08.16 (3 entries); *FA* (BMD) 12.08.16; *FFP* 12.08.16; *FFP* (BMD) 12.08.16; *FA* (RoH) 16.09.16; *FFP* (RoH) 16.09.16; *FA* 23.09.16; *FFP* 23.09.16; *FFP* (RoH) 30.12.16; *FA* (Service List) 13.01.17; *FA* 14.07.17 (KHS War Honours); *FA* (FRoH) 23.11.18; *FA* (KHS RoH) 29.03.19; *FA* 19.11.21; *MRoM*; Wauchope Vol 2

Bell, Alexander Whitehead: Private (S/16773 Black Watch [8th]); DOW, 09.04.17, 26 years; 6 Miller Street, Kirkcaldy; St Michael's Church Memorial Plaque; Haute-Avesnes British Cemetery, Pas de Calais, France. Grave B.12; Kirkcaldy War Memorial; *Soldiers Died* Part 46; *FA* 28.04.17; *FFP* 28.04.17; *FFP* 05.05.17; *FFP* (BMD) 05.05.17; *FA* (CasList) 12.05.17; *FFP* (CasList) 12.05.17; *FA* (RoH) 19.05.17; *FFP* (RoH) 19.05.17; *FFP* (BMD) 06.04.18; *FA* (FRoH) 30.11.18; Wauchope Vol 3

Bell, Andrew Robertson: 2nd Lieutenant (RAF; 28th Squadron); KIA Italian Front, 22.09.18, 19 years; 19 David Street/Craiglea, Abbotshall Road, Kirkcaldy; St Brycedale Church Plaque. Kirkcaldy High School War Memorial; Montecchio Precalcino Communal Cemetery Extension, Italy. Grave 5.B.3; Kirkcaldy War Memorial; *FA* 05.10.18; *FFP* 05.10.18; RFC/RAF RoH; *Cross of Sacrifice Vol 2*; *FA* 28.09.18; *FA* (BMD) 28.09.18; *FFP* 28.09.18; *FFP* (BMD) 28.09.18; *FA* 05.10.18; *FFP* 05.10.18; *FA* (RoH) 19.10.18; *FA* (FRoH) 14.12.18; *FA* (KHS RoH) 29.03.19; *FA* (KHS RoH) 19.07.19; *FA* (BMD) 20.09.19

Bell, James: Private (S/17546 Black Watch [8th]); KIA, 23.03.18; 44 Overton Road, Kirkcaldy; Pozieres Memorial, Somme, France. Panels 49-50; Kirkcaldy War Memorial; *Soldiers Died* Part 46; *FA* 27.04.18; *FFP* (RoH) 27.04.18; *FA* 04.05.18; *FA* (RoH) 18.05.18; *FFP* (RoH) 18.05.18; *FA* (FRoH) 07.12.18; Wauchope Vol 3

Bell, Levi: Private (40145 Royal Scots [11th]. Formerly 3498 F & F Yeo & 26739 KOSB); KIA, 22.03.18, 21 years; 6 Millar Street, Kirkcaldy; St Michael's Church Memorial Plaque; Gouzeaucourt New British Cemetery, Nord, France. Grave II.A.12; Kirkcaldy War Memorial; ‡; *Soldiers Died* Part 6

Bell, William: Private (S/41031 A & S Hldrs [1/8th]); KIA, 19.09.18, 30 years; 45 Pratt Street, Kirkcaldy; Noeux-Les-Mines Communal Cemetery & Extension, Pas de Calais, France. Grave V.A.11; Kirkcaldy War Memorial; *Soldiers Died* Part 70; *FFP* (BMD) 12.10.18

Bennet, George: Private (S/3698 Gordon Hldrs [8th]); Brother of Thomas Bennet; KIA Loos, 25.09.15, 19 years; 85 Balsusney Road, Kirkcaldy; Loos Memorial, Pas de Calais, France. Panels 115-119; Kirkcaldy War Memorial; *FFP* 07.09.18; *Soldiers Died* Part 65; *FA* 11.11.16; *FA* (RoH) 18.11.16; *FFP* (RoH) 18.11.16; *FFP* (RoH) 30.12.16; *FFP* 24.08.18; *FA* 31.08.18

Bennet, Thomas: Private (S/13355 Gordon Hldrs [5th] [Machine Gun Section]); Brother of George Bennet; KIA, 28.07.18, 24 years; 85 Balsusney Road, Kirkcaldy; Soissons Memorial, Aisne, France; Kirkcaldy War Memorial; *FFP* 07.09.18; *Soldiers Died* Part 65; *FFP* 24.08.18; *FA* 31.08.18; *FA* (RoH) 14.09.18; *FA* (FRoH) 14.12.18

Bett, Charles Pratt: Bombardier (344154 RGA [249 Seige Batt'y] [Forth]); Brother-in-law of Robert Graham; KIA, 25.10.17, 34 years; 19 Harcourt Road, Kirkcaldy; Forth RGA Plaque. Old Parish Church Memorial Panel; Huts Cemetery, Dickebusch, Kemmel, Belgium. Grave XII.B.1; Kirkcaldy War Memorial; ‡; *Soldiers Died* Part 3; *FA* 03.11.17; *FFP* 03.11.17; *FFP* (RoH) 17.11.17; *FFP* (BMD) 17.11.17; *FA* 28.09.18; *FA* (FRoH) 07.12.18

Beveridge, Henry: Trooper (2489 F & F Yeo [1st]); KIA Suvla Bay, Gallipoli, 21.10.15, 19 years; 40 Union Street, Kirkcaldy; Gravestone in Dysart Cemetery. Pathhead Parish Church Memorial Plaques & Windows; Green Hill Cemetery, Turkey. Grave I.E.18; Kirkcaldy War Memorial; *Soldiers Died* Part 1; War Album 15/16; *FA* 06.11.15; *FA* (RoH) 13.11.15; *FFP* 05.08.16 Roll of the Brave; *FFP* (BMD) 21.10.16; *FA* (Service List) 17.03.17; *FA* (FRoH) 16.11.18; Ogilvie

Beveridge, Robert De'ath: Private (S/40126 Black Watch [1/6th]); DOW German Hospital, Wreschen, Germany, 21.06.18, 33 years; 15 Victoria Road, Kirkcaldy; Poznan Old Garrison Cemetery, Poland. Grave I.B.9; Kirkcaldy War Memorial; *Soldiers Died* Part 46; *FFP* 04.01.19; *FFP* (BMD) 04.01.19; *FA* 11.01.19; *FA* (RoH) 18.01.19; Wauchope Vol 2

Birrell, Christopher (Charles?) Greig: Private (S/20418 A & S Hldrs [2nd]); MIA, 25.09.17; 231 St Clair Street, Kirkcaldy; Tyne Cot Memorial, Zonnebeke, West Vlaanderen, Belgium. Panels 141-143 & 162; Kirkcaldy War Memorial; *Soldiers Died* Part 70; *FFP* (RoH) 23.03.18; *FFP* 03.08.18; *FA* 10.08.18; *FA* (RoH) 14.09.18; *FFP* (RoH) 14.09.18; *FA* (FRoH) 14.12.18

Birrell, Henry: Lance Corporal (S/3528 Seaforth Hldrs [8th]); MIA Loos, 25.09.15, 23 years; 278 Rosslyn Street, Kirkcaldy; Loos Memorial, Pas de Calais, France. Panels 112-115; Kirkcaldy War Memorial; *Soldiers Died* Part 64; War Album 15/16; *Scotsman* 15.11.15; *FA* 20.11.15; *FA* (RoH) 18.12.15; *FFP* 05.08.16 Roll of the Brave; *FFP* 07.10.16; *FFP* (BMD) 07.10.16; *FA* 14.10.16; *FFP* 25.11.16; *FA* (Service List) 09.12.16; *FA* (FRoH) 16.11.18

Bisset, Samuel: Sergeant (7479 KOSB [6th]); KIA, 25.09.15; 12 Lorne Street, Kirkcaldy; St Michael's Church Memorial Plaque; Loos Memorial, Pas de Calais, France. Panels 53-56; Kirkcaldy War Memorial; *FA* 30.10.15; *Soldiers Died* Part 30; War Album 15/16; *Scotsman* 27.10.15; *FA* 30.10.15; *FFP* 30.10.15; *FA* (RoH) 13.11.15; *FFP* 05.08.16 Roll of the Brave; *FA* (Service List) 03.02.17; *FA* (FRoH) 16.11.18

Black, James: Stoker 1st Class (299558; Royal Navy; HMS *Achates*); Brother of Robert Black; Drowned, 17.02.17, 36 years; Links Street, Kirkcaldy; Chatham Memorial, Kent. Panel 23; Kirkcaldy War Memorial; *Cross of Sacrifice Vol 4*; *FA* 24.02.17; *FA* (BMD) 24.02.17; *FFP* 24.02.17; *FFP* (BMD) 24.02.17; *FA* (RoH) 17.03.17; *FA* (FRoH) 30.11.18

Black, James: Pioneer (217485 Royal Engineers [Carrier Pigeon Service]); Died of pneumonia, 30.01.19, 31 years; 24 Mill Street, Kirkcaldy; Gravestone in Bennochy Cemetery; Bennochy Cemetery, Kirkcaldy. Grave FF.161; Kirkcaldy War Memorial; *FFP* (BMD) 01.02.19; *FA* (RoH) 15.02.19

Black, John: Private (3/2614 Black Watch [2nd]); KIA Persian Gulf, 22.04.16, 19 years; 3 Church Lane, Oswald Wynd, Kirkcaldy; Amara War Cemetery, Iraq. Grave XVII.E.7; Kirkcaldy War Memorial; *FA* 22.04.16; *FA* 03.06.16; *Soldiers Died* Part 46; *FA* 03.06.16; *FA* (BMD) 03.06.16; *FFP* 03.06.16; *FFP* (BMD) 03.06.16; *FA* (RoH) 17.06.16; *FFP* (RoH) 17.06.16; *FA* 24.06.16; *FA* (CasList) 01.07.16; *FFP* 05.08.16 Roll of the Brave; *FA* (Memorial Service) 06.01.17; *FA* (Service List) 20.01.17; *FFP* (BMD) 21.04.17; *FFP* (BMD) 20.04.18; *FA* (FRoH) 23.11.18; Wauchope Vol 1

Private John **Black** enlisted in the Black Watch "to uphold the honour of the regiment", as he told his father, who had also served in the Black Watch.

John was wounded on 4th July 1915, but saved from more serious injury because the bullet hit the wristwatch his mother had given him for his 18th birthday. John was killed a year later, aged 19.

Black, John: Private (1682 Royal Scots [5th]); KIA Dardanelles, Gallipoli, 19.06.15, 21 years; Fitzroy Street, Dysart; St Serf's Church Family Memorial Lectern; Twelve Tree Copse Cemetery, Gallipoli, Turkey. Grave I.B.4; Kirkcaldy War Memorial; *Soldiers Died* Part 6; *FFP* (BMD) 10.07.15; *FA* 24.07.15; *FFP* 24.07.15; *FFP* (BMD) 24.06.16; *FFP* 05.08.16 Roll of the Brave

Black, Joseph: Private (S/2048 Gordon Hldrs (8/10th]); KIA, 26.05.16, 22 years; 170 Overton Road, Kirkcaldy; Gravestone in Dysart Cemetery; Dud Corner Cemetery, Loos, Pas de Calais, France. Grave III.A.17; Kirkcaldy War Memorial; *Soldiers Died* Part 65; *FFP* 01.07.16; *FFP* (BMD) 01.07.16; *FA* (CasList) 08.07.16; *FA* (RoH) 15.07.16; *FFP* 05.08.16 Roll of the Brave; *FA* (Service List) 18.11.16; *FFP* (BMD) 26.05.17; *FFP* (BMD) 25.05.18; *FA* (FRoH) 23.11.18

Black, Robert: Private (7657 Cameron Hldrs [1st]); Brother of James Black; KIA, 25.09.14, 29 years; 34 Links Street/ 28 Bridgeton, Kirkcaldy; La Ferte-Sous-Jouarre Memorial, Seine-et-Marne, France; Kirkcaldy War Memorial; *FA* 04.03.16; *Soldiers Died* Part 66; *FA* (CasList) 20.02.15; *FA* 26.02.16; *FA* (BMD) 26.02.16; *FFP* 26.02.16; *FFP* (BMD) 26.02.16; *FFP* 05.08.16 Roll of the Brave; *FA* (Service List) 02.12.16; *FA* 24.02.17; *FA* (FRoH) 23.11.18

Black, Robert M.: Private (S/20983 A & S Hldrs [10th]); KIA France, 12.10.17, 35 years; 50 Lorne Street, Kirkcaldy; Tyne Cot Memorial, Zonnebeke, West Vlaanderen, Belgium. Panels 114-143 & 162; Kirkcaldy War Memorial; *Soldiers Died* Part 70; *FA* 10.11.17; *FA* (RoH) 17.11.17; *FFP* 17.11.17; *FFP* (RoH) 17.11.17; *FFP* (CasList) 01.12.17; *FA* (FRoH) 07.12.18

Black, William: Private (2631 Black Watch [1st]); KIA Ypres, 27.10.14, 21 years; 2 Gaswork Place/Gas Houses, 3 Gas Wynd, Kirkcaldy; Ypres (Menin Gate) Memorial, Ieper, West Vlaanderen, Belgium. Panel 37; Kirkcaldy War Memorial; *Soldiers Died* Part 46; War Album 14/15; *FFP* (BMD) 05.12.14; *FA* 12.12.14; *FA* (CasList) 19.12.14; *FA* 02.01.15; *FA* (CasList) 20.02.15; *FFP* 05.08.16 Roll of the Brave; *FA* (Service List) 04.11.16; *FA* (Service List) 23.12.16; *FA* (Service List) 06.01.17; *FA* (Service List) 27.01.17; *FA* (FRoH) 16.11.18; Wauchope Vol 1

Blackwood, Alexander: Private (3/992 Black Watch [3rd] att'd [1st]); In Wauchope as 31992. Brother of W. Blackwood; KIA Ypres, 09.11.14, 26 years; 33 Nicol Street, Kirkcaldy; St Michael's Church Memorial Plaque; Ypres (Menin Gate) Memorial, Ieper, West Vlaanderen, Belgium. Panel 37; Kirkcaldy War Memorial; *Soldiers Died* Part 46; War Album 14/15; *Dundee Advertiser* 03.12.14; *FFP* 05.12.14; *FA* 12.12.14; *Dundee Advertiser* 14.12.14; *FA* 19.12.14; *FA* (CasList) 19.12.14; *FA* 02.01.15; *FA* (CasList) 20.02.15; *FA* 29.07.16; *FFP* 05.08.16 Roll of the Brave; *FA* (BMD) 11.11.16; *FA* (Service List) 18.11.16; Wauchope Vol 1; RoH Dunnikier Colliery

Blackwood, William: Lance Corporal (19447 Royal Scots Fusiliers (6/7th]); Brother of Alexander Blackwood. In papers as D. Blackwood; KIA, 22.08.17, 25 years; 185 Links Street, Kirkcaldy; Tyne Cot Memorial, Zonnebeke, West Vlaanderen, Belgium. Panels 60-61; Kirkcaldy War Memorial; *FA* 22.09.17; *Soldiers Died* Part 26; *FA* 15.09.17; *FFP* 15.09.17; *FA* 22.09.17; *FFP* (CasList) 06.10.17; *FA* 13.10.17; *FFP* (RoH) 13.10.17; *FA* (FRoH) 07.12.18

Blake, George: Private (S/40697 Black Watch [8th]. Formerly 2632 F & F Yeo); KIA, 12.10.17, 29 years; 29 Tolbooth Street, Kirkcaldy/119 High Binn, Burntisland; Tyne Cot Memorial, Zonnebeke, West Vlaanderen, Belgium. Panels 94-96; Kirkcaldy War Memorial; *FA* 17.11.17; *Soldiers Died* Part 46; *FA* 17.11.17; *FA* (BMD) 17.11.17; *FFP* (CasList) 17.11.17; *FA* (BMD) 01.12.17; *FA* (RoH) 15.12.17; *FFP* (RoH) 15.12.17; *FA* (FRoH) 07.12.18; Wauchope Vol 3

Blake, James: Private (44092 KOSB [2nd]. Formerly 2252 HCB); KIA, 03.09.16, 19 years; 114 Rosslyn Street, Kirkcaldy; Delville Wood Cemetery, Longueval, Somme, France. Grave XXVIII.A.1; Kirkcaldy War Memorial; *Soldiers Died* Part 30; *FA* 07.10.16; *FFP* 07.10.16; *FA* (RoH) 14.10.16; *FFP* (RoH) 14.10.16; *FFP* (CasList) 14.10.16; *FA* (Service List) 09.12.16; *FFP* (RoH) 30.12.16; *FA* (FRoH) 23.11.18

Bloomfield, William: Private (3/2575 Black Watch [1st]); KIA, 09.05.15, 20 years; 25 Tolbooth Street, Kirkcaldy; Le Touret Memorial, Pas de Calais, France. Panels 24-26; Kirkcaldy War Memorial; *Soldiers Died* Part 46; War Album 15; *FA* 19.06.15; *FFP* 19.06.15; *Scotsman* 19.06.15; *FFP* (BMD) 26.06.15; *FFP* (CasList) 03.07.15; *FA* (RoH) 17.07.15; *FFP* 05.08.16 Roll of the Brave; *FA* (Service List) 04.11.16; *FA* (Service List) 27.01.17; *FA* (FRoH) 16.11.18; Wauchope Vol 1

Blount, James: Private (192998; CEF; Canadian Infantry [13th] 1st Div 3rd Bde. [Quebec Regt] [Royal Hldrs of Canada]); KIA, 12.12.17, 24 years; 4 Meldrum Place, Quality Street, Kirkcaldy/Hamilton, Ontario; Whytescauseway Baptist Church Memorial Plaque; Sucrerie Cemetery, Ablain-St Nazaire, Pas de Calais, France. Grave III.A.1; Kirkcaldy War Memorial; *FA* 04.11.16; *CBoR* Page 203; *FFP* 05.01.18; *FFP* (BMD) 05.01.18; *FA* 12.01.18; *FA* (RoH) 19.01.18; *FA* 06.04.18; *FA* (FRoH) 07.12.18

Blyth, John Christie Mackie: Private (44101 KOSB [2nd]. Formerly 2424 HCB); KIA, 03.09.16, 19 years; 1 Matthew Street, Kirkcaldy; Gravestone in Bennochy Cemetery; Thiepval Memorial, Somme, France. Pier & Face 4A & 4D; Kirkcaldy War Memorial; *Soldiers Died* Part 30; *FA* 30.09.16; *FFP* 07.10.16; *FFP* (BMD) 07.10.16; *FA* (RoH) 14.10.16; *FFP* (RoH) 14.10.16; *FFP* (RoH) 30.12.16; *FA* (Service List) 24.03.17; *FFP* (BMD) 08.09.17; *FA* (FRoH) 23.11.18

Boag, David: Private (44091 KOSB [2nd]. Formerly 2242 HCB); KIA, 04.10.17; St Columba's Church Memorial Plaque; Tyne Cot Memorial, Zonnebeke, West Vlaanderen, Belgium. Panels 66-68; Kirkcaldy War Memorial; *Soldiers Died* Part 30; *FA* 10.11.17

Bogie, Alexander: Private (27929 Royal Scots [16th]); KIA, 01.07.16, 20 years; 213 Links Street, Kirkcaldy; Gravestone in Bennochy Cemetery. Raith Church Memorial Plaque; Thiepval Memorial, Somme, France. Pier & Face 6D & 7D; Kirkcaldy War Memorial; *FA* 05.08.16; *Soldiers Died* Part 6; *FA* 29.07.16; *FFP* 29.07.16; *FA* (RoH) 05.08.16; *FFP* 05.08.16 Roll of the Brave; *FA* (RoH) 16.09.16; *FFP* (RoH) 16.09.16; *FA* (Service List) 25.11.16; *FA* (Service List) 02.12.16; *FFP* (RoH) 30.12.16; *FA* (BMD) 30.06.17; *FA* (BMD) 06.07.18; *FA* (FRoH) 23.11.18

Bogie, George: Private (3259 RDC [National Reservists] Black Watch [2/7th]. No 1 Supernumerary Coy); Died Edinburgh, 05.05.15; 21/24 Quality Street, Nicol Street, Kirkcaldy; Comely Bank Cemetery, Edinburgh. Grave D.26; Kirkcaldy War Memorial; *Soldiers Died* Part 46; War Album 15; *FA* 15.05.15; *FFP* (CasList) 05.06.15; *FFP* 05.08.16 Roll of the Brave; *FA* (Service List) 25.11.16; *FA* (FRoH) 16.11.18; Wauchope Vol 2

Bogie, William Nicol: Sapper (44738 Royal Engineers [15th Div Signals Coy]); KIA, 11.10.18, 21 years; 53 Nether Street, Kirkcaldy; Gravestone in Dysart Cemetery; Inchy Communal Cemetery Extension, France. Grave B.13; Kirkcaldy War Memorial; *FA* 26.10.18; *Soldiers Died* Part 4; *FA* 19.10.18; *FA* (RoH) 16.11.18; *FFP* (RoH) 16.11.18; *FFP* (BMD) 16.11.18; *FA* (FRoH) 14.12.18

Borthwick, Alfred George: Private (267207 Royal Warwickshire Regt [2/7th]. Formerly 781 HCB); KIA, 13.10.17, 21 years; 25 Octavia Street, Kirkcaldy; Pathhead Parish Church Memorial Plaques & Windows; Brown's Copse Cemetery, Roeux, Pas de Calais, France. Grave IV.B.29; Kirkcaldy War Memorial; *Soldiers Died* Part 11; *FA* 20.10.17; *FFP* 20.10.17; *FFP* (BMD) 20.10.17; *FA* (BMD) 27.10.17; *FA* (RoH) 17.11.17; *FFP* (CasList) 17.11.17; *FFP* (RoH) 17.11.17; *FFP* (BMD) 12.10.18; *FA* (FRoH) 07.12.18

Bowie, Peter Gibson: Private (7327 KOSB [2nd] "A" Coy); KIA Hill 60, Ypres, 18.04.15, 28 years; 5 Heggie's Square, Kirkcaldy; Ypres (Menin Gate) Memorial, Ieper, West Vlaanderen, Belgium. Panel 22; Kirkcaldy War Memorial; *FA* 08.05.15; *Soldiers Died* Part 30; War Album 15; *FA* 08.05.15; *FFP* 05.08.16 Roll of the Brave; *FA* (Service List) 28.10.16; *FA* (Service List) 06.01.17; *FA* (FRoH) 16.11.18

Bradley, Michael J.: Private (Royal Dublin Fusiliers); Not identified on CWGC web site; Kirkcaldy War Memorial

Brady, Thomas: Private (21245 Black Watch [1st]); MIA Ypres, 11.11.14, 20 years; 54 St Clair Street, Kirkcaldy; Ypres (Menin Gate) Memorial, Ieper, West Vlaanderen, Belgium. Panel 37; Kirkcaldy War Memorial; *Soldiers Died* Part 46; *FA* 08.05.15; *FA* 22.05.15; *FA* 28.10.16; *FFP* 28.10.16; *FFP* (BMD) 28.10.16; *FA* (RoH) 18.11.16; *FFP* (RoH) 18.11.16; *FA* (Service List) 02.12.16; *FFP* (RoH) 30.12.16; *FA* 10.02.17; *FFP* 10.02.17; *FA* (FRoH) 16.11.18; *FA* (FRoH) 23.11.18; Wauchope Vol 1

Braid, David: Private (345332 Black Watch [14th] [F & F Yeo Bn]); KIA Egypt, 06.11.17, 21 years; 83 Mid Street, Kirkcaldy; Pathhead Parish Church Memorial Plaques & Windows; Beersheba War Cemetery, Israel. Grave L.I; Kirkcaldy War Memorial; *Soldiers Died* Part 46; *FA* 24.11.17; *FFP* 24.11.17; *FA* 01.12.17; *FFP* (BMD) 01.12.17; *FA* (RoH) 15.12.17; *FFP* (RoH) 15.12.17; *FA* (FRoH) 07.12.18; *FFP* 21.06.24; Wauchope Vol 3; Ogilvie

Braid, James: Private (2656 Black Watch [1st]); KIA, 25.09.15, 19 years; Albert Terrace, 75 Dunnikier Road, Kirkcaldy; St Andrew's Church Memorial Plaque; Loos Memorial, Pas de Calais, France. Panels 78-83; Kirkcaldy War Memorial; *Soldiers Died* Part 46; War Album 15/16; *FFP* 09.10.15; *Scotsman* 11.10.15; *FA* 16.10.15; *FA* (RoH) 16.10.15; *FFP* (RoH) 16.10.15; *FFP* 05.08.16 Roll of the Brave; *FFP* (BMD) 23.09.16; *FA* (Service List) 16.12.16; *FFP* (BMD) 22.09.17; *FFP* (BMD) 28.09.18; *FA* (FRoH) 16.11.18; Wauchope Vol 1

Breen, Charles: Private (9240 Black Watch [1st]); KIA, 12.11.14; 159 Links Street/3 Heggie's Wynd, Kirkcaldy; Ypres (Menin Gate) Memorial, Ieper, West Vlaanderen, Belgium. Panel 37; Kirkcaldy War Memorial; *FA* 23.01.15; *FA* 18.03.16; *Soldiers Died* Part 46; *FA* (CasList) 20.02.15; *FFP* 11.03.16; *FA* 18.03.16; *FA* (RoH) 15.04.16; *FFP* (CasList) 15.04.16; *FFP* 05.08.16 Roll of the Brave; *FA* (Service List) 04.11.16; *FA* (Service List) 25.11.16; *FA* (Service List) 02.12.16; *FA* (Service List) 30.12.16; *FA* (FRoH) 23.11.18; Wauchope Vol 1

Breslin, Matthew: Private (202279 Black Watch (4/5th]); KIA, 31.10.17, 32 years; 159 Links Street/15 Park Road, Kirkcaldy; Tyne Cot Memorial, Zonnebeke, West Vlaanderen, Belgium. Panels 94-96; Kirkcaldy War Memorial; *FA* 17.07.15; *Soldiers Died* Part 46; *Scotsman* 20.07.15; *FA* 10.11.17; *FA* (RoH) 17.11.17; *FFP* (RoH) 17.11.17; *FFP* (CasList) 08.12.17; *FA* (FRoH) 07.12.18; Wauchope Vol 2

Bristow, Frederick C.: Private (L/6021 Middlesex Regt [2nd]); Brother-in-law of Robert Chapman; Died at home, 02.11.14; 7 Meldrum Road/69 Viceroy Street, Kirkcaldy; Portsdown (Christ Church) Military Cemetery, Hampshire. Grave D.6; Kirkcaldy War Memorial; *Soldiers Died* Part 56; *FA* 07.11.14; *FA* 04.12.15; *FA* 24.02.17; *FA* (Service List) 17.03.17

Brown, Andrew: Lance Corporal (12348 HLI [1st]); KIA, 08.03.16, 21 years; 29 Oswald Road, Kirkcaldy; Basra Memorial, Iraq. Panels 35 & 64; Kirkcaldy War Memorial; *Soldiers Died* Part 63; *FA* 15.04.16; *FA* (RoH) 15.04.16; *FFP* 15.04.16; *FFP* (CasList) 15.04.16; *FFP* 05.08.16 Roll of the Brave; *FA* (Service List) 24.03.17; *FA* (FRoH) 23.11.18

Brown, Andrew Henderson: Private (S/31515 Cameron Hldrs [5th]. Formerly 6639 Lovat Scouts & 4103 F & F Yeo); KIA Pozieres Ridge, 23.03.18; Pozieres Memorial, Somme, France. Panel 74; Kirkcaldy War Memorial; *Soldiers Died* Part 66

Brown, Charles, MM: Sergeant (45954 Royal Engineers [25th Div Signals Coy]); DOW 2nd Canadian CCS, 02.05.18, 26 years; Abbotshall House, 44 Nicol Street, Kirkcaldy; Abbotshall Parish Church Memorial Plaque; Esquelbecq Military Cemetery, Nord, France. Grave II.B.4; Kirkcaldy War Memorial; *Soldiers Died* Part 4; *FA* 18.05.18; *FA* (BMD) 18.05.18; *FFP* (BMD) 18.05.18; *FA* (RoH) 15.06.18; *FFP* (RoH) 15.06.18; *FA* 26.10.18; *FA* (FRoH) 14.12.18; *FA* (BMD) 03.05.19; *FA* 19.11.21

Brown, George: Private (3688; AIF; Australian Infantry [46th]); Died a PoW in Germany, 11.04.17, 25 years; 37 Aitken Street, Kirkcaldy; Gallatown Church Roll of Honour; Villers-Bretonneux Memorial, Somme, France; Australian War Memorial web site; Kirkcaldy War Memorial; *FFP* (BMD) 27.10.17; *FA* (BMD) 03.11.17; *FFP* (RoH) 17.11.17; *FA* (FRoH) 07.12.18

Brown, George Allan: Driver (M/282164 RASC [781st MT Coy]); Died of pneumonia at Salonika, 02.11.18; 20 Milton Road, Kirkcaldy; Raith Church Memorial Plaque; Mikra British Cemetery, Kalamaria, Greece. Grave 1917; Kirkcaldy War Memorial; *Soldiers Died* Part 78; *FFP* (BMD) 23.11.18; *FA* 07.12.18; *FFP* 07.12.18; *FA* (FRoH) 14.12.18; *FFP* (RoH) 14.12.18

Brown, James: Corporal (7755 Cameron Hldrs [2nd] "B" Coy); KIA Salonika, 04.10.16, 28 years; 252 Links Street, Kirkcaldy; Struma Military Cemetery, Kalocastron, Greece. Grave V.B.14; Kirkcaldy War Memorial; *FA* 28.10.16; *Soldiers Died* Part 66; *FA* 21.10.16; *FA* 28.10.16; *FFP* 28.10.16; *FFP* (CasList) 11.11.16; *FA* (RoH) 18.11.16; *FFP* (RoH) 18.11.16; *FFP* (RoH) 30.12.16; *FA* (FRoH) 30.11.18; Kirkcaldy Council Memorial Scroll

Brown, Norman McLeod: Sergeant (1057 London Regt [14th] [County of London] [London Scottish] "C" Coy); KIA Givenchy, 24.12.14, 27 years; 70 High Street, Kirkcaldy; Gravestone in Bennochy Cemetery. Kirkcaldy High School War Memorial; Arras Road Cemetery, Roclincourt, Pas de Calais, France. Grave III.N.29; Kirkcaldy War Memorial; *Soldiers Died* Part 76; War Album 14/15; *FA* 02.01.15; *FFP* 02.01.15; *FA* 16.01.15; *FFP* (RoH) 30.01.15; *FA* (CasList) 20.02.15; *FFP* 05.08.16 Roll of the Brave; *FA* (Service List) 28.10.16; *FA* (Service List) 09.12.16; *FA* (FRoH) 16.11.18; *FA* (KHS RoH) 29.03.19; Kirkcaldy Council Memorial Scroll

Brown, Ramsay: Private (2135 Black Watch [1/7th]); KIA, 30.07.16; 4 Randolph Road, Kirkcaldy; Caterpillar Valley Cemetery, Longueval, Somme, France. Grave 16.F.36; Kirkcaldy War Memorial; ‡; *Soldiers Died* Part 46; *FA* 12.08.16; *FFP* 26.08.16; *FFP* (BMD) 26.08.16; *FA* 02.09.16; *FFP* 02.09.16; *FA* (CasList) 09.09.16; *FFP* (CasList) 09.09.16; *FA* (RoH) 16.09.16; *FFP* (RoH) 16.09.16; *FFP* (RoH) 30.12.16; *FA* (Service List) 31.03.17; *FA* (FRoH) 23.11.18; Wauchope Vol 2

Brown, Robert Ewan: Private (290768 Black Watch [1/7th] att'd 2nd); DOW Fulham Military Hospital, 04.11.18, 27 years; 75 St Clair Street, Kirkcaldy; Barony Church Plaque; Bennochy Cemetery, Kirkcaldy. Grave FF.64; Kirkcaldy War Memorial; *Soldiers Died* Part 46; *FA* 09.11.18; *FA* (RoH) 16.11.18; *FFP* (RoH) 16.11.18; *FA* (FRoH) 14.12.18; Wauchope Vol 2

Brown, William, MM & Bar: Private (290298 Black Watch [7th]); DOW, 21.03.18, 21 years; 9 Harriet Street, Kirkcaldy; Arras Memorial, Pas de Calais, France. Bay 6; Kirkcaldy War Memorial; *Soldiers Died* Part 46; *FFP* 13.03.18; *FA* 20.04.18; Wauchope Vol 2

Brown, William: Private (S/13343 Black Watch [8th]); KIA, 17.10.16, 19 years; 2 Junction Road, Kirkcaldy; Thiepval Memorial, Somme, France. Pier & Face 10A; Kirkcaldy War Memorial; *FFP* 04.11.16; *Soldiers Died* Part 46; *FA* 28.10.16; *FFP* 28.10.16; *FFP* 04.11.16; *FA* (RoH) 18.11.16; *FFP* (RoH) 18.11.16; *FFP* (BMD) 18.11.16; *FA* (CasList) 25.11.16; *FFP* (CasList) 25.11.16; *FFP* (BMD) 25.11.16; *FFP* (RoH) 30.12.16; *FA* (Service List) 03.02.17; *FA* (FRoH) 23.11.18; Wauchope Vol 3

Bruce, John: Corporal (S/1785 Gordon Hldrs [8/10th]); KIA France, 01.08.17, 28 years; 64 Overton Road, Kirkcaldy; Pathhead Parish Church Memorial Plaques & Windows; Tyne Cot Memorial, Zonnebeke, West Vlaanderen, Belgium. Panels 135-136; Kirkcaldy War Memorial; *FA* 01.01.16; *FA* 18.08.17; *FA* 15.09.17; *FFP* (CasList) 15.09.17; *FFP* (RoH) 15.09.17; *FA* (BMD) 27.07.18; *FFP* (BMD) 27.07.18; *FA* (FRoH) 21.12.18

Bruce, William: Trooper (2020 F & F Yeo [1/1st]); Died of accidental injuries, 20.05.15, 35 years; 212 Rosslyn Street, Kirkcaldy; Gravestone in Dysart Cemetery; Dysart Cemetery, Kirkcaldy. Grave 27.25. North; Kirkcaldy War Memorial; *Soldiers Died* Part 1; *FA* (Service List) 09.12.16

Bryce, William: Sapper (Royal Engineers); 18 Rosslyn Street, Kirkcaldy; Not identified on CWGC web site; Kirkcaldy War Memorial; *FA* (RoH) 15.12.17; *FFP* (RoH) 15.12.17; *FA* (FRoH) 07.12.18

Buchan, Andrew: Private (44069 KOSB [2nd]. Formerly 1939 HCB); MIA, 03.09.16, 31 years; 125 St Clair Street, Kirkcaldy; Barony Church Plaque; Thiepval Memorial, Somme, France. Pier & Face 4A & 4D; Kirkcaldy War Memorial; *Soldiers Died* Part 30; *FFP* 07.10.16; *FA* 14.10.16; *FFP* (BMD) 21.10.16; *FFP* 28.10.16; *FFP* (CasList) 04.11.16; *FA* (RoH) 18.11.16; *FFP* (RoH) 18.11.16; *FFP* (RoH) 30.12.16; *FFP* (BMD) 08.09.17; *FFP* (BMD) 07.09.18; *FA* (FRoH) 30.11.18

Buchanan, George: Private (S/41031 Gordon Hldrs [2nd]); KIA, 26.10.17, 34 years; 48 Cowan Street, Kirkcaldy; Raith Church Memorial Plaque; Tyne Cot Memorial, Zonnebeke, West Vlaanderen, Belgium. Panels 135-136; Kirkcaldy War Memorial; *Soldiers Died* Part 65; *FA* 02.11.18

Buchanan, James H.: Private (27781 KOSB [2nd]. Formerly 2881 F & F Yeo); Died of acute bronchitis at 24th General Hospital, Etaples, 20.12.16, 26 years; 77 Nicol Street, Kirkcaldy; Raith Church Memorial Plaque; Etaples Military Cemetery, Pas de Calais, France. Grave XXI.J.6; Kirkcaldy War Memorial; *Soldiers Died* Part 30; *FA* 23.12.16; *FFP* (BMD) 23.12.16; *FA* (BMD) 30.12.16; *FFP* (RoH) 30.12.16; *FA* (RoH) 13.01.17; *FFP* (RoH) 13.01.17; *FA* (CasList) 03.02.17; *FFP* (CasList) 03.02.17; *FFP* (BMD) 22.12.17; *FA* (FRoH) 30.11.18

Buchanan, Thomas: Private (353003 Royal Scots [9th]. Formerly 2173 Lothian & Borders Horse); MIA Roeux Wood, 25.04.17, 26 years; 6 Rosebank Terrace, Kirkcaldy; St Brycedale Church Plaque. Gravestone in Bennochy Cemetery (Photo); Arras Memorial, Pas de Calais, France. Bays 1 & 2; Kirkcaldy War Memorial; *Soldiers Died* Part 6; *FA* 02.06.17; *FFP* (Memorial List) 05.01.18; *FA* 09.02.18; *FA* (BMD) 09.02.18; *FFP* (RoH) 09.02.18; *FFP* (BMD) 09.02.18; *FA* (RoH) 16.02.18; *FFP* (RoH) 16.02.18; *FFP* (BMD) 16.02.18; *FA* (BMD) 23.02.18; *FA* (FRoH) 07.12.18

Burnett, David G.: Private (S/15224 Cameron Hldrs [1st]); CWGC has his number as S/15924; KIA Loos, 25.09.15, 26 years; 19 Harriet Street, Kirkcaldy; Pathhead Parish Church Memorial Plaques & Windows; Ninth Avenue Cemetery, Haisnes, Pas de Calais, France. Sp. Mem.1; Kirkcaldy War Memorial; *Soldiers Died* Part 66; War Album 15/16; *FA* 06.11.15; *FA* (RoH) 13.11.15; *FFP* 18.12.15 (Pathhead Church Memorial); *FFP* 05.08.16 Roll of the Brave; *FA* (Service List) 20.01.17; *FFP* (BMD) 28.09.18; *FA* (FRoH) 16.11.18

Burt, David: Rifleman (S/9249 Rifle Brigade [8th Bn]); Returned from America to join army; KIA, 03.05.17, 22 years; 36 Viceroy Street, Kirkcaldy; Barony Church Plaque; Albuera Cemetery, Bailleul-Sire-Berthoult, Pas de Calais, France. Grave G.5; Kirkcaldy War Memorial; *Soldiers Died* Part 74; *FA* 12.05.17; *FFP* 12.05.17; *FFP* (BMD) 12.05.17; *FA* 19.05.17; *FA* (RoH) 19.05.17; *FFP* (RoH) 19.05.17; *FFP* (CasList) 09.06.17; *FFP* 28.07.17; *FA* (FRoH) 30.11.18

Burt, James: 2nd Lieutenant (Black Watch [3rd] att'd 8th); KIA, 19.07.18, 20 years; 184 High Street, Kirkcaldy; Gravestone in Abbotshall Churchyard (Photo). St Brycedale Church Plaque. Kirkcaldy High School War Memorial; Meteren Military Cemetery, Nord, France. Grave II.B.87; Kirkcaldy War Memorial; *FFP* 03.08.18; *Officers Died*; *Cross of Sacrifice Vol 1*; *FA* 27.07.18; *FFP* 27.07.18; *FFP* (BMD) 27.07.18; *FA* 03.08.18 (2 entries); *FA* 24.08.18; *FA* (RoH) 14.09.18; *FFP* (RoH) 14.09.18; *FA* (FRoH) 14.12.18; *FA* (KHS RoH) 29.03.19; *FA* (KHS RoH) 19.07.19; *FA* (BMD) 19.07.19; Wauchope Vol 3

Butchart, Malcolm G.: Private (291159 Black Watch [8th]); KIA, 12.10.17, 19 years; 42 Maryhall Street, Kirkcaldy; Bethelfield Church Plaque; Tyne Cot Memorial, Zonnebeke, West Vlaanderen, Belgium. Panels 94-96; Kirkcaldy War Memorial; *FA* 03.11.17; *Soldiers Died* Part 46; *FA* 03.11.17; *FA* (BMD) 03.11.17; *FFP* 03.11.17; *FFP* (BMD) 03.11.17; *FA* (RoH) 17.11.17; *FFP* (CasList) 17.11.17; *FFP* (RoH) 17.11.17; *FA* (BMD) 12.10.18; *FFP* (BMD) 12.10.18 (2 entries); *FA* (FRoH) 07.12.18; *FA* (BMD) 11.10.19; Wauchope Vol 3

Butterfield, William: Corporal (43210 Royal Scots [2nd]); KIA near Lens, 26.08.17, 21 years; Late of 14 Harriet Street, Kirkcaldy; St Michael's Church Memorial Plaque; Lebucquiere Communal Cemetery Extension, Pas de Calais, France. Grave I.D.10; Kirkcaldy War Memorial; *Soldiers Died* Part 6; *FA* 08.09.17; *FFP* 08.09.17; *FFP* (BMD) 08.09.17; *FFP* 20.10.17; *FA* (RoH) 17.11.17; *FFP* (RoH) 17.11.17; *FFP* (BMD) 31.08.18; *FA* (FRoH) 07.12.18

Butters, William: Private (43195 North Staffordshire Regt [13th Garrison Bn] [Labour Corps]); 04.01.19, 43 years; 6 Harriet Street, Kirkcaldy; Gravestone in Dysart Cemetery; Dysart Cemetery, Kirkcaldy. Grave 8.J. Middle; Kirkcaldy War Memorial; *FA* (RoH) 15.02.19

Byrne, Peter Joseph: Private (18172 Royal Munster Fusiliers [2nd]. Formerly 26837 Royal Dublin Fusiliers [10th & 11th]); DOW whilst PoW, 23.03.18, 20 years; 13 Sang Road/Douglasfield, Abbotshall Road, Kirkcaldy; Kirkcaldy High School War Memorial; Honnechy British Cemetery, Nord, France. Grave II.D.6; Kirkcaldy War Memorial; *Soldiers Died* Part 72; *FA* 18.05.18; *FA* 01.06.18; *FFP* 01.06.18; *FA* (RoH) 15.06.18; *FFP* (RoH) 15.06.18; *FA* 13.07.18; *FA* (FRoH) 14.12.18; *FA* (KHS RoH) 29.03.19

Cadger, James: Private (S/18778 Black Watch [8th]); CWGC gives his number as S/118778; KIA, 21.03.18, 19 years; 2 Pillan's Buildings, Sands Road, Kirkcaldy; Pozieres Memorial, Somme, France. Panels 49-50; Kirkcaldy War Memorial; *Soldiers Died* Part 46; *FA* 04.05.18; *FFP* (BMD) 04.05.18; *FFP* (RoH) 11.05.18; *FA* (RoH) 18.05.18; *FFP* (RoH) 18.05.18; *FA* (FRoH) 07.12.18; Wauchope Vol 3

Caird, John: Private (10868 Royal Scots Fusiliers [2nd]); KIA, 12.03.15, 31 years; 10 Stewart's Lane, Kirkcaldy; Gravestone in Bennochy Cemetery; Le Touret Memorial, Pas de Calais, France. Panels 12-13; Kirkcaldy War Memorial; *FFP* 10.04.15; *FA* 17.04.15; *Soldiers Died* Part 26; War Album 15; *FA* 03.04.15; *FFP* (BMD) 03.04.15; *FA* 29.07.16; *FFP* 05.08.16 Roll of the Brave; *FA* (Service List) 04.11.16; *FA* (Service List) 03.02.17; *FA* (FRoH) 16.11.18

Cairns, James: Private (44050 KOSB [2nd]. Formerly 1285 HCB); KIA, 03.09.16, 41 years; 56 Rosabelle Street, Kirkcaldy; Pathhead Parish Church Memorial Plaques & Windows; Delville Wood Cemetery, Longueval, Somme, France. Grave XXIII.K.1; Kirkcaldy War Memorial; *FFP* 18.11.16; *Soldiers Died* Part 30; *FA* 23.09.16; *FFP* 30.09.16; *FFP* (BMD) 07.10.16; *FA* (RoH) 14.10.16; *FA* (BMD) 14.10.16; *FFP* (RoH) 14.10.16; *FFP* (RoH) 30.12.16; *FA* (Service List) 17.03.17; *FFP* (BMD) 01.09.17; *FFP* (BMD) 07.09.18; *FA* (FRoH) 23.11.18; *FFP* 21.06.24

Calder, John: Private (290230 Black Watch [7th]); KIA Arras, 20.04.17, 20 years; 77 Links Street, Kirkcaldy; St Columba's Church Memorial Plaque; Arras Memorial, Pas de Calais, France. Bay 6; *FA* 11.12.15; *FA* 12.05.17; *Soldiers Died* Part 46; War Album 15/16; *FFP* 12.05.17; *FA* (RoH) 19.05.17; *FA* (CasList) 26.05.17; *FFP* (CasList) 26.05.17; *FFP* (BMD) 26.05.17; *FA* (BMD) 20.04.18; *FA* (FRoH) 30.11.18; *FA* (BMD) 19.04.19; Wauchope Vol 2

Cameron, William Hendry: Lance Corporal (47308 RAMC [Woolwich Dispensary] [8th Fld Amb]); DOW in hospital, St Jean, Arras, 11.05.17, 24 years; 81 Dunnikier Road, Kirkcaldy; Dunnikier Church Roll of Honour. Kirkcaldy High School War Memorial; Faubourg D'Amiens Cemetery, Arras, Pas de Calais, France. Grave V.D.33; Kirkcaldy War Memorial; *Soldiers Died* Part 79; *FA* 19.05.17; *FA* (BMD) 19.05.17; *FFP* 19.05.17; *FFP* (BMD) 19.05.17; *FA* (RoH) 16.06.17; *FFP* (CasList) 16.06.17; *FFP* (RoH) 16.06.17; *FA* 14.07.17 (KHS War Honours); *FA* (BMD) 11.05.18; *FFP* (BMD) 11.05.18; *FA* (FRoH) 30.11.18; *FA* (KHS RoH) 29.03.19; *FA* 26.04.19; *FA* (BMD) 10.05.19

Campbell, Francis: Private (5591 Royal Warwickshire Regt [2/7th]. Formerly 2164 HCB); DOW, 08.08.16; 56 Lorne Street, Kirkcaldy; Barony Church Plaque; Merville Communal Cemetery, Nord, France. Grave XI.B.9; Kirkcaldy War Memorial; *Soldiers Died* Part 11; *FA* 12.08.16; *FFP* 19.08.16; *FA* (BMD) 02.09.16; *FFP* (BMD) 02.09.16; *FA* (BMD) 09.09.16; *FA* (CasList) 16.09.16; *FA* (RoH) 16.09.16; *FFP* (RoH) 16.09.16; *FFP* (RoH) 30.12.16; *FA* (Service List) 03.02.17; *FFP* (BMD) 11.08.17; *FA* (BMD) 18.08.17; *FA* (FRoH) 23.11.18

Campbell, Robert: Private (S/1717 Gordon Hldrs [8th]); KIA Loos, 25.09.15, 21 years; 28 St Clair Street, Kirkcaldy/1 Kirkgate, Burntisland; Chocques Military Cemetery, Pas de Calais, France. Grave I.E.27; Kirkcaldy War Memorial; *Soldiers Died* Part 65; *FFP* 05.08.16 Roll of the Brave; *FA* (FRoH) 23.11.18; Kirkcaldy Council Memorial Scroll

Canavan, Richard: Private (3/1618 Black Watch [1st]); Referred to as Cavanagh in some local news items; KIA at Neuve Chapelle, 09.05.15, 22 years; 2 Gow's Square, Glasswork Street, Kirkcaldy; Le Touret Memorial, Pas de Calais, France. Panels 24-26; Kirkcaldy War Memorial; *FA* 08.07.16; *Soldiers Died* Part 46; *FA* 19.06.15; *FA* 08.07.16; *FA* (RoH) 15.07.16; *FFP* 05.08.16 Roll of the Brave; *FA* (Service List) 27.01.17; *FFP* (BMD) 12.05.17; Wauchope Vol 1

Cargill, James R.: Gunner (RGA); Whytescauseway Baptist Church Memorial Plaque; Not identified on CWGC web site; Kirkcaldy War Memorial

Carlyle, Thomas: Private (292112 Black Watch [7th]); KIA, 26.03.18, 19 years; 4 Mill Street, Kirkcaldy; St Columba's Church Memorial Plaque; Arras Memorial, Pas de Calais, France. Bay 6; Kirkcaldy War Memorial; *Soldiers Died* Part 46; *FA* 11.05.18; *FA* (BMD) 12.07.19; Wauchope Vol 2

Carmichael, Andrew: Private (241204 Black Watch [9th]. Formerly F & F Yeo); KIA, 26.08.17, 22 years; 11 Maryhall Street, Kirkcaldy; St Peter's Church Memorial Plaque; Tyne Cot Memorial, Zonnebeke, West Vlaanderen, Belgium. Panels 94-96; Kirkcaldy War Memorial; *Soldiers Died* Part 46; *FA* 15.09.17; *FA* (BMD) 15.09.17; *FFP* 15.09.17; *FFP* (BMD) 15.09.17; *FFP* (CasList) 29.09.17; *FA* 13.10.17; *FFP* (RoH) 13.10.17; *FA* (FRoH) 07.12.18; Wauchope Vol 3

Carr, Alexander: Private (Gordon Hldrs); Died, 31.07.18; 51 Victoria Road, Kirkcaldy; Not identified on CWGC web site; Kirkcaldy War Memorial; *FA* 03.08.18

Carswell, Robert Reid: Trooper (301486 Staffordshire Yeomanry Hussars [1/1st]. Formerly F & F Yeo); KIA Palestine, 14.11.17, 38 years; 50/78 Salisbury Street, Kirkcaldy; Invertiel Parish Church Memorial Table; Ramleh War Cemetery, Israel. Grave E.72; Kirkcaldy War Memorial; *Soldiers Died* Part 1; *FA* 01.12.17; *FFP* 01.12.17; *FFP* (BMD) 01.12.17; *FA* (RoH) 15.12.17; *FA* (FRoH) 16.11.18; *FA* (FRoH) 07.12.18

Carter, George: Private (S/17059 Black Watch [8th]); KIA, 19.07.18, 20 years; 23 Ramsay Road, Kirkcaldy; Gravestone in Dysart Cemetery; Meteren Military Cemetery, Nord, France. Grave II.G.205; Kirkcaldy War Memorial; *Soldiers Died* Part 46; *FA* 03.08.18; *FFP* 10.08.18; *FFP* (BMD) 10.08.18; *FA* (BMD) 17.08.18; *FA* (RoH) 14.09.18; *FFP* (RoH) 14.09.18; *FA* (FRoH) 14.12.18; Wauchope Vol 3

Cathro, Albert, MM: Lance Corporal (238127 Cameronians [Scottish Rifles] [9th] [Signals Section]. Formerly 1160 HCB); KIA by a sniper, France, 25.10.18, 20 years; 32 Viceroy Street, Kirkcaldy; Pathhead Parish Church Memorial Plaques & Windows; Ingoyghem Military Cemetery, Anzegem, West Vlaanderen, Belgium. Grave B.9; Kirkcaldy War Memorial; *Soldiers Died* Part 31; *FA* (BMD) 16.11.18; *FA* (BMD) 30.11.18; *FA* 07.12.18; *FA* (BMD) 07.12.18; *FFP* 07.12.18; *FA* (FRoH) 14.12.18; *FFP* (RoH) 14.12.18; *FFP* (BMD) 23.10.20

Chalmers, Alexander: Private (S/27703 Black Watch [9th]); DOW Australian base hospital, 15.11.18, 19 years; 447 High Street, Kirkcaldy; Terlincthun British Cemetery, Wimille, Pas de Calais, France. Grave X.F.24; Kirkcaldy War Memorial; *Soldiers Died* Part 46; *FFP* 23.11.18; *FFP* 07.12.18; *FA* (FRoH) 14.12.18; *FFP* (RoH) 14.12.18; Wauchope Vol 3

Chalmers, Harry: Sergeant (43305 Royal Scots Fusiliers [2nd] "A" Coy, 4th Platoon. Formerly HLI); MIA, 12.10.16, 21 years; 24 Stewart's Lane, Kirkcaldy; St Peter's Church Memorial Plaque; Thiepval Memorial, Somme, France. Pier & Face 3C; Kirkcaldy War Memorial; *FA* 18.11.16; *Soldiers Died* Part 26; *FA* 18.11.16; *FA* (CasList) 03.02.17; *FA* (Service List) 03.02.17; *FA* 14.07.17; *FFP* (CasList) 14.07.17; *FFP* (BMD) 14.07.17; *FFP* 21.07.17

Chalmers, Thomas: Private (622109; CEF; 3rd Div 8th Bde. 1st Canadian Mounted Rifles [Saskatchewan Regt]. Formerly Canadian Bn [44th]. Winnipeg Rifles); Brother of James Chalmers. Late of Thornton; 02.06.16, 20 years; Rosabelle Street, Gallatown, Kirkcaldy/229 St Mary's Road, Norwood, Winnipeg; Ypres (Menin Gate) Memorial, Ieper, West Vlaanderen, Belgium. Panels 30-32; Kirkcaldy War Memorial; *CBoR* Page 65; *FA* 08.07.16; *FFP* 08.07.16; *FFP* 12.05.17; *FA* 19.05.17; *FA* (RoH) 16.06.17; *FFP* (RoH) 16.06.17; *FFP* (RoH) 20.04.18; *FA* 27.04.18; *FA* (FRoH) 30.11.18; Kirkcaldy Council Memorial Scroll

Chapman, Andrew Ramsey: Private (33032 RAMC [43rd Fld Amb]); KIA, 21.03.18; 23 Forth Avenue South/37 West Smeaton Street, Kirkcaldy; Pathhead Parish Church Memorial Plaques & Windows. St Columba's Church Memorial Plaque; Pozieres Memorial, Somme, France. Panel 95; Kirkcaldy War Memorial; *Soldiers Died* Part 79; *FFP* (RoH) 20.04.18; *FA* 27.04.18; *FA* 14.09.18; *FFP* 11.01.19; *FA* (RoH) 15.02.19; *FFP* 21.06.24

Chapman, Robert Ednie: Private (1799; AIF; Australian Infantry [17th]); Brother-in-law of Fred Bristow; KIA, 04.02.17, 27 years; 7 Meldrum Road, Kirkcaldy/Redfern NSW, Australia; Gravestone in Abbotshall Churchyard; Villers-Bretonneux Memorial, Somme, France. Panel 26; Australian War Memorial web site; Kirkcaldy War Memorial; *FA* 24.02.17; *FFP* 03.03.17; *FFP* (BMD) 03.03.17; *FA* (RoH) 17.03.17; *FFP* (BMD) 09.02.18; *FA* (FRoH) 30.11.18

Chisholm, Alexander: Able Seaman (R/2174; Royal Navy; RNVR [RND] [Howe Bn]); KIA France, 26.10.17, 36 years; 38 Overton Road, Kirkcaldy; Tyne Cot Memorial, Zonnebeke, West Vlaanderen, Belgium. Panels 2-3 & 162-162A; Kirkcaldy War Memorial; *Cross of Sacrifice Vol 4*; *FA* 10.11.17; *FA* (RoH) 17.11.17; *FFP* 17.11.17; *FFP* (RoH) 17.11.17; *FA* (FRoH) 07.12.18

Christie, Alexander: Lance Corporal (21379 Cheshire Regt [16th] [Lewis Gun Section]); KIA, 19.08.17, 19 years; 12 Berwick Place, Dysart; St Brycedale Church Plaque; Templeux-Le-Guerard British Cemetery, France. Grave II.G.4; Kirkcaldy War Memorial; *Soldiers Died* Part 27; *FFP* 08.09.17; *FFP* (BMD) 08.09.17; *FA* 15.09.17; *FA* (BMD) 15.09.17; *FFP* (RoH) 15.09.17; *FFP* (CasList) 22.09.17; *FFP* (Memorial List) 05.01.18; *FFP* (BMD) 17.08.18

Christie, Andrew: Gunner (156104 RFA [50th Bde] "C" Batt'y. Formerly 2377 Horsekeeper, RAVC); KIA, 08.05.18, 28 years; 89 Sutherland Street, Kirkcaldy; Lijssenthoek Military Cemetery, Poperinge, West Vlaanderen, Belgium. Grave XXVIII.H.3; Kirkcaldy War Memorial; *Soldiers Died* Part 2; *FA* (BMD) 25.05.18; *FFP* 08.06.18; *FFP* (BMD) 08.06.18; *FA* 15.06.18; *FA* (RoH) 15.06.18; *FA* (BMD) 15.06.18; *FFP* (RoH) 15.06.18; *FA* (FRoH) 14.12.18

Christie, David: Private (15409 KOSB [7/8th] "I" Coy); KIA Somme, 09.08.16, 23 years; 90 Meldrum Road, Kirkcaldy; Thiepval Memorial, Somme, France. Pier & Face 4A & 4D; Kirkcaldy War Memorial; *Soldiers Died* Part 30; *FA* 26.08.16; *FA* (BMD) 26.08.16; *FFP* (BMD) 26.08.16; *FFP* 02.09.16; *FA* (RoH) 16.09.16; *FFP* 16.09.16; *FFP* (CasList) 16.09.16; *FFP* (RoH) 16.09.16; *FFP* (RoH) 30.12.16; *FA* (Service List) 17.03.17; *FFP* (BMD) 11.08.17; *FA* (FRoH) 23.11.18

Christie, George: Private (S/40829 A & S Hldrs [10th]); KIA, 30.08.18, 34 years; 31 Maryhall Street, Kirkcaldy; Old Parish Church Memorial Panel; Roye New British Cemetery, Somme, France. Grave III.D.16; Kirkcaldy War Memorial; *Soldiers Died* Part 70; *FA* 07.09.18; *FA* (BMD) 14.09.18; *FFP* 14.09.18; *FFP* (BMD) 21.09.18; *FA* (RoH) 16.11.18; *FFP* (RoH) 16.11.18; *FA* (FRoH) 14.12.18

Christie, James Whyte: Trooper (2530 F & F Yeo); Died at Kirkcaldy Hospital, 10.02.16, 27 years; 87 Balsusney Road, Kirkcaldy; Bennochy Cemetery, Kirkcaldy. Grave O.394; Kirkcaldy War Memorial; *Soldiers Died* Part 1; *FFP* 12.02.16; *FFP* (BMD) 12.02.16; *FA* 19.02.16; *FA* (BMD) 19.02.16; *FFP* 05.08.16 Roll of the Brave; *FA* (FRoH) 16.11.18

Christie, John: Lance Sergeant (S/3193 Black Watch [8th]); KIA, 14.07.16, 30 years; 86 East Smeaton Street, Kirkcaldy; Thiepval Memorial, Somme, France. Pier & Face 10A; Kirkcaldy War Memorial; *Soldiers Died* Part 46; *FA* 29.07.16; *FFP* 29.07.16; *FA* 05.08.16; *FA* (RoH) 05.08.16; *FFP* 05.08.16 Roll of the Brave; *FFP* (CasList) 02.09.16; *FA* (RoH) 16.09.16; *FFP* (RoH) 16.09.16; *FFP* (RoH) 30.12.16; *FA* (Service List) 17.02.17; *FA* (FRoH) 23.11.18; Wauchope Vol 3

Christie, John: Private (S/4152 Black Watch [9th]); Brother-in-law of P. Izatt, killed on the same day; KIA by a shell near Loos, 25.09.15, 34 years; 80 Kidd Street, Kirkcaldy; Philosophe British Cemetery, Mazingarbe, Pas de Calais, France. Grave III.H.2; Kirkcaldy War Memorial; *FA* 18.09.15; *Soldiers Died* Part 46; War Album 15/16; *FFP* 30.10.15; *FFP* (BMD) 30.10.15; *Scotsman* 01.11.15; *FA* 06.11.15; *FA* (BMD) 06.11.15; *FA* (RoH) 13.11.15; *FFP* 05.08.16 Roll of the Brave; *FFP* (BMD) 23.09.16; *FFP* (BMD) 30.09.16; *FA* (Service List) 27.01.17; *FFP* (BMD) 29.09.17; *FFP* (BMD) 28.09.18; *FA* (FRoH) 16.11.18; Wauchope Vol 3

John **Christie** and his brother-in-law, Peter Izatt, both of 9th Black Watch, were killed on the same day, 25th September 1915. Christie's step-brother, also serving in the same regiment, was wounded on that day.

Christie, William Alison: Private (16549 KOSB [7th]); Would appear to be same person as William Christie Alison on *Soldiers Died* and CWGC; 25.09.15; 149 Rosslyn Street, Kirkcaldy; Loos Memorial, Pas de Calais, France. Panels 53-56; Kirkcaldy War Memorial; *Soldiers Died* Part 30; *FA* 19.08.16; *FA* (RoH) 16.09.16; *FFP* (RoH) 16.09.16; *FA* (Service List) 09.12.16; *FFP* (RoH) 30.12.16; *FA* (FRoH) 23.11.18

Clack, Edward: Private (12765 KOSB [6th]); KIA, 25.09.15, 19 years; 312 St Clair Street, Kirkcaldy; Loos Memorial, Pas de Calais, France. Panels 53-56; Kirkcaldy War Memorial; *Soldiers Died* Part 30; *FA* (RoH) 18.11.16; *FFP* (RoH) 18.11.16; *FFP* (RoH) 30.12.16; *FA* (FRoH) 30.11.18

Clark, Andrew: Lance Corporal (201603 A & S Hldrs [1/5th]); KIA Egypt, 08.11.17; Gaza War Cemetery, Israel. Grave XII.F.6; Kirkcaldy War Memorial; *Soldiers Died* Part 70

Clark, David: Driver (6737 RFA [13th Batt'y 17th Bde]); KIA, 28.09.18, 23 years; 80 Salisbury Street, Kirkcaldy; Pathhead Parish Church Memorial Plaques & Windows; Hooge Crater Cemetery, Ieper, West Vlaanderen, Belgium. Grave II.H.10; Kirkcaldy War Memorial; *Soldiers Died* Part 2; *FA* 02.11.18; *FA* 16.11.18; *FA* (RoH) 16.11.18; *FFP* (RoH) 16.11.18; *FFP* 21.06.24

Clark, David W.: Trooper (1496 F & F Yeo [1st]); KIA Suvla Bay, Gallipoli, 28.10.15, 22 years; Les Oiseaux, 11 Rue Alphonse Brault, Choisy-le-Roi (Seine), France; Gravestone in Bennochy Cemetery; Green Hill Cemetery, Turkey. Grave I.E.15; Kirkcaldy War Memorial; *Soldiers Died* Part 1; *FA* 27.11.15; *FA* (CasList) 15.01.16; *FA* 05.02.16; *FFP* 12.02.16; *FFP* 12.08.16 Roll of The Brave; *FFP* (BMD) 28.10.16; Ogilvie

Clark, George, DCM & MID: Corporal (9774 Black Watch [2nd] att'd [1st]); Gassed 18.04.18. Died at 2/1 General Hospital, Dudley Road, Birmingham. Buried in Kirkcaldy, 11.06.18, 32 years; Lochgelly/2 Buccleuch Place, Burntisland. Formerly 29 Rosslyn Street, Kirkcaldy; Gravestone in Abbotshall Churchyard; Abbotshall Parish Churchyard, Kirkcaldy. Grave New. (C.) 389; Kirkcaldy War Memorial; *Soldiers Died* Part 46; *FA* 15.06.18; *FFP* 15.06.18; *FFP* (BMD) 15.06.18; *FA* 22.06.18 (2 entries); *FA* (BMD) 22.06.18; *FA* (RoH) 13.07.18; *FA* (FRoH) 14.12.18; Wauchope Vol 1

Clark, Henry: Private (115 Cameronians [Scottish Rifles] [8th] "1" Coy, 4th Platoon); First man to enlist from the Pannie Pit; KIA, 28.06.15; c/o Mrs. Mackie, 27 Dunnikier Road, Kirkcaldy; Helles Memorial, Gallipoli, Turkey. Panels 92-97; Kirkcaldy War Memorial; *Soldiers Died* Part 31; *FA* 28.08.15; *FFP* 28.08.15; *FA* 30.10.15; *FA* (Service List) 16.12.16

Clark, James: Private (3/1572 Black Watch [3rd] "C" Coy, att'd [1st]); KIA Ypres, 29.10.14, 24 years; 8 The Braes, Dysart; Gravestone in Strathmiglo Churchyard; Ypres (Menin Gate) Memorial, Ieper, West Vlaanderen, Belgium. Panel 37; Kirkcaldy War Memorial. Dysart War Memorial; *Soldiers Died* Part 46; *FA* 13.03.15; *FFP* 27.03.15; *FFP* 29.04.16; *FA* 06.05.16; *FFP* 05.08.16 Roll of the Brave; Wauchope Vol 1

Clark, James: Private (44098 KOSB [2nd]. Formerly 2287 HCB); KIA, 03.09.16, 19 years; 234 St Clair Street, Kirkcaldy; Delville Wood Cemetery, Longueval, Somme, France. Grave XXVII.L.6; Kirkcaldy War Memorial; *FA* 25.11.16; *FA* 11.08.17; *Soldiers Died* Part 30; *FA* 18.11.16; *FA* 25.11.16; *FA* 11.08.17; *FA* 15.09.17; *FFP* (RoH) 15.09.17

Clark, Peter: Private (S/24042 Seaforth Hldrs [6th]. Formerly TR/1/18660 TR Bn); KIA, 09.04.18, 19 years; 29 Rose Street, Kirkcaldy; Loos Memorial, Pas de Calais, France. Panels 112-115; Kirkcaldy War Memorial; *Soldiers Died* Part 64; *FA* (BMD) 02.08.19

Clark, William: Private (202496 Cameronians [Scottish Rifles] [5/6th]. Formerly 3606 Royal Scots); KIA, 16.04.18, 32 years; 7 Charlotte Street, Kirkcaldy; Bethelfield Church Plaque; Ploegsteert Memorial, Comines-Warneton, Hainault, Belgium. Panel 5; Kirkcaldy War Memorial; *Soldiers Died* Part 31; *FA* 11.05.18; *FFP* (RoH) 11.05.18; *FFP* (BMD) 11.05.18; *FA* (RoH) 18.05.18; *FA* (RoH) 18.05.18; *FFP* (RoH) 18.05.18; *FA* (FRoH) 14.12.18; Martin

Clephane, Charles Thomas: Private (S/42106 Gordon Hldrs [1st] "B" Coy); DOW, 25.07.18, 18 years; 2 Gow Square, Glasswork Street, Kirkcaldy; Sandpits British Cemetery, Labeuvriere, Pas de Calais, France. Grave III.D.10; Kirkcaldy War Memorial; *Soldiers Died* Part 65; *FFP* 17.08.18; *FA* 24.08.18; *FA* (RoH) 14.09.18; *FFP* (RoH) 14.09.18; *FA* (FRoH) 14.12.18

Clunie, David: Private (S/10317 Seaforth Hldrs [2nd] "B" Coy. Formerly 6534 Res Cavalry Regt); Uncle of Isaac Connell; Died at No 12 General Hospital, Rouen of appendicitis, 08.02.16, 34 years; 3 Meldrum Place/18 Wemyss Place, Quality Street, Kirkcaldy; St Sever Cemetery, Rouen, Seine-Maritime, France. Grave A.17.12; Kirkcaldy War Memorial; *Soldiers Died* Part 64; *FFP* (BMD) 19.02.16; *FA* 26.02.16; *FA* 01.04.16; *FFP* 05.08.16 Roll of the Brave; *FFP* (BMD) 09.02.18; *FFP* (BMD) 09.03.18; *FA* (FRoH) 16.11.18

Coleman, John: Private (3/2186 Black Watch [1st]); Spelling in some newspapers is Colman. *FFP* (BMD) 12.12.14 has 3rd Bn Black Watch; KIA by sniper fire, 09.11.14, 21 years; 1 Gow Square, Glasswork Street, Kirkcaldy; Ypres (Menin Gate) Memorial, Ieper, West Vlaanderen, Belgium. Panel 37; *Soldiers Died* Part 46; *FFP* (BMD) 12.12.14; *Scotsman* 00.01.15; *FA* 06.02.15; *FA* (CasList) 20.02.15; *FFP* 12.08.16 Roll of the Brave; *FA* (Service List) 27.01.17

Collier, Walter B.: Corporal (Gordon Hldrs. Formerly Seaforth Hldrs); KIA France, 31.07.17, 22 years; 21 Anderson Street, Kirkcaldy; Pathhead Parish Church Memorial Plaques & Windows; Not identified on CWGC web site; Kirkcaldy War Memorial; *FA* 11.08.17; *FFP* 11.08.17; *FA* 18.08.17; *FFP* (BMD) 25.08.17; *FA* 15.09.17; *FFP* (RoH) 15.09.17; *FFP* (BMD) 27.07.18; *FFP* 21.06.24

Collins, Andrew P.: Private (S/18451 Black Watch [2nd]); Died in military hospital, 13.11.18, 22 years; 259 Rosslyn Street, Kirkcaldy; Cairo War Memorial Cemetery, Egypt. Grave Q.106; Kirkcaldy War Memorial; *FFP* (RoH) 14.12.18; *FA* (FRoH) 14.12.18

Collins, John: Private (S/7051 Gordon Hldrs [2nd]. Formerly Cameron Hldrs); KIA, 05.11.14, 36 years; 3 Stewart's Lane/17 Overton Road, Kirkcaldy; St Peter's Church Memorial Plaque; Ypres (Menin Gate) Memorial, Ieper, West Vlaanderen, Belgium. Panel 38; Kirkcaldy War Memorial; *FA* 27.02.15; *Soldiers Died* Part 65; War Album 15; *FA* 20.02.15; *FA* (CasList) 20.02.15; *FA* 15.05.15; *FFP* (CasList) 05.06.15; *FA* 26.06.15; *FFP* 05.08.16 Roll of the Brave; *FA* (Service List) 04.11.16; *FA* (Service List) 03.02.17; *FA* (FRoH) 16.11.18

Collins, Thomas: Lance Corporal (17594 Royal Scots [15th]); His brother was also killed; KIA, 01.07.16; High School, Carlyle Road, Kirkcaldy; Old Parish Church Memorial Panel. Kirkcaldy High School War Memorial; Thiepval Memorial, Somme, France. Pier & Face 6D & 7D; Kirkcaldy War Memorial; *Soldiers Died* Part 6; *FA* 12.08.16; *FFP* 19.08.16; *FA* 16.09.16; *FA* (RoH) 16.09.16; *FFP* (RoH) 16.09.16; *FA* 14.10.16; *FA* 11.11.16; *FFP* 11.11.16; *FFP* (RoH) 30.12.16; *FA* (Service List) 06.01.17; *FA* 14.07.17 (KHS War Honours); *FA* (BMD) 18.08.17; *FA* (FRoH) 23.11.18; *FA* (KHS RoH) 29.03.19

Colthart, Robert Herd, MID (2), Captain & Adjutant: (Black Watch [14th] [F & F Yeo Bn]); DOW, 02.11.18, 25 years; 9 Montgomery Street, Kirkcaldy/256 Vernon Drive, Vancouver, Canada; Fretin Communal Cemetery, France. Grave 6; Kirkcaldy War Memorial; *Officers Died*; *Cross of Sacrifice Vol 1*; *FA* 09.11.18; *FA* (RoH) 16.11.18; *FFP* (RoH) 16.11.18; *FA* (FRoH) 14.12.18; *FFP* 14.12.18; Ogilvie; Wauchope Vol 3

Colville, James: Stoker 1st Class (3780/S; Royal Navy; RNR (HMS *Defence*]); Drowned, Battle of Jutland, 31.05.16, 26 years; 147 Ramsay Road, Kirkcaldy; Raith Church Memorial Plaque; Portsmouth Naval Memorial, Hampshire. Plate 23; Kirkcaldy War Memorial; *FA* 23.10.15; *FA* 10.06.16; *Cross of Sacrifice Vol 4*; *FA* 10.06.16; *FA* (BMD) 10.06.16; *FFP* 10.06.16; *FFP* (BMD) 10.06.16; *FA* (RoH) 17.06.16; *FFP* (RoH) 17.06.16; *FFP* 24.06.16; *FFP* 05.08.16 Roll of the Brave; *FA* 26.08.16; *FA* (Service List) 16.12.16; *FA* (BMD) 02.06.17 (2 entries); *FFP* (BMD) 02.06.17; *FA* (FRoH) 23.11.18; Jutland Roll of Honour

Connell, Isaac: Private (8816 HLI [1st]); Cousin of Isaac Connell, Royal Engineers and nephew of David Clunie; KIA Mesopotamia, 08.03.16, 24 years; Palm Villa, 40 Links Street, Kirkcaldy; Whytescauseway Baptist Church Memorial Plaque; Basra Memorial, Iraq. Panels 35 & 64; Kirkcaldy War Memorial; *FA* 01.01.16; *FA* 01.04.16; *Soldiers Died* Part 63; *FA* 01.04.16; *FFP* 08.04.16; *FFP* (BMD) 08.04.16; *FA* (RoH) 15.04.16; *FA* (BMD) 15.04.16; *FFP* (CasList) 15.04.16; *FFP* 05.08.16 Roll of the Brave; *FA* (Service List) 02.12.16; *FFP* (BMD) 10.03.17; *FFP* (BMD) 09.03.18; *FA* (FRoH) 23.11.18

Connell, Isaac: Corporal (79847 Royal Engineers [175th Tunneling Coy]. Formerly 12974 KOSB); Cousin of Isaac Connell, HLI; 26.01.16, 28 years; 229 Rosslyn Street, Kirkcaldy; Railway Dugouts Burial Ground, Zillebeke, Ieper, West Vlaanderen, Belgium. Grave I.L.24; Kirkcaldy War Memorial; *Soldiers Died* Part 4; *FFP* 05.02.16; *FA* 12.02.16; *FFP* 12.02.16; *FA* (BMD) 19.02.16; *FA* 01.04.16; *FFP* 08.04.16; *FFP* 05.08.16 Roll of the Brave; *FA* (Service List) 09.12.16; *FA* (FRoH) 16.11.18

Cook, Hector: Private (1633; AIF; Australian Infantry [36th]); KIA, 23.01.17, 26 years; Dunnikier Road, Kirkcaldy; Cite Bonjean Military Cemetery, Armentieres, Nord, France. Grave III.D.21; Australian War Memorial web site; Kirkcaldy War Memorial; *FA* 24.02.17; *FA* (BMD) 24.02.17; *FFP* (BMD) 24.02.17; *FFP* 03.03.17; *FA* (RoH) 17.03.17; *FA* (FRoH) 30.11.18

Cook, James: Private (S/9584 Black Watch [4/5th]); DOW CCS, 30.08.18, 41 years; 38 Rosabelle Street, Kirkcaldy; Pernes British Cemetery, Pas de Calais, France. Grave IV.B.35; Kirkcaldy War Memorial; *Soldiers Died* Part 46; *FA* 07.09.18; *FA* (RoH) 14.09.18; *FA* (BMD) 14.09.18; *FFP* 14.09.18; *FFP* (RoH) 14.09.18; *FFP* (BMD) 14.09.18; *FA* (FRoH) 14.12.18; Wauchope Vol 2

Cooper, John: Private (10410 HLI [1st] Indian Expeditionary Force); KIA Neuve Chapelle, 24.03.15, 31 years; 18 Nicol Street, Kirkcaldy; Vieille-Chapelle New Military Cemetery, Lacouture, Pas de Calais, France. Grave VI.E.13; Kirkcaldy War Memorial; *Soldiers Died* Part 63; War Album 15; *FA* 10.04.15; *FFP* 10.04.15; *FFP* 05.08.16 Roll of the Brave; *FA* (FRoH) 16.11.18

Cormie, David Bell: Lance Corporal (12882 Royal Scots Fusiliers [7th]); Died of pneumonia at No. 9 CCS, 24.01.16, 29 years; Alexandra Street/48/99 Harcourt Rd, Kirkcaldy; Union Church Plaque; Lillers Communal Cemetery & Extension, Lillers, Pas-de-Calais, France. Grave IV.E.14; Kirkcaldy War Memorial; ‡; *Soldiers Died* Part 26; *FFP* (BMD) 05.02.16; *FA* 12.02.16; *FFP* (BMD) 27.01.17; *FA* (Service List) 03.03.17

Costello, George: Private (9274 Cameron Hldrs [1st]); KIA, 24.10.14, 20 years; 36 Commercial Street/144 Den Road, Kirkcaldy; Ypres (Menin Gate) Memorial, Ieper, West Vlaanderen, Belgium. Panels 38 & 40; Kirkcaldy War Memorial; *Soldiers Died* Part 66; War Album 14/15; *FA* 05.12.14; *FA* (CasList) 19.12.14; *FA* 02.01.15; *FA* (CasList) 20.02.15; *FA* (BMD) 23.10.15; *FFP* 05.08.16 Roll of the Brave; *FA* (BMD) 21.10.16; *FA* (Service List) 04.11.16; *FA* (Service List) 16.12.16; *FA* (Service List) 10.02.17; *FA* (FRoH) 16.11.18

Coupar, James Whyte: Private (135681; CEF; Canadian Infantry [1st] 1st Div 1st Bde. [Western Ontario Regt]. Formerly 74th Bn); KIA Ypres, 13.06.16, 23 years; 24 Forth Avenue North, Kirkcaldy; Abbotshall Parish Church Memorial Plaque; Ypres (Menin Gate) Memorial, Ieper, West Vlaanderen, Belgium. Panels 10-26-28; Kirkcaldy War Memorial; *FA* 01.07.16; *CBoR* Page 71; *FA* 01.07.16 (2 entries); *FA* (BMD) 01.07.16; *FFP* (BMD) 01.07.16; *FFP* 08.07.16; *FA* (RoH) 15.07.16; *FFP* 05.08.16 Roll of the Brave; *FA* (Service List) 17.02.17; *FFP* (BMD) 16.06.17; *FA* (FRoH) 23.11.18; *FA* 19.11.21; CEF Official List of Casualties

Couper, David: Lance Corporal (9832 Cameron Hldrs [1st] "D" Coy); KIA, 09.05.15, 18 years; 23 Charlotte Street, Kirkcaldy; Le Touret Memorial, Pas de Calais, France. Panels 41-42; Kirkcaldy War Memorial; *FA* 29.05.15; *Soldiers Died* Part 66; War Album 15; *FA* 29.05.15; *FFP* 19.06.15; *FFP* (BMD) 19.06.15; *Scotsman* 21.06.15; *FFP* 24.07.15; *FFP* (BMD) 13.05.16; *FFP* 05.08.16 Roll of the Brave; *FA* (Service List) 27.01.17; *FFP* (BMD) 12.05.17; *FA* (FRoH) 16.11.18

Couper, Roger Aytoun Whyte: Corporal (S/4571; CEF; Canadian Infantry. No. 2 District Depot); Died of phthisis, 18.12.19, 32 years; 24 Forth Avenue North, Kirkcaldy/225 Wallace Avenue, Toronto; Abbotshall Parish Church Memorial Plaque; Toronto (Prospect) Cemetery, Ontario. Lot 95. Sec.16; Kirkcaldy War Memorial; *CBoR* Page 532; *FA* 19.11.21

Cowen, Archibald Johnstone: Driver (T2/016833 RAMC att'd RASC [41st Fld Amb]); Died of cholera at Station Hospital, Bangalore, 24.08.18, 29 years; 34 Miller Street, Kirkcaldy; Gallatown Church Roll of Honour; Madras 1914-18 War Memorial, Chennai, India. Face 26. Buried Bangalore (Hosur Road Cemetery); Kirkcaldy War Memorial; *Soldiers Died* Part 79; *FFP* 07.09.18; *FA* 14.09.18; *FFP* 14.09.18; *FA* 21.09.18; *FA* (RoH) 16.11.18; *FFP* (RoH) 16.11.18; *FA* (FRoH) 14.12.18; *FA* (BMD) 30.08.19

Cowie, James: Private (44068 KOSB [2nd]. Formerly 1924 HCB); KIA, 03.09.16, 20 years; 9 Rosslyn Street, Kirkcaldy; Barony Church Plaque; Carnieres Communal Cemetery, Nord, France. Grave XXVII.A.2; Kirkcaldy War Memorial; *FA* 14.10.16; *Soldiers Died* Part 30; *FFP* 30.09.16; *FA* 07.10.16; *FA* (RoH) 14.10.16; *FFP* 14.10.16; *FFP* (CasList) 14.10.16; *FFP* (RoH) 14.10.16; *FA* (Service List) 09.12.16; *FFP* (RoH) 30.12.16

Cox, John Alonzo, DSO, MID: Major (HLI [12th]. Formerly HCB [1st]); KIA France, 29.09.18, 31 years; High Street, Kirkcaldy; St Peter's Church Memorial Plaque; Aeroplane Cemetery, Ieper, West Vlaanderen, Belgium. Grave VII.A.22; Kirkcaldy War Memorial; *FA* 31.07.15; *Officers Died*; *Cross of Sacrifice* Vol 1; *FA* 14.08.15; *FFP* 12.10.18; *FA* (RoH) 19.10.18; *FA* 26.10.18 (2 entries); *FA* 16.11.18; *FA* (FRoH) 14.12.18; *FFP* 04.01.19; *FA* 11.01.19

Crabbe, Alexander: Private (260211 Gordon Hldrs [5th]. Formerly HCB); On CWGC as Crabb; KIA, 20.11.17, 20 years; 5 Anderson Street, Kirkcaldy; Gravestone in Bennochy Cemetery; Ribecourt Road Cemetery, Trescault, Pas de Calais, France. Grave I.B.7; Kirkcaldy War Memorial; *Soldiers Died* Part 65; *FA* 15.12.17; *FA* (BMD) 15.12.17; *FFP* 15.12.17; *FFP* (BMD) 15.12.17; *FA* (RoH) 19.01.18; *FA* (FRoH) 07.12.18

Crawford, Alexander: Private (8133 Seaforth Hldrs [2nd]); Brother of James Crawford and brother-in-law of James Duncan; Missing at Vielsay. Died of pneumonia at Chemnitz in Saxony whilst a PoW, 31.10.18; 265 Rosslyn Street/6 Pool Lane, Gallatown, Kirkcaldy; Gallatown Church Roll of Honour; Berlin South-Western Cemetery, Brandenburg, Germany. Grave II.G.7; Kirkcaldy War Memorial; *FFP* 10.10.14; *FA* 27.11.15; *FFP* 25.01.19; *Soldiers Died* Part 64; *FFP* 23.09.14; *FA* (CasList) 20.02.15; *FA* (Service List) 09.12.16; *FFP* 25.01.19; *FA* (RoH) 15.02.19

Crawford, David: Private (16807 Royal Scots Fusiliers [1st]); KIA Loos, 25.09.15, 18 years; 155 Rosslyn Street, Kirkcaldy; Perth Cemetery (China Wall), Zillebeke, Ieper, West Vlaanderen, Belgium. Grave XI.A.4; Kirkcaldy War Memorial; *Soldiers Died* Part 26; War Album 15/16; *FFP* 09.10.15; *FA* 27.11.15; *FA* (RoH) 18.12.15; *FFP* 05.08.16 Roll of the Brave; *FFP* (BMD) 30.09.16; *FA* (Service List) 09.12.16; *FA* (FRoH) 16.11.18

Crawford, David: Private; KIA, 01.10.15, 18 years; Not identified on CWGC web site; Kirkcaldy War Memorial

Crawford, James: Private (15648 Royal Scots [1st]); Brother of Alexander Crawford & brother-in-law of James Duncan; KIA Salonika, 01.10.16; 6 Pool Lane, Gallatown, Kirkcaldy; Gallatown Church Roll of Honour; Doiran Memorial, Greece; Kirkcaldy War Memorial; *Soldiers Died* Part 6; *FA* (RoH) 15.02.19

Crichton, George: Private (40997 KOSB [6th]. Formerly 2415 F & F Yeo); KIA Arras, 03.05.17, 26 years; Seaforth Lodge, Loughborough Road, Kirkcaldy; Gravestone in Dysart Cemetery. Pathhead Parish Church Memorial Plaques & Windows; Arras Memorial, Pas de Calais, France. Bay 6; Kirkcaldy War Memorial; *Soldiers Died* Part 30; *FFP* 09.06.17; *FA* 16.06.17; *FA* 02.03.18; *FFP* (RoH) 02.03.18; *FFP* (BMD) 02.03.18; *FA* (BMD) 09.03.18; *FA* (RoH) 16.03.18; *FFP* (RoH) 16.03.18; *FA* (FRoH) 07.12.18; *FFP* 21.06.24

Crichton, Robert: Lance Corporal (S/15998 A & S Hldrs [10th]); KIA, 30.09.18, 29 years; 57 Ramsay Road, Kirkcaldy; Gravestone in Abbotshall Churchyard. Invertiel Parish Church Memorial Table; Joncourt British Cemetery, Aisne, France. Grave B.11; Kirkcaldy War Memorial; *Soldiers Died* Part 70; *FFP* (BMD) 26.10.18; *FA* (RoH) 16.11.18; *FFP* (RoH) 16.11.18; *FA* (FRoH) 14.12.18

Crombie, Alexander: Private (PLY/17027; Royal Navy; Royal Marine Light Infantry [RND] [Deal Bn] [1st]); KIA, 17.02.17, 19 years; 103 Links Street, Kirkcaldy; Queens Cemetery, Bucquoy, Somme, France. Grave II.H.15; Kirkcaldy War Memorial; ‡; *FA* 10.07.15; *FA* 24.03.17; *Cross of Sacrifice Vol 4*; RMD; *FFP* 17.03.17; *FFP* 24.03.17; *FA* (RoH) 14.04.17; *FA* (FRoH) 30.11.18

Crombie, John: Private (350119 Black Watch [8th]. Formerly 1007 HCB); KIA, 12.10.17; Tyne Cot Memorial, Zonnebeke, West Vlaanderen, Belgium. Panels 94-96; Kirkcaldy War Memorial; *Soldiers Died* Part 46; Wauchope Vol 3

Crombie, William: Private (3218 Black Watch [2/7th] No 1 Supernumerary Coy); Fell off a roof in Dunfermline. Died at the Red Cross Hospital, Dunfermline, 09.05.15, 40 years; 27/77 Victoria Road, Kirkcaldy; Bethelfield Church Plaque; Bennochy Cemetery, Kirkcaldy. Grave N.306; Kirkcaldy War Memorial; *Soldiers Died* Part 46; War Album 15; *FA* 15.05.15; *FA* (BMD) 15.05.15; *FFP* (CasList) 05.06.15; *FFP* 05.08.16 Roll of the Brave; *FA* (Service List) 02.12.16; *FA* (FRoH) 16.11.18; Wauchope Vol 2

Crutchlow, John Stewart: Corporal (196 52nd Lowland Divisional Cyclist Coy. Formerly 638 HCB); KIA, 04.08.16, 20 years; Mayview, 20 Windmill Road, Dysart; Gravestone in Dysart Cemetery. Kirkcaldy High School War Memorial. Gallatown Church Roll of Honour; Kantara War Memorial Cemetery, Egypt. Grave E.237; Kirkcaldy War Memorial; *Soldiers Died* Part 77; *FA* 26.08.16; *FA* (BMD) 26.08.16; *FFP* 26.08.16; *FFP* (BMD) 26.08.16; *FA* (RoH) 16.09.16; *FFP* (RoH) 16.09.16; *FFP* (CasList) 23.09.16; *FFP* (RoH) 30.12.16; *FA* (Service List) 31.03.17; *FA* 14.07.17 (KHS War Honours); *FFP* (BMD) 03.08.18; *FA* (FRoH) 23.11.18; *FA* (KHS RoH) 29.03.19

Cunningham, George: Private (44030 KOSB [2nd]. Formerly 722 HCB); KIA, 03.09.16, 22 years; Barony Church Plaque; Serre Road Cemetery No 2, Somme, France. Grave XXX.E.1; Kirkcaldy War Memorial; *Soldiers Died* Part 30

Cunningham, Robert: Private (6056 Royal Irish Regt [2nd]. Formerly 6511 Connaught Rangers); KIA, 21.08.18; AIF Burial Ground, Flers, Somme, France. Grave X.G.8; Kirkcaldy War Memorial; *Soldiers Died* Part 23

Cunningham, Thomas: Private (3/2569 Black Watch [2nd]); KIA Persian Gulf, 22.04.16, 18 years; 32 St Clair Street/58 Oswald Road, Kirkcaldy; Amara War Cemetery, Iraq. Grave XVII.E.13; Kirkcaldy War Memorial; *FA* 24.06.16; *Soldiers Died* Part 46; *FA* (BMD) 03.06.16; *FA* 24.06.16; *FA* 01.07.16; *FA* (CasList) 01.07.16; *FA* (RoH) 15.07.16; *FFP* 05.08.16 Roll of the Brave; *FA* (Service List) 24.03.17; *FFP* (BMD) 21.04.17; *FFP* (BMD) 20.04.18; *FA* (FRoH) 23.11.18; Wauchope Vol 1

Curran, Richard: Private (3/2392 Black Watch [1st]); KIA Neuve Chapelle, 09.05.15, 19 years; 120 Park Road, Kirkcaldy; Le Touret Memorial, Pas de Calais, France. Panels 24-26; Kirkcaldy War Memorial; *FA* 25.03.16; *Soldiers Died* Part 46; War Album 15; *Dundee Advertiser* 24.05.15; *FA* 29.05.15; *FFP* (CasList) 05.06.15; *FA* (RoH) 17.07.15; *FA* 18.03.16; *FFP* 25.03.16; *FFP* 05.08.16 Roll of the Brave; *FA* (Service List) 24.03.17; *FA* (FRoH) 16.11.18; Wauchope Vol 1

Curran, William John: Private (71892 Royal Defence Corps [350th Protection Coy]. Formerly 45962 Royal Engineers); Died at Prees Heath Hospital, Shropshire, 24.07.18, 48 years; 87 Lorne Street, Kirkcaldy; Gravestone in Dysart Cemetery; Dysart Cemetery, Kirkcaldy. Grave 57.II.Middle; Kirkcaldy War Memorial; *FA* 25.03.16; *Soldiers Died* Part 77; *FFP* (BMD) 27.07.18; *FA* (RoH) 14.09.18; *FFP* (RoH) 14.09.18; *FA* (FRoH) 14.12.18

Currie, Alexander: Acting Corporal (S/42449 Black Watch [9th]); CWGC has his number as S/43449; KIA Arras, 23.04.17, 21 years; 19 Smeaton Road, Kirkcaldy; Gravestone in Dysart Cemetery. Pathhead Baptist Church War Memorial Roll of Honour; Gemappe British Cemetery, Wancourt, Pas de Calais, France. Grave I.C.1; Kirkcaldy War Memorial; *Soldiers Died* Part 46; *FA* 12.05.17; *FFP* 12.05.17; *FFP* (BMD) 12.05.17; *FA* 19.05.17; *FA* (RoH) 19.05.17; *FFP* (RoH) 19.05.17; *FA* (CasList) 02.06.17; *FFP* (CasList) 02.06.17; *FA* (FRoH) 30.11.18; Wauchope Vol 3

Currie, Patrick: Private (3/271 Black Watch [3rd] att'd [1st]); Brother of Thomas Currie; KIA Ypres, 29.10.14, 24 years; 6 Sands Road/9 Gas Wynd, Kirkcaldy; Ypres (Menin Gate) Memorial, Ieper, West Vlaanderen, Belgium. Panel 37; Kirkcaldy War Memorial; *FA* 30.01.15; *Soldiers Died* Part 46; War Album 14/15; *FA* 02.01.15; *FA* 16.01.15 (2 entries); *Dundee Advertiser* 08.02.15; *FA* (CasList) 20.02.15; *FA* 12.02.16; *FFP* 05.08.16 Roll of the Brave; *FFP* (BMD) 28.10.16; *FA* (Service List) 04.11.16; *FA* (Service List) 23.12.16; *FA* (BMD) 03.11.17; *FA* (BMD) 02.11.18; *FA* (FRoH) 16.11.18; Wauchope Vol 1

Currie, Thomas: Private (8174 Black Watch [3rd] att'd [1st]); Brother of Patrick Currie; KIA, 16.09.14, 33 years; 6 Mill Vennel/36 Nicol Street, Kirkcaldy; La Ferte-Sous-Jouarre Memorial, Seine-et-Marne, France; Kirkcaldy War Memorial; *FA* 12.02.16; *Soldiers Died* Part 46; *FA* 31.10.14; *Scotsman* 17.11.14; *FA* (CasList) 20.02.15; *FA* 12.02.16; *FA* (BMD) 12.02.16; *FFP* (BMD) 12.02.16; *FFP* 05.08.16 Roll of the Brave; *FA* (FRoH) 16.11.18; *FA* (Service List) 18.11.16; Wauchope Vol 1

Currie, Thomas: Private (S/40037 Black Watch [8th]); DOW 22nd General Hospital, Camiers, 08.12.17, 19 years; 148 Dunnikier Road, Kirkcaldy; Etaples Military Cemetery, Pas de Calais, France. Grave XXXI.B.5; Kirkcaldy War Memorial; *Soldiers Died* Part 46; *FA* 08.12.17; *FA* 15.12.17; *FFP* 15.12.17; *FFP* (BMD) 15.12.17; *FFP* 22.12.17; *FFP* (Memorial List) 05.01.18; *FA* (RoH) 19.01.18; *FA* (FRoH) 07.12.18; *FFP* (BMD) 07.12.18; Wauchope Vol 3

Curror, Alexander Thomson Lesslie: Corporal (474128; CEF; Canadian Infantry [72nd] [British Columbia Regt]. Formerly 65th Battalion); KIA Vimy Ridge, 01.03.17, 25 years; Newton House, Nicol Street, Kirkcaldy/Banchory Farm, Elstow, Saskatchewan; Kirkcaldy High School War Memorial; Cabaret-Rouge British Cemetery, Souchez, Pas de Calais, France. Grave XII.F.5; Kirkcaldy War Memorial; *CBoR* Page 224; *FA* 15.03.19; *FA* (BMD) 15.03.19; *FA* (KHS RoH) 29.03.19; *FA* (KHS RoH) 19.07.19

Cuthill, Alexander: Private (Machine Gun Corps); Barony Church Plaque; Not identified on CWGC web site; Kirkcaldy War Memorial

Dand, Henry: Private (3/2312 Black Watch [2nd]); Brother of John Dand; DOW Persian Gulf, 24.04.16, 22 years; 19 Invertiel Road, Kirkcaldy; Invertiel Parish Church Memorial Table; Basra War Cemetery, Iraq. Grave VI.Q.2; Kirkcaldy War Memorial; *FA* 13.05.16; *Soldiers Died* Part 46; *Despatch* 23.11.14; *FA* 06.05.16; *FFP* 06.05.16; *FA* 13.05.16; *FA* (RoH) 13.05.16; *FFP* 05.08.16 Roll of the Brave; *FA* (Service List) 03.03.17; *FFP* (BMD) 13.04.18; *FA* (FRoH) 23.11.18; Wauchope Vol 1

Dand, John: Private (1174 Black Watch [2nd]); Brother of Henry Dand; KIA Hill 60, Ypres, 12.04.15; 19 Invertiel Road, Kirkcaldy; Le Touret Memorial, Pas de Calais, France. Panels 24-26; Kirkcaldy War Memorial; *FA* 13.05.16; *Soldiers Died* Part 46; War Album 15; *FFP* 01.05.15; *Evening News* 01.05.15; *FA* 08.05.15; *FA* 05.02.16; *FFP* (BMD) 15.04.16; *FFP* 06.05.16; *FA* 13.05.16; *FFP* 05.08.16 Roll of the Brave; *FA* (Service List) 28.10.16; *FA* (Service List) 03.03.17; *FFP* (BMD) 13.04.18; *FA* (FRoH) 16.11.18; Wauchope Vol 1

Daniel, James Dalgliesh, DCM & Bar: Lance Corporal (1731 Black Watch [1st] Depot Regt); DOW 3rd Southern General Hospital, Oxford, 06.06.15, 25 years; 49 Meldrum Road, Kirkcaldy; Gravestone in Bennochy Cemetery. Bethelfield Church Plaque; Bennochy Cemetery, Kirkcaldy. Grave M.774; Kirkcaldy War Memorial; *Soldiers Died* Part 46; War Album 15; *FA* 20.02.15; *Dundee Advertiser* 09.06.15; *Scotsman* 09.06.15; *Dundee Advertiser* 10.06.15; *FA* 12.06.15; *FA* (BMD) 12.06.15; *FFP* 12.06.15; *FFP* (BMD) 12.06.15; *FFP* (CasList) 03.07.15; *FA* (RoH) 17.07.15; *FFP* (BMD) 10.06.16; *FFP* 05.08.16 Roll of the Brave; *FA* 30.09.16; *FA* (Service List) 17.03.17; *FA* (FRoH) 16.11.18; Wauchope Vol 1

Davidson, John: Corporal (S/43351 Cameron Hldrs [5th]. Formerly 126130 Lovat Scouts); KIA Zonnebeke, 28.09.18, 20 years; Cemetery Lodge, Bennochy Road, Kirkcaldy; Gravestone in Bennochy Cemetery. Abbotshall Parish Church Memorial Plaque; Aeroplane Cemetery, Ieper, West Vlaanderen, Belgium. Grave V.B.8; Kirkcaldy War Memorial; *Soldiers Died* Part 66; *FA* 26.10.18; *FA* (BMD) 02.11.18; *FA* (RoH) 16.11.18; *FFP* (RoH) 16.11.18; *FA* (FRoH) 14.12.18; *FA* 19.11.21

Dawson, James: Private (Cameron Hldrs); Died suddenly at Stirling Royal Infirmary. Buried Kirkcaldy, 29.06.17, 17 years; 48 Sutherland Street, Kirkcaldy; Not identified on CWGC web site; Kirkcaldy War Memorial; *FA* 14.07.17; *FFP* 14.07.17

Deas, James H.: Sergeant (S/5594 Gordon Hldrs [10th]); On CWGC as 8th Bn; DOW Merryflatts Hospital, Glasgow, 30.09.16, 41 years; 91/99 High Street, Kirkcaldy; St Andrew's Church Memorial Plaque; Abbotshall Parish Churchyard, Kirkcaldy. Grave Raith 43; Kirkcaldy War Memorial; *Soldiers Died* Part 65; *FA* 07.10.16; *FA* (BMD) 07.10.16; *FFP* 07.10.16; *FFP* (BMD) 07.10.16; *FA* (RoH) 14.10.16; *FFP* 14.10.16; *FFP* (RoH) 14.10.16; *FA* 21.10.16; *FFP* 21.10.16; *FA* (Service List) 28.10.16; *FFP* (CasList) 28.10.16; *FA* (Service List) 09.12.16; *FFP* (RoH) 30.12.16

Deas, William Darling: Lieutenant (A & S Hldrs [11th]); Wounded at Loos. Died a PoW in German Hospital at Wahn, Valenciennes, 30.09.15, 27 years; Victoria Villa, Victoria Road, Kirkcaldy; Gravestone in Bennochy Cemetery (Photo). Dunnikier Church Roll of Honour. Kirkcaldy High School War Memorial; Valenciennes (St Roch) Communal Cemetery, Nord, France. Grave IV.B.10; Kirkcaldy War Memorial; *FA* 25.09.15; *FA* 09.10.15; *FFP* 09.10.15; *Officers Died*; War Album 15/16; *Cross of Sacrifice Vol 1*; *FA* 02.10.15; *FA* 09.10.15 (2 entries); *FA* (BMD) 09.10.15; *FFP* 09.10.15 (2 entries); *FFP* (BMD) 09.10.15 (2 entries); *FA* 16.10.15 (2 entries); *FA* (RoH) 16.10.15; *FFP* (RoH) 16.10.15; *FA* 20.11.15; *FFP* 05.08.16 Roll of the Brave; *FA* (BMD) 30.09.16; *FFP* (BMD) 30.09.16; *FA* (Service List) 02.12.16; *FA* (BMD) 29.09.17; *FFP* (BMD) 29.09.17; *FA* (BMD) 28.09.18; *FFP* (BMD) 28.09.18; *FA* (FRoH) 16.11.18; *FA* (KHS RoH) 29.03.19; *FA* 26.04.19; *FA* (BMD) 27.09.19

Death, Charles: Private (6840 Royal Scots [2nd]); Died in Kirkcaldy Sanitorium, 12.05.16, 36 years; 13 Factory Square, Kirkcaldy; Gravestone in Dysart Cemetery; Dysart Cemetery, Kirkcaldy. Grave 4.10.Middle; Kirkcaldy War Memorial; *FA* 31.10.14; *FFP* (BMD) 20.05.16; *FA* (RoH) 17.06.16; *FFP* (RoH) 17.06.16; *FFP* 05.08.16 Roll of the Brave; *FA* (Service List) 31.03.17; *FA* (FRoH) 23.11.18

Dempster, Charles: Gunner (7883 RFA (73rd Bde]); Kicked by a horse on Salisbury Plain. Died at Tidworth Hospital, 11.03.15, 22 years; 6 Allison Street, Kirkcaldy; Bulford Church Cemetery, Bulford, Wiltshire. Grave 4.I.4; Kirkcaldy War Memorial; *FA* 13.03.15; *Soldiers Died* Part 2; War Album 15; *FA* 13.03.15; *FA* (BMD) 13.03.15; *FFP* 13.03.15; *FFP* (BMD) 13.03.15; *FFP* (CasList) 27.03.15; *FA* 17.06.16; *FFP* 05.08.16 Roll of the Brave; *FA* (Service List) 16.12.16; *FA* (FRoH) 16.11.18

Dempster, James: Private (3/2862 Black Watch [1st]); KIA La Bassee, 25.01.15, 36 years; 242 Links Street, Kirkcaldy; Le Touret Memorial, Pas de Calais, France. Panels 24-26; Kirkcaldy War Memorial; *Soldiers Died* Part 46; War Album 14/15; *FA* 13.02.15; *FA* (CasList) 20.02.15; *FFP* 20.02.15; *FFP* 05.08.16 Roll of the Brave; *FA* (Service List) 26.11.16; *FA* (Service List) 02.12.16; *FA* (FRoH) 16.11.18; Wauchope Vol 1

Dewar, Alexander: Corporal (8575 Royal Scots [2nd]); Brother of Andrew Dewar; KIA, 15.10.14, 28 years; 5 Buchanan Street, Kirkcaldy; Raith Church Memorial Plaque; Y Farm Military Cemetery, Bois-Grenier, Nord, France. Grave J.47. (Buried Nearby); Kirkcaldy War Memorial; *FA* 17.10.14; *FA* 10.06.16; *Soldiers Died* Part 6; War Album 14/15; *FFP* 31.10.14; *FA* (RoH) 07.11.14; *FA* 14.11.14; *FA* (CasList) 21.11.14; *FA* 02.01.15; *FA* (CasList) 20.02.15; *FFP* 27.05.16; *FA* 10.06.16; *FFP* 10.06.16; *FFP* 05.08.16 Roll of the Brave; *FA* (Service List) 04.11.16; *FA* (Service List) 30.12.16; *FA* (FRoH) 16.11.18

Dewar, Andrew: Private (10717 Royal Scots [11th]. Formerly 1863 Black Watch); Brother of Alexander Dewar; KIA, 13.05.16, 22 years; 2 Buchanan Street, Kirkcaldy; Rifle House Cemetery, Comines-Warneton, Hainaut, Belgium. Grave I.C.5; Kirkcaldy War Memorial; *FA* 10.06.16; *Soldiers Died* Part 6; *FFP* 27.05.16; *FA* 03.06.16 (2 entries); *FFP* 03.06.16; *FFP* 10.06.16; *FA* (RoH) 17.06.16; *FFP* (RoH) 17.06.16; *FFP* 05.08.16 Roll of the Brave; *FA* (Service List) 30.12.16; *FA* (FRoH) 23.11.18

Dewar, David: Private (S/41384 Gordon Hldrs [5th]. Formerly A & S Hldrs); KIA, 14.09.17, 20 years; 26 East Smeaton Street, Kirkcaldy; New Irish Farm Cemetery, Ieper, West Vlaanderen, Belgium. Grave XII.E.5; Kirkcaldy War Memorial; *Soldiers Died* Part 65; *FA* 29.09.17; *FFP* 06.10.17; *FFP* (CasList) 27.10.17

Dewar, David C.: Corporal (A/450; CEF; 1st Div 1st Bde. 1st Infantry Bn [Western Ontario Regt]); KIA France, 16.03.16, 27 years; 13 Ava Street, Kirkcaldy; Gravestone in Abbotshall Churchyard. Bethelfield Church Plaque; Dranoutre Military Cemetery, Heuvelland, West Vlaanderen, Belgium. Grave I.A.15; Kirkcaldy War Memorial; *CBoR* Page 77; *FA* 25.03.16; *FFP* 01.04.16; *FFP* (BMD) 01.04.16; *FA* (RoH) 15.04.16; *FFP* 05.08.16 Roll of the Brave; *FFP* (BMD) 17.03.17; *FFP* (BMD) 23.03.18; *FA* (FRoH) 23.11.18

Dewar, George McNeil: Private (9876 Black Watch [1st]); Brother of Martin Dewar; Died as a PoW, Germany, 21.06.15, 28 years; 8 Quality Street, Kirkcaldy; Ypres (Menin Gate) Memorial, Ieper, West Vlaanderen, Belgium. Panel 59 (Addenda); Kirkcaldy War Memorial; *FA* 05.02.16; *Soldiers Died* Part 46; *FA* 05.02.16; *FFP* 05.08.16 Roll of the Brave; *FFP* 11.11.16; *FA* (FRoH) 16.11.18; Army Returns 1914-1918 (SRO); Wauchope Vol 1

Dewar, Martin: Private (44079 KOSB [2nd]. Formerly 2101 HCB); Brother of George Dewar; KIA, 03.09.16, 28 years; Stocks Buildings, 274 Links Street, Kirkcaldy; Thiepval Memorial, Somme, France. Pier & Face 4A & 4D; Kirkcaldy War Memorial; *Soldiers Died* Part 30; *FA* 05.02.16; *FA* 23.09.16; *FFP* 23.09.16; *FFP* 11.11.16

Dewar, William: Corporal (9779 Seaforth Hldrs [2nd]); KIA France, 04.10.17, 33 years; 19 Den Road, Kirkcaldy; Pathhead Parish Church Memorial Plaques & Windows; Tyne Cot Memorial, Zonnebeke, West Vlaanderen, Belgium. Panels 132-135 & 162A; Kirkcaldy War Memorial; *Soldiers Died* Part 64; *FA* 20.10.17; *FFP* 27.10.17; *FFP* 03.11.17; *FFP* (BMD) 03.11.17; *FA* 10.11.17; *FA* (BMD) 10.11.17; *FFP* (CasList) 17.11.17; *FFP* 21.06.24

Dick, David: Private (34037 HLI [15th]. Formerly 33461 Royal Scots); KIA, 02.10.18, 27 years; 96 Overton Road, Kirkcaldy; Sequehart British Cemetery No. 2, Aisne, France. Grave A.6; Kirkcaldy War Memorial; *Soldiers Died* Part 63; *FA* (RoH) 16.11.18; *FFP* (RoH) 16.11.18; *FFP* (BMD) 16.11.18

Dick, John: Private (44058 KOSB [2nd]. Formerly 1405 HCB); KIA, 03.09.16; 57 East Smeaton Street, Kirkcaldy; Delville Wood Cemetery, Longueval, Somme, France. Grave XXIV.D.4; Kirkcaldy War Memorial; *FA* 21.10.16; *Soldiers Died* Part 30; *FFP* 07.10.16; *FA* 14.10.16; *FA* (RoH) 14.10.16; *FFP* (RoH) 14.10.16; *FFP* (CasList) 11.11.16; *FFP* (RoH) 30.12.16; *FA* (Service List) 17.02.17; *FFP* (BMD) 01.09.17; *FA* (FRoH) 23.11.18

Dick, John: Private (S/41458 Seaforth Hldrs [1/6th]. Formerly 12613 Lovat Scouts & S/31824 Cameron Hldrs); KIA, 09.04.18, 18 years; 82/94 Lorne Street, Kirkcaldy; Gravestone in Dysart Cemetery; Loos Memorial, Pas de Calais, France. Panels 112-115; Kirkcaldy War Memorial; *Soldiers Died* Part 64; *FFP* 25.01.19; *FA* 09.08.19; *FA* (RoH) 13.09.19

Dickie, John Duncan: Private (51018; NZEF; Wellington Infantry Regt [2nd]); KIA, 05.04.18; Sucrerie Military Cemetery, Colincamps, Somme, France. Grave I.J.49; Kirkcaldy War Memorial; NZEF Roll of Honour

Dickson, David: Private (345353 Black Watch [14th] [F & F Yeo Bn]. Formerly 2524 F & F Yeo); Ogilvie gives number as 345352; KIA Palestine, 01.12.17; 41 Bridgeton, Kirkcaldy; Jerusalem Memorial, Israel. Panel 33; Kirkcaldy War Memorial; *FFP* 19.01.18; *Soldiers Died* Part 46; *FA* 22.12.17; *FFP* 22.12.17; *FFP* 19.01.18; *FFP* (RoH) 19.01.18; *FA* (RoH) 16.02.18; *FFP* (RoH) 16.02.18; *FA* (FRoH) 07.12.18; Wauchope Vol 3; Ogilvie

Dingwall, Henry: Private (S/41018 Seaforth Hldrs [1/6th]. Formerly S/18569 Black Watch); KIA, 16.05.17, 33 years; 84 Nether Street, Kirkcaldy; Gravestone in Feuars Burial Ground, Pathhead. Pathhead Parish Church Memorial Plaques & Windows; Brown's Copse Cemetery, Roeux, Pas de Calais, France. Grave III.A.24; Kirkcaldy War Memorial; *FA* 09.06.17; *Soldiers Died* Part 64; *FA* 09.06.17; *FFP* 09.06.17; *FA* 16.06.17; *FA* (RoH) 16.06.17; *FFP* (RoH) 16.06.17; *FFP* (CasList) 23.06.17; *FA* (BMD) 11.05.18; *FFP* (BMD) 11.05.18; *FA* (FRoH) 30.11.18; *FFP* 21.06.24

Dixon, Henry Edward: Private (12396 Royal Scots Fusiliers [2nd]); DOW France & Flanders, 25.04.15, 35 years; Wigton Cemetery, Cumberland. Grave 2.M. "U".27; Kirkcaldy War Memorial; *Soldiers Died* Part 26

Doggart, Norman Alexander: Captain (Cameronians [Scottish Rifles] att'd RAF [33rd Training Depot]); Killed in a flying accident at Witney, Oxford, 10.10.18, 27 years; Townsend Cottage, Townsend Place, Kirkcaldy; St Brycedale Church Plaque. Kirkcaldy High School War Memorial. Gravestone in St Andrews Western Cemetery; Oxford (Botley) Cemetery. Grave 11.125; Kirkcaldy War Memorial; *FA* 19.10.18; *Cross of Sacrifice Vol 1*; RFC/RAF RoH; *FA* 19.06.15; *FA* 19.10.18; *FA* (RoH) 19.10.18; *FA* (BMD) 19.10.18; *FA* (FRoH) 14.12.18; *FA* (KHS RoH) 29.03.19; *FA* (KHS RoH) 19.07.19

Doig, Thomas Melville: Private (S/3741 Black Watch [8th] "A" Coy); KIA Loos, 25.09.15, 19 years; 83 Victoria Road, Kirkcaldy; Gravestone in Bennochy Cemetery. Old Parish Church Memorial Panel; Loos Memorial, Pas de Calais, France. Panels 78-83; Kirkcaldy War Memorial; *FFP* 02.10.15; *FA* 09.10.15; *FA* 23.10.15; *FFP* 23.10.15; *Soldiers Died* Part 46; War Album 15/16; *FA* (BMD) 09.10.15; *FFP* 09.10.15; *FFP* (BMD) 09.10.15; *FA* (RoH) 16.10.15; *FFP* (RoH) 16.10.15; *FA* 23.10.15 (2 entries); *FFP* 23.10.15; *FA* (CasList) 13.05.16; *FFP* 05.08.16 Roll of the Brave; *FFP* (BMD) 23.09.16; *FA* (Service List) 02.12.16; *FFP* (BMD) 29.09.17; *FFP* (BMD) 28.09.18; *FA* (FRoH) 16.11.18; Wauchope Vol 3

Donaldson, David B.: Lance Corporal (27788 KOSB [7/8th]. Formerly 2918 F & F Yeo); DOW, 06.08.18, 26 years; St Sever Cemetery Extension, Rouen, Seine-Maritime, France. Grave Q.III.M.22; Kirkcaldy War Memorial; *Soldiers Died* Part 30; *FFP* (RoH) 14.09.18

Donaldson, Robert Hunter: Private (S/24766 Seaforth Hldrs [7th]. Formerly A & S Hldrs); KIA France, 20.09.18, 19 years; 33 Cowan Street, Kirkcaldy; Hagle Dump Cemetery, Elverdinge, Flanders, Belgium. Grave VI; *FA* 12.09.18; Kirkcaldy War Memorial; *Soldiers Died* Part 64; *FA* 12.09.18; *FFP* 05.10.18; *FA* (BMD) 12.10.18; *FFP* 12.10.18; *FFP* (BMD) 12.10.18; *FA* (RoH) 19.10.18; *FA* (FRoH) 14.12.18

Donaldson, Thomas: Private (21324 Royal Scots [17th]); DOW, 28.07.16, 20 years; 216 Rosslyn Street, Kirkcaldy; Sinclairtown Parish Church War Memorial Chair; La Neuville British Cemetery, Corbie, Somme, France. Grave I.D.73; Kirkcaldy War Memorial; *Soldiers Died* Part 6; *FA* 12.08.16; *FFP* 19.08.16; *FA* (BMD) 26.08.16; *FA* (CasList) 02.09.16; *FFP* (CasList) 02.09.16; *FA* (RoH) 16.09.16; *FFP* (RoH) 16.09.16; *FA* (Service List) 09.12.16; *FFP* (RoH) 30.12.16; *FA* (FRoH) 23.11.18

Donaldson, William: Private (16143 KOSB [6th]); KIA, 19.07.16; 60 East Smeaton Street, Kirkcaldy; Thiepval Memorial, Somme, France. Pier & Face 4A & 4D; Kirkcaldy War Memorial; *Soldiers Died* Part 30; *FA* 12.08.16; *FFP* 19.08.16; *FA* (CasList) 02.09.16; *FFP* (CasList) 02.09.16; *FA* (RoH) 16.09.16; *FFP* (RoH) 16.09.16; *FFP* (RoH) 30.12.16; *FA* (Service List) 17.02.17; *FA* (FRoH) 23.11.18

Donelly, Thomas: Private (3/2594 Black Watch [1st] "D" Coy); MIA, 09.05.15, 21 years; 164 Links Street, Kirkcaldy; Le Touret Memorial, Pas de Calais, France. Panels 24-26; Kirkcaldy War Memorial; *FA* 30.10.15; *Soldiers Died* Part 46; War Album 15/16; *FA* 09.10.15; *FFP* 05.08.16 Roll of the Brave; *FA* (CasList) 16.09.16; *FFP* (CasList) 16.09.16; *FA* (Service List) 26.11.16; *FA* (Service List) 02.12.16; *FA* (FRoH) 16.11.18; Wauchope Vol 1

Donnachie, Hugh: Private (6113 Border Regt [2nd] 7th Div "A" Coy); KIA, 16.05.15, 28 years; 8/10 Sands Road, Kirkcaldy; Le Touret Memorial, Pas de Calais, France. Panels 19-20; Kirkcaldy War Memorial; *Soldiers Died* Part 39; War Album 15; *FFP* (BMD) 12.06.15; *FA* 19.06.15; *FA* (RoH) 17.07.15; *FFP* 05.08.16 Roll of the Brave; *FA* (Service List) 06.01.17; *FA* (FRoH) 16.11.18

Dorward, David: Private (S/3930 Black Watch [9th]); KIA Loos, 25.09.15; 2 Balfour Street, Kirkcaldy; Loos Memorial, Pas de Calais, France. Panels 78-83; Kirkcaldy War Memorial; *Soldiers Died* Part 46; War Album 15/16; *FA* (RoH) 13.11.15; *FFP* 05.08.16 Roll of the Brave; *FFP* (BMD) 23.09.16; *FA* (Service List) 18.11.16; *FA* (FRoH) 16.11.18; Wauchope Vol 3

Dorward, James, MM: Sergeant (14703; CEF; Motor Machine Gun Bde [1st]); 24.03.18, 28 years; Vimy Memorial, Pas de Calais, France; Kirkcaldy War Memorial; *CBoR* Page 399

Dougall, George: Private (351175 Black Watch [4/5th]. Formerly HCB); DOW CCS, 03.08.18, 25 years; 116 Mid Street, Kirkcaldy; Pathhead Parish Church Memorial Plaques & Windows; Senlis French National Cemetery, Oise, France. Grave III.A.113; Kirkcaldy War Memorial; *Soldiers Died* Part 46; *FFP* 17.08.18; *FFP* (BMD) 17.08.18; *FA* 24.08.18; *FA* (BMD) 24.08.18; *FA* (RoH) 14.09.18; *FA* (FRoH) 14.12.18; *FFP* 21.06.24; Wauchope Vol 2

Douglas, Henry James Wilkie: Driver (T4/083264 RASC [22nd Div Train]); Died of malaria in Salonika Camp Hospital, 13.07.16, 40 years; 17 Young's Terrace, Maria Street, Kirkcaldy; Gravestone in Bennochy Cemetery; Salonika (Lembet Road) Military Cemetery, Salonika, Greece. Grave 243; Kirkcaldy War Memorial; *Soldiers Died* Part 78; *FA* 29.07.16; *FA* (BMD) 29.07.16; *FFP* 29.07.16; *FFP* (BMD) 29.07.16; *FA* (RoH) 05.08.16; *FFP* 05.08.16 Roll of the Brave; *FA* (CasList) 02.09.16; *FFP* (CasList) 02.09.16; *FA* (RoH) 16.09.16; *FFP* (RoH) 16.09.16; *FFP* (RoH) 30.12.16; *FA* (FRoH) 23.11.18

Dow, Adam James: Private (9436 Black Watch [1st] "A" Coy); Brother of Drummond Dow; KIA rescuing wounded comrades, 09.05.15, 30 years; 118 Links Street, Kirkcaldy; Le Touret Memorial, Pas de Calais, France. Panels 24-26; Kirkcaldy War Memorial; *FA* 26.06.15; *Soldiers Died* Part 46; War Album 15; *FA* 22.05.15; *Dundee Advertiser* 24.05.15; *FFP* (CasList) 05.06.15; *FA* 26.06.15; *FFP* 05.08.16 Roll of the Brave; *FA* (Service List) 25.11.16; *FA* (Service List) 02.12.16; *FFP* 23.06.17; *FA* (FRoH) 16.11.18; Wauchope Vol 1

Private Adam **Dow** had been discharged from the Black Watch in January 1914, having served for thirteen years. He rejoined his regiment in August 1914 and by May 1915 was the only survivor of his section.

Dow went out four times, under heavy fire, to rescue wounded comrades. He was killed on his fourth attempt.

His brother, Drummond Dow, came over from Canada to enlist and was reported missing, believed killed, in 1914. In June 1917, his parents received a letter from him saying he was well but making no mention of what had happened in the intervening months. It was assumed that he had suffered a loss of memory.

Downie, Andrew: Sergeant (828 Black Watch [2nd]); DOW Mesopotamia, 01.05.16, 25 years; 22 Factory Road, Kirkcaldy; Gravestone in Bennochy Cemetery; Amara War Cemetery, Iraq. Grave II.C.7; Kirkcaldy War Memorial; *FA* 20.05.16; *Soldiers Died* Part 46; *FA* 06.05.16; *FFP* 13.05.16; *FA* 20.05.16; *FA* (BMD) 20.05.16; *FA* (RoH) 17.06.16; *FFP* (RoH) 17.06.16; *FA* (CasList) 24.06.16; *FA* 08.07.16; *FFP* 08.07.16; *FFP* 05.08.16 Roll of the Brave; *FA* 12.08.16; *FA* (Service List) 06.01.17; *FFP* (BMD) 05.05.17; *FFP* (BMD) 04.05.18; *FA* (FRoH) 23.11.18; Wauchope Vol 1

Downie, Peter: Pioneer (44735 Royal Engineers [17th Signals Coy]); KIA Somme, 12.11.16, 21 years; 52 Dunnikier Road,Kirkcaldy; Gravestone in Bennochy Cemetery; AIF Burial Ground, Flers, Somme, France. Grave 1.F.6; Kirkcaldy War Memorial; *Soldiers Died* Part 4; *FA* 25.11.16; *FA* (BMD) 25.11.16; *FFP* 25.11.16; *FFP* (BMD) 25.11.16; *FFP* 02.12.16; *FA* (RoH) 16.12.16; *FA* (CasList) 23.12.16; *FFP* (CasList) 23.12.16; *FFP* (RoH) 30.12.16; *FFP* (BMD) 10.11.17; *FA* (FRoH) 30.11.18

Doyle, Charles: Private (17709 HLI [12th]); KIA, 26.09.15, 18 years; 24 Forth Avenue South, Kirkcaldy; Loos Memorial, Pas de Calais, France. Panels 108-112; Kirkcaldy War Memorial; *FFP* 25.12.15; *Soldiers Died* Part 63; War Album 15/16; *FFP* 04.12.15; *FA* 11.12.15; *FA* (RoH) 18.12.15; *FFP* 25.12.15; *FFP* 05.08.16 Roll of the Brave; *FA* (Service List) 17.02.17; *FA* (FRoH) 16.11.18

Drummond, Duncan: Private (3/2666 Black Watch [1st] att'd Royal Engineers); KIA, 28.04.16; 39 Nicol Street, Kirkcaldy; St Patrick's Cemetery, Loos, Pas de Calais, France. Grave III.D.6; Kirkcaldy War Memorial; *FA* 13.05.16; *Soldiers Died* Part 46; *FFP* 06.05.16; *FA* 13.05.16; *FA* (RoH) 13.05.16; *FA* 20.05.16; *FFP* 20.05.16; *FFP* 05.08.16 Roll of the Brave; *FA* (Service List) 18.11.16; *FA* (FRoH) 23.11.18; Wauchope Vol 1

Dryburgh, Charles: Private (S/3461 Black Watch [8th]); KIA, 09.04.17, 36 years; 44 Overton Road, Kirkcaldy; St Catherine British Cemetery, Pas de Calais, France. Grave L.11; Kirkcaldy War Memorial; *Soldiers Died* Part 46; *FA* 19.05.17; *FA* (RoH) 19.05.17; *FFP* 19.05.17; *FFP* (CasList) 19.05.17; *FFP* (RoH) 19.05.17; *FA* (FRoH) 30.11.18; Wauchope Vol 3

Dryburgh, David: Lance Corporal (9926 Black Watch [1st]); KIA, 09.05.15, 28 years; 115 Nether Street, Kirkcaldy; Pathhead Baptist Church War Memorial Roll of Honour (As Daniel); Le Touret Memorial, Pas de Calais, France. Panels 24-26; Kirkcaldy War Memorial; *FA* 11.03.16; *Soldiers Died* Part 46; *FA* 28.08.15; *FFP* 28.08.15; *FA* 04.03.16; *FA* (BMD) 04.03.16; *FFP* 04.03.16; *FFP* (BMD) 04.03.16; *FFP* 11.03.16; *FFP* 05.08.16 Roll of the Brave; *FA* (Service List) 30.12.16; *FA* (FRoH) 23.11.18; Wauchope Vol 1

Dryburgh, John: Sapper (46820 Royal Engineers [Signal Service Training Centre]); 24.02.19; Gravestone in Old Parish Churchyard; Old Parish Churchyard, Kirkcaldy. Northwest side of church; Kirkcaldy War Memorial

Dudgeon, W.: Lance Corporal (KOSB); DOW; St Clair Street, Kirkcaldy; Not identified on CWGC web site; Kirkcaldy War Memorial; *FFP* 08.01.16; *FA* (FRoH) 16.11.18

Duff, Alexander: Private (335584 Royal Scots [9th]); DOW, 22.01.18, 24 years; 25 Union Street, Kirkcaldy; Barony Church Plaque; St Sever Cemetery Extension, Rouen, Seine-Maritime, France. Grave P.VI.G.1A; Kirkcaldy War Memorial; *Soldiers Died* Part 6; *FFP* (RoH) 26.01.18; *FFP* (BMD) 26.01.18; *FA* (BMD) 02.02.18; *FA* (RoH) 16.02.18; *FFP* (RoH) 16.02.18; *FA* (FRoH) 07.12.18

Duff, David: Private (S/13565 Gordon Hldrs [8/10th] "D" Coy); DOW No 8 General Hospital, Rouen, 22.10.16, 34 years; 122 Institution Street, Kirkcaldy; Boisguillaume Communal Cemetery, Rouen, Seine-Maritime, France. Grave II.B.4; Kirkcaldy War Memorial; *Soldiers Died* Part 65; *FA* 28.10.16; *FA* (BMD) 28.10.16; *FFP* 28.10.16; *FFP* (BMD) 28.10.16; *FA* (CasList) 18.11.16; *FA* (RoH) 18.11.16; *FFP* (CasList) 18.11.16; *FFP* (RoH) 18.11.16; *FFP* (RoH) 30.12.16; *FA* (Service List) 24.02.17; *FFP* (BMD) 20.10.17; *FA* (FRoH) 30.11.18; *FA* 26.04.19; *FFP* (BMD) 23.10.20

Dunbar, James: Private (39171 Royal Scots [13th]. Formerly S/14594 Black Watch); Died of pneumonia, 22.04.17, 20 years; 57 High Street, Kirkcaldy; St Hilaire Cemetery, Frevent, Pas de Calais, France. Grave II.H.4; Kirkcaldy War Memorial; *Soldiers Died* Part 6; *FA* 28.04.17; *FFP* 05.05.17; *FA* (RoH) 19.05.17; *FFP* (RoH) 19.05.17; *FFP* (CasList) 26.05.17; *FA* (FRoH) 30.11.18

Duncan, Alexander: Private (34361 RDC [205th Protection Coy]. Formerly 20149 A & S Hldrs); Died at home, 16.11.16; Falkirk Cemetery. Grave B.778; Kirkcaldy War Memorial; *Soldiers Died* Part 77

Duncan, Henry: Private (202008 Black Watch [4/5th]); KIA, 01.08.18, 40 years; 465 High Street, Kirkcaldy; Raperie British Cemetery, Villemontoire, Aisne, France. Grave III.E.4; Kirkcaldy War Memorial; *Soldiers Died* Part 46; *FFP* 24.08.18; *FFP* (BMD) 24.08.18; *FA* 31.08.18; *FA* (RoH) 14.09.18; *FFP* (RoH) 14.09.18; *FA* (FRoH) 14.12.18; Wauchope Vol 2

Duncan, James: Private (Black Watch); Brother-in-law of Alexander Crawford & James Crawford; KIA France; Not identified on CWGC web site; Kirkcaldy War Memorial; *FFP* 25.01.19

Duncan, John: Private (Royal Scots [2nd]); 47 Victoria Road, Kirkcaldy; Not identified on CWGC web site; Kirkcaldy War Memorial; *FA* 03.10.14

Dunn, Thomas Low, MM: Lance Corporal (S/17401 Seaforth Hldrs [6th]. Formerly S/9716 Gordon Hldrs); DOW, 31.08.18, 24 years; 21 Greenhill Place, Kirkcaldy; Plaque in Ceres Church; Perreuse Chateau Franco British National Cemetery, Seine-et-Marne, France. Grave I.A.53; Kirkcaldy War Memorial. Ceres War Memorial; *Soldiers Died* Part 64; *FFP* (BMD) 14.09.18; *FA* (RoH) 16.11.18; *FFP* (RoH) 16.11.18; *FA* (FRoH) 14.12.18

Dunsire, Alexander: Private (351519 Royal Scots [11th]); DOW 18th CCS, 20.08.18, 26 years; 15 Sang Place, Kirkcaldy; Gravestone in Kinghorn Cemetery. Kirkcaldy High School War Memorial; Longuenesse (St Omer) Souvenir Cemetery, Pas de Calais, France. Grave V.D.75; Kirkcaldy War Memorial; *Soldiers Died* Part 6; *FA* 31.08.18; *FFP* 31.08.18; *FA* (KHS RoH) 29.03.19; *FA* 26.04.19; *FA* (KHS RoH) 19.07.19

Dunsire, Robert Anderson, VC: Lance Corporal (18274 Royal Scots [13th]); Brother-in-law of Ralph Pitt; DOW, 30.01.16, 24 years; 107/210 Denbeath, Methil/Commercial Street, Kirkcaldy; E.U. Congregational Church Memorial Plaque. Buckhaven Higher Grade School War Memorial; Mazingarbe Communal Cemetery, Pas de Calais, France. Grave 18; Kirkcaldy War Memorial. Methil War Memorial; ‡; *Soldiers Died* Part 6; *FA* 20.11.15; *FA* 27.11.15 (2 entries); *FA* 04.12.15; *FA* 11.12.15; *FA* 08.01.16; *FA* 15.01.16; *FA* 22.01.16; *FA* 12.02.16 (2 entries); *FFP* 12.02.16; *FA* (BMD) 19.02.16; *FFP* 05.08.16; *FA* 26.08.16; *FFP* 02.09.16; *FFP* 09.09.16; *FFP* 16.09.16; *FA* 30.09.16; *FA* (Service List) 04.11.16; *FA* (Service List) 16.12.16; *FA* (BMD) 02.03.17; *FA* (BMD) 02.02.18; *FA* (FRoH) 16.11.18; *FA* 21.12.18; *FFP* (BMD) 25.01.19

Easson, Robert: Private (65301; CEF; Canadian Infantry [24th] 2nd Div 5th Bde. [Victoria Rifles]); KIA, 15.04.16, 35 years; 18 Thistle Street, Kirkcaldy; Ypres (Menin Gate) Memorial, Ieper, West Vlaanderen, Belgium. Panels 24-26-28-30; Kirkcaldy War Memorial; *FA* 20.05.16; *CBoR* Page 81; *FFP* 06.05.16; *FA* 13.05.16; *FA* (RoH) 13.05.16; *FA* 29.07.16; *FFP* 05.08.16 Roll of the Brave; *FFP* (RoH) 16.09.16; *FA* (FRoH) 23.11.18; CEF Official List of Casualties

Edgar, George: Private (2081 Black Watch [1st] "B" Coy); Missing at Mons. DOW whilst PoW in Germany, 21.06.15, 22 years; 41 Bridgeton, Kirkcaldy; Le Touret Memorial, Pas de Calais, France. Panels 24-26; Kirkcaldy War Memorial; *FA* 07.08.15; *Soldiers Died* Part 46; *FA* 26.06.15; *Scotsman* 30.06.15; *FFP* 03.07.15; *FA* 07.08.15; *FFP* 14.08.15; *FA* (RoH) 18.09.15; *FFP* 05.08.16 Roll of the Brave; *FA* (Service List) 28.10.16; *FA* (Service List) 24.02.17; *FA* (FRoH) 16.11.18; Wauchope Vol 1; Army Returns 1914-1918 (SRO)

Ednie, John Law: Guardsman (13904 Scots Guards [2nd]); KIA, 04.04.18, 24 years; 42 Market Street, Kirkcaldy; Gravestones in Bennochy Cemetery & Abbotshall Churchyard. Old Parish Church Memorial Plaque; Arras Memorial, Pas de Calais, France. Bay 1; Kirkcaldy War Memorial; *Soldiers Died* Part 5; *FA* 13.04.18; *FA* (BMD) 04.05.18; *FFP* (BMD) 04.05.18; *FA* (RoH) 18.05.18; *FFP* (RoH) 18.05.18; *FA* (FRoH) 07.12.18; *FA* (FRoH) 21.12.18

Edwards, Percy E.: Private (3/2579 Black Watch [10th]); MIA Salonika, 08.05.17, 23 years; 4 Quality Street, Kirkcaldy; Doiran Memorial, Greece; Kirkcaldy War Memorial; *Soldiers Died* Part 46; *FA* 16.06.17; *FA* (CasList) 16.06.17; *FA* 24.08.18; *FFP* 24.08.18; *FA* 31.08.18; *FA* (RoH) 14.09.18; *FFP* 14.09.18; *FFP* (RoH) 14.09.18; *FA* (FRoH) 14.12.18; Wauchope Vol 3

Elder, Alexander Lawson: Private (4511; AIF; Australian Infantry (45th]); Served as Alexander Croydon; KIA, 28.04.18, 29 years; 93 Salisbury Street, Kirkcaldy. Native of Pitlessie; Adelaide Cemetery, Villers-Bretonneux, Somme, France. Grave III.P.8; Australian War Memorial web site; Kirkcaldy War Memorial; *FFP* 13.07.18; *FA* (RoH) 14.09.18; *FFP* (RoH) 14.09.18; *FA* (FRoH) 14.12.18

Elder, David: Private (RAVC); DOW German Hospital, 23.01.17; 92 Alexandra Street, Kirkcaldy; Not identified on CWGC web site; Kirkcaldy War Memorial; *FA* 15.04.16; *FA* 27.01.17; *FA* (BMD) 27.01.17; *FFP* (BMD) 19.01.18; *FFP* (BMD) 25.01.19

Elder, James A.: Captain (Merchant Navy; *The Baron Wemyss*); Missing after being taken prisoner. Now reported killed, 07.03.17; 1 Montgomery Street, Kirkcaldy; Tower Hill Memorial, London; Kirkcaldy War Memorial; *Cross of Sacrifice Vol 5*; *FFP* 15.12.17; *FFP* (BMD) 15.12.17; *FA* 22.12.17; *FA* (BMD) 22.12.17

Robert Dunsire, VC, visiting his old school, Pathhead School, Kirkcaldy. The lady on his right is his wife. The photograph was taken during his visit following his award of the VC by the King.

Andrew **Elshender** was killed in action when he was returning from accompanying his wounded officer to medical help. He had taken part in a dawn attack and was to be recommended "as he had done excellent work that morning".

Elshender is a good example of how difficult it was to get accurate information about serving soldiers, as he is variously listed under Elshender, Elfinder and Andrew E. Shender!

Elliot, John Service: Private (33422 HLI [16th]. Formerly HCB & S/15777Black Watch); MIA, 18.11.16, 29 years; 81 Sutherland Street, Kirkcaldy; Pathhead Parish Church Memorial Plaques & Windows; New Munich Trench British Cemetery, Beaumont-Hamel, Somme, France. Grave E.16; Kirkcaldy War Memorial; *Soldiers Died* Part 63; *FA* (CasList) 13.01.17; *FFP* (BMD) 21.07.17; *FA* (BMD) 28.07.17; *FFP* 28.07.17; *FA* 15.09.17; *FFP* (RoH) 15.09.17; *FFP* (BMD) 17.11.17; *FFP* (BMD) 16.11.18; *FFP* 21.06.24

Ellis, Allan: Private (S/25770 Seaforth Hldrs [2nd]. Formerly TR/9728 TR Bn); Also listed as Alex Ellis; KIA, 17.04.18, 19 years; 39 Balfour Street, Kirkcaldy; Chocques Military Cemetery, Pas de Calais, France. Grave II.D.8; Kirkcaldy War Memorial; *Soldiers Died* Part 64; *FA* 04.05.18; *FFP* (RoH) 04.05.18; *FA* (RoH) 18.05.18; *FFP* 18.05.18; *FFP* (RoH) 18.05.18; *FFP* (BMD) 18.05.18; *FA* (FRoH) 14.12.18

Ellis, James Patterson: CSM (108209; CEF; 3rd Div 8th Bde. 2nd Canadian Mounted Rifles [British Columbia Regt]); Drowned in West Wemyss Harbour, 25.12.18, 33 years; 10 St Clair Place, Bridgeton, Kirkcaldy/Coronation, Alberta, Canada; Gravestone in Bennochy Cemetery; Bennochy Cemetery, Kirkcaldy. Grave EE.251; Kirkcaldy War Memorial; *CBoR* Page 404; *FA* 18.11.16; *FA* 28.12.18; *FA* (RoH) 18.01.19

Elshender, Andrew: Private (43244 HLI [17th]. Formerly 1498 HCB); On CWGC web site as Elfhender; KIA, 01.04.17, 19 years; 5 Coal Wynd/High Street/Thistle Street, Kirkcaldy; Raith Church Memorial Plaque; Thiepval Memorial, Somme, France. Pier & Face 15C; Kirkcaldy War Memorial; *Soldiers Died* Part 63; *FA* 15.01.16; *FA* 14.04.17; *FA* (BMD) 21.04.17; *FFP* 21.04.17; *FFP* (BMD) 21.04.17; *FA* (CasList) 12.05.17; *FFP* (CasList) 12.05.17; *FA* (RoH) 19.05.17; *FFP* (RoH) 19.05.17; *FA* (FRoH) 30.11.18

English, John: Private (2657 Black Watch [7th]); KIA, 26.03.18; Old Parish Church Memorial Panel; Arras Memorial, Pas de Calais, France. Bay 6; Kirkcaldy War Memorial; *Soldiers Died* Part 46; Wauchope Vol 2

Erskine, Henry: Corporal (290419 Black Watch [7th]); Brother of William Erskine; KIA Arras, 25.04.17, 23 years; 256 Links Street, Kirkcaldy; Brown's Copse Cemetery, Roeux, Pas de Calais, France. Grave II.B.35; Kirkcaldy War Memorial; *Soldiers Died* Part 46; *FA* 21.07.17; *FFP* 28.07.17; *FFP* 25.08.17; *FA* 01.09.17; *FA* 15.09.17; *FFP* (RoH) 15.09.17; *FFP* (BMD) 04.05.18; Wauchope Vol 2

Erskine, William: Private (3/2807 Black Watch [9th]); Brother of Henry Erskine; MIA, 25.09.15, 19 years; 256 Links Street, Kirkcaldy; Loos Memorial, Pas de Calais, France. Panels 78-83; Kirkcaldy War Memorial; *Soldiers Died* Part 46; *FA* 21.07.17; *FFP* 28.07.17; *FFP* 25.08.17; *FA* 01.09.17; *FA* 15.09.17; *FFP* (RoH) 15.09.17; Wauchope Vol 3

Espie, Leonard: Private (13869 Hussars [13th]); Died at Connaught Hospital, Aldershot, 07.04.17, 43 years; Links Street, Kirkcaldy; Kensal Green (St Mary's) Roman Catholic Cemetery, London. Grave 3.2862; Kirkcaldy War Memorial; *Soldiers Died* Part 1; *FFP* 14.04.17; *FA* 21.04.17; *FA* (BMD) 21.04.17; *FA* (RoH) 19.05.17; *FFP* (RoH) 19.05.17; *FA* (FRoH) 30.11.18

Faichney, John: Gunner (344042 RGA [261st Siege Batt'y] [Forth]); KIA, 27.08.18; Forth RGA Plaque. St Peter's Church Memorial Plaque; Lijssenthoek Military Cemetery, Poperinge, West Vlaanderen, Belgium. Grave XXV.A.26a; Kirkcaldy War Memorial; *Soldiers Died* Part 3

Fair, James: Private (Black Watch); Would appear to be Private James Phair 3/3024; 09.05.15, 33 years; Kirkcaldy War Memorial

Fairgrieve, Robert: Corporal (40186 Royal Scots Fusiliers [1st]); MIA France, 26.09.17, 20 years; 52 Glebe Park, Kirkcaldy; West End Congregational Church Memorial Plaque; Tyne Cot Memorial, Zonnebeke, West Vlaanderen, Belgium. Panels 60-61; Kirkcaldy War Memorial; *Soldiers Died* Part 26; *FA* 10.08.18; *FFP* 10.08.18; *FFP* (BMD) 10.08.18; *FA* 17.08.18; *FA* (BMD) 17.08.18; *FA* (RoH) 14.09.18; *FFP* (RoH) 14.09.18; *FA* (FRoH) 14.12.18

Farmer, John: Private (S/15987 A & S Hldrs [14th]); DOW, 05.07.17, 26 years; 17 Alexandra Street/Bell Wynd, Kirkcaldy; Union Church Plaque; Fins New British Cemetery, Sorel-Le-Grand, Somme, France. Grave I.A.10; Kirkcaldy War Memorial; *Soldiers Died* Part 70; *FFP* 14.07.17; *FA* 21.07.17; *FFP* (BMD) 21.07.17; *FA* (BMD) 28.07.17; *FFP* 28.07.17; *FA* 15.09.17; *FFP* (RoH) 15.09.17; *FFP* (BMD) 06.07.18

Farmer, Robert Burt: Private (S/32023 Cameron Hldrs [3rd]). Formerly 126137 Lovat Scouts & 4121 F & F Yeo); DOW Butterbank Military Hospital, Ireland, 04.11.18, 20 years; 177 Park Road, Kirkcaldy; Gravestone in Dysart Cemetery; Dysart Cemetery, Kirkcaldy. Grave 22.18.South; Kirkcaldy War Memorial; *Soldiers Died* Part 66; *FA* 16.11.18; *FA* (RoH) 16.11.18; *FA* (BMD) 16.11.18; *FFP* 16.11.18; *FFP* (RoH) 16.11.18; *FA* (FRoH) 14.12.18

Fearns, Charles: Private (S/11128 Black Watch [1st]); KIA, 24.12.16; Thiepval Memorial, Somme, France. Pier & Face 10A; Kirkcaldy War Memorial; *Soldiers Died* Part 46; *FA* (CasList) 27.01.17; *FFP* (CasList) 27.01.17; Wauchope Vol 1

Ferguson, Robert: Signaller; (345445 Black Watch [14th] [F & F Yeo Bn]. Formerly 2711 F & F Yeo); KIA Palestine while serving with the Egyptian Expeditionary Force, 26.03.18, 26 years; 7 Russell Place, Kirkcaldy; Gravestone in Bennochy Cemetery; Jerusalem War Cemetery, Israel. Grave L.66; Kirkcaldy War Memorial; *Soldiers Died* Part 46; *FA* 13.04.18; *FA* (BMD) 13.04.18; *FFP* 13.04.18; *FFP* (BMD) 13.04.18; *FFP* (RoH) 20.04.18; *FFP* (BMD) 20.04.18; *FA* (RoH) 18.05.18; *FFP* (RoH) 18.05.18; *FA* (FRoH) 07.12.18; Wauchope Vol 3; Ogilvie

Ferguson, Thomas Anderson: Lance Corporal (7529 Black Watch [1st] "B" Coy); Brother-in-law of William Adams & William Thain; Died as PoW in Germany, 21.06.15, 32 years; 1 Little Lane, High Street, Kirkcaldy; Dunnikier Church Roll of Honour; Ypres (Menin Gate) Memorial, Ieper, West Vlaanderen, Belgium. Panel 57 (Addenda); Kirkcaldy War Memorial; *Soldiers Died* Part 46; War Album 15/16; *FA* (CasList) 20.02.15; *FA* 24.07.15; *FA* (BMD) 24.07.15; *FFP* 24.07.15; *FFP* (BMD) 24.07.15; *Scotsman* 26.07.15; *FA* (RoH) 18.09.15; *FA* 16.10.15; *FA* 25.12.15; *FA* 29.07.16; *FFP* 05.08.16 Roll of the Brave; *FA* (Service List) 04.11.16; *FA* (Service List) 20.01.17; *FA* 15.09.17; *FFP* 15.09.17; *FA* (FRoH) 16.11.18; *FA* 26.04.19; Wauchope Vol 1

Fernie, George: Private (44061 KOSB [2nd]. Formerly 1519 HCB); Brother of John Fisher Fernie; KIA Guillemont, 03.09.16, 23 years; 4 Pottery Road, Links Street, Kirkcaldy; Invertiel Parish Church Memorial Table; Thiepval Memorial, Somme, France. Pier & Face 4A & 4D; Kirkcaldy War Memorial; *FA* 14.10.16; *Soldiers Died* Part 30; *FA* 14.10.16; *FFP* 14.10.16; *FA* (BMD) 28.10.16; *FFP* (CasList) 28.10.16; *FFP* (BMD) 28.10.16; *FA* (Service List) 04.11.16; *FA* (RoH) 18.11.16; *FFP* (RoH) 18.11.16; *FFP* (RoH) 30.12.16; *FA* (Service List) 13.01.17; *FFP* (BMD) 01.09.17; *FFP* (BMD) 07.09.18; *FA* (FRoH) 30.11.18

Fernie, George: Gunner (6631 RFA [56th Div] [Ammunition Column]); DOW, 25.06.16, 19 years; 24 Sutherland Street, Kirkcaldy; St Andrew's Church Memorial Plaque; Couin British Cemetery, Pas de Calais, France. Grave I.A.13; Kirkcaldy War Memorial; *Soldiers Died* Part 2; *FFP* 08.07.16; *FFP* 29.07.16; *FFP* (BMD) 29.07.16; *FA* (RoH) 05.08.16; *FA* (BMD) 05.08.16; *FFP* 05.08.16 Roll of the Brave; *FFP* 12.08.16; *FA* (RoH) 16.09.16; *FFP* (RoH) 16.09.16; *FFP* (CasList) 14.10.16; *FFP* (RoH) 30.12.16; *FA* (Service List) 03.03.17; *FA* (FRoH) 23.11.18

Fernie, John Fisher: Sergeant (21350 Royal Scots [17th] Rosebery Bantam Bn); Brother of George Fernie; DOW Lahore British Hospital, Calais as the result of an accident, 29.03.16, 18 years; 4 Pottery Road, Links Street, Kirkcaldy; Invertiel Parish Church Memorial Table; Calais Southern Cemetery, Pas de Calais, France. Grave C.I.11; Kirkcaldy War Memorial; *FA* 25.03.16; *Soldiers Died* Part 6; *FA* 18.03.16; *FA* 25.03.16; *FFP* 25.03.16; *FA* 01.04.16; *FFP* 08.04.16; *FFP* (BMD) 08.04.16; *FA* (RoH) 15.04.16; *FA* (BMD) 15.04.16; *FFP* (CasList) 15.04.16; *FA* 17.06.16; *FFP* 05.08.16; *FA* 14.10.16; *FFP* 14.10.16; *FA* (Service List) 04.11.16; *FA* (Service List) 13.01.17; *FFP* (BMD) 24.03.17; *FFP* (BMD) 07.09.18; *FA* (FRoH) 23.11.18

Ferns, Cornelius: Private (3/2581 Black Watch [1st]); DOW, 03.09.16; Warlencourt British Cemetery, Pas de Calais, France. Grave I.H.39; Kirkcaldy War Memorial; *Soldiers Died* Part 46; Wauchope Vol 1

Ferrier, George: Private (S/10052 Cameron Hldrs [6th]); KIA Loos, 26.09.15; 152 Overton Road, Kirkcaldy; Sinclairtown Parish Church War Memorial Chair; Loos Memorial, Pas de Calais, France. Panels 119-124; Kirkcaldy War Memorial; *FFP* 23.10.15; *Soldiers Died* Part 66; War Album 15/16; *FFP* 09.10.15; *Scotsman* (CasList) 11.10.15; *FA* 16.10.15; *FA* (RoH) 16.10.15; *FFP* (RoH) 16.10.15; *FFP* 05.08.16 Roll of the Brave; *FA* 12.08.16; *FA* (Service List) 18.11.16; *FA* (FRoH) 16.11.18

Finlay, Thomas: Private (B/21327 HLI [1st]. Formerly Dragoon Guards [5th]); KIA Mesopotamia, 15.04.16, 23 years; 190 Overton Road, Kirkcaldy; Basra Memorial, Iraq. Panels 35 & 64; Kirkcaldy War Memorial; *Soldiers Died* Part 63; *FFP* 13.05.16; *FFP* (BMD) 13.05.16; *FA* 20.05.16; *FA* (BMD) 20.05.16; *FA* (RoH) 17.06.16; *FFP* 05.08.16 Roll of the Brave; *FA* (Service List) 18.11.16; *FA* (FRoH) 23.11.18

Finley, David L.: Lance Corporal (14059 KOSB [7th]); Name variously spelt Findlay, Finlay, Finley; DOW, 28.04.16, 28 years; 75 Rosslyn Street, Kirkcaldy; Sinclairtown Parish Church War Memorial Chair; Vermelles British Cemetery, Pas de Calais, France. Grave II.G.36; Kirkcaldy War Memorial; *FA* 13.05.16; *FFP* 13.05.16; *Soldiers Died* Part 30; *FFP* 06.05.16; *FA* 13.05.16; *FA* (RoH) 13.05.16; *FFP* 13.05.16; *FA* (CasList) 20.05.16; *FFP* (BMD) 20.05.16; *FFP* 05.08.16 Roll of the Brave; *FA* (Service List) 09.12.16; *FA* (FRoH) 23.11.18

Fisher, James: Private (S/2181 Seaforth Hldrs [8th]); Brother-in-law of Charles Petrie; MIA Loos, 25.09.15, 24 years; 23 High Street, Kirkcaldy; E.U. Congregational Church Memorial Plaque; Loos Memorial, Pas de Calais, France. Panels 112-115; Kirkcaldy War Memorial; *FA* 06.11.15; *Soldiers Died* Part 64; *FA* 29.07.16; *FA* 04.11.16; *FFP* 04.11.16; *FA* (RoH) 18.11.16; *FFP* (RoH) 18.11.16; *FA* (Service List) 09.12.16; *FFP* (RoH) 30.12.16; *FFP* (BMD) 22.09.17; *FA* (FRoH) 30.11.18

Fisher, James Anderson: Private (1001186; CEF; Canadian Infantry [16th] 1st Div 3rd Bde. [Canadian Scottish] [Manitoba Regt]. Formerly 226th Bn); CWGC gives number as 1001188.; DOW CCS, 13.08.17; 63 Commercial Street, Kirkcaldy; Noeux-les-Mines Communal Cemetery & Extension, Pas de Calais, France. Grave II.H.26; Kirkcaldy War Memorial; *CBoR* Page 237; *FFP* (CasList) 18.08.17; *FA* 25.08.17; *FA* 15.09.17; *FFP* (RoH) 15.09.17; *FFP* 29.09.17; *FFP* (BMD) 17.08.18; Urquhart

Fisher, Joseph: Private (S/40557 Black Watch [8th]); KIA, 19.10.16, 26 years; Rosebank, Victoria Road, Kirkcaldy; Thiepval Memorial, Somme, France. Pier & Face 4A & 4D; Kirkcaldy War Memorial; *Soldiers Died* Part 46; *FFP* (BMD) 11.11.16; *FA* (RoH) 18.11.16; *FA* (BMD) 18.11.16; *FFP* (RoH) 18.11.16; *FA* (CasList) 25.11.16; *FFP* (CasList) 25.11.16; *FFP* (RoH) 30.12.16; *FFP* (BMD) 20.10.17; *FA* (FRoH) 30.11.18; Wauchope Vol 3

Fleming, John Crawford: Private (412223; CEF; Canadian Infantry [26th] 2nd Div 5th Bde. [New Brunswick Regt] [PPCLI]. Formerly 39th Bn); KIA France, 06.03.16, 21 years; 27 Balfour Street, Kirkcaldy; La Laiterie Miltary Cemetery, Heuvelland, West Vlaanderen, Belgium. Grave II.B.12; Kirkcaldy War Memorial; *CBoR* Page 86; *FA* 25.03.16; *FFP* 25.03.16; *FFP* (BMD) 25.03.16; *FA* (RoH) 15.04.16; *FFP* (RoH) 15.04.16; *FFP* 05.08.16 Roll of the Brave; *FA* (Service List) 18.11.16; *FA* (FRoH) 23.11.18; CEF Official List of Casualties

Foreman, John Scott, MM: Private (40529 Royal Scots [17th]. Formerly 9189 Reserve Cavalry Regt [5th]); DOW CCS, Arneke, 06.08.18, 21 years; New Buildings, Springfield, Cupar; E.U. Congregational Church Memorial Plaque; Arneke British Cemetery, Nord, France. Grave III.C.4; Kirkcaldy War Memorial; *Soldiers Died* Part 6

Forrest, David, DCM: Private (7831 Seaforth Hldrs [2nd] "A" Coy); 06.06.15; 31 years; Wemyss' Close, 19 Mid Street, Pathhead, Kirkcaldy; Barony Church Plaque; Bard Cottage Cemetery, Boezinge, Ieper, West Vlaanderen, Belgium. Grave VI.C.21; Kirkcaldy War Memorial; *FA* 12.09.14; *Soldiers Died* Part 64; War Album 14/15; War Album 15; *FA* 19.06.15; *FFP* 19.06.15; *FFP* (CasList) 03.07.15; *FA* (RoH) 17.07.15; *FFP* (BMD) 10.06.16 (2 entries); *FFP* 05.08.16 Roll of the Brave; *FA* (Service List) 28.10.16; *FA* (Service List) 06.01.17; *FFP* 08.06.18; *FA* (FRoH) 16.11.18; RoH Dunnikier Colliery

---

Private David **Forrest** won the DCM for carrying wounded comrade, James Henderson, also of Kirkcaldy, to safety under heavy fire. Forrest was killed by a shell burst on his way to the forward trenches a few months later.

Forrester, Robert: Private (14190 Cameronians [Scottish Rifles] [10th]); KIA Loos, 25.09.15, 19 years; 7 Nairn Street, Kirkcaldy; Barony Church Plaque; Loos Memorial, Pas de Calais, France. Panels 57-59; Kirkcaldy War Memorial; *FA* 27.11.15; *Soldiers Died* Part 31; War Album 15/16; *FA* 20.11.15; *FA* (BMD) 20.11.15; *FA* (RoH) 18.12.15; *FFP* 05.08.16 Roll of the Brave; *FFP* (BMD) 23.09.16; *FA* (Service List) 04.11.16; *FA* (Service List) 13.01.17; *FFP* (BMD) 28.09.18; *FA* (FRoH) 16.11.18

Forsyth, D.: Guardsman (Scots Guards); DOW France; 109/125 Nether Street, Kirkcaldy; Not identified on CWGC web site; Kirkcaldy War Memorial; War Album 15/16; *FA* 04.09.15; *FA* (RoH) 18.09.15; *FFP* 05.08.16 Roll of the Brave; *FA* (Service List) 28.10.16; *FA* (Service List) 30.12.16; *FA* (FRoH) 16.11.18; Kirkcaldy Council Memorial Scroll

Foster, Andrew: Lance Corporal (3509 Black Watch [2/7th] 2nd Support Coy); Died of appendicitis at Eastern Hospital, Hove, Brighton, 22.10.15, 47 years; 17 Glasswork Street, Kirkcaldy; Gravestone in Bennochy Cemetery. Bethelfield Church Plaque; Bennochy Cemetery, Kirkcaldy. Grave O.242; Kirkcaldy War Memorial; *FA* 27.11.15; *Soldiers Died* Part 46; War Album 15/16; *FA* 23.10.15; *FFP* (BMD) 23.10.15; *FA* 30.10.15; *FA* (RoH) 13.11.15; *FFP* 05.08.16 Roll of the Brave; *FFP* (BMD) 21.10.16; *FA* (Service List) 27.01.17; *FA* (FRoH) 16.11.18; Wauchope Vol 2

Foster, Harry: Private (14377 KOSB [7/8th]); Brother of Robert Foster; DOW, 08.07.16, 26 years; 6 Invertiel Road, Kirkcaldy; Vermelles British Cemetery, Pas de Calais, France. Grave IV.E.48; Kirkcaldy War Memorial; *FA* 05.08.16; *Soldiers Died* Part 30; *FFP* 09.10.15; *FA* 29.07.16 (2 entries); *FFP* 29.07.16; *FA* 05.08.16; *FFP* 05.08.16; *FFP* 05.08.16 Roll of the Brave; *FFP* (CasList) 26.08.16; *FA* (RoH) 16.09.16; *FFP* (RoH) 16.09.16; *FA* (Service List) 28.10.16; *FFP* (RoH) 30.12.16; *FA* (Service List) 03.03.17; *FA* 23.06.17; *FFP* 30.06.17; *FFP* 29.12.17; *FA* (FRoH) 23.11.18

Foster, Robert: Corporal (CH/1035 [S]; Royal Navy; Royal Marine Light Infantry [RND] [RM Bn] [1st]); Brother of Harry Foster; MIA, 28.04.17; 6 Invertiel Road, Kirkcaldy; Arras Memorial, Pas de Calais, France. Bay 1; Kirkcaldy War Memorial; *FA* 05.08.16; *Cross of Sacrifice Vol 4*; RMD; *FA* 05.08.16; *FA* 23.06.17; *FA* 22.12.17; *FFP* 29.12.17; *FA* (RoH) 19.01.18; *FA* (FRoH) 07.12.18

Foulis, Richard R.: Private (S/11087 A & S Hldrs [2nd]. Formerly Scots Greys); DOW, 24.04.17, 23 years; 47 Market Street, Kirkcaldy; Heninel-Croisilles Road Cemetery, France. Grave I.C.3; Kirkcaldy War Memorial; *Soldiers Died* Part 70; *FFP* 05.05.17; *FA* (RoH) 19.05.17; *FFP* (RoH) 19.05.17; *FA* 16.06.17; *FA* (CasList) 16.06.17; *FA* 07.07.17; *FFP* (CasList) 14.07.17; *FFP* 11.08.17; *FA* (FRoH) 30.11.18

Fowler, Harry Scott: Lance Corporal (1984 Black Watch [1/7th]); KIA, 30.07.16, 21 years; Balwearie by Kirkcaldy; Gravestone in Abbotshall Chuchyard. Abbotshall Parish Church Memorial Plaque; Thiepval Memorial, Somme, France. Pier & Face 10A; Kirkcaldy War Memorial; *Soldiers Died* Part 46; *FA* 12.08.16; *FFP* 12.08.16; *FA* 19.08.16; *FA* 26.08.16; *FA* (BMD) 26.08.16; *FFP* 26.08.16; *FFP* 02.09.16; *FA* (CasList) 09.09.16; *FFP* 09.09.16; *FA* (RoH) 16.09.16; *FFP* (RoH) 16.09.16; *FFP* (RoH) 30.12.16; *FA* (Service List) 20.01.17; *FFP* (BMD) 04.08.17; *FFP* (BMD) 03.08.18; *FA* (FRoH) 23.11.18; *FA* 19.11.21; Wauchope Vol 2

Fox, Peter: Private (S/23894 Black Watch [1st]); KIA, 30.09.18, 35 years; 9 Glebe Park, Kirkcaldy; Vis-En-Artois Memorial, Haucourt, Pas de Calais, France. Panel 7; Kirkcaldy War Memorial; *Soldiers Died* Part 46; *FA* 12.10.18; *FFP* 12.10.18; *FA* (RoH) 19.10.18; *FA* 26.10.18; *FA* (BMD) 26.10.18; *FA* (FRoH) 14.12.18; Wauchope Vol 1

France, Thomas: Private (3/2604 Black Watch [8th]); KIA, 25.09.15, 19 years; 32 Bridgeton, Kirkcaldy; Loos Memorial, Pas de Calais, France. Panels 78-83; Kirkcaldy War Memorial; *FA* 30.10.15; *Soldiers Died* Part 46; War Album 15/16; *Scotsman* 27.10.15; *FA* 30.10.15; *FFP* 30.10.15; *FA* (RoH) 13.11.15; *FFP* 05.08.16 Roll of the Brave; *FA* (Service List) 28.10.16; *FA* (Service List) 24.02.17; *FA* (FRoH) 16.11.18; Wauchope Vol 3

Francis, William Pollock: Lieutenant (Royal Scots [12th] [Trench Mortar Batt'y]. Formerly HCB); KIA Kronprinz Farm, Ypres, 22.10.17, 20 years; Raith Manse, Milton Road, Kirkcaldy; Gravestone in Abbotshall Churchyard. Raith Church Memorial Plaque. Kirkcaldy High School War Memorial; Tyne Cot Memorial, Zonnebeke, West Vlaanderen, Belgium. Panels 11-14 & 162; Kirkcaldy War Memorial; *Officers Died*; *Cross of Sacrifice Vol 1*; *FA* 03.11.17; *FA* (BMD) 03.11.17; *FFP* 03.11.17; *FFP* (BMD) 03.11.17; *FA* (RoH) 17.11.17; *FFP* (RoH) 17.11.17; *FA* 08.12.17; *FA* 13.07.18; *FA* (BMD) 26.10.18; *FA* (FRoH) 07.12.18; *FA* (KHS RoH) 29.03.19; *MRoM*

Fraser, Alexander: Private (8047 KOSB [1st]); KIA Dardanelles, 04.06.15; 155 Overton Road, Kirkcaldy; Helles Memorial, Gallipoli, Turkey. Panels 84-92 or 220-222; Kirkcaldy War Memorial; *Soldiers Died* Part 30; *FA* (Service List) 18.11.16

Fraser, Andrew, MC & Bar: Captain (Cameron Hldrs [2nd]); Brother of W. B. Fraser & cousin of W. B. Paterson; DOW 57th CCS, 20.04.18, 29 years; 391 High Street/109 Links Street/Hendry Road, Kirkcaldy; Gravestone in Bennochy Cemetery (Photo). Abbotshall Parish Church Memorial Plaque; Aubigny Communal Cemetery Extension, Pas de Calais, France. Grave V.B.24; Kirkcaldy War Memorial; *Officers Died*; *Cross of Sacrifice Vol 1*; *FA* 29.04.16; *FFP* 05.08.16; *FA* 04.05.18; *FFP* 04.05.18; *FFP* (RoH) 11.05.18; *FA* (RoH) 18.05.18; *FFP* (RoH) 18.05.18; *FA* 03.08.18; *FFP* 03.08.18; *FA* 26.10.18; *FA* (FRoH) 07.12.18; *FA* 19.11.21

Fraser, Annan: Private (277380 A & S Hldrs [1/7th]); KIA "The Labyrinth", near Thelus, on the first day of the Battle of the Scarpe, 09.04.17, 28 years; 48 Market Street, Kirkcaldy; Arras Memorial, Pas de Calais, France. Bay 9; Kirkcaldy War Memorial; *FA* 28.04.17; *Soldiers Died* Part 70; *FA* 21.04.17; *FFP* 28.04.17; *FA* (RoH) 19.05.17; *FFP* (RoH) 19.05.17; *FFP* (CasList) 19.05.17; *FA* (FRoH) 30.11.18

Fraser, Daniel: Sergeant (9108 Gordon Hldrs [1st]); KIA Flanders, 12.10.14; Kirkcaldy; Vieille-Chapelle New Military Cemetery, Lacouture, Pas de Calais, France. Grave IV.C.18; Kirkcaldy War Memorial; *Soldiers Died* Part 65; War Album 14/15; *FA* 05.12.14; *FA* (CasList) 19.12.14; *FA* (BMD) 19.12.14; *StAC* (BMD) 19.12.14; *FA* 02.01.15; *FA* (CasList) 20.02.15; *FFP* 05.08.16 Roll of the Brave; *FA* (FRoH) 16.11.18

Fraser, William Brown: Private (420284; CEF; Canadian Infantry [16th] 1st Div 3rd Bde. [Canadian Scottish] [Manitoba Regt]. Formerly 43rd Bn); Brother of Andrew Fraser & cousin of W.B. Paterson; KIA St Eloi, 17.04.16, 24 years; 109 Links Street, Kirkcaldy; Abbotshall Parish Church Memorial Plaque; Woods Cemetery, Ieper, West Vlaanderen, Belgium. Grave IV.A.3; Kirkcaldy War Memorial; *FA* 29.04.16; *CBoR* Page 88; *FA* 29.04.16; *FA* (BMD) 29.04.16; *FA* (RoH) 13.05.16; *FFP* 13.05.16; *FFP* (BMD) 13.05.16; *FFP* 05.08.16 Roll of the Brave; *FA* (Service List) 02.12.16; *FFP* (BMD) 21.04.17; *FFP* (BMD) 20.04.18; *FFP* 04.05.18; *FA* (FRoH) 23.11.18; Urquhart; CEF Official List of Casualties

Fyfe, Robert: Corporal (15747 Royal Scots Fusiliers [1/4th]); Drowned when the troopship, *Arcadian*, was sunk, 15.04.17, 20 years; 20 Ava Street, Kirkcaldy; Abbotshall Parish Church Memorial Plaque. Kirkcaldy High School War Memorial; Mikra Memorial, Greece; Kirkcaldy War Memorial; *Soldiers Died* Part 26; *FA* 28.04.17; *FFP* 05.05.17; *FA* (RoH) 19.05.17; *FFP* (RoH) 19.05.17; *FA* 14.07.17 (KHS War Honours); *FA* 21.07.17; *FA* (BMD) 21.07.17; *FFP* (BMD) 21.07.17; *FFP* 28.07.17; *FA* (FRoH) 30.11.18; *FA* (KHS RoH) 29.03.19; *FA* 19.11.21

Gair, David Scott: Private (202490 Black Watch [4/5th]); DOW, 07.10.17, 22 years; 95 Mid Street, Kirkcaldy; Wimereux Communal Cemetery, Pas de Calais, France. Grave VI.C.12; Kirkcaldy War Memorial; *Soldiers Died* Part 46; *FA* 13.10.17; *FFP* 20.10.17; *FA* (RoH) 17.11.17; *FFP* (RoH) 17.11.17; *FFP* (BMD) 05.10.18; *FA* (FRoH) 07.12.17; Wauchope Vol 2

Galloway, David: Private (1826 Black Watch [1/7th]); KIA, 30.07.16, 20 years; 270 St Clair Street, Kirkcaldy; Serre Road Cemetery No. 2, Somme, France. Grave XVIII.F.9; Kirkcaldy War Memorial; *Soldiers Died* Part 46; *FA* 12.08.16; *FA* (RoH) 16.09.16; *FFP* (RoH) 16.09.16; *FFP* (RoH) 30.12.16; *FA* (FRoH) 23.11.18; Wauchope Vol 2

Galloway, Henry D.: BQMS (344043 RGA [Siege Batt'y] [Forth]); DOW France, 29.06.17; 53 Alexandra Street, Kirkcaldy; Gravestone in Dysart Cemetery. Forth RGA Plaque. Old Parish Church Memorial Plaque; Bus House Cemetery, Ieper, West Vlaanderen, Belgium. Grave D.9; Kirkcaldy War Memorial; *FA* 07.07.17; *Soldiers Died* Part 3; *FA* 07.07.17; *FA* (BMD) 07.07.17; *FFP* (BMD) 07.07.17; *FA* 14.07.17; *FFP* 14.07.17; *FFP* (CasList) 04.08.17; *FFP* (Memorial List) 05.01.18; *FA* (BMD) 29.06.18; *FA* 06.07.18; *FA* (BMD) 28.06.19

Gayner, Luke: Private (S/11046 Seaforth Hldrs [9th]); Also spelt Gainer; DOW. Buried at Amiens Field Hospital Cemetery, 16.07.16; 111 Overton Road, Kirkcaldy; St Pierre Cemetery, Amiens, France. Grave I.E.6; Kirkcaldy War Memorial; *Soldiers Died* Part 64; *FA* (BMD) 05.08.16; *FFP* 05.08.16 Roll of the Brave; *FA* 12.08.16; *FA* (BMD) 12.08.16; *FFP* 12.08.16; *FA* (CasList) 19.08.16; *FFP* (CasList) 19.08.16; *FA* (RoH) 16.09.16; *FFP* (RoH) 16.09.16; *FA* (Service List) 18.11.16; *FFP* 30.12.16; *FA* (FRoH) 23.11.18

Gentle, Robert: Lance Corporal (16545 Royal Scots Fusiliers [1st]); On CWGC as James Brown Gentle; DOW 6th CCS, 31.05.18, 30 years; 73 Nether Street, Kirkcaldy; Pernes British Cemetery, Pas de Calais, France. Grave II.E.22; Kirkcaldy War Memorial; *Soldiers Died* Part 26; *FA* 22.06.18; *FFP* 22.06.18; *FFP* (BMD) 22.06.18; *FA* 29.06.18; *FA* (BMD) 29.06.18; *FA* (RoH) 13.07.18; *FA* (FRoH) 14.12.18

George, Archibald: Private (S/41457 Seaforth Hldrs [1/6th]. Formerly 6662 Lovat Scouts & 126142 Cameron Hldrs); KIA, 25.10.18, 20 years; Almasi, 15 Novar Crescent, Kirkcaldy; Raith Church Memorial Plaque; Maing Communal Cemetery Extension, Nord, France. Grave A.5; Kirkcaldy War Memorial; *Soldiers Died* Part 64; *FA* (RoH) 16.11.18; *FA* (BMD) 16.11.18; *FFP* (RoH) 16.11.18; *FA* (FRoH) 14.12.18

Gibson, Andrew: Private (S/40201 HCB att'd Black Watch [1st]); DOW No 45 CCS, 26.09.16, 20 years; 144 High Street, Kirkcaldy; Abbotshall Parish Church Memorial Plaque; Dernancourt Communal Cemetery Extension, Somme, France. Grave III.B.24; Kirkcaldy War Memorial; *Soldiers Died* Part 46; *FA* 07.10.16; *FA* (BMD) 07.10.16; *FFP* 07.10.16; *FFP* (BMD) 07.10.16; *FA* (RoH) 14.10.16; *FFP* 14.10.16; *FFP* (RoH) 14.10.16; *FA* (Service List) 28.10.16; *FFP* (CasList) 28.10.16; *FA* (Service List) 09.12.16; *FFP* (RoH) 30.12.16; *FA* (FRoH) 23.11.18; *FA* 19.11.21; Wauchope Vol 1

Gibson, George: Private (43420 Cameronians [Scottish Rifles] [9th]); KIA, 28.12.16, 19 years; 65 Overton Road, Kirkcaldy; Faubourg D'Amiens Cemetery, Arras, Pas de Calais, France. Grave III.A.18; Kirkcaldy War Memorial; *Soldiers Died* Part 31; *FFP* (CasList) 03.02.17; *FA* (RoH) 17.02.17; *FFP* (RoH) 17.02.17; *FA* (FRoH) 30.11.18

Gibson, James Burton: Private (21155; NZEF; Auckland Infantry Regt); DOW at sea, 05.09.15, 26 years; 39 Pratt Street, Kirkcaldy; Kirkcaldy High School War Memorial. West End Congregational Church Memorial Plaque; Lone Pine Memorial, Gallipoli, Turkey. Panel 72; Kirkcaldy War Memorial; *FA* 25.09.15; *FFP* 25.09.15; NZEF Roll of Honour; War Album 15/16; *FA* 18.09.15; *FA* (BMD) 18.09.15; *FFP* 18.09.15; *FFP* (BMD) 18.09.15; *FFP* 25.09.15; *FA* (RoH) 16.10.15; *FFP* (RoH) 16.10.15; *FFP* 05.08.16 Roll of the Brave; *FA* (Service List) 16.12.16; *FA* (FRoH) 16.11.18; *FA* (KHS RoH) 29.03.19

Gibson, John Smith: Private (G/67548 Royal Fusiliers [London Regt] [2/2nd]); KIA, 16.09.17, 19 years; 78 Balfour Street, Kirkcaldy; St Brycedale Church Plaque; Track "X" Cemetery, Ieper, West Vlaanderen, Belgium. Grave B.6; Kirkcaldy War Memorial; *FA* 06.10.17; *FA* 29.09.17; *FFP* 29.09.17; *FA* 06.10.17; *FA* (BMD) 06.10.17; *FFP* 06.10.17; *FA* 13.10.17; *FFP* (RoH) 13.10.17; *FFP* (Memorial List) 05.01.18; *FFP* (BMD) 21.09.18; *FA* (FRoH) 07.12.18

Gilbertson, John William: Private (47328 Royal Inniskilling Fusiliers [13th]. Formerly 8984 Army Service Corps); KIA France, 27.08.18, 41 years; 51 Beatty Crescent/455 Pottery Street, Gallatown, Kirkcaldy; Pathhead Baptist Church War Memorial Roll of Honour; Ploegsteert Memorial, Comines-Warneton, Hainaut, Belgium. Panel 5; Kirkcaldy War Memorial; *Soldiers Died* Part 32; *FFP* (BMD) 28.09.18; *FA* 05.10.18; *FA* (BMD) 05.10.18; *FFP* 05.10.18

Gilfillan, John: Private (3/2633 Black Watch [2nd] No. 4 Coy, 7th Meerut Div, Indian Expeditionary Force); KIA, 12.04.15, 20 years; 124 Den Road, Kirkcaldy; Le Touret Memorial, Pas de Calais, France. Panels 24-26; Kirkcaldy War Memorial; *Soldiers Died* Part 46; War Album 15; *FA* 24.04.15; *Dundee Courier* 26.04.15; *FFP* 01.05.15; *FFP* 05.08.16 Roll of the Brave; *FA* (Service List) 10.02.17; *FA* (FRoH) 16.11.18; Wauchope Vol 1

Gillespie, David: Driver (80846 RFA [14th Bde] [97th Batt'y]); Brother of Edward Gillespie and John Gillespie; 07.10.18, 24 years; 56 Links Street, Kirkcaldy; Bucquoy Road Cemetery, Ficheux, Pas de Calais, France. Grave IV.E.4; Kirkcaldy War Memorial; *FA* 28.10.16; *Soldiers Died* Part 2; *FA* 26.10.18; *FA* (BMD) 26.10.18; *FA* (RoH) 16.11.18; *FFP* (RoH) 16.11.18; *FA* (FRoH) 14.12.18; *FA* (FRoH) 28.12.18

Gillespie, Edward: Corporal (11305 KOSB [2nd] "C" Coy); Brother of David Gillespie and John Gillespie; KIA, 28.10.14; 23 years; 56 Links Street, Kirkcaldy; Le Touret Memorial, Pas de Calais, France. Panel 15; Kirkcaldy War Memorial; *FA* 28.10.16; *Soldiers Died* Part 30; War Album 14/15; *FA* 12.12.14; *FA* (CasList) 19.12.14; *FA* (BMD) 19.12.14; *FFP* (BMD) 19.12.14; *Despatch* 21.12.14; *FA* 02.01.15; *FA* (CasList) 20.02.15; *FA* 08.07.16; *FFP* 05.08.16 Roll of the Brave; *FA* (BMD) 28.10.16; *FA* (Service List) 02.12.16; *FA* 18.08.17; *FA* 26.10.18; *FA* (BMD) 26.10.18; *FA* (FRoH) 16.11.18

Gillespie, John: Private (S/40709 Black Watch [6th]. Formerly F & F Yeo); CWGC says 3rd Black Watch. Brother of Peter Gillespie; DOW Highland Fld Amb, 21.07.18, 32 years; 17 Oswald's Wynd/69 Bridgeton, Kirkcaldy; St Imoges Churchyard, Marne, France. Grave C.17; Kirkcaldy War Memorial; *FA* 01.04.16; *Soldiers Died* Part 46; *FFP* 03.08.18; *FFP* (BMD) 03.08.18; *FA* 10.08.18; *FA* (BMD) 10.08.18; *FFP* 10.08.18; *FFP* (BMD) 10.08.18; *FFP* 24.08.18; *FA* (RoH) 14.09.18; *FFP* (RoH) 14.09.18; *FA* (FRoH) 14.12.18; *FA* 21.12.18; Wauchope Vol 2

Gillespie, John: Private (17595 Royal Scots Fusiliers [2nd]); Brother of David Gillespie and Edward Gillespie; KIA, 31.07.17, 19 years; 56 Links Street, Kirkcaldy; Ypres (Menin Gate) Memorial, Ieper, West Vlaanderen, Belgium. Panels 19 & 33; Kirkcaldy War Memorial; *FA* 28.10.16; *FA* 18.08.17; *Soldiers Died* Part 26; *FA* 18.08.17; *FA* (CasList) 01.09.17; *FFP* (CasList) 08.09.17; *FA* 26.10.18; *FA* (BMD) 26.10.18; *FA* (FRoH) 28.12.18

Gillespie, Peter: Private (S/30776 Cameron Hlds [5th]); Brother of John Gillespie; Died of pneumonia at home, 12.12.18, 35 years; 17 Oswald's Wynd, Kirkcaldy; Gravestone in Abbotshall Churchyard; Abbotshall Parish Churchyard, Kirkcaldy. Grave New. (S.) 81; Kirkcaldy War Memorial; *FA* 01.04.16; *Soldiers Died* Part 66; *FFP* 14.12.18; *FFP* (BMD) 14.12.18; *FA* 21.12.18 (2 entries); *FA* (FRoH) 21.12.18; *FA* (BMD) 21.12.18; *FA* (RoH) 18.01.19

Gillies, James: Private (S/40558 Black Watch [1st]); DOW 36th CCS, France; 02.04.18, 31 years; 21 Tolbooth Street, Kirkcaldy; Bethelfield Church Plaque; Haringhe (Bandaghem) Military Cemetery, Poperinge, West Vlaanderen, Belgium. Grave II.B.1; Kirkcaldy War Memorial; *Soldiers Died* Part 46; *FA* 13.04.18; *FA* (BMD) 13.04.18; *FFP* 13.04.18; *FFP* (BMD) 13.04.18; *FFP* (RoH) 20.04.18; *FFP* (BMD) 20.04.18; *FA* (RoH) 18.05.18; *FFP* (RoH) 18.05.18; *FA* (FRoH) 07.12.18; Wauchope Vol 1

Glasgow, Robert: Private (391 AIF; Australian Infantry [3rd] 1st Infantry Bde); KIA Sari Bair, 27.04.15, 36 years; Invertiel Manse, Kirkcaldy; Gravestone in Abbotshall Churchyard. Invertiel Parish Church Memorial Table. Kirkcaldy High School War Memorial; Lone Pine Memorial, Gallipoli, Turkey. Panel 20; Australian War Memorial web site; Kirkcaldy War Memorial; War Album 15; *FA* 29.05.15; *FA* (BMD) 29.05.15; *FFP* (CasList) 05.06.15; *FA* 05.02.16; *FFP* 05.08.16 Roll of the Brave; *FA* (Service List) 16.12.16; *FA* (FRoH) 16.11.18; *FA* (KHS RoH) 29.03.19; *MRoM*

Glen, Andrew C.: Private (S/21479 Seaforth Hldrs [1/4th]. Formerly TR/1/13040 TR Bn); DOW 42nd CCS, 02.06.18, 32 years; 7 Page's Pend, Heggie's Wynd, Kirkcaldy; St Columba's Church Memorial Plaque; Aubigny Communal Cemetery Extension, Pas de Calais, France. Grave IV.H.27; Kirkcaldy War Memorial; *Soldiers Died* Part 64; *FFP* 08.06.18; *FA* 15.06.18; *FA* 06.07.18; *FA* (BMD) 06.07.18; *FA* (RoH) 13.07.18; *FA* (FRoH) 14.12.18

Glen, James: Private (S/14276 Gordon Hldrs [9th]); KIA, 22.04.17; 126 Links Street, Kirkcaldy; Feuchy Chapel British Cemetery, Wancourt, Pas de Calais, France. Grave I.B.32; Kirkcaldy War Memorial; *FA* 05.05.17; *Soldiers Died* Part 65; *FA* 05.05.17; *FFP* 05.05.17; *FA* (RoH) 19.05.17; *FFP* (RoH) 19.05.17; *FFP* (CasList) 26.05.17; *FA* (FRoH) 30.11.18

Glen, James: Sapper (79062 Royal Engineers [179th Tunnelling Coy]. Formerly 16201 KOSB); KIA East Albert, 21.11.15, 36 years; 17 Stewarts Lane/9 Kirk Wynd, Kirkcaldy; Albert Communal Cemetery Extension, Albert, Somme, France. Grave I.A.17; Kirkcaldy War Memorial; *FA* 18.12.15; *Soldiers Died* Part 4; War Album 15/16; *FA* 11.12.15; *FFP* 11.12.15; *FA* (RoH) 18.12.15; *FA* (BMD) 18.12.15; *FA* 19.02.16; *FA* 11.03.16; *FFP* 05.08.16 Roll of the Brave; *FA* (Service List) 04.11.16; *FFP* (BMD) 18.11.16; *FFP* (BMD) 25.11.16; *FA* (Service List) 03.02.17; *FFP* (BMD) 17.11.17; *FA* (FRoH) 16.11.18; *FFP* (BMD) 23.11.18

Glen, John: Private (9070 HLI [2nd]); KIA Aisne, 17.09.14; 48 Cowan Street, Kirkcaldy; St Brycedale Church Plaque; La Ferte-Sous-Jouarre Memorial, Seine-et-Marne, France; Kirkcaldy War Memorial; *Soldiers Died* Part 63; War Abum 14/15; *FA* 31.10.14; *FFP* (BMD) 31.10.14; *FA* (RoH) 07.11.14; *FA* (CasList) 21.11.14; *FA* (CasList) 19.12.14; *FA* 02.01.15; *FA* (CasList) 20.02.15; *FFP* 05.08.16 Roll of the Brave; *FA* (Memorial Service) 06.01.17; *FA* (Service List) 03.02.17; *FA* (FRoH) 16.11.18

Goodsir, Robert M.: Private (17249 KOSB [6th]); Wounded at Loos, captured and died in a German Hospital, 09.10.15, 34 years; 80 Overton Road, Kirkcaldy; Pathhead Parish Church Memorial Plaques & Windows. Sinclairtown Parish Church War Memorial Chair; Phalempin Communal Cemetery, Nord, France. Grave D.6; Kirkcaldy War Memorial; *FA* 30.10.15; *FFP* 30.10.15; *FA* 20.11.15; *Soldiers Died* Part 30; War Album 15/16; *FA* 30.10.15; *FA* (BMD) 30.10.15; *FFP* 30.10.15; *FFP* (BMD) 30.10.15; *FA* (RoH) 13.11.15; *FA* 20.11.15; *FA* 04.12.15; *FFP* 11.12.15; *FFP* (BMD) 11.12.15; *FFP* 18.12.15; *FA* (CasList) 17.06.16; *FFP* 05.08.16 Roll of the Brave; *FFP* (BMD) 14.10.16; *FA* (Service List) 18.11.16; *FFP* (BMD) 12.10.18; *FA* (FRoH) 16.11.18; *FFP* 21.06.24

Goodsir, William Michie, MM: Private (24546 Machine Gun Corps [51st Bn]. Formerly 709 HCB); DOW Cambrai at 1st CCS. Interred at Les Cadoeuvres Convent Cemetery, 25.10.18, 22 years; 8 Novar Crescent, Kirkcaldy; Gravestone in Dysart Cemetery; Ramillies British Cemetery, Nord, France. Grave F.15; Kirkcaldy War Memorial; *Soldiers Died* Part 75; *FA* (BMD) 09.11.18; *FA* (RoH) 16.11.18; *FFP* (RoH) 16.11.18; *FA* (FRoH) 14.12.18; *FFP* (BMD) 23.10.20

Goodwin, William B.: Private (2114 Black Watch [2nd]); KIA, 09.05.15; 71 Nether Street, Kirkcaldy; Le Touret Memorial, Pas de Calais, France. Panels 24-26; Kirkcaldy War Memorial; *Soldiers Died* Part 46; War Album 15; *Dundee Advertiser* 20.05.15; *Dundee Courier* 20.05.15; *FA* 26.06.15; *FFP* 05.08.16 Roll of the Brave; *FA* (Service List) 28.10.16; *FA* (Service List) 30.12.16; *FFP* (BMD) 26.05.17; *FA* (FRoH) 16.11.18; Wauchope Vol 1

Gourlay, Alexander: Private (S/40716 Black Watch [8th]. Formerly F & F Yeo); KIA Arras, 09.04.17, 19 years; 24 Bank Street, Kirkcaldy; Gravestone in Dysart Cemetery. Pathhead Parish Church Memorial Plaques & Windows; Cabaret-Rouge British Cemetery, Souchez, Pas de Calais, France. Grave XV.Q.4; Kirkcaldy War Memorial; *Soldiers Died* Part 46; *FA* 28.04.17; *FFP* 28.04.17; *FA* (RoH) 19.05.17; *FFP* (CasList) 19.05.17; *FFP* (RoH) 19.05.17; *FA* (FRoH) 30.11.18; Wauchope Vol 3

Gourlay, Andrew Archibald: Private (6229 Black Watch [1/7th]. Formerly F & F Yeo); DOW Boulogne Hospital, 18.11.16, 22 years; 41 High Street, Kirkcaldy; Gravestone in Abbotshall Churchyard. Abbotshall Parish Church Memorial Plaque; Boulogne Eastern Cemetery Extension, France. Grave VIII.D.211; Kirkcaldy War Memorial; *FA* 25.11.16; *Soldiers Died* Part 46; *FA* 25.11.16; *FA* (BMD) 25.11.16; *FFP* (BMD) 25.11.16; *FFP* (CasList) 02.12.16; *FA* (Service List) 09.12.16; *FA* (RoH) 16.12.16; *FA* (CasList) 23.12.16; *FFP* (CasList) 23.12.16; *FFP* (RoH) 30.12.16; *FFP* (BMD) 17.11.17; *FFP* (BMD) 16.11.18; *FA* (FRoH) 30.11.18; *FA* 19.11.21; Wauchope Vol 2

Gourlay, George: Private (3086 AIF; Australian Infantry [47th]); DOW, 08.08.16; Alexandra Street, Kirkcaldy; Warloy-Baillon Communal Cemetery Extension, Somme, France. Grave VII.B.8; Australian War Memorial web site; Kirkcaldy War Memorial; *FA* 23.09.16; *FFP* 23.09.16 (2 entries); *FA* (RoH) 14.10.16; *FFP* (RoH) 14.10.16; *FFP* (RoH) 30.12.16; *FA* (FRoH) 23.11.18

Gourlay, George: Lance Corporal (S/18149 Black Watch [8th]); KIA, 30.09.18; Dadizeele New British Cemetery, Moorslede, West Vlaanderen, Belgium. Grave V.E.9; Kirkcaldy War Memorial; *Soldiers Died* Part 46; Wauchope Vol 3

Gourlay, George: 2nd Lieutenant (Machine Gun Corps [73rd] [Irish Regt]); KIA, 14.11.17, 24 years; 33 Alexandra Street, Kirkcaldy; Gravestone in Abbotshall Churchyard (Photo). Whytescauseway Baptist Church Memorial Plaque; Roisel Communal Cemetery Extension, Somme, France. Grave III.C.1.E; Kirkcaldy War Memorial; *Officers Died*; *Cross of Sacrifice Vol 1*; *FA* 24.11.17; *FA* (BMD) 24.11.17; *FFP* 24.11.17; *FFP* (BMD) 24.11.17; *FA* (RoH) 15.12.17; *FFP* (RoH) 15.12.17; *FA* (FRoH) 07.12.18

Gourlay, James: Private (2947 Black Watch [1/7th]); KIA, 31.07.16, 39 years; 205 St Clair Street, Kirkcaldy; Gravestone in Dysart Cemetery. Barony Church Plaque; Thiepval Memorial, Somme, France. Pier & Face 10A; Kirkcaldy War Memorial; *FA* 19.08.16; *Soldiers Died* Part 46; *FA* 12.08.16; *FFP* 12.08.16; *FA* 19.08.16; *FFP* 19.08.16; *FA* (CasList) 09.09.16; *FFP* (CasList) 09.09.16; *FA* (RoH) 16.09.16; *FFP* (RoH) 16.09.16; *FFP* 23.09.16; *FA* 30.09.16; *FFP* (RoH) 30.12.16; *FFP* (BMD) 04.08.17; *FFP* (BMD) 03.08.18; *FA* (FRoH) 23.11.18; Wauchope Vol 2

Gourlay, John: Private (S/41432 Gordon Hldrs [7th]); KIA, 26.03.18, 34 years; 15 Quality Street, Kirkcaldy; Arras Memorial, Pas de Calais, France. Bays 8 & 9; Kirkcaldy War Memorial; *Soldiers Died* Part 65; *FFP* (RoH) 20.04.18; *FFP* (BMD) 20.04.18; *FA* 27.04.18; *FFP* (CasList) 11.05.18; *FA* (RoH) 18.05.18; *FFP* (RoH) 18.05.18; *FA* (FRoH) 07.12.18

Gourlay, Thomas: Private (225 52nd Lowland Divisional Cyclist Coy. Formerly 1987 HCB); KIA, 04.08.16, 24 years; 188 Links Street, Kirkcaldy; Kantara War Memorial Cemetery, Egypt. Grave E.313; Kirkcaldy War Memorial; *FA* 16.09.16; *Soldiers Died* Part 77; *FA* 26.08.16; *FA* 02.09.16; *FFP* 02.09.16; *FA* 09.09.16; *FFP* (BMD) 09.09.16; *FA* (RoH) 16.09.16; *FA* (BMD) 16.09.16; *FFP* (RoH) 16.09.16; *FFP* (CasList) 23.09.16; *FA* 14.10.16; *FA* 18.11.16; *FFP* (RoH) 30.12.16; *FA* (FRoH) 23.11.18

Graham, David H. L. N.: Private (40173 Royal Scots [11th]. Formerly 2381 F & F Yeo & 26769 KOSB); Brother of James Graham; KIA, 09.04.17, 22 years; 341 High Street, Kirkcaldy; Point-Du-Jour Military Cemetery, Athies, Pas de Calais, France. Grave I.C.2; Kirkcaldy War Memorial; *FA* 28.04.17; *Soldiers Died* Part 6; *FA* 28.04.17; *FA* (RoH) 19.05.17; *FFP* (RoH) 19.05.17; *FFP* (CasList) 19.05.17; *FA* (FRoH) 30.11.18

Graham, James Niven: Private (S/4448 Seaforth Hldrs [7th]); Brother of David Graham; KIA, 12.09.15, 20 years; 341 High Street, Kirkcaldy; Vermelles British Cemetery, Pas de Calais, France. Grave I.C.20; Kirkcaldy War Memorial; *FA* 25.09.15; *Soldiers Died* Part 64; War Album 15/16; *FA* 25.09.15; *FFP* 25.09.15; *FA* (RoH) 16.10.15; *FA* 01.01.16; *FFP* 05.08.16 Roll of the Brave; *FA* (BMD) 16.09.16; *FA* (Service List) 28.10.16; *FA* (Service List) 09.12.16; *FA* 28.04.17; *FA* (FRoH) 16.11.18

Graham, John: Private (202081 Black Watch [4/5th]); MIA France. Killed on his birthday, 27.09.17, 22 years; 41 Bridgeton, Kirkcaldy; Tyne Cot Memorial, Zonnebeke, West Vlaanderen, Belgium. Panels 94-96; Kirkcaldy War Memorial; *Soldiers Died* Part 46; *FA* 27.10.17; *FA* 25.05.18; *FFP* 03.08.18; *FA* (CasList) 14.09.18; *FFP* (RoH) 14.09.18; *FA* (FRoH) 14.12.18; Wauchope Vol 2

John **Graham** was killed in 1917 on his 22nd birthday.

Graham, John Gourlay: Pioneer (44925 Royal Engineers [218 Fld Coy]); Brother of William Graham; Died of pneumonia whilst on leave, 15.11.18, 25 years; 20 Forth Avenue North, Kirkcaldy; Gravestone in Abbotshall Churchyard. Abbotshall Parish Church Memorial Plaque; Abbotshall Parish Churchyard, Kirkcaldy. Grave Old. (C.) 450; Kirkcaldy War Memorial; *FA* 22.07.16; *FA* 23.09.16; *FA* 23.09.16; *FA* 23.11.18; *FFP* 23.11.18; *FA* (FRoH) 14.12.18; *FFP* (RoH) 14.12.18; *FA* (BMD) 13.09.19; *FA* 19.11.21

Graham, Nigel: Corporal (9120 Cameron Hlds [1st]. Formerly 3/1751 Black Watch); KIA Battle of the Lys, 22.10.14, 19 years; 228 Links Street, Kirkcaldy; St Columba's Church Memorial Plaque; Perth Cemetery (China Wall), Zillebeke, Ieper, West Vlaanderen, Belgium. Grave German Cem. Mem.93; Kirkcaldy War Memorial; *FFP* 14.11.14; *Soldiers Died* Part 66; War Album 14/15; *Dundee Advertiser* 11.11.14; *FA* 14.11.14; *FFP* 14.11.14; *FA* (CasList) 21.11.14; *FA* (CasList) 19.12.14; *FA* 02.01.15; *FA* (CasList) 20.02.15; *FFP* 05.08.16 Roll of the Brave; *FFP* (BMD) 21.10.16; *FA* (Service List) 25.11.16; *FA* (Service List) 02.12.16; *FA* (FRoH) 16.11.18; *FFP* 23.10.20

Graham, Robert: Corporal (43310 HLI [12th]. Formerly 1716 HCB); Brother-in-law of Charles Bett; MIA, 27.03.18; 19 Harcourt Road, Kirkcaldy; West End Congregational Church Memorial Plaque; Beacon Cemetery, Sailly-Laurette, Somme, France. Grave IV.B.10; Kirkcaldy War Memorial; *Soldiers Died* Part 63; *FA* 28.09.18; *FFP* 05.10.18; *FA* (RoH) 16.11.18; *FFP* (RoH) 16.11.18; *FA* (FRoH) 14.12.18

Graham, William: Private (293263 Black Watch [6th]); KIA, 21.03.18, 34 years; 109 High Street, Kirkcaldy; Gravestone in Bennochy Cemetery (Photo); Arras Memorial, Pas de Calais, France. Bay 6; Kirkcaldy War Memorial; *Soldiers Died* Part 46; *FA* 20.04.18; *FFP* (RoH) 20.04.18; Wauchope Vol 2

Graham, William: Gunner (344359 RGA [153 Siege Batt'y] [Forth]); Brother of John Graham; DOW. Buried at Le Mesnil, France, 09.09.18, 23 years; Hunter's Buildings, Sands Road, Kirkcaldy; Gravestone in Abbotshall Churchyard. Forth RGA Plaque. Abbotshall Parish Church Memorial Plaque; Vis-En-Artois Memorial, Pas de Calais, France. Panel 3; Kirkcaldy War Memorial; *FA* 22.07.16; *Soldiers Died* Part 3; *FA* 23.09.16; *FA* (BMD) 05.10.18; *FFP* (BMD) 05.10.18; *FFP* 12.10.18; *FA* 19.10.18; *FA* (RoH) 19.10.18; *FA* 23.11.18; *FFP* 23.11.18; *FA* (FRoH) 14.12.18; *FA* (BMD) 13.09.19; *FA* 19.11.21

Grainger, George, MM: Sapper (6595 Royal Engineers [69th Fld Coy]); KIA on the first anniversary of the award of his Military Medal, 13.10.16, 35 years; 279 Links Street, Kirkcaldy; Longueval Road Cemetery, Somme, France. Grave C.1; Kirkcaldy War Memorial; *Soldiers Died* Part 4; *FA* 22.01.16; *FFP* 21.10.16; *FA* (BMD) 28.10.16; *FA* (RoH) 18.11.16; *FFP* (RoH) 18.11.16; *FA* (Service List) 02.12.16; *FFP* (RoH) 30.12.16; *FA* (FRoH) 30.11.18

George **Grainger** was killed in action in 1916, on the first anniversary of the award of his Military Medal.

Grainger, Harry Cook Wilson: Private (S/12953 Black Watch [1st]); KIA, 27.10.18, 33 years; 18 Forth Avenue North, Kirkcaldy; Vis-en-Artois Memorial, Pas de Calais, France. Panel 7; Kirkcaldy War Memorial; *Soldiers Died* Part 46; *FA* 14.12.18; *FA* (FRoH) 14.12.18; *FFP* 14.12.18; *FA* (RoH) 18.01.19; Wauchope Vol 1

Grant, George Murray: Private (2785 Black Watch [1/7th] 5th Platoon); KIA, 04.09.15; 2a West Albert Road, Kirkcaldy; Old Parish Church Memorial Panel; Becourt Military Cemetery, Becordel-Becourt, Somme, France. Grave I.B.11; Kirkcaldy War Memorial; *FA* 11.09.15; *FFP* 11.09.15; *FA* 14.10.16; *Soldiers Died* Part 46; War Album 15/16; *Scotsman* 09.09.15; *FA* 11.09.15 (2 entries); *FA* (BMD) 11.09.15; *FFP* (BMD) 11.09.15; *FA* 18.09.15; *FA* (RoH) 18.09.15; *FA* 15.07.16; *FFP* 05.08.16 Roll of the Brave; *FFP* (BMD) 02.09.16; *FA* (Service List) 30.12.16; *FFP* (BMD) 07.09.18; *FA* (FRoH) 16.11.18; *FA* (BMD) 06.09.19; Wauchope Vol 2

Grant, George Thomson: Private (3081153; CEF; Canadian Infantry [87th] 4th Div 11th Bde. [Quebec Regt]); KIA, 02.09.18, 32 years; 13 East Smeaton St, Kirkcaldy; Dury Mill British Cemetery, Pas de Calais, France. Grave II.B.II; Kirkcaldy War Memorial; *CBoR* Page 418; *FFP* 21.09.18; *FA* 28.09.18; *FA* (RoH) 19.10.18; *FA* (FRoH) 14.12.18

Gray, David Proudfoot: Driver (8629; AIF; Australian Field Artillery [5th Bde]); KIA, 19.10.17, 33 years; 50 Rosabelle Street, Kirkcaldy; Gallatown Church Roll of Honour; Perth Cemetery (China Wall), Zillebeke, Ieper, West Vlaanderen, Belgium. Grave IV.K.5; Australian War Memorial web site; Kirkcaldy War Memorial; *FA* 10.11.17; *FFP* 10.11.17; *FFP* (RoH) 17.11.17; *FA* (FRoH) 07.12.18

Gray, Frederick Colin: Private (277206 A & S Hldrs [1/7th]); MIA, 15.11.16, 24 years; The Manse, Pathhead U.F. Church, St Ives, Loughborough Road, Kirkcaldy; Kirkcaldy High School War Memorial. Pathhead Parish Church Memorial Plaques & Windows; Thiepval Memorial, Somme, France. Pier & Face 15A & 16C; Kirkcaldy War Memorial; *Soldiers Died* Part 70; *FA* 09.12.16; *FFP* 09.12.16; *FA* (CasList) 13.01.17; *FA* (Service List) 17.02.17; *FA* 29.12.17; *FA* (BMD) 29.12.17 (2 entries); *FFP* 29.12.17; *FFP* (BMD) 29.12.17; *FA* (RoH) 19.01.18; *FA* 13.07.18; *FA* (FRoH) 07.12.18; *FA* (KHS RoH) 29.03.19

Gray, John: Private (21695; CEF; Canadian Infantry [10th] [Alberta Regt]); MIA Hill 60, 23.04.15, 45 years; 58/154 Commercial Street/18 Institution Street, Kirkcaldy; Ypres (Menin Gate) Memorial, Ieper, West Vlaanderen, Belgium. Panels 24-28-30; Kirkcaldy War Memorial; *CBoR* Page 94; War Album 15/16; *FA* 08.05.15; *FA* (RoH) 18.09.15; *FFP* 05.08.16 Roll of the Brave; *FA* (Service List) 04.11.16; *FA* (Service List) 16.12.16; *FA* (Service List) 24.02.17; *FA* (FRoH) 16.11.18; Kirkcaldy Council Memorial Scroll

Gray, Thomas: Ordinary Seaman (Merchant Navy; SS *Fingal* [Leith]); Drowned as a result of an attack by an enemy submarine, 15.03.15, 19 years; 41 Sutherland Street, Kirkcaldy; Gallatown Church Roll of Honour; Tower Hill Memorial, London; Kirkcaldy War Memorial; *Cross of Sacrifice Vol 5*; *FA* 20.03.15

Gregor, John: Corporal (43056 HLI [16th]. Formerly 1305 HCB); Also listed as McGregor in *FA* (RoH); KIA, 16.08.16, 27 years; 13 Quality Street, Kirkcaldy; Cambrin Churchyard Extension, Pas de Calais, France. Grave Q.6; Kirkcaldy War Memorial; *Soldiers Died* Part 63; *FFP* 09.09.16; *FFP* (BMD) 09.09.16; *FA* 16.09.16; *FA* (RoH) 16.09.16; *FA* (CasList) 23.09.16; *FFP* (CasList) 23.09.16; *FA* (FRoH) 23.11.18

Greig, Robert Simpson: Private (43346 HLI [17th]. Formerly 1854 HCB); KIA Beaumont-Hamel, 18.11.16, 19 years; 6 Oswald's Wynd, Kirkcaldy; Gravestone in Bennochy Cemetery; New Munich Trench British Cemetery, Beaumont-Hamel, Somme, France. Grave F.13; Kirkcaldy War Memorial; *FA* 02.12.16; *Soldiers Died* Part 63; *FA* 02.12.16; *FA* (BMD) 02.12.16; *FFP* 02.12.16; *FFP* (BMD) 02.12.16; *FA* (RoH) 16.12.16; *FFP* (RoH) 30.12.16; *FA* 06.01.17; *FFP* (CasList) 06.01.17; *FA* (BMD) 17.11.17; *FFP* (BMD) 17.11.17; *FA* 18.05.18; *FFP* (BMD) 16.11.18; *FA* (FRoH) 30.11.18; *FA* 26.04.19

Greig, Thomas: Private (S/18665 Cameron Hldrs [5th]. Formerly Black Watch); MIA Loos, 25.09.15, 17 years; 257/265 Links Street, Kirkcaldy; Loos Memorial, Pas de Calais, France. Panels 119-124; Kirkcaldy War Memorial; *FA* 03.03.17; *Soldiers Died* Part 66; *FA* 27.11.15; *FA* (Service List) 26.11.16; *FA* (Service List) 02.12.16; *FA* 03.03.17; *FFP* (BMD) 10.03.17; *FA* (RoH) 17.03.17; *FA* (FRoH) 30.11.18

Greig, William Thomson: Sergeant (345342 Black Watch [14th] [F & F Yeo Bn]. Formerly 2507 F & F Yeo); DOW Southern General Hospital, Birmingham, 06.12.18, 23 years; 66 Overton Road, Kirkcaldy; Dysart Cemetery, Kirkcaldy. Grave1.4.Middle; Kirkcaldy War Memorial; *Soldiers Died* Part 46; *FFP* (BMD) 14.12.18; *FA* (BMD) 21.12.18; *FFP* 04.01.19; *FA* (RoH) 18.01.19; Wauchope Vol 3

Grey, Andrew Ramsay: Private (45326 Royal Scots [1st Garrison Bn]. Formerly 1827 F & F Yeo); On CWGC as R. Gray (45326). On *Soldiers Died* as R. Grey (45320); Accidentally drowned, 19.08.17, 19 years; 19 Victoria Road, Kirkcaldy; Alexandria (Hadra) War Memorial Cemetery, Egypt. Grave A.63; Kirkcaldy War Memorial; *Soldiers Died* Part 6; *FA* 15.09.17; *FFP* 15.09.17; *FFP* (CasList) 15.09.17; *FFP* (BMD) 15.09.17; *FA* 13.10.17; *FFP* (RoH) 13.10.17; *FFP* (BMD) 24.08.18; *FFP* (BMD) 31.08.18; *FA* (FRoH) 07.12.18

Grierson, William: Signaller (Clyde Z/7977; Royal Navy; RNVR [HM Drifter *Our Allies*]); Died of influenza, 22.10.18, 21 years; 4 Battery Place, Glasswork Street, Kirkcaldy; Gravestone in Abbotshall Churchyard. Invertiel Parish Church Memorial Table. Kirkcaldy High School War Memorial; Gallipoli Communal Cemetery, Italy. Grave 3; Kirkcaldy War Memorial; *Cross of Sacrifice Vol 4*; *FA* (BMD) 09.11.18; *FA* (RoH) 16.11.18; *FFP* (RoH) 16.11.18; *FA* (FRoH) 14.12.18; *FA* (KHS RoH) 19.07.19; *FFP* (BMD) 23.10.20

Grieve, Arthur: Corporal (S/9847 Gordon Hldrs [2nd] [Lewis Gun Section]); KIA, 05.09.16; 101 Balsusuney Road/2 Abden Terrace, Kirkcaldy; Bethelfield Church Plaque; Thiepval Memorial, Somme, France. Pier & Face 15B & 15C; Kirkcaldy War Memorial; *Soldiers Died* Part 65; *FA* 16.09.16; *FFP* 16.09.16; *FFP* (BMD) 30.09.16; *FA* (RoH) 14.10.16; *FFP* (RoH) 14.10.16; *FFP* (CasList) 14.10.16; *FA* (Service List) 18.11.16; *FFP* (RoH) 30.12.16; *FA* 06.04.18; *FA* 26.10.18; *FA* (FRoH) 23.11.18

Grieve, James: Private (S/13338 Black Watch [8th]); MIA, 09.04.17, 20 years; 7 Bank Street, Kirkcaldy; Sinclairtown Parish Church War Memorial Chair; Arras Memorial, Pas de Calais, France. Bay 6; Kirkcaldy War Memorial; *Soldiers Died* Part 46; *FFP* (RoH) 16.03.18; *FFP* (BMD) 16.03.18; *FFP* (RoH) 23.03.18; *FA* (RoH) 13.04.18; *FA* (FRoH) 07.12.18; Wauchope Vol 3

Grieve, John: Corporal (345331 Black Watch [14th] [F & F Yeo Bn]. Formerly 2487 F & F Yeo); Died at sea when *Aragon* was lost, 30.12.17, 26 years; 23 Viewforth Terrace, Viewforth Street, Kirkcaldy; Gravestone in Dysart Cemetery; Chatby Memorial, Egypt; Kirkcaldy War Memorial; *Soldiers Died* Part 46; *FA* 02.02.18; *FFP* (RoH) 02.02.18; *FA* 09.02.18; *FA* (RoH) 16.02.18; *FA* (FRoH) 07.12.18; *FFP* (BMD) 28.12.18; *FA* 26.04.19; Wauchope Vol 3

Grieve, Peter: Able Seaman ([Bugler]; Clyde 4/2305; Royal Navy; RNVR [RND] [*Howe* Bn]); KIA Dardanelles, 20.05.15, 20 years; 34 Links Street, Kirkcaldy. Parents at 18 Carmichael Street, Glasgow; Helles Memorial, Gallipoli, Turkey. Panels 8-15; *FA* 12.06.15; Kirkcaldy War Memorial; *Cross of Sacrifice Vol 4*; War Album 15; *Dundee Advertiser* 09.06.15; *FA* 12.06.15 (2 entries); *FFP* 12.06.15; *FFP* (BMD) 12.06.15; *FFP* 19.06.15; *FFP* (CasList) 03.07.15; *FFP* 20.05.16; *FFP* 05.08.16 Roll of the Brave; *FA* (Service List) 02.12.16; *FFP* (BMD) 26.05.17; *FA* (FRoH) 16.11.18

Grieve, Robert: Private (33569 Royal Scots Fusiliers [2nd]); DOW, 26.12.16; 234 St Clair Street, Kirkcaldy; Varennes Military Cemetery, Somme, France. Grave I.F.14; Kirkcaldy War Memorial; *Soldiers Died* Part 26; *FFP* 06.01.17; *FA* 13.01.17; *FA* (RoH) 13.01.17; *FFP* (RoH) 13.01.17; *FA* (CasList) 27.01.17; *FFP* (CasList) 27.01.17; *FA* (FRoH) 30.11.18

Grieve, William: Lance Corporal (28659 KOSB [7/8th]. Formerly 3344 F & F Yeo); KIA, 23.07.18, 26 years; 266/ 366 High Street, Kirkcaldy; Buzancy Military Cemetery, Aisne, France. Grave I.C.30; Kirkcaldy War Memorial; *Soldiers Died* Part 30; *FA* 10.08.18; *FFP* 10.08.18; *FFP* (BMD) 10.08.18; *FA* 17.08.18; *FA* (RoH) 14.09.18; *FFP* (RoH) 14.09.18; *FA* (FRoH) 14.12.18

Grubb, Richard Smith: Private (3/3866 Black Watch [1st]); KIA Ypres, 09.05.15, 34 years; 350/397/447 High Street/177 Commercial Street, Kirkcaldy; St Brycedale Church Plaque. Gravestone in Bennochy Cemetery (Photo); Le Touret Memorial, Pas de Calais, France. Panels 24-26; Kirkcaldy War Memorial; *Soldiers Died* Part 46; War Album 15; *FA* 29.05.15; *FA* 05.06.15 (2 entries); *FA* (BMD) 05.06.15; *FFP* (CasList) 05.06.15; *FFP* (BMD) 05.06.15; *FFP* 05.08.16 Roll of the Brave; *FA* (Service List) 28.10.16; *FA* (Service List) 09.12.16; *FA* (Memorial Service) 06.01.17; *FA* (FRoH) 16.11.18; Wauchope Vol 1

Guyan, David: Private (345713 Black Watch [14th] [F & F Yeo Bn]. Formerly 2490 Black Watch [3rd]); Brother of William Guyan; DOW Sheria, 11.11.17, 22 years; 34 Bridgeton/181 Links Street/9 Mill Street, Kirkcaldy; Kantara War Memorial Cemetery, Egypt. Grave E.215; Kirkcaldy War Memorial; *FA* 17.11.17; *Soldiers Died* Part 46; *Despatch* 26.11.14; *Scotsman* 26.11.14; *FFP* 28.11.14; *FA* 19.06.15; *FA* 17.11.17; *FA* (BMD) 17.11.17; *FFP* 17.11.17; *FFP* (CasList) 08.12.17; *FA* (RoH) 15.12.17; *FFP* (RoH) 15.12.17; *FA* (BMD) 09.11.18 (2 entries); *FA* (FRoH) 07.12.18; Wauchope Vol 3; Ogilvie

Guyan, William Reid: Private (3/2223 Black Watch [1st] "A" Coy); Previously wounded at Ypres. Brother of David Guyan; 09.05.15; 20/21 Mill Street, Kirkcaldy; Le Touret Memorial, Pas de Calais, France. Panels 24-26; Kirkcaldy War Memorial; *Soldiers Died* Part 46; War Album 15; *Despatch* 26.11.14; *Scotsman* 26.11.14; *FFP* 28.11.14; *FA* 05.06.15; *Dundee Advertiser* 09.06.15; *FFP* 12.06.15; *FA* 19.06.15 (2 entries); *FA* (BMD) 19.06.15; *Scotsman* 21.06.15; *FFP* 26.06.15; *FFP* (CasList) 03.07.15; *FA* (RoH) 17.07.15; *FFP* 05.08.16 Roll of the Brave; *FA* (Service List) 13.01.17; *FA* (BMD) 12.05.17; *FA* 17.11.17; *FA* (BMD) 11.05.18; *FA* (BMD) 09.11.18; *FA* (FRoH) 16.11.18; Wauchope Vol 1

Haggart, James: Private (41810 Royal Scots Fusiliers [2nd]); KIA, 18.08.18, 31 years; 38 Cloanden Place, Kirkcaldy/Kingskettle; Gravestone in Kettle Cemetery. Raith Church Memorial Plaque; Meteren Military Cemetery, Nord, France. Grave V.H.801; Kirkcaldy War Memorial; *Soldiers Died* Part 26; *FA* (BMD) 14.09.18 (2 entries); *FA* (RoH) 16.11.18; *FFP* (RoH) 16.11.18; *FA* (FRoH) 14.12.18

Haig, David: 2nd Lieutenant (Black Watch [4/5th]. Formerly HCB); Accidentally killed, 05.07.18, 32 years; Bemersyde, St Brycedale Road, Kirkcaldy; Gravestones in Dysart Cemetery and MacDuff Cemetery, East Wemyss. Old Parish Church Memorial Panel; St Sever Cemetery, Rouen, Seine-Maritime, France. Grave Officers, B.9.3; Kirkcaldy War Memorial; *Officers Died*; *Cross of Sacrifice Vol 1*; *FA* 13.07.18; *FA* 20.07.18; *FA* (BMD) 20.07.18; *FFP* 20.07.18; *FFP* (BMD) 20.07.18; *FA* (RoH) 14.09.18; *FFP* (RoH) 14.09.18; *FA* (FRoH) 14.12.18

Haig, William: Private (S/13003 Black Watch [8th]); DOW, 09.04.17; 6 Heggie's Wynd, Kirkcaldy; Haute-Avesnes British Cemetery, Pas de Calais, France. Grave B.14; Kirkcaldy War Memorial; *Soldiers Died* Part 46; *FA* 12.05.17; *FA* (CasList) 12.05.17; *FFP* (CasList) 12.05.17; *FA* (RoH) 19.05.17; *FFP* (RoH) 19.05.17; *FA* (FRoH) 30.11.18; Wauchope Vol 3

Halket, William: Private (2707 Black Watch [1st]); KIA, 29.10.14; 132 Den Road, Kirkcaldy; Ypres (Menin Gate) Memorial, Ieper, West Vlaanderen, Belgium. Panel 37; Kirkcaldy War Memorial; *FFP* 26.02.16; *Soldiers Died* Part 46; *FA* 05.02.16; *Scotsman* 24.02.16; *FFP* 26.02.16; *FFP* 05.08.16 Roll of the Brave; *FA* 12.08.16; *FA* (Service List) 10.02.17; *FA* (FRoH) 16.11.18; Wauchope Vol 1

Halkett, Alexander: Private (PLY/17028; Royal Navy; Royal Marine Light Infantry [RND] [Deal Bn]); KIA, 17.02.17, 19 years; 42 Links Street, Kirkcaldy; Queens Cemetery, Bucquoy, Pas de Calais, France. Grave II.H.15; Kirkcaldy War Memorial; ‡; *FA* 22.01.16; *FA* 10.03.17; *Cross of Sacrifice Vol 4*; *FA* 22.01.16; *FA* (BMD) 10.03.17; *FA* (RoH) 17.03.17; *FFP* 17.03.17; *FA* 24.03.17; *FA* (FRoH) 30.11.18

Hamilton, George: Corporal (17891 Royal Scots Fusiliers [6/7th]); KIA, 22.03.18, 23 years; 48/77 Links Street, Kirkcaldy; Arras Memorial, Pas de Calais, France. Bay 5; Kirkcaldy War Memorial; *Soldiers Died* Part 26; *FA* 20.04.18; *FA* (RoH) 18.05.18; *FFP* (RoH) 18.05.18; *FA* (FRoH) 14.12.18

Hamilton, George Bill: Air Mechanic 2nd Class (118487; RAF; 105th Squadron); Accidentally drowned at Armagh, 21.05.18, 18 years; 154 Mid Street, Kirkcaldy; E.U. Congregational Church Memorial Plaque; Dysart Cemetery, Kirkcaldy. Grave 4.5.Middle; Kirkcaldy War Memorial; *Cross of Sacrifice Vol 4*; *FA* 25.05.18; *FFP* 25.05.18; *FFP* (BMD) 25.05.18; *FA* 01.06.18 (2 entries); *FA* (BMD) 01.06.18; *FA* (RoH) 15.06.18; *FFP* (RoH) 15.06.18; *FA* (FRoH) 14.12.18

Hamilton, William: Sergeant (D/6727 Royal Scots Greys [2nd Dragoons]); DOW No 5 Clearing Hospital, 03.12.17, 27 years; 81 Dunnikier Road/57 Salisbury Street, Kirkcaldy; Tincourt New British Cemetery, Somme, France. Grave III.C.18; Kirkcaldy War Memorial; ‡; *FFP* 22.12.17; *Soldiers Died* Part 1; *FA* 15.12.17; *FA* (BMD) 15.12.17; *FFP* 15.12.17; *FFP* (BMD) 22.12.17; *FFP* (CasList) 12.01.18; *FA* (RoH) 19.01.18; *FA* 07.12.18; *FA* (FRoH) 07.12.18; *FA* (BMD) 07.12.18; *FFP* (BMD) 07.12.18

Handy, Thomas Bernard: Private (3/2639 Black Watch [1st] "C" Coy); Brother of Bernard Handy; DOW, 07.09.16, 31 years; 52 Nairn Street/34 Bridgeton, Kirkcaldy; Heilly Station Cemetery, Mericourt-L'Abbe, Somme, France. Grave IV.A.37; Kirkcaldy War Memorial; *Soldiers Died* Part 46; *FA* 16.09.16; *FFP* 16.09.16; *FA* (CasList) 30.09.16; *FFP* (CasList) 30.09.16; *FA* (RoH) 14.10.16; *FFP* (RoH) 14.10.16; *FA* (Service List) 04.11.16; *FFP* (RoH) 30.12.16; *FA* (Service List) 13.01.17; *FA* (Service List) 24.02.17; *FA* 04.05.18; *FA* (FRoH) 23.11.18; Wauchope Vol 1

Harley, Archibald Brown Low: Trooper (2129 F & F Yeo [1st] "B" Squadron); Died of typhoid fever in Zagazig Government Hospital, Port Said, 18.11.15, 20 years; 50 Townsend Place, Kirkcaldy; Union Church Plaque. Kirkcaldy High School War Memorial; Tel El Kebir War Memorial Cemetery, Egypt. Grave 54; Kirkcaldy War Memorial; *Soldiers Died* Part 1; *War Album* 15/16; *FA* 20.11.15; *FA* (BMD) 20.11.15; *FA* (RoH) 18.12.15; *FFP* 05.08.16 Roll of the Brave; *FA* 14.10.16; *FA* (Service List) 30.12.16; *FA* 12.05.17; *FA* (FRoH) 16.11.18; *FA* (KHS RoH) 29.03.19; Ogilvie

Harley, Charles: Private (40040 Royal Scots [13th]); KIA, 11.05.16, 30 years; 1 Junction Road, Kirkcaldy; Bethelfield Church Plaque. Kirkcaldy High School War Memorial; Thiepval Memorial, Somme, France. Pier & Face 6D & 7D; Kirkcaldy War Memorial; *Soldiers Died* Part 6; *FA* 01.04.16; *FA* 30.09.16; *FFP* 30.09.16 (2 entries); *FA* (RoH) 14.10.16; *FFP* (RoH) 14.10.16; *FA* 21.10.16; *FA* (BMD) 21.10.16; *FFP* (BMD) 21.10.16; *FFP* (CasList) 04.11.16; *FFP* (RoH) 30.12.16; *FA* (Service List) 03.02.17; *FA* (FRoH) 23.11.18

Harley, Frederick William: Lieutenant (Black Watch [7th] att'd RFC [70th Squadron]); Killed while flying, 03.06.17, 28 years; Blinkbonny, Kirkcaldy; St Brycedale Church Plaque. Kirkcaldy High School War Memorial. Gravestone in Bennochy Cemetery (Photo); Menin Communal Cemetery, Ieper, West Vlaanderen, Belgium. Grave III.A.9/10; Kirkcaldy War Memorial; *Dinna Forget*; *Officers Died*; *Cross of Sacrifice Vol 1*; *FFP* 09.10.15; *FA* 09.06.17; *FFP* 16.06.17; *FA* 30.06.17; *FA* (BMD) 30.06.17; *FFP* 30.06.17; *FFP* (BMD) 30.06.17; *FA* 14.07.17; *FA* 14.07.17 (KHS War Honours); *FA* 28.07.17; *FFP* (Memorial List) 05.01.18; *FA* (FRoH) 30.11.18; *FA* (KHS RoH) 29.03.19; RFC/RAF RoH; Wauchope Vol 2

Harley, Peter Robert: Private (43026 HLI [16th]. Formerly 2052 HCB); On CWGC as R. Harley; MIA, 18.11.16, 33 years; 20 Charlotte Street, Kirkcaldy; Thiepval Memorial, Somme, France. Pier & Face 15C; Kirkcaldy War Memorial; *Soldiers Died* Part 63; *FA* 16.12.16; *FA* (CasList) 13.01.17; *FA* 02.06.17; *FFP* 02.06.17; *FFP* (BMD) 02.06.17; *FA* (RoH) 16.06.17; *FFP* (RoH) 16.06.17; *FFP* (CasList) 16.06.17; *FFP* (BMD) 17.11.17; *FA* (FRoH) 30.11.18

Harrison, Neil: Guardsman (4398 Scots Guards [2nd]); DOW, 12.10.18, 33 years; 55 Pratt Street, Kirkcaldy; St Columba's Church Memorial Plaque; Carnieres Communal Cemetery, Nord, France. Grave I.A.8; Kirkcaldy War Memorial; *FA* 25.03.16; *FA* 26.10.18; *Soldiers Died* Part 5; *FA* 26.10.18; *FA* (RoH) 16.11.18; *FA* (BMD) 16.11.18; *FFP* (RoH) 16.11.18; *FA* (FRoH) 14.12.18

Harvey, Robert: Private (S/9233 Gordon Hldrs [1st]); KIA, 20.05.18, 22 years; 54 Nicol Street, Kirkcaldy; Sandpits British Cemetery, Labouvriere, Pas de Calais, France. Grave I.J.9; Kirkcaldy War Memorial; *Soldiers Died* Part 65; *FFP* 15.06.18; *FA* 22.06.18; *FFP* 22.06.18; *FA* 29.06.18; *FA* (RoH) 13.07.18; *FA* (FRoH) 14.12.18

Haxton, Thomas, MM: Private (437254; CEF; Canadian Infantry [7th] [British Columbia Regt]); 06.10.18; 86 Mid Street, Kirkcaldy; Pathhead Parish Church Memorial Plaques & Windows; Queant Road Cemetery, Buissy, Pas de Calais, France. Grave VII.G.34; Kirkcaldy War Memorial; *CBoR* Page 426; *FA* 19.10.18; *FA* (RoH) 16.11.18; *FFP* (RoH) 16.11.18; *FA* (FRoH) 14.12.18

Hay, James Morgan: Private (16229 KOSB [7/8th]); DOW France, 28.09.17, 31 years; 30 Overton Road, Kirkcaldy; St Serf's Church Memorial Plaque; Dozinghem Military Cemetery, Poperinge, West Vlaanderen, Belgium. Grave VI.H.23; Kirkcaldy War Memorial; *FA* 20.10.17; *Soldiers Died* Part 30; *FFP* 06.10.17; *FA* 13.10.17; *FFP* 13.10.17; *FFP* (RoH) 13.10.17; *FA* (BMD) 20.10.17; *FFP* (CasList) 03.11.17; *FFP* 10.11.17; *FA* (FRoH) 07.12.18

Healds, Frederick, Medal of St George, IV Class (Russia): Leading Seaman (178988; Royal Navy; HMS *Mary Rose*); KIA protecting convoy in North Sea, 21.10.17, 38 years; 10 Coal Wynd, Kirkcaldy; Old Parish Church Memorial Panel; Chatham Memorial, Kent. Panel 21; Kirkcaldy War Memorial; *FA* 12.09.14; *FA* 17.06.16; *FA* 27.10.17; *Cross of Sacrifice Vol 4*; *FA* 04.12.15; *FA* 27.10.17; *FFP* 27.10.17; *FA* (BMD) 03.11.17; *FA* (RoH) 17.11.17; *FFP* (RoH) 17.11.17; *FA* 16.02.18; *FA* 03.08.18; *FFP* 03.08.18; *FA* (FRoH) 07.12.18

Heggie, James: Lance Corporal (422461 Royal Engineers [416th Fld Coy]); Died of influenza at Craigleith Military Hospital whilst on leave, 02.11.18, 36 years; 18 Balsusney Road, Kirkcaldy; Gravestone in Abbotshall Churchyard. St Andrew's Church Memorial Plaque. Kirkcaldy High School War Memorial; Abbotshall Parish Churchyard, Kirkcaldy. Grave New. (N).206; Kirkcaldy War Memorial; *Soldiers Died* Part 4; *FA* 09.11.18; *FA* (RoH) 16.11.18; *FFP* (RoH) 16.11.18; *FA* (FRoH) 14.12.18; *FA* (KHS RoH) 29.03.19

Henderson, Alfred: Private (7751 Black Watch [1st]); KIA, 07.10.14, 45 years; 14/20 Flesh Wynd, Kirkcaldy; La Ferte-Sous-Jouarre Memorial, Seine-et-Marne, France; Kirkcaldy War Memorial; *FA* 16.01.15; *Soldiers Died* Part 46; War Album 14/15; *FA* 07.11.14; *FA* (RoH) 07.11.14; *FA* (CasList) 21.11.14; *FA* 02.01.15; *FA* (CasList) 20.02.15; *FFP* (BMD) 09.10.15; *FFP* 05.08.16 Roll of the Brave; *FA* (Service List) 28.10.16; *FA* (Service List) 06.01.17; *FA* (FRoH) 16.11.18; Wauchope Vol 1

Henderson, Andrew: Private (8061 Black Watch [1st] "B" Coy); KIA Aisne, 15.09.14, 36 years; 30 St Clair Street, Kirkcaldy; Gravestone in Bennochy Cemetery; La Ferte-Sous-Jouarre Memorial, Seine-et-Marne, France; Kirkcaldy War Memorial; *FA* 02.10.15; *Soldiers Died* Part 46; *FFP* 17.10.14; *FFP* 24.10.14; *FA* 31.10.14; *FFP* 23.01.15; *FA* (CasList) 20.02.15; *FFP* 20.03.15; *FA* (Service List) 02.12.16; Wauchope Vol 1

Henderson, Andrew: Private (7764 Black Watch [1st] "C" Coy); KIA Ypres, 29.10.14, 32 years; 45 Links Street, Kirkcaldy; St Michael's Church Memorial Plaque; Ypres (Menin Gate) Memorial, Ieper, West Vlaanderen, Belgium. Panel 37; Kirkcaldy War Memorial; *Soldiers Died* Part 46; *FA* 03.04.15; *FA* (FRoH) 23.11.18; Wauchope Vol 1

Henderson, Andrew Smith: Private (S/12588 A & S Hldrs [14th]); KIA, 24.04.17, 23 years; 42 Maria Street, Kirkcaldy; Gravestone in Falkland Cemetery. Whytescauseway Baptist Church Memorial Plaque; Thiepval Memorial, Somme, France. Pier & Face 15A & 16C; Kirkcaldy War Memorial; *Soldiers Died* Part 70; *FA* 05.05.17; *FA* 12.05.17 (2 entries); *FA* (BMD) 12.05.17; *FFP* (BMD) 12.05.17; *FA* (RoH) 19.05.17; *FFP* (RoH) 19.05.17; *FA* (CasList) 02.06.17; *FFP* (CasList) 02.06.17; *FA* (FRoH) 30.11.18; *FA* (FRoH) 07.12.18

Henderson, Archibald: Private (351226 Black Watch [4th/5th]. Formerly 3184 HCB); KIA, 14.11.17, 35 years; 25 Glebe Park/77 Sutherland Street, Kirkcaldy; Tyne Cot Memorial, Zonnebeke, West Vlaanderen, Belgium. Panels 94-96; Kirkcaldy War Memorial; *Soldiers Died* Part 46; *FA* 01.12.17; *FFP* 01.12.17; *FFP* (BMD) 01.12.17; *FA* (RoH) 15.12.17; *FFP* (CasList) 15.12.17; *FA* 11.05.18; *FA* (FRoH) 07.12.18; *FA* 26.04.19; Wauchope Vol 2

Henderson, Charles: Gunner (4316 RGA [118th Siege Batt'y] [Forth]); DOW, 16.10.16, 28 years; 20 Buchanan Street/56 Nicol Street, Kirkcaldy; Forth RGA Plaque. Raith Church Memorial Plaque; Longueval Road Cemetery, Somme, France. Grave D.1; Kirkcaldy War Memorial; ‡; *Soldiers Died* Part 3; *FA* 28.10.16; *FFP* 28.10.16; *FA* (Service List) 04.11.16; *FA* (RoH) 18.11.16; *FFP* (RoH) 18.11.16; *FA* (CasList) 23.12.16; *FFP* (CasList) 23.12.16; *FA* (Service List) 30.12.16; *FFP* (RoH) 30.12.16; *FFP* (BMD) 20.10.17; *FA* (FRoH) 30.11.18

Henderson, Christopher Phillips: Private (19501 Royal Scots [16th]); KIA, 01.07.16, 21 years; 1 Seaforth Place, Kirkcaldy; Sinclairtown Parish Church War Memorial Chair; Thiepval Memorial, Somme, France. Pier & Face 6D & 7D; Kirkcaldy War Memorial; *Soldiers Died* Part 6; *FA* 29.07.16; *FFP* 29.07.16; *FA* (RoH) 05.08.16; *FFP* 05.08.16 Roll of the Brave; *FFP* (CasList) 09.09.16; *FA* (RoH) 16.09.16; *FFP* (RoH) 16.09.16; *FFP* (RoH) 30.12.16; *FA* (Service List) 31.03.17; *FA* (FRoH) 23.11.18

Henderson, David: Private (291803 Black Watch [7th] "A" Coy, 2nd Platoon); KIA, 26.03.18, 27 years; 7 Rosebank Cottages, Victoria Road, Kirkcaldy; Gravestone in Abbotshall Churchyard. Abbotshall Parish Church Memorial Plaque; Arras Memorial, Pas de Calais, France. Bay 6; Kirkcaldy War Memorial; *FA* 08.02.19; *FA* 28.06.19; *Soldiers Died* Part 46; *FA* 04.05.18; *FA* 11.05.18; *FA* 25.01.19; *FA* 08.02.19; *FFP* 08.02.19; *FA* 28.06.19; *FA* (BMD) 28.06.19; *FA* 19.11.21; Wauchope Vol 2

Henderson, David: Private (28662 KOSB [6th]. Formerly 3537 F & F Yeo); KIA, 25.04.18; 6 Regent Place, Dysart; Barony Church Plaque; Tyne Cot Memorial, Zonnebeke, West Vlaanderen, Belgium. Panels 66-68; Kirkcaldy War Memorial; *Soldiers Died* Part 30; *FA* (RoH) 13.09.19

Henderson, Francis Alexander: Private (S/7125 Seaforth Hldrs [9th] [Pioneers]); KIA Ypres, 28.09.17, 25 years; Craigholm, 150 Dunnikier Road, Kirkcaldy; Gravestone in Dysart Cemetery. St Andrew's Church Memorial Plaque; Ypres Reservoir Cemetery, Ieper, West Vlaanderen, Belgium. Grave 1.F.25; Kirkcaldy War Memorial; *Soldiers Died* Part 64; *FFP* 06.10.17; *FFP* (BMD) 06.10.17; *FA* 13.10.17; *FA* (BMD) 13.10.17; *FFP* (RoH) 13.10.17; *FFP* (CasList) 03.11.17; *FFP* (BMD) 28.09.18; *FA* (FRoH) 07.12.18

Henderson, George: Private (696 Black Watch [3rd] att'd [1st]); DOW base hospital, Boulogne, 26.10.14, 33 years; 17 Stewart's Lane, Kirkcaldy; Old Parish Church Memorial Panel; Boulogne Eastern Cemetery, Pas de Calais, France. Grave III.B.6; Kirkcaldy War Memorial; *FA* 22.08.14; *Soldiers Died* Part 46; War Album 14/15; *FA* 14.11.14; *FFP* 14.11.14; *FA* (CasList) 21.11.14; *FA* (CasList) 19.12.14; *FA* 02.01.15; *FA* (CasList) 20.02.15; *FFP* 05.08.16 Roll of the Brave; *FA* (Service List) 04.11.16; *FA* (Service List) 03.02.17; *FA* (FRoH) 16.11.18; Wauchope Vol 1

Henderson, John: Private (S/44787 Gordon Hldrs [1st]); KIA, 23.10.18, 18 years; 27 Glasswork Street, Kirkcaldy; Romeries Communal Cemetery Extension, Nord, France. Grave VII.D.16; Kirkcaldy War Memorial; *Soldiers Died* Part 65; *FA* (RoH) 16.11.18; *FA* (BMD) 16.11.18; *FFP* 16.11.18; *FFP* (RoH) 16.11.18; *FA* (FRoH) 14.12.18; *FFP* (BMD) 23.10.20

Henderson, William: Private (7759 Black Watch [1st]); KIA Aisne, 15.09.14, 36 years; 465 High Street/Volunteers Green, Kirkcaldy; Raith Church Memorial Plaque; La Ferte-Sous-Jouarre Memorial, Seine-et-Marne, France; Kirkcaldy War Memorial; *FA* 31.10.14; *Soldiers Died* Part 46; *FA* 31.10.14; *FFP* 31.10.14; *FA* (RoH) 07.11.14; *FA* (BMD) 07.11.14; *FFP* (BMD) 07.11.14; *FA* 14.11.14; *Scotsman* (CasList) 19.11.14; *FA* (CasList) 21.11.14; *FFP* 05.08.16 Roll of the Brave; *FA* (Service List) 27.01.17; *FA* (FRoH) 16.11.18; Wauchope Vol 1

Henderson, William Francis: Private (43197 HLI [16th]. Formerly 1526 HCB); 18.11.16, 20 years; 2 Kidd Street, Kirkcaldy; Pathhead Parish Church Memorial Plaques & Windows; Waggon Road Cemetery, Beaumont-Hamel, Somme, France. Grave C.14; Kirkcaldy War Memorial; *Soldiers Died* Part 63; *FA* (CasList) 13.01.17; *FFP* 21.04.17; *FA* (RoH) 19.05.17; *FFP* (RoH) 19.05.17; *FA* (FRoH) 30.11.18; *FFP* 21.06.24

Hepburn, Andrew, MM, DCM: Pioneer (48019 Royal Engineers [14th Signals Coy]); DOW, 04.04.18, 22 years; 31 Lady Helen Street, Kirkcaldy; Gravestone in Bennochy Cemetery. Bethelfield Church Plaque. Buckhaven Higher Grade School War Memorial; Pozieres Memorial, Somme, France. Panels 10-13; Kirkcaldy War Memorial; *FA* 13.05.16; *Soldiers Died* Part 4; *FA* 13.05.16; *FA* 27.04.18; *FFP* 27.04.18; *FA* 11.05.18; *FA* 12.04.19; *FA* (BMD) 12.04.19

Herd, Alexander: Lance Corporal (267243 Royal Warwickshire Regt [2/7th]. Formerly 2144 HCB); KIA, 23.03.18, 26 years; 60 Links Street, Kirkcaldy; St Brycedale Church Plaque; Roye New British Cemetery, Somme, France. Grave III.A.14; Kirkcaldy War Memorial; *Soldiers Died* Part 11; *FA* 06.04.18; *FFP* (RoH) 13.04.18; *FA* 11.05.18

Herd, Herbert John Humphries, DSO: Lieutenant (Black Watch [3rd] att'd Royal Engineers [17th Coy]); Brother of Oswald A. Herd; Whytebank, Dunnikier Road, Kirkcaldy; Not identified on CWGC web site; Kirkcaldy War Memorial; *FA* 06.05.16; *FA* 24.06.16 (3 entries); *FFP* 05.08.16; *FA* 30.09.16; *FA* 06.01.17

Herd, Oswald Alexander, DSO: Captain (Durham Light Infantry [14th]); Brother of Herbert J. H. Herd; KIA, 24.09.16, 25 years; Whytebank, Dunnikier Road, Kirkcaldy; Bethelfield Church Plaque. Kirkcaldy High School War Memorial; Guards' Cemetery, Lesboeufs, Somme, France. Grave XII.K.9; Kirkcaldy War Memorial; *FA* 30.09.16; *Officers Died*; *Cross of Sacrifice Vol 1*; *FA* 30.09.16; *FA* (BMD) 30.09.16; *FFP* 30.09.16; *FA* 14.10.16; *FA* (RoH) 14.10.16; *FFP* 14.10.16; *FFP* (RoH) 14.10.16; *FA* (Service List) 16.12.16; *FFP* (RoH) 30.12.16; *FA* 21.04.17; *FFP* 21.04.17; *FA* 14.07.17 (KHS War Honours); *FA* (FRoH) 23.11.18; *FA* (KHS RoH) 29.03.19

Herd, William: Private (291519 Black Watch [9th]); Died Parchin Stamlager, Germany, 28.05.18, 20 years; 14 Dunnikier Row, Kirkcaldy; Cabaret-Rouge British Cemetery, Souchez, Pas de Calais, France. Grave XXI. A.A.25; Kirkcaldy War Memorial; *Soldiers Died* Part 46; *FA* 21.09.18; *FA* (BMD) 21.09.18; *FFP* 21.09.18; *FFP* (BMD) 21.09.18; *FA* 19.10.18; *FA* (FRoH) 14.12.18; Wauchope Vol 3

Herd, William Bain: Corporal (S/6867 A & S Hldrs [2nd]); KIA, 22.09.18, 38 years; Hoosick Falls, New York State, U.S.A. Formerly 15 Nairn St, Kirkcaldy; Pathhead Parish Church Memorial Plaques & Windows; Villers Hill British Cemetery, Villers-Guislain, Nord, France. Grave I.D.6; Kirkcaldy War Memorial; *Soldiers Died* Part 70; *FA* (RoH) 16.11.18; *FA* (BMD) 16.11.18; *FFP* (RoH) 16.11.18; *FFP* (BMD) 16.11.18; *FA* (FRoH) 14.12.18

Hill, James: Private (43025 Cameronians [Scottish Rifles] [9th]. Formerly 29723 Royal Scots); Nephew of William Hill; KIA France, 20.09.17, 21 years; $5^{1}/_{2}$ Dysart Road, Pathhead, Kirkcaldy; E.U. Congregational Church Memorial Plaque; Tyne Cot Memorial, Zonnebeke, West Vlaanderen, Belgium. Panels 68-70 & 162-162A; Kirkcaldy War Memorial; *Soldiers Died* Part 31; *FFP* 27.10.17; *FFP* (BMD) 27.10.17; *FA* 03.11.17 (2 entries); *FFP* (CasList) 10.11.17; *FA* (RoH) 17.11.17; *FFP* (RoH) 17.11.17; *FFP* (BMD) 21.09.18; *FA* (BMD) 12.10.18; *FA* (FRoH) 07.12.18

Hill, William Francis: Driver (6731 RFA [9th Div] [Ammunition Column]); Uncle of James Hill; DOW France, 12.09.17, 30 years; 121 East Smeaton Street, Kirkcaldy; E.U. Congregational Church Memorial Plaque; Mendingham Military Cemetery, Poperinge, West Vlaanderen, Belgium. Grave IV.D.13; Kirkcaldy War Memorial; *Soldiers Died* Part 2; *FA* 22.09.17; *FFP* 22.09.17; *FFP* (BMD) 29.09.17; *FA* (BMD) 06.10.17; *FA* 13.10.17; *FFP* (RoH) 13.10.17; *FFP* 27.10.17; *FA* 03.11.17 (2 entries); *FFP* (BMD) 14.09.18; *FA* (FRoH) 07.12.18

Hitchin, Chalmers: Private (20996 HLI [16th]); Died of influenza 61st CCS, 14.11.18; 17 Hill Place, Kirkcaldy; Premont British Cemetery, Aisne, France. Grave III.D.2; Kirkcaldy War Memorial; *FA* 07.12.18; *FA* (FRoH) 14.12.18

Hogg, John: Private (S/12989 Black Watch [8th]); MIA, 19.10.16, 27 years; Fish Wynd/84 East Smeaton Street, Kirkcaldy; Thiepval Memorial, Somme, France. Pier & Face 10A; Kirkcaldy War Memorial; *Soldiers Died* Part 46; *FA* 21.04.17; *FFP* 11.08.17; *FFP* (BMD) 11.08.17; *FA* 18.08.17; *FA* (BMD) 18.08.17; *FA* 15.09.17; *FFP* (RoH) 15.09.17; *FFP* (BMD) 20.10.17; *FFP* (BMD) 23.10.20; Wauchope Vol 3

Holborn, Alexander: Private (31293 Royal Scots [11th] "C" Coy); Brother of Charles Holborn; KIA, 05.04.17, 19 years; Formerly 90 Kidd Street, Kirkcaldy. Lived in Dundee; St Nicolas British Cemetery, Pas de Calais, France. Grave I.D.13; Kirkcaldy War Memorial; *Soldiers Died* Part 6; *FA* 28.04.17; *FFP* 28.04.17; *FFP* (BMD) 28.04.17; *FFP* 05.05.17; *FA* (RoH) 19.05.17; *FFP* (RoH) 19.05.17; *FA* (FRoH) 30.11.18

Holborn, Charles: Sergeant (S/1858 Gordon Hldrs [8th]); Brother of Alexander Holborn; DOW Boulogne Hospital, 03.06.15, 24 years; 90 Kidd Street, Kirkcaldy; Boulogne Eastern Cemetery, Pas de Calais, France. Grave VIII.A.66; Kirkcaldy War Memorial; *FA* 12.06.15; *FFP* 19.06.15; *Soldiers Died* Part 65; War Album 15; *FFP* (BMD) 05.06.15; *FA* 12.06.15 (2 entries); *FFP* 12.06.15; *FFP* (BMD) 12.06.15; *FFP* 19.06.15; *FFP* (CasList) 03.07.15; *FFP* 18.03.16; *FFP* (BMD) 03.06.16; *FFP* 05.08.16 Roll of the Brave; *FA* (Service List) 27.01.17; *FA* 28.04.17; *FFP* (BMD) 26.05.17; *FA* (FRoH) 16.11.18

Honeyman, Andrew: Private (43027 HCB att'd HLI [16th]); Brother of James Honeyman; DOW, 10.02.17, 19 years; 2 Factory Square, Rosslyn Street, Kirkcaldy; Gallatown Church Roll of Honour; Varennes Military Cemetery, Somme, France. Grave I.D.6; Kirkcaldy War Memorial; *FA* 17.02.17; *FFP* 24.02.17; *FA* (CasList) 10.03.17; *FFP* (CasList) 10.03.17; *FA* (RoH) 17.03.17; *FA* (Service List) 31.03.17; *FFP* 15.06.18; *FA* 22.06.18; *FA* (FRoH) 30.11.18

Honeyman, Christopher Thomson: Private (2792 Black Watch [1/7th]); DOW, 19.06.15, 23 years; 27/83 Victoria Road, Kirkcaldy; Hinges Military Cemetery, Pas de Calais, France. Grave B.17; *FA* 08.07.16; *Soldiers Died* Part 46; Kirkcaldy War Memorial; War Album 15; *Scotsman* 07.06.15; *FA* 26.06.15; *FFP* (CasList) 03.07.15; *FFP* (BMD) 03.07.15; *FA* (RoH) 17.07.15; *FFP* (BMD) 24.06.16; *FA* 08.07.16; *FFP* 05.08.16 Roll of the Brave; *FA* (Service List) 02.12.16; *FFP* (BMD) 23.06.17; *FA* (FRoH) 16.11.18; Wauchope Vol 2

Honeyman, James: Private (S/29660 Cameron Hldrs [6th]); Brother of Andrew Honeyman; DOW 50th CCS, 14.05.18, 23 years; 2 Factory Square, Rosslyn Street, Kirkcaldy; Gallatown Church Roll of Honour; Aubigny Communal Cemetery Extension, Pas de Calais, France. Grave IV.K.6; Kirkcaldy War Memorial; *Soldiers Died* Part 66; *FFP* 15.06.18; *FA* 22.06.18; *FA* (RoH) 13.07.18; *FA* (FRoH) 14.12.18

Honeyman, Walter Baillie: Lance Corporal (486334 Labour Corps [962nd Area Employment Coy]. Formerly 13835 Royal Dublin Fusiliers [7th]); Died of pneumonia, in hospital, Taranto, Italy, 13.10.18, 39 years; Kirkcaldy High School War Memorial. St Peter's Church Memorial Plaque; Taranto Town Cemetery Extension, Taranto, Italy. Grave IV.A.8; Kirkcaldy War Memorial; *Soldiers Died* Part 80; *FA* 04.09.15; *FA* 18.09.15; *FA* 26.10.18; *FA* (BMD) 26.10.18; *FA* (KHS RoH) 29.03.19; *FA* (KHS RoH) 19.07.19

Hood, James Swirles: 2nd Lieutenant (CEF; Canadian Infantry [3rd] 1st Div 1st Bde. [Central Ontario Regt]); KIA, 03.05.17, 24 years; 252D High Street/Townsend Place, Kirkcaldy; Gravestone in Bennochy Cemetery. Old Parish Church Memorial Panel. Kirkcaldy High School War Memorial; Orchard Dump Cemetery, Arleux-en-Gohelle, Pas de Calais, France. Grave V.C.29; Kirkcaldy War Memorial; *CBoR* Page 258; *Cross of Sacrifice Vol 3*; *FA* 12.05.17; *FFP* 12.05.17; *FA* (RoH) 19.05.17; *FFP* (RoH) 19.05.17; *FA* 14.07.17 (KHS War Honours); *FA* (FRoH) 30.11.18; *FA* (KHS RoH) 29.03.19

Horne, Alexander: Private (4159 Black Watch [7th]); KIA, 13.11.16, 32 years; 12 Links Street, Kirkcaldy; Gravestone in Bennochy Cemetery. Whytescauseway Baptist Church Memorial Plaque; Y Ravine Cemetery, Beaumont-Hamel, Somme, France; Kirkcaldy War Memorial; *Soldiers Died* Part 46; *FA* (BMD) 09.12.16; *FFP* 09.12.16; *FFP* (BMD) 09.12.16; *FA* (RoH) 16.12.16; *FFP* (RoH) 30.12.16; *FA* (CasList) 13.01.17; *FFP* (CasList) 13.01.17; *FA* (FRoH) 30.11.18; Wauchope Vol 2

Horne, Andrew Thomson: Private (43135 Royal Scots Fusiliers [8th]); KIA Salonika, 19.09.18, 39 years; 19 Pringle's Buildings, Overton Road, Kirkcaldy; Doiran Military Cemetery, Greece. Grave I.E.7; Kirkcaldy War Memorial; *Soldiers Died* Part 26; *FFP* (BMD) 12.10.18; *FA* (RoH) 19.10.18; *FA* (FRoH) 14.12.18

Howie, James: Gunner (118665 RGA [191st Siege Batt'y]); DOW, 29.04.18, 21 years; 3 Balfour Place, Kirkcaldy; Lijssenthoek Military Cemetery, Poperinge, West Vlaanderen, Belgium. Grave XXVIII.E.12A; Kirkcaldy War Memorial; *FA* 17.02.17; *Soldiers Died* Part 3; *FFP* 25.05.18; *FA* 01.06.18; *FFP* 01.06.18; *FFP* (BMD) 01.06.18; *FA* (BMD) 08.06.18; *FA* (RoH) 15.06.18; *FFP* (RoH) 15.06.18; *FFP* (CasList) 22.06.18; *FA* (FRoH) 14.12.18

Hudghton, James: BQMS (344282 RGA [237th Batt'y] [Forth]); KIA France, 17.03.17, 28 years; 18 Glebe Park, Kirkcaldy; Forth RGA Plaque; Vlamertinghe Military Cemetery, Ieper, West Vlaanderen, Belgium. Grave VI.C.11; Kirkcaldy War Memorial; *Soldiers Died* Part 3; *FA* 24.03.17; *FFP* 24.03.17; *FA* (BMD) 31.03.17; *FFP* 31.03.17; *FA* (RoH) 14.04.17; *FA* (FRoH) 30.11.18

Hughes, Andrew: Private (13439 Cameronians [Scottish Rifles] [10th]); DOW Canadian CCS, 01.08.17, 39 years; 9 Rosslyn Street, Kirkcaldy; Lijssenthoek Military Cemetery, Poperinge, West Vlaanderen, Belgium. Grave XVI.G.15; Kirkcaldy War Memorial; *Soldiers Died* Part 31; *FA* 18.08.17; *FA* (BMD) 25.08.17; *FFP* (BMD) 25.08.17; *FFP* (CasList) 08.09.17; *FA* 15.09.17; *FFP* (RoH) 15.09.17

Hughes, Andrew: Private (43345 HLI [17th]); Brothers James, Thomas & William also killed; KIA Beaumont Hamel, 18.11.16, 19 years; Floral Nursery, Hendry Road, Kirkcaldy; New Munich Trench British Cemetery, Beaumont-Hamel, Somme, France. Grave E.8; Kirkcaldy War Memorial; *Soldiers Died* Part 63; *FA* 06.01.17; *FA* (Service List) 06.01.17; *FFP* (CasList) 06.01.17; *FFP* (RoH) 27.04.18; *FA* 04.05.18; *FFP* 04.05.18; *FFP* (Memorial Service) 04.05.18; *FA* 26.04.19

Hughes, James: Private (CEF; Canadian Horse); Brothers Andrew, Thomas & William also killed; KIA; Floral Nursery, Hendry Road, Kirkcaldy; Not identified on CWGC web site; Kirkcaldy War Memorial; *CBoR* Page 433; *FA* 26.10.18; *FA* (RoH) 16.11.18; *FFP* (RoH) 16.11.18; *FA* (FRoH) 14.12.18

Hughes, John: Corporal (260198 Gordon Hldrs [5th]. Formerly HCB and Black Watch); KIA, 21.03.18, 37 years; 465 High Street, Kirkcaldy; St Andrew's Church Memorial Plaque; Pozieres Memorial, Somme, France. Panel 73; Kirkcaldy War Memorial; *FA* 20.04.18; *Soldiers Died* Part 65; *FA* 20.04.18; *FFP* 20.04.18; *FFP* (BMD) 20.04.18; *FFP* (BMD) 27.04.18; *FA* (BMD) 04.05.18; *FA* (RoH) 18.05.18; *FFP* (RoH) 18.05.18; *FA* (FRoH) 07.12.18

Hughes, Thomas: Private (266609 Black Watch [6th]); Brothers Andrew, James & William also killed; KIA, 10.04.18; Floral Nursery, Hendry Road, Kirkcaldy; Loos Memorial, Pas de Calais, France. Panels 78-83; Kirkcaldy War Memorial; *Soldiers Died* Part 46; *FA* 25.05.18; *FA* 26.04.19; Wauchope Vol 2

Hughes, William: Lance Corporal (1856 Black Watch [2nd]); KIA Mesopotamia, 21.01.16, 22 years; 14 Denburn Place, Kirkcaldy; Basra Memorial, Iraq. Panels 25 & 63; Kirkcaldy War Memorial; *FA* 19.02.16; *Soldiers Died* Part 46; *Scotsman* 16.02.16; *FA* 19.02.16; *FA* (BMD) 19.02.16; *FFP* 19.02.16; *FFP* (BMD) 19.02.16; *FFP* 26.02.16; *FFP* 05.08.16 Roll of the Brave; *FFP* (BMD) 20.01.17; *FFP* (BMD) 02.02.18; *FA* (FRoH) 23.11.18; *FFP* (BMD) 25.01.19; Wauchope Vol 1

Hughes, William: 2nd Lieutenant (Manchester Regt [10th] att'd [1/9th]); Brothers Andrew, James & Thomas also killed; KIA, 26.03.18, 27 years; Floral Nursery, Hendry Road, Kirkcaldy; Pozieres Memorial, Somme, France. Panels 64-67; Kirkcaldy War Memorial; *Officers Died*; *Cross of Sacrifice Vol 1*; *FFP* (RoH) 27.04.18; *FFP* (BMD) 27.04.18; *FA* 04.05.18; *FA* (BMD) 04.05.18; *FFP* (Memorial Service) 04.05.18; *FFP* (RoH) 04.05.18; *FA* (RoH) 18.05.18; *FFP* (RoH) 18.05.18; *FA* (FRoH) 07.12.18; *FA* 26.04.19

Hunter, Andrew: Private (288063 Gordon Hldrs [6th]); Cousin of Andrew Hunter (288078); DOW, 23.11.17, 18 years; 4 Buchanan Street, Kirkcaldy; Rocquigny-Equancourt Road British Cemetery, Manancourt, Somme, France. Grave IV.B.13; Kirkcaldy War Memorial; *Soldiers Died* Part 65; *FFP* 08.12.17; *FA* 15.12.17; *FA* (RoH) 15.12.17; *FFP* 15.12.17; *FFP* (RoH) 15.12.17; *FA* 22.12.17; *FFP* 12.01.18; *FA* (FRoH) 07.12.18; MacKenzie

Two cousins of the same name, Andrew **Hunter**, and same age, both serving in the Gordon Highlanders were killed on the same day, 23rd November, 1917.

Hunter, Andrew: Lance Corporal (288078 Gordon Hldrs [6th]. Formerly F & F Yeo); In *FA* (RoH) as Henry Hunter. Cousin of Andrew Hunter (288063); KIA Cambrai, 23.11.17, 19 years; 5 Cameron's Buildings, Sands Road, Kirkcaldy; Flesquieres Hill British Cemetery, Nord, France. Grave VIII.G.4; Kirkcaldy War Memorial; *FFP* 05.01.18; *Soldiers Died* Part 65; *FA* 15.12.17; *FFP* 15.12.17; *FFP* (BMD) 29.12.17; *FA* (BMD) 05.01.18; *FFP* (RoH) 05.01.18; *FFP* (CasList) 12.01.18; *FA* (RoH) 19.01.18; *FFP* (BMD) 23.11.18; *FA* (FRoH) 07.12.18; MacKenzie

Hunter, David: Private (3/2669 Black Watch [1st] "B" Coy, 5th Platoon); DOW, 16.05.15, 18 years; 16 Hill Place, Kirkcaldy; Bethune Town Cemetery, Pas de Calais, France. Grave III.C.75; Kirkcaldy War Memorial; *FA* 03.07.15; *Soldiers Died* Part 46; *War Album 15*; *FFP* 12.06.15; *FFP* 19.06.15; *FA* 26.06.15; *FA* 03.07.15; *FFP* (CasList) 03.07.15; *FA* (RoH) 17.07.15; *FFP* 05.08.16 Roll of the Brave; *FA* (Service List) 04.11.16; *FA* (Service List) 27.01.17; *FA* (FRoH) 16.11.18; Wauchope Vol 1

Hunter, David: Private (3/2615 Black Watch [1st] "D" Coy); Brother of George Hunter; Died in hospital of wounds received at Neuve Chapelle, 09.05.15, 22 years; 95 Overton Road, Kirkcaldy; Le Touret Memorial, Pas de Calais, France. Panels 24-26; Kirkcaldy War Memorial; *FA* 31.07.15; *Soldiers Died* Part 46; *FA* 19.06.15; *FA* 18.03.16; *FFP* 25.03.16; *FA* (RoH) 15.04.16; *FFP* (CasList) 15.04.16; *FFP* 05.08.16 Roll of the Brave; *FA* (Service List) 18.11.16; *FA* (FRoH) 23.11.18; Wauchope Vol 1

Hunter, David: Private (28664 KOSB [2nd]. Formerly 2254 F & F Yeo); KIA, 27.02.17; 9 Rosslyn Street, Kirkcaldy; Brown's Road Military Cemetery, Festubert, Pas de Calais, France. Grave I.H.20; Kirkcaldy War Memorial; *Soldiers Died* Part 30; *FA* 10.03.17; *FFP* (BMD) 10.03.17; *FA* (RoH) 17.03.17; *FA* (FRoH) 30.11.18

Hunter, George: Private (12515 KOSB [6th]); Brother of David Hunter; KIA Loos, 25.09.15, 25 years; 95 Overton Road, Kirkcaldy; Loos Memorial, Pas de Calais, France. Panels 53-56; Kirkcaldy War Memorial; *Soldiers Died* Part 30; *FA* 19.06.15; *FA* 18.03.16; *FFP* 25.03.16; *FA* (RoH) 15.04.16; *FFP* (CasList) 15.04.16; *FFP* 05.08.16 Roll of the Brave; *FA* (Service List) 18.11.16; *FA* (FRoH) 23.11.18

Hunter, James: Driver (7419 RFA [83rd Bde] "B" Batt'y); KIA, 24.04.18; 10 Fish Wynd, Kirkcaldy; Pozieres Memorial, Somme, France. Panels 7-10; Kirkcaldy War Memorial; *Soldiers Died* Part 2; *FA* (BMD) 18.05.18; *FFP* 18.05.18; *FA* 25.05.18; *FA* (RoH) 15.06.18; *FFP* (RoH) 15.06.18; *FFP* (CasList) 22.06.18; *FA* (FRoH) 14.12.18

Hunter, John: Lance Corporal (Black Watch); Not identified on CWGC web site; Kirkcaldy War Memorial

Hunter, John: Lance Corporal (15464 Royal Engineers [23rd Fld Coy]); 25.09.15; 124/126 Den Road, Kirkcaldy; Dud Corner Cemetery, Loos, Pas de Calais, France. Grave VI.B.9; Kirkcaldy War Memorial; *Soldiers Died* Part 4; War Album 15/16; *FA* 23.10.15; *FA* (RoH) 13.11.15; *FFP* 05.08.16 Roll of the Brave; *FA* (Service List) 10.02.17; *FA* (FRoH) 16.11.18

Hunter, Peter: Private (S/4914 Black Watch [9th]); KIA Loos, 25.09.15; 23 Smeaton Road, Kirkcaldy; Philosophe British Cemetery, Mazingarbe, Pas de Calais, France. Grave II.H.15; Kirkcaldy War Memorial; *Soldiers Died* Part 46; War Album 15/16; *FA* (RoH) 13.11.15; *FFP* 05.08.16Roll of the Brave; *FFP* (BMD) 23.09.16; *FA* (Service List) 04.11.16; *FA* (Service List) 10.02.17; *FFP* (BMD) 29.09.17; *FFP* (BMD) 28.09.18; *FA* (FRoH) 16.11.18; Wauchope Vol 3

Hunter, Thomas: Private (43358 Royal Scots Fusiliers [2nd]); KIA, 23.04.17, 22 years; 165 Den Road, Kirkcaldy. Late of Balwearie Mills; Arras Memorial, Pas de Calais, France. Bay 5; Kirkcaldy War Memorial; *Soldiers Died* Part 26; *FFP* 02.06.17; *FFP* (BMD) 02.06.17; *FA* 09.06.17; *FA* (BMD) 09.06.17; *FA* (CasList) 16.06.17; *FA* (RoH) 16.06.17; *FFP* (CasList) 16.06.17; *FFP* (RoH) 16.06.17; *FA* 15.09.17; *FFP* (RoH) 15.09.17; *FFP* (BMD) 20.04.18; *FFP* (BMD) 27.04.18; *FA* (FRoH) 30.11.18

Hush, John Dick: Lance Corporal (601 Black Watch [2nd]); MIA, 25.09.15; 21 Quality Street, Kirkcaldy; Loos Memorial, Pas de Calais, France. Panels 78-83; Kirkcaldy War Memorial; *FA* 30.10.15; *Soldiers Died* Part 46; *FA* 23.10.15; *FA* (Service List) 25.11.16; *FA* 23.12.16; *FA* (BMD) 23.12.16; *FFP* 30.12.16; *FA* (RoH) 13.01.17; *FFP* (RoH) 13.01.17; *FA* (FRoH) 30.11.18; Wauchope Vol 1

Hutcheson, Samuel: Sapper (151232 Royal Engineers [173rd Tunnelling Coy]. Formerly 7347 A & S Hldrs); On CWGC as 11232; KIA, 17.04.16, 34 years; 240 Links Street, Kirkcaldy; Loos Memorial, Pas de Calais, France. Panels 4 & 5; Kirkcaldy War Memorial; *Soldiers Died* Part 4; *FA* 29.04.16; *FFP* 29.04.16; *FA* (RoH) 13.05.16; *FFP* 05.08.16 Roll of the Brave; *FA* (FRoH) 23.11.18

Hutchison, Alexander: Sapper (216142 Royal Engineers [440th Cheshire Fld Coy]); Wounded in billet in France. Died Lowestoft Military Hospital. Buried Kirkcaldy, 12.04.17, 31 years; 56 East March Street, Kirkcaldy; Gravestone in Dysart Cemetery. Gallatown Church Roll of Honour; Dysart Cemetery, Kirkcaldy. Grave 50.Y. North; Kirkcaldy War Memorial; *Soldiers Died* Part 4; *FA* 14.04.17; *FA* (BMD) 14.04.17; *FFP* (BMD) 14.04.17; *FA* 21.04.17; *FA* (RoH) 19.05.17; *FFP* (RoH) 19.05.17; *FFP* (BMD) 13.04.18; *FA* (FRoH) 30.11.18

Hutchison, William: Private (S/19712 A & S Hldrs [11th]); KIA France, 22.08.17, 24 years; 1 East Smeaton Street, Kirkcaldy; Raith Church Memorial Plaque; Artillery Wood Cemetery, Boezinge, Ieper, West Vlaanderen, Belgium. Grave XII.D.4; Kirkcaldy War Memorial; *FFP* 22.09.17; *Soldiers Died* Part 70; *FA* 22.09.17; *FA* (BMD) 22.09.17; *FFP* (BMD) 22.09.17; *FA* 13.10.17; *FFP* (RoH) 13.10.17; *FFP* (BMD) 24.08.18; *FA* (FRoH) 07.12.18

Hutchison, William Rintoul: Private (6020; AIF; Australian Infantry [4th]); KIA, 06.05.17, 26 years; 74 Sutherland Street, Kirkcaldy; Gravestone in Dysart Cemetery. Barony Church Plaque; Villers-Bretonneux Memorial, Somme, France; Australian War Memorial web site; Kirkcaldy War Memorial; *FA* 02.06.17; *FA* (BMD) 02.06.17; *FFP* (BMD) 02.06.17; *FA* (RoH) 16.06.17; *FFP* (RoH) 16.06.17; *FFP* (BMD) 04.05.18; *FA* (FRoH) 30.11.18

Imrie, Robert: Private (S/6472 Black Watch [8th]); DOW, 03.10.15; 157 Rosslyn Street/42 Miller Street, Kirkcaldy; Barony Church Plaque; Chocques Military Cemetery, Pas de Calais, France. Grave I.C.126; Kirkcaldy War Memorial; *FFP* 23.10.15; *Soldiers Died* Part 46; War Album 15/16; *FFP* 09.10.15; *Scotsman* (CasList) 11.10.15; *FA* 16.10.15; *FA* (RoH) 16.10.15; *FA* (BMD) 16.10.15; *FFP* (RoH) 16.10.15; *FFP* 05.08.16 Roll of the Brave; *FFP* 19.08.16; *FA* (Service List) 09.12.16; *FA* (Service List) 31.03.17; *FA* (FRoH) 16.11.18; Wauchope Vol 3

Inglis, James Kinnear: Lance Corporal (43257 Royal Scots [16th]); KIA, 26.08.17, 27 years; 24/30 St Clair Place, Bridgeton, Kirkcaldy; Hargicourt British Cemetery, Aisne, France. Grave I.D.24; Kirkcaldy War Memorial; *Soldiers Died* Part 6; *FA* 29.09.17; *FFP* 29.09.17; *FA* 13.10.17; *FFP* (RoH) 13.10.17; *FA* (FRoH) 07.12.18

Inglis, John: Private (French Army); DOW in hospital at Torquay; Links Street, Kirkcaldy; Not identified on CWGC web site; Kirkcaldy War Memorial; *FA* 06.05.16; *FFP* 13.05.16; *FA* (RoH) 17.06.16; *FFP* (RoH) 17.06.16; *FFP* 05.08.16 Roll of the Brave; *FA* (FRoH) 23.11.18

Innes, George C.: Private (8/928; NZEF; Otago Infantry Regt [10th]); Reported missing & DOW Gallipoli, 30.08.15, 28 years; 86 Overton Road, Kirkcaldy; Gravestone in Dysart Cemetery; Chunuk Bair (New Zealand) Memorial, Turkey; Kirkcaldy War Memorial; *FA* 22.04.16; NZEF Roll of Honour; *FFP* 09.10.15; *FFP* 15.04.16; *FA* 22.04.16; *FFP* 22.04.16; *FA* (RoH) 13.05.16; *FFP* 05.08.16 Roll of the Brave; *FA* (Service List) 18.11.16; *FA* (FRoH) 23.11.18

Innes, James: Private (S/155551 Black Watch [8th]); KIA, 23.04.17, 33 years; Links Street, Kirkcaldy; Wancourt British Cemetery, Pas de Calais, France. Grave IV.E.27; Kirkcaldy War Memorial; *Soldiers Died* Part 46; *FA* 19.05.17; *FA* (BMD) 19.05.17; *FFP* 19.05.17; *FFP* (BMD) 19.05.17; *FA* (CasList) 26.05.17; *FFP* (CasList) 26.05.17; *FA* (RoH) 16.06.17; *FFP* (RoH) 16.06.17; *FA* (FRoH) 30.11.18; Wauchope Vol 3

Innes, John Boyd: Bombardier (344080 RGA [210th Seige Batt'y] [Forth]); Relative of Alexander Petrie; DOW, 21.05.17, 32 years; 25/37 Rosabelle Street, Kirkcaldy; Gravestone in Dysart Cemetery. Forth RGA Plaque; Sunken Road Cemetery, Boisleux-St Marc, Pas de Calais, France. Grave I.A.10; Kirkcaldy War Memorial; *FA* 02.06.17; *Soldiers Died* Part 3; *FA* 02.06.17; *FA* (BMD) 02.06.17; *FFP* 02.06.17; *FA* (RoH) 16.06.17; *FFP* (RoH) 16.06.17; *FFP* (CasList) 23.06.17; *FA* 03.08.18; *FA* (FRoH) 30.11.18

Innes, William: Private (S/21615 Black Watch [4/5th]); KIA, 01.04.18; St Clair Street/120 Institution Street/29 Rosabelle Street, Kirkcaldy; Pozieres Memorial, Somme, France. Panels 49-50; Kirkcaldy War Memorial; *FA* 08.02.19; *Soldiers Died* Part 46; *FA* 08.02.19; *FA* (BMD) 12.07.19; Wauchope Vol 2

Ireland, John Landels: Private (Royal Irish Fusiliers [9th]. Formerly HCB); Brother of Lockhart Landels Ireland; 01.07.16; Gravestone in Bennochy Cemetery. Abbotshall Parish Church Memorial Plaque. Whytescauseway Baptist Church Memorial Plaque. Kirkcaldy High School War Memorial; Not identified on CWGC web site; Kirkcaldy War Memorial; *FA* 05.08.16 (2 entries); *FA* (Service List) 20.01.17; *FA* (KHS RoH) 29.03.19; *FA* 19.11.21

Ireland, Lockhart Landels: Private (S/13479 Gordon Hldrs [8/10th]); Brother of John Landels Ireland;KIA, 25.07.16, 29 years; 23 Abbotshall Road, Kirkcaldy; Gravestone in Bennochy Cemetery. Whytescauseway Baptist Church Memorial Plaque. Kirkcaldy High School War Memorial; Flatiron Copse Cemetery, Mametz, Somme, France. Grave VI.C.8; Kirkcaldy War Memorial; *FA* 05.08.16; *Soldiers Died* Part 65; *FA* 11.03.16; *FA* 25.03.16; *FA* 05.08.16; *FA* (RoH) 05.08.16; *FA* (BMD) 05.08.16; *FFP* 05.08.16; *FFP* 05.08.16 Roll of the Brave; *FA* (RoH) 16.09.16; *FFP* (RoH) 16.09.16; *FA* 25.11.16; *FFP* (RoH) 30.12.16; *FA* (Service List) 20.01.17; *FA* 14.07.17 (KHS War Honours); *FA* 03.11.17; *FA* 10.11.17; *FA* 24.11.17; *FA* 04.05.18 (2 entries); *FA* (FRoH) 23.11.18; *FA* (KHS RoH) 29.03.19

Irvine, Duncan: Private (4132 Black Watch [1/7th]); DOW, 31.07.16, 20 years; 9 Pratt Street, Kirkcaldy; St Columba's Church Memorial Plaque; Dernancourt Communal Cemetery, Somme, France. Grave J.5; Kirkcaldy War Memorial; *Soldiers Died* Part 46; *FA* 12.08.16; *FFP* 12.08.16; *FA* 26.08.16; *FA* (BMD) 26.08.16; *FFP* 26.08.16; *FFP* 02.09.16; *FA* (RoH) 16.09.16; *FFP* (CasList) 16.09.16; *FA* (Service List) 16.12.16; *FFP* (RoH) 30.12.16; *FA* (FRoH) 23.11.18; Wauchope Vol 2

Irvine, Watson: Private (292281 Black Watch [6th]); KIA, 21.03.18; Beaumetz-Les-Cambrai Military Cemetery No. 1, Pas de Calais, France. Grave II.B; Kirkcaldy War Memorial; *Soldiers Died* Part 46; Wauchope Vol 2

Jack, Alexander: Private (27913 Royal Scots [12th]); KIA, 16.07.16, 23 years; 93 Sutherland Street, Kirkcaldy; Pathhead Parish Church Memorial Plaques & Windows; Thiepval Memorial, Somme, France. Pier & Face 6D & 7D; Kirkcaldy War Memorial; *Soldiers Died* Part 6; *FA* 12.08.16; *FA* (BMD) 12.08.16; *FFP* 12.08.16; *FFP* (BMD) 12.08.16; *FA* (CasList) 26.08.16; *FFP* (CasList) 26.08.16; *FA* 16.09.16; *FA* (RoH) 16.09.16; *FFP* (RoH) 16.09.16; *FFP* (RoH) 30.12.16; *FA* (Service List) 03.03.17; *FFP* (BMD) 21.07.17; *FA* (BMD) 18.08.17; *FA* (FRoH) 23.11.18

Jack, Andrew: Private (345964 Black Watch [14th] [F & F Yeo Bn]. Formerly 1877 Black Watch); KIA Zeitun, Palestine, 27.12.17, 22 years; 49/145 Ramsay Road, Kirkcaldy; Gravestone in Abbotshall Churchyard. Raith Church Memorial Plaque; Jerusalem War Cemetery, Israel. Grave D.64; Kirkcaldy War Memorial; *Soldiers Died* Part 46; *FA* 15.04.16; *FA* 19.01.18; *FA* (BMD) 19.01.18; *FFP* (RoH) 19.01.18; *FFP* (BMD) 19.01.18; *FA* (RoH) 16.02.18; *FFP* (RoH) 16.02.18; *FA* (FRoH) 07.12.18; Wauchope Vol 3; Ogilvie

---

Lockhart Landels **Ireland** had shown promise as an artist and author. During the war he regularly sent articles and drawings to the local paper. Despite being seriously wounded in February, 1916, he was soon back in the firing line and was killed in action in July, 1916. His writings, "Private John Maclean of the Black Watch & other sketches" were posthumously published.

His brother, John Ireland, was also killed in July, 1916.

Jack, Robert: Carpenter's Mate (Merchant Navy; SS *Aragon* [Belfast]); Went down with his ship, 30.12.17; Abbotshall Parish Church Memorial Plaque; Tower Hill Memorial, London; Kirkcaldy War Memorial; *Cross of Sacrifice Vol 5*; *FFP* (BMD) 04.01.19; *FA* 19.11.21

Jackson, John Stewart Walker: Private (TR/1/29826 Gordon Hldrs [51st]); On CWGC as S.W. Jackson; Died Thetford Military Hospital, 21.07.18, 18 years; 64 Commercial Street, Kirkcaldy; Gravestone in Falkland Cemetery. Barony Church Plaque; Falkland Cemetery. Grave N.35; Kirkcaldy War Memorial; *Soldiers Died* Part 65; *FA* (BMD) 27.07.18; *FFP* (BMD) 27.07.18; *FA* (RoH) 14.09.18; *FFP* (RoH) 14.09.18; *FA* (FRoH) 14.12.18

Jarvis, William Dewar: Private (S/41883 Black Watch [1/6th]. Formerly 32025 Cameron Hldrs & Lovat Scouts); KIA, 10.09.18, 19 years; 1 Cameron's Buildings, Sands Road, Kirkcaldy; Raith Church Memorial Plaque; Brown's Copse Cemetery, Roeux, Pas de Calais, France. Grave V.C.17; Kirkcaldy War Memorial; *Soldiers Died* Part 46; *FA* 28.09.18; *FFP* 05.10.18; *FA* (RoH) 19.10.18; *FA* (FRoH) 14.12.18; Wauchope Vol 2

Johnston, James Rae: Private (345247 Black Watch [14th] [F & F Yeo Bn]); KIA Egypt, 06.11.17, 28 years; 16 Kidd Street, Kirkcaldy; Pathhead Parish Church Memorial Plaques & Windows; Beersheba War Cemetery, Israel. Grave L.2; Kirkcaldy War Memorial; *Soldiers Died* Part 46; *FA* 24.11.17; *FFP* (BMD) 01.12.17; *FA* (RoH) 15.12.17; *FFP* (RoH) 15.12.17; *FA* (FRoH) 07.12.18; *FFP* 21.06.24; Wauchope Vol 3; Ogilvie

Johnston, William: Lance Corporal (13791 Scots Guards [1st]); MIA, 15.09.16, 28 years; 8 Pool Lane, Gallatown, Kirkcaldy; Gallatown Church Roll of Honour; Thiepval Memorial, Somme, France. Pier & Face 7D; Kirkcaldy War Memorial; *Soldiers Died* Part 5; *FA* 07.07.17; *FA* (BMD) 07.07.17; *FFP* 07.07.17; *FFP* (BMD) 07.07.17; *FA* 14.07.17; *FFP* (CasList) 14.07.17; *FFP* (BMD) 14.07.17; *FFP* (BMD) 14.09.18; *FA* (FRoH) 07.12.18

Jones, James: Private (S/16729 Cameron Hldrs [6th]); Adopted brother of John Wotherspoon; KIA by shellfire, 30.06.16; 171 Den Road, Kirkcaldy; Pathhead Parish Church Memorial Plaques & Windows; Loos Memorial, Pas de Calais, France. Panels 119-124; Kirkcaldy War Memorial; *Soldiers Died* Part 66; *FFP* 08.07.16; *FA* 15.07.16; *FA* (RoH) 15.07.16; *FFP* 05.08.16 Roll of the Brave; *FFP* 12.08.16; *FA* (Service List) 10.02.17; *FA* (FRoH) 23.11.18; *FFP* 21.06.24

Kay, George Mathieson: Sapper (4/767; NZEF; Royal New Zealand Engineers); On *FA* (Service List) 17.03.17 as McKay; KIA, 20.09.16, 30 years; 29 Aitken Street, Kirkcaldy; AIF Burial Ground, Flers, Somme, France. Grave I.E.II; Kirkcaldy War Memorial; NZEF Roll of Honour; *FFP* 30.09.16; *FFP* (BMD) 30.09.16; *FA* 07.10.16; *FA* (BMD) 07.10.16; *FA* (RoH) 14.10.16; *FFP* 14.10.16; *FFP* (RoH) 14.10.16; *FFP* (RoH) 30.12.16; *FA* (Service List) 17.03.17; *FFP* (BMD) 22.09.17; *FA* (FRoH) 23.11.18; *FA* 26.04.19

Kay, James Wilson: Corporal (S/8955 Black Watch [8th]); KIA Arras, 09.04.17, 24 years; 154 Institution Street, Kirkcaldy; Mindel Trench British Cemetery, St Laurent-Blangy, Pas de Calais, France. Grave B.24; Kirkcaldy War Memorial; *Soldiers Died* Part 46; *FA* 21.04.17; *FFP* 21.04.17; *FFP* (BMD) 28.04.17; *FA* (BMD) 05.05.17; *FA* (RoH) 19.05.17; *FFP* (CasList) 19.05.17; *FFP* (RoH) 19.05.17; *FFP* (BMD) 13.04.18; *FFP* (BMD) 20.04.18; *FA* (FRoH) 30.11.18; Wauchope Vol 3

Kay, Robert Murray: Private (12188 Nothumberland Fusiliers [9th] "B" Coy); 06.10.15, 22 years; Northall, Victoria Road, Kirkcaldy; Old Parish Church Memorial Panel. Kirkcaldy High School War Memorial; Ypres (Menin Gate) Memorial, Ieper, West Vlaanderen, Belgium. Panels 8 & 12; Kirkcaldy War Memorial; *Soldiers Died* Part 10; War Album 15/16; *FA* 16.10.15; *FA* (BMD) 16.10.15; *FFP* 16.10.15; *FA* (RoH) 13.11.15; *FFP* 05.08.16 Roll of the Brave; *FA* (Service List) 02.12.16; *FA* (FRoH) 16.11.18; *FA* (FRoH) 28.12.18; *FA* (KHS RoH) 29.03.19

Keddie, James: Lance Corporal (43103 HLI [16th]. Formerly 2329 HCB); DOW France, 09.07.17, 21 years; 52 Kidd Street, Kirkcaldy; Coxyde Military Cemetery, Koksijde, West Vlaanderen, Belgium. Grave I.D.42; Kirkcaldy War Memorial; *Soldiers Died* Part 63; *FA* 28.07.17; *FFP* (BMD) 28.07.17; *FA* (BMD) 04.08.17; *FA* 15.09.17; *FFP* (RoH) 15.09.17; *FFP* (BMD) 13.07.18

Private James **Jones** was killed by a shell in June, 1916, when taking two wounded men to a dressing station. His adopted brother, Private James Wotherspoon, had been killed in March of the same year.

Keith, William: Sergeant (345390 Black Watch [14th] [F & F Yeo Bn] "A" Coy); KIA Moislains, 02.09.18, 21 years; 11 Rossend Terrace, Nether Street, Kirkcaldy; Fins New British Cemetery, Sorel-Le-Grand, Somme, France. Grave VIII.H.14; Kirkcaldy War Memorial; *Soldiers Died* Part 46; *FFP* 21.09.18; *FFP* 12.10.18; *FA* 19.10.18; *FA* (RoH) 19.10.18; *FA* (FRoH) 14.12.18; Wauchope Vol 3; Ogilvie

Kelly, John: Private (11934 HLI [1st]); KIA, 21.12.14, 21 years; 154 Den Road, Kirkcaldy; Le Touret Memorial, Pas de Calais, France. Panels 37-38; Kirkcaldy War Memorial; *Soldiers Died* Part 63; War Album 14/15; *FA* 16.01.15 (2 entries); *FFP* 16.01.15; *FFP* (RoH) 30.01.15; *FA* (CasList) 20.02.15; *FFP* (BMD) 25.12.15; *FFP* 05.08.16 Roll of the Brave; *FA* (Service List) 10.02.17; *FA* (FRoH) 16.11.18; *FFP* (BMD) 21.12.18

Kelock, John: Lance Corporal (442706; CEF; Canadian Infantry [2nd] 1st Div 1st Bde. [Eastern Ontario Regt]); KIA, 09.08.18, 34 years; 131 Mid Street/3 Kirk Wynd, Kirkcaldy; Rosieres Communal Cemetery Extension, Somme, France. Grave I.B.16; Kirkcaldy War Memorial; *CBoR*; *FA* (BMD) 24.08.18; *FFP* 24.08.18; *FFP* (BMD) 24.08.18; *FA* 31.08.18; *FA* (RoH) 14.09.18; *FFP* (RoH) 14.09.18; *FA* (FRoH) 14.12.18

Kennedy, Alexander: Private (31456 Lancashire Fusiliers [16th]. Formerly 7841 RAVC); DOW, 03.04.17, 38 years; 62 Balsusney Road, Kirkcaldy; Abbotshall Parish Church Memorial Plaque; Foreste Communal Cemetery, Aisne, France. Grave II.A.27; Kirkcaldy War Memorial; *Soldiers Died* Part 25; *FA* 21.04.17; *FFP* 21.04.17; *FA* (BMD) 28.04.17; *FFP* (BMD) 28.04.17; *FA* (RoH) 19.05.17; *FFP* (RoH) 19.05.17; *FFP* (BMD) 30.03.18; *FA* (FRoH) 30.11.18; *FA* 19.11.21

Kennedy, John: Private (351082 Black Watch [7th] "B" Coy. Formerly HCB); DOW, 24.07.18, 19 years; 16 Cloanden Place, Kirkcaldy/Skene Street, Strathmiglo; Abbotshall Parish Church Memorial Plaque; Terlincthun British Cemetery, Wimille, Pas de Calais, France. Grave XV.1.C.24; Kirkcaldy War Memorial; *Soldiers Died* Part 46; *FFP* 24.08.18; *FA* 31.08.18 (2 entries); *FFP* (BMD) 31.08.18; *FA* (RoH) 14.09.18; *FFP* (RoH) 14.09.18; *FA* (FRoH) 14.12.18; *FA* 19.11.21; Wauchope Vol 2

Kennedy, John: Leading Seaman (R/2107 Royal Navy; RNVR [RND] [Drake Bn]. Formerly HCB); KIA, 30.12.17, 19 years; 68 Sutherland Street, Kirkcaldy; Pathhead Parish Church Memorial Plaques & Windows; Thiepval Memorial, Somme, France. Pier & Face 1A; Kirkcaldy War Memorial; *Cross of Sacrifice Vol 4*; *FFP* (RoH) 16.02.18; *FFP* (BMD) 16.02.18; *FA* 23.02.18; *FFP* (RoH) 16.03.18; *FA* (FRoH) 07.12.18; *FFP* 21.06.24

Kenny, James: Private (S/10863 Gordon Hldrs [2nd]); Died, 03.04.17, 30 years; 201 Links Street, Kirkcaldy; Ervillers Military Cemetery, Pas de Calais, France. Grave A.5; Kirkcaldy War Memorial; *Soldiers Died* Part 65; *FFP* (CasList) 02.06.17

Kidd, George: Stoker 1st Class (299560 Royal Navy; HMS *Aboukir*); KIA in the North Sea, 22.09.14, 32 years; 4 Hendry's Wynd, Kirkcaldy; Raith Church Memorial Plaque; Chatham Memorial, Kent. Panel 5; *FA* 03.10.14; *FA* 10.10.14; *FFP* 10.10.14; Kirkcaldy War Memorial; *Cross of Sacrifice Vol 4*; War Album 14/15; *FFP* 26.09.14; *FFP* 03.10.14; *FA* 10.10.14; *FFP* 10.10.14; *FA* (CasList) 21.11.14; *FA* 02.01.15; *FA* (CasList) 20.02.15; *FFP* 05.08.16 Roll of the Brave; *FFP* (BMD) 23.09.16; *FA* (Service List) 04.11.16; *FA* (Service List) 23.12.16; *FA* (FRoH) 16.11.18; RoH Dunnikier Colliery

Kidd, Neil Cameron: Lance Corporal (24536 Machine Gun Corps [45th Coy]. Formerly 1176 HCB); DOW Clipstone Military Hospital, Nottinghamshire, 17.06.17; 7 Garnock's Lane, Kirkcaldy; Gravestone in Dysart Cemetery. Barony Church Plaque; Dysart Cemetery, Kirkcaldy. Grave 55.7.South; Kirkcaldy War Memorial. Springfield War Memorial; *Soldiers Died* Part 75; *FA* (BMD) 30.06.17; *FFP* (BMD) 30.06.17; *FA* 14.07.17; *FFP* 14.07.17; *FFP* (CasList) 21.07.17; *FA* (FRoH) 07.12.18

Kidd, William Kirk: Gunner (183022 RGA [Signals Section]); KIA, 25.05.18, 35 years; 40 Glebe Park, Kirkcaldy; Gravestone in Bennochy Cemetery. West End Congregational Church Memorial Plaque; Warloy-Baillon Communal Cemetery Extension, Somme, France. Grave IV.F.12; Kirkcaldy War Memorial; *Soldiers Died* Part 3; *FA* 01.06.18; *FFP* 01.06.18; *FFP* (BMD) 01.06.18; *FA* (BMD) 08.06.18; *FA* (RoH) 15.06.18; *FFP* (RoH) 15.06.18; *FA* (FRoH) 14.12.18

Kilgour, Alexander: Lieutenant (Black Watch [1/7th] att'd [2nd]. Formerly F & F Yeo); KIA Battle of the Lys, Givenchy, 18.04.18, 22 years; Craig-Gowan, Loughborough Road, Kirkcaldy; Gravestone in Dysart Cemetery. Dunnikier Church Roll of Honour. Kirkcaldy High School War Memorial; Guards Cemetery, Windy Corner, Cuinchy, Pas de Calais, France. Grave V.F.8; Kirkcaldy War Memorial; *Officers Died*; *Cross of Sacrifice Vol 1*; *FA* 27.04.18; *FFP* (RoH) 27.04.18; *FFP* (BMD) 27.04.18; *FA* 04.05.18; *FA* (BMD) 04.05.18; *FFP* (RoH) 04.05.18; *FFP* (Memorial Service) 04.05.18; *FA* (RoH) 18.05.18; *FFP* (RoH) 18.05.18; *FA* 13.07.18; *FA* (FRoH) 07.12.18; *FA* (KHS RoH) 29.03.19; *FA* 26.04.19; Wauchope Vol 1 & 2

Kilgour, James: Private (51084 Royal Scots Fusiliers [1st]. Formerly HLI); KIA, 28.03.18, 19 years; 44 Commercial Street, Kirkcaldy; Arras Memorial, Pas de Calais, France. Bay 5; Kirkcaldy War Memorial; *Soldiers Died* Part 26; *FA* 20.04.18; *FFP* (BMD) 20.04.18; *FA* (BMD) 27.04.18; *FFP* (CasList) 11.05.18; *FA* 18.05.18; *FFP* (RoH) 18.05.18; *FA* (FRoH) 14.12.18

Kilpatrick, William: Lance Corporal (345404 Black Watch [14th] [F & F Yeo Bn]. Formerly 2601 F & F Yeo); *Soldiers Died* gives number as 315404; DOW Beitania, Egypt, 29.12.17, 24 years; 35 Mitchell Street, Kirkcaldy; St Andrew's Church Memorial Plaque; Jerusalem War Cemetery, Israel. Grave D.27; Kirkcaldy War Memorial; *FFP* 19.01.18; *FFP* 16.02.18; *Soldiers Died* Part 46; *FA* 19.01.18; *FFP* (RoH) 19.01.18; *FFP* (BMD) 19.01.18; *FA* (BMD) 26.01.18; *FA* (RoH) 16.02.18; *FFP* (RoH) 16.02.18; *FA* (FRoH) 07.12.18; *FFP* (BMD) 04.01.19; Wauchope Vol 3; Ogilvie

King, James: Private (Black Watch [1/7th]); 109/125 Nether Street, Kirkcaldy; Not identified on CWGC web site; Kirkcaldy War Memorial; War Album 15; *Dundee Courier* 22.06.15; *FA* 26.06.15; *FFP* 26.06.15; *FFP* (CasList) 03.07.15; *FA* (RoH) 17.07.15; *FFP* 05.08.16 Roll of the Brave; *FA* (Service List) 28.10.16; *FA* (Service List) 30.12.16; *FA* (FRoH) 16.11.18

King, John: Private (6842 Labour Corps [12th Coy]. Formerly 2798 Black Watch); Died of influenza Leven Military Hospital, 29.11.18, 30 years; Scoonie Cemetery, Leven. Grave 13.85; Kirkcaldy War Memorial; *FFP* (BMD) 14.12.18; *FA* (RoH) 18.01.19

King, John Alexander: 2nd Lieutenant (Gordon Hldrs [4th]); KIA, 12.09.16, 30 years; High School, Carlyle Road, Kirkcaldy; Kirkcaldy High School War Memorial; Cité Bonjean Military Cemetery, Armentières, Nord, France. Grave II.F.28; Kirkcaldy War Memorial; *Officers Died*; *Cross of Sacrifice Vol 1*; *FA* 23.09.16; *FFP* 23.09.16; *FA* 14.10.16; *FA* (RoH) 14.10.16; *FFP* (RoH) 14.10.16; *FFP* (RoH) 30.12.16; *FA* (Service List) 06.01.17; *FA* 14.07.17 (KHS War Honours); *FA* (FRoH) 23.11.18; *FA* (KHS RoH) 29.03.19

Kinnaird, Andrew: Staff Sergeant (SE/7195 RAVC [16th Veterinary Hospital]); Died of bronchial pneumonia, 25.12.18, 44 years; 69 Victoria Road, Kirkcaldy; Gravestone in Bennochy Cemetery. Old Parish Church Memorial Panel; Kantara War Memorial Cemetery, Egypt. Grave F.332; Kirkcaldy War Memorial; *Soldiers Died* Part 80; *FA* (RoH) 18.01.19; *FFP* 11.01.19

Kinnear, Robert G.: Private (50769 North Staffordshire Regt [2/5th]. Formerly T/4/056927 RASC); DOW, 02.12.17, 33 years; 10 Fish Wynd, Kirkcaldy; Rocquigny-Equancourt Road British Cemetery, Manancourt Somme, France. Grave VI.E.13; Kirkcaldy War Memorial; *Soldiers Died* Part 60; *FFP* 22.12.17; *FFP* (BMD) 22.12.17; *FA* 29.12.17; *FA* (RoH) 19.01.18; *FA* (FRoH) 07.12.18; *FFP* (BMD) 07.12.18

Kinnell, John: Gunner (4234 RGA [108th Siege Batt'y] Labour Corps [Irish Command Labour Centre]); Died Edinburgh Royal Infirmary, 25.01.19, 36 years; Back Lane, Sinclairtown, Kirkcaldy; Gravestone in Dysart Cemetery; Dysart Cemetery, Kirkcaldy. Grave 49.V.Middle; Kirkcaldy War Memorial; *FFP* (BMD) 01.02.19; *FA* (RoH) 15.02.19

Kinninmonth, Ronald: Private (29660 Royal Scots [15th]) KIA near Arras, 09.04.17, 25 years; Lothriebank Wemyssfield, Kirkcaldy; Gravestone in Bennochy Cemetery. St Brycedale Church Plaque. Kirkcaldy High School War Memorial; Roclincourt Valley Cemetery, Pas de Calais, France. Grave IV.A.6; Kirkcaldy War Memorial; *Soldiers Died* Part 6; *FFP* 28.04.17; *FA* (BMD) 12.05.17; *FFP* (BMD) 12.05.17; *FA* (RoH) 19.05.17; *FFP* (RoH) 19.05.17; *FA* (CasList) 26.05.17; *FFP* (CasList) 26.05.17; *FA* 14.07.17 (KHS War Honours); *FFP* (Memorial List) 05.01.18; *FFP* (RoH) 13.04.18; *FA* (FRoH) 30.11.18; *FA* (KHS RoH) 29.03.19

Kinsman, Samuel Thomas: Guardsman (17369 Scots Guards [1st]); KIA, 27.09.18, 19 years; 3 Victoria Road, Kirkcaldy; Gravestone in Bennochy Cemetery. Old Parish Church Memorial Panel. Kirkcaldy High School War Memorial; Flesquieres Hill British Cemetery, Nord, France. Grave VIII.F.18; Kirkcaldy War Memorial; *Soldiers Died* Part 5; *FA* 05.10.18; *FFP* 05.10.18; *FFP* (BMD) 12.10.18; *FA* (RoH) 19.10.18; *FA* (FRoH) 14.12.18; *FA* (KHS RoH) 29.03.19; *FA* (KHS RoH) 19.07.19

Knox, Alexander: Lance Corporal (S/22512 Gordon Hldrs [4th]); KIA, 25.07.18; School Lane, Gallatown, Kirkcaldy; Soissons Memorial, Aisne, France; Kirkcaldy War Memorial; *Soldiers Died* Part 65; *FA* 09.11.18

Kyles, George: Private (7625 Seaforth Hldrs [13th] [Labour Corps]. Formerly 19205 Labour Coy); 09.01.18; Duhallow ADS Cemetery, Ieper, West Vlaanderen, Belgium. Grave II.F.12; Kirkcaldy War Memorial; *Soldiers Died* Part 80

Laing, David Davidson: Private (4132 Royal Scots [9th]); Wounded France. Died Western General Hospital, Cardiff. Buried Abbotshall, 15.10.16, 21 years; Swan Road/16 James Grove, Kirkcaldy; Gravestone in Abbotshall Churchyard. Kirkcaldy High School War Memorial; Abbotshall Parish Churchyard, Kirkcaldy. Grave Raith.27; Kirkcaldy War Memorial; *Soldiers Died* Part 6; *FA* 07.10.16; *FA* 21.10.16; *FA* (BMD) 21.10.16; *FFP* 21.10.16 (2 entries); *FFP* (BMD) 21.10.16; *FA* (RoH) 18.11.16; *FFP* (RoH) 18.11.16; *FFP* (RoH) 30.12.16; *FA* (Service List) 10.02.17; *FA* 14.07.17 (KHS War Honours); *FA* (BMD) 20.10.17; *FFP* (BMD) 20.10.17; *FA* (BMD) 19.10.18; *FA* (FRoH) 30.11.18; *FA* (KHS RoH) 29.03.19; *FA* (BMD) 18.10.19

Laing, Thomas: Private (Black Watch); Not identified on CWGC web site; Kirkcaldy War Memorial

Lambert, David Eadie: Lance Corporal (S/3735 Black Watch [8th] "A" Coy); KIA Ypres, 14.10.15, 20 years; 21 Victoria Road, Kirkcaldy; Railway Dugouts Burial Ground, Zillebeke, Ieper, West Vlaanderen, Belgium. Grave I.B.8; Kirkcaldy War Memorial; *FA* 23.10.15; *Soldiers Died* Part 46; War Album 15/16; *FA* 23.10.15; *FFP* 23.10.15; *FFP* (BMD) 23.10.15; *Scotsman* (CasList) 25.10.15; *FA* (RoH) 13.11.15; *FFP* 05.08.16 Roll of the Brave; *FFP* (BMD) 14.10.16; *FA* 24.08.18; *FA* (FRoH) 16.11.18; Wauchope Vol 3

Lang, Charles F.: Lance Corporal (19991 HLI [12th]); Killed Hill 70, Loos, 25.09.15; The Cottage, Kinghorn Road, Kirkcaldy; Invertiel Parish Church Memorial Table; Loos Memorial, Pas de Calais, France. Panels 108-112; Kirkcaldy War Memorial; *Soldiers Died* Part 63; *FFP* 30.10.15; *FFP* 08.01.16; *FA* (RoH) 15.01.16 (2 items); *FFP* 15.01.16; *FA* 05.02.16; *FFP* 05.08.16 Roll of the Brave; *FA* 26.08.16; *FA* (FRoH) 16.11.18

Lang, George Boak, MM: Sergeant (49849 Royal Engineers [93rd Fld Coy]); KIA Cambrai. Buried Audencourt, 14.10.18, 23 years; Langside, 110 Dunnikier Road, Kirkcaldy; Gravestone in Bennochy Cemetery. Kirkcaldy High School War Memorial; Coudry British Cemetery, Nord, France. Grave III.F.7; Kirkcaldy War Memorial; *FA* 02.11.18; *Soldiers Died* Part 4; *FA* 26.10.18; *FA* 02.11.18; *FA* (BMD) 02.11.18; *FA* (RoH) 16.11.18; *FFP* (RoH) 16.11.18; *FA* (FRoH) 14.12.18; *FA* (FRoH) 21.12.18; *FA* (KHS RoH) 29.03.19; *FA* (KHS RoH) 19.07.19; *FA* (BMD) 11.10.19; *FA* 01.11.19

Langslow, William: Private (3/2121 Black Watch [3rd] att'd [1st]); DOW, 25.10.14, 21 years; 65 Rosabelle Street, Kirkcaldy; Cement House Cemetery, Langemark-Poelcapelle, West Vlaanderen, Belgium. Grave VIIA.E.4; Kirkcaldy War Memorial; *Soldiers Died* Part 46; War Album 14/15; *Dundee Advertiser* 03.12.14; *FA* (BMD) 05.12.14; *FFP* 05.12.14 (2 entries); *FFP* (BMD) 05.12.14; *FA* (CasList) 19.12.14; *FA* 02.01.15; *FA* (CasList) 20.02.15; *FFP* (BMD) 02.10.15; *FFP* 05.08.16 Roll of the Brave; *FFP* (BMD) 28.10.16; *FA* (Service List) 20.01.17; *FA* (Service List) 17.03.17; *FFP* (BMD) 27.10.17; *FA* (FRoH) 16.11.18; Wauchope Vol 1; RoH Dunnikier Colliery

Lascelles, George Kilgour: Private (S/29668 Cameron Hldrs [6th]); Brother of Robert Lascelles; KIA, 28.03.18, 20 years; 233 High Street, Kirkcaldy; Gravestone in Dysart Cemetery; Arras Memorial, Pas de Calais, France. Bay 9; Kirkcaldy War Memorial; *Soldiers Died* Part 66; *FFP* 12.10.18; *FA* 19.10.18

Mystery surrounded the death of Private George **Lascelles**. Having been wounded in action, Lascelles was put into an ambulance, but there is no record of him being admitted to any hospital thereafter. The Red Cross wrote to the family to report that there was heavy shelling in the area at the time and it is assumed that the ambulance he was in was blown up, but there is no direct evidence of this. George's brother, Robert, was killed four days previously.

Lascelles, Robert: Private (15907 KOSB [6th]); Brother of George Lascelles; KIA, 24.03.18, 22 years; 233 High Street, Kirkcaldy; Gravestone in Dysart Cemetery; Pozieres Memorial, Somme, France. Panel 37; Kirkcaldy War Memorial; *Soldiers Died* Part 30; *FFP* 12.10.18; *FA* 19.10.18; *FA* (RoH) 13.09.19

Latto, George: Private (S/10504 Cameron Hldrs [2nd] "C" Coy); Brother-in-law of George Bain; MIA Salonika, 16.03.17; 21 years; 20 Buchanan Street, Kirkcaldy; Gravestone in Bennochy Cemetery. Raith Church Memorial Plaque; Doiran Memorial, Greece; Kirkcaldy War Memorial; *FA* 12.05.17; *Soldiers Died* Part 66; *FA* (CasList) 14.04.17; *FA* 05.05.17; *FFP* 26.05.17; *FFP* 27.07.18; *FFP* (BMD) 27.07.18; *FA* 03.08.18; *FA* (RoH) 14.09.18; *FFP* (RoH) 14.09.18; *FA* (FRoH) 14.12.18

Lauder, Leslie: Lance Corporal (S/13566 Gordon Hldrs [8/10th] [Machine Gun Section]); Listed in *FA* (CasList) 30.09.16 as Lander. Brother of Robert Lauder; KIA, 30.08.16, 22 years; Theatre Buildings, 258a High Street, Kirkcaldy; St Brycedale Church Plaque; Thiepval Memorial, Somme, France. Pier & Face 15B & 15C; Kirkcaldy War Memorial; *Soldiers Died* Part 65; *FFP* 16.09.16; *FA* 23.09.16; *FFP* 23.09.16; *FA* (CasList) 30.09.16; *FFP* (CasList) 30.09.16; *FA* (RoH) 14.10.16; *FFP* (RoH) 14.10.16; *FA* 28.10.16; *FA* (Service List) 09.12.16; *FFP* (RoH) 30.12.16; *FA* (Memorial Service) 06.01.17; *FA* (BMD) 30.06.17; *FFP* 30.06.17; *FFP* (BMD) 30.06.17; *FFP* (BMD) 24.08.18; *FA* (FRoH) 23.11.18

Lauder, Robert E.: Private (S/9584 Gordon Hldrs [1st]); Brother of Leslie Lauder; KIA, 18.07.16, 20 years; Theatre Buildings, 258a High Street, Kirkcaldy; St Brycedale Church Plaque; Thiepval Memorial, Somme, France. Pier & Face 15B & 15C; Kirkcaldy War Memorial; *Soldiers Died* Part 65; *FFP* 16.09.16; *FA* 23.09.16; *FA* (CasList) 23.09.16; *FFP* 23.09.16; *FA* (Service List) 28.10.16; *FA* (Service List) 09.12.16; *FA* (Memorial Service) 06.01.17; *FA* (BMD) 30.06.17; *FFP* 30.06.17; *FFP* (BMD) 30.06.17; *FA* 14.07.17; *FFP* 14.07.17; *FFP* (BMD) 24.08.18; *FA* (FRoH) 07.12.18

Laurie, Alexander: Sergeant (7967; Cameron Hldrs [5th]. Formerly 280 Black Watch); KIA. On CWGC as Lawre; 25.09.15; Loos Memorial, Pas de Calais, France. Panels 119-124; Kirkcaldy War Memorial; *Soldiers Died* Part 66

Laverance, William: Lance Corporal (S/7404 Gordon Hldrs [2nd] [Lewis Gun Section]); Brother-in-law of Hugh McDade. Referred to as Lawrence in *FA* 16.11.18; KIA, 07.05.17, 41 years; 7 Garnock's Lane, Kirkcaldy; Arras Memorial, Pas de Calais, France. Bays 8 & 9; Kirkcaldy War Memorial; *FA* 30.09.16; *Soldiers Died* Part 65; *FA* 19.05.17; *FFP* 26.05.17; *FA* 02.06.17; *FFP* (BMD) 02.06.17; *FA* (BMD) 09.06.17; *FA* (RoH) 16.06.17; *FFP* (CasList) 16.06.17; *FFP* (RoH) 16.06.17; *FFP* (BMD) 11.05.18; *FA* 16.11.18; *FA* (FRoH) 30.11.18; *FFP* 30.11.18

Laverty, Frank Scott: Private (2356 Black Watch [1st]); KIA, 26.09.15, 24 years; 203/234 Links Street, Kirkcaldy; Loos Memorial, Pas de Calais, France. Panels 78-83; Kirkcaldy War Memorial; *Soldiers Died* Part 46; War Album 15/16; *FA* 16.10.15; *FA* (RoH) 13.11.15; *Scotsman* 15.11.15; *FA* 20.11.15; *FFP* 05.08.16 Roll of the Brave; *FA* 12.08.16; *FA* (Service List) 25.11.16; *FA* (Service List) 02.12.16; *FA* (FRoH) 16.11.18; Wauchope Vol 1

Law, George: Private (8332 HLI [12th]); DOW, 28.05.16, 31 years; Balfour Street/13 Nile Street, Kirkcaldy; St Brycedale Church Plaque; Lillers Communal Cemetery & Extension, Pas de Calais, France. Grave V.C.11; Kirkcaldy War Memorial; *Soldiers Died* Part 63; *FFP* 10.06.16; *FA* 17.06.16; *FA* (RoH) 17.06.16; *FFP* (RoH) 17.06.16; *FFP* 05.08.16 Roll of the Brave; *FA* (Memorial Service) 06.01.17; *FA* (Service List) 24.03.17; *FA* (FRoH) 23.11.18

Lawrence, Henry: Private (186 RAMC [Fld Amb] Scottish Horse [2nd]); DOW Salonika, 25.11.16, 27 years *Fifeshire Advertiser*, Kirkcaldy; Abbotshall Parish Church Memorial Plaque; Struma Military Cemetery Kalocastron, Greece. Grave III.A.3; Kirkcaldy War Memorial; *FA* 30.12.16; *Soldiers Died* Part 79; *FA* 30.12.16; *FA* (RoH) 13.01.17; *FFP* (RoH) 13.01.17; *FA* 24.02.17; *FA* 20.07.18; *FA* (FRoH) 30.11.18; *FA* 19.11.21

Lawson, Alexander: Private (S/9211 Black Watch [9th]); Brother of John Lawson;KIA, 17.08.16, 32 years; 34 Nicol Street, Kirkcaldy; Bethelfield Church Plaque; Thiepval Memorial, Somme, France. Pier & Face 10A; Kirkcaldy War Memorial; *Soldiers Died* Part 46; *FA* (BMD) 09.09.16; *FFP* 09.09.16; *FFP* (BMD) 09.09.16; *FA* (CasList) 16.09.16; *FA* (RoH) 16.09.16; *FFP* (CasList) 16.09.16; *FFP* (RoH) 16.09.16; *FA* 14.10.16; *FA* (Service List) 18.11.16; *FFP* (RoH) 30.12.16; *FA* (Service List) 17.02.17; *FFP* 16.06.17; *FFP* (BMD) 16.06.17; *FA* (BMD) 23.06.17; *FA* (BMD) 07.07.17; *FFP* (BMD) 07.07.17; *FFP* (BMD) 27.04.18; *FA* (FRoH) 23.11.18; Wauchope Vol 3

Lawson, Andrew: Private (41059 KOSB [6th]. Formerly 2541 F & F Yeo); KIA France, 13.10.17, 22 years; 5 Quality Street, Kirkcaldy; Raith Church Memorial Plaque; Tyne Cot Memorial, Zonnebeke, West Vlaanderen, Belgium. Panel 66-68; Kirkcaldy War Memorial; *FA* 10.11.17; *Soldiers Died* Part 30; *FA* 03.11.17; *FFP* 03.11.17; *FFP* (BMD) 03.11.17; *FA* (BMD) 10.11.17; *FFP* (BMD) 10.11.17; *FA* (RoH) 17.11.17; *FFP* (RoH) 17.11.17; *FFP* (CasList) 24.11.17; *FA* (FRoH) 07.12.18

Lawson, James: Private (S/11478 A & S Hldrs [1/8th]); KIA Bois Gerard, 28.07.18, 27 years; 5 Masereene Road/ Mitchell Street, Kirkcaldy; Buzancy Military Cemetery, Aisne, France. Grave II.E.11/15; Kirkcaldy War Memorial; *Soldiers Died* Part 70; *FA* 12.08.16; *FFP* 19.08.16; *FFP* 17.08.18; *FFP* 24.08.18; *FFP* 24.08.18; *FFP* (BMD) 24.08.18; *FA* (BMD) 31.08.18; *FA* (RoH) 14.09.18; *FFP* (RoH) 14.09.18; *FA* (FRoH) 14.12.18

Lawson, James: Private (S/31547 Cameron Hldrs [6th]. Formerly 6675 Lovat Scouts); KIA, 21.03.18, 19 years; Sutherland Street/11 Park Road, Kirkcaldy; Monchy British Cemetery, Monchy le Preux, Pas de Calais, France. Grave II.C.21; Kirkcaldy War Memorial; *Soldiers Died* Part 66; *FA* 13.04.18; *FFP* (RoH) 13.04.18; *FA* (RoH) 18.05.18; *FFP* (RoH) 18.05.18; *FA* (FRoH) 16.11.18; *FA* (FRoH) 07.12.18

Lawson, James: Private (16123 KOSB [1st]); Drowned when the *Royal Edward* was sunk in the Aegean, 13.08.15, 23 years; 109 Nether Street, Kirkcaldy; Gravestone in Dysart Cemetery; Helles Memorial, Gallipoli, Turkey. Panels 84-92 or 220-222; Kirkcaldy War Memorial; *FA* 04.09.15; *FFP* 04.09.15; *Soldiers Died* Part 30; War Album 15/16; *FA* 21.08.15; *FFP* 28.08.15; *FA* 04.09.15; *FFP* 04.09.15; *FA* (RoH) 18.09.15; *FFP* 05.08.16 Roll of the Brave; *FA* 12.08.16; *FFP* (BMD) 19.08.16; *FA* (Service List) 28.10.16; *FA* (Service List) 30.12.16; *FFP* (BMD) 18.08.17; *FFP* (BMD) 17.08.18; *FA* (FRoH) 16.11.18

Lawson, James Betts M., MC: Lieutenant (AIF; Australian Infantry [41st]); Native of Edentown, Fife. On Australian War Memorial as John Betts Lawson. Brother of William Lawson; KIA, 29.09.18, 26 years; Villers-Bretonneux Memorial, Somme, France. Panel 134; Australian War Memorial web site; Kirkcaldy War Memorial; *FA* 19.10.18; *FA* 12.10.18; *FA* (BMD) 12.10.18; *FFP* 12.10.18; *FFP* (BMD) 12.10.18; *FA* (RoH) 19.10.18; *FA* (FRoH) 14.12.18

Lawson, John: Sergeant (734 Black Watch [1st]); KIA Ypres, 10.11.14, 24 years; 17 Coal Wynd, Kirkcaldy; Ypres (Menin Gate) Memorial, Ieper, West Vlaanderen, Belgium. Panel 37; Kirkcaldy War Memorial; *FA* 10.10.14; *FA* 12.12.14; *FFP* 12.12.14; *Soldiers Died* Part 46; War Album 14/15; *Daily Telegraph* 00.12.14; *FA* 12.12.14; *FFP* 12.12.14; *FFP* (BMD) 12.12.14; *FA* (CasList) 19.12.14; *FA* 02.01.15; *FFP* 09.01.15; *FA* (CasList) 20.02.15; *FFP* 05.08.16 Roll of the Brave; *FA* (Service List) 04.11.16; *FA* (Memorial Service) 06.01.17; *FA* (Service List) 03.02.17; *FA* (FRoH) 16.11.18; Wauchope Vol 1

Lawson, John: Private (S/12364 Seaforth Hldrs [8th]); Brother of Alexander Lawson;KIA, 23.04.17; 31 East Smeaton Street, Kirkcaldy; Guemappe British Cemetery, Wancourt, Pas de Calais, France. Grave I.C.20; Kirkcaldy War Memorial; *Soldiers Died* Part 64; *FA* (Service List) 17.02.17; *FA* (CasList) 02.06.17; *FFP* (CasList) 02.06.17; *FFP* 16.06.17; *FFP* (BMD) 16.06.17; *FA* (BMD) 23.06.17; *FA* (BMD) 07.07.17; *FFP* (BMD) 07.07.17; *FA* 14.07.17; *FFP* 14.07.17; *FFP* (BMD) 27.04.18; *FA* (FRoH) 07.12.18

Lawson, Johnstone: Private (S/8706 Seaforth Hldrs [1st]); KIA Mesopotamia, 05.11.17; 33 Oswald Road, Kirkcaldy; Basra Memorial, Iraq. Panels 37 & 64; Kirkcaldy War Memorial; *Soldiers Died* Part 64; *FFP* 01.12.17; *FFP* (CasList) 08.12.17; *FA* (RoH) 15.12.17; *FFP* (CasList) 15.12.17; *FFP* (RoH) 15.12.17; *FA* (FRoH) 07.12.18

Lawson, Michael Brodie: Private (27098 Royal Scots [12th]); KIA Arras, 12.04.17, 20 years; 4 Malcolm's Wynd, Kirkcaldy; Union Church Plaque; Point-Du-Jour Military Cemetery, Athies, Pas de Calais, France. Grave Sp. Mem. B.8; Kirkcaldy War Memorial; *Soldiers Died* Part 6; *FA* 19.05.17; *FA* (BMD) 19.05.17; *FFP* 19.05.17; *FFP* (BMD) 19.05.17; *FA* (CasList) 02.06.17; *FFP* (CasList) 02.06.17; *FA* (RoH) 16.06.17; *FFP* (RoH) 16.06.17; *FFP* (BMD) 13.04.18; *FA* (FRoH) 30.11.18

Lawson, William: Private (S/4069 Seaforth Hldrs [9th]); Brother of James Betts M. Lawson;DOW, 06.06.17, 23 years; 33 Oswald Road, Kirkcaldy; St Nicolas British Cemetery, Pas de Calais, France. Grave I.L.16; Kirkcaldy War Memorial; *Soldiers Died* Part 64; *FFP* (CasList) 07.07.17; *FA* 14.07.17; *FFP* 14.07.17; *FA* 13.07.18; *FA* 12.10.18; *FA* (FRoH) 07.12.18

Leighton, John: Private (352 Cameronians [Scottish Rifles] [8th]); In *FFP* (BMD) 28.10.16 under mother's name Latto, KIA Dardanelles, 28.06.15, 22 years; 18 Doctor's Row, Gallatown, Kirkcaldy; Barony Church Plaque; Helles Memorial, Gallipoli, Turkey. Panels 92-97; Kirkcaldy War Memorial; *Soldiers Died* Part 31; *FFP* 09.10.15; *FA* 23.09.16; *FA* (BMD) 23.09.16; *FFP* 23.09.16; *FA* (RoH) 14.10.16; *FFP* (RoH) 14.10.16; *FFP* (BMD) 28.10.16 ; *FA* (Service List) 09.12.16; *FFP* (RoH) 30.12.16; *FA* (Service List) 31.03.17; *FFP* (BMD) 07.07.17; *FA* (FRoH) 23.11.18

Leishman, Alexander: Private (S/32027 Cameron Hldrs [6th]. Formerly Lovat Scouts); KIA, 23.07.18, 19 years; 97 Balsusney Road, Kirkcaldy; Kirkcaldy High School War Memorial; Soissons Memorial, Aisne, France; Kirkcaldy War Memorial; *Soldiers Died* Part 66; *FA* 10.08.18; *FFP* 10.08.18; *FFP* (BMD) 10.08.18; *FA* (BMD) 17.08.18; *FA* (RoH) 14.09.18; *FFP* (RoH) 14.09.18; *FA* (FRoH) 14.12.18; *FA* (KHS RoH) 29.03.19

Leitch, John: Sergeant (4852 Black Watch [1/7th]. Formerly F & F Yeo); DOW, 30.07.16, 20 years; 37 Balfour Street, Kirkcaldy; Gravestone in Bennochy Cemetery. Kirkcaldy High School War Memorial; Albert Communal Cemetery Extension, Albert, Somme, France. Grave I.L.53; Kirkcaldy War Memorial; *FA* 19.08.16; *Soldiers Died* Part 46; *FA* 12.08.16; *FA* (BMD) 19.08.16; *FFP* 19.08.16; *FFP* (BMD) 19.08.16; *FA* (BMD) 26.08.16; *FA* (RoH) 16.09.16; *FFP* (CasList) 16.09.16; *FFP* (RoH) 16.09.16; *FA* (Service List) 18.11.16; *FFP* (RoH) 30.12.16; *FA* 14.07.17 (KHS War Honours); *FFP* (BMD) 28.07.17; *FFP* (BMD) 27.07.18; *FA* (FRoH) 23.11.18; *FA* (KHS RoH) 29.03.19; Wauchope Vol 2

Lendrum, Alfred Atkinson: Private (3030217; CEF; CCRC [15th Bn] [Central Ontario Regt]); KIA, 02.09.18; Denend, Kirkcaldy; Kirkcaldy High School War Memorial; Dominion Cemetery, Hendecourt-Les-Cagnicourt, Pas de Calais, France. Grave II.C.6; Kirkcaldy War Memorial; *CBoR* Page 448; *FA* (BMD) 21.09.18; *FFP* (BMD) 21.09.18

Lennie, Lawrence: Lance Corporal (S/4447 Seaforth Hldrs [9th]); KIA, 24.03.18; 29 Bank Street, Kirkcaldy Sinclairtown Parish Church War Memorial Chair Pozieres Memorial, Somme, France. Panels 72-73 Kirkcaldy War Memorial; *Soldiers Died* Part 64; *FA* 25.05.18; *FA* (RoH) 13.09.19

Lennox, George Charles Pennycook: Private (S/3153 Cameron Hldrs [5th]. Formerly 4140 Lovat Scouts & 676 Machine Gun Corps); DOW, 20.04.18, 19 years Rosebank, 137 Dunnikier Road, Kirkcaldy; Barony Church Plaque. Kirkcaldy High School War Memorial Gravestone in MacDuff Cemetery, East Wemyss Haringhe (Bandaghem) Military Cemetery Poperinge, West Vlaanderen, Belgium. Grave V.C.24 Kirkcaldy War Memorial; *Soldiers Died* Part 66; *FA* 04.05.18; *FFP* (RoH) 04.05.18; *FA* (RoH) 18.05.18 *FFP* 18.05.18; *FA* (FRoH) 07.12.18; *FA* (KHS RoH) 29.03.19; *FA* (BMD) 19.04.19

Leslie, William: Lance Corporal (124 Black Watch [1st] "A" Coy); KIA, 09.05.15, 28 years; 116 Mid Street/42 West Smeaton Street, Kirkcaldy; Barony Church Plaque Gravestone in Dysart Cemetery; Le Touret Memorial Pas de Calais, France. Panels 24-26; Kirkcaldy War Memorial; *Soldiers Died* Part 46; War Album 15; *FA* 05.06.15; *FFP* (BMD) 05.06.15; *Dundee Advertiser* 05.06.15; *Scotsman* 05.06.15; *FFP* 12.06.15; *FA* 19.06.15 *FFP* (CasList) 03.07.15; *FFP* (BMD) 13.05.16 (2 entries) *FFP* 05.08.16 Roll of the Brave; *FA* (Service List) 28.10.16; *FA* (Service List) 23.12.16; *FA* (Service List) 24.02.17; *FFP* (BMD) 12.05.17; *FA* (FRoH) 16.11.18 Wauchope Vol 1

Lessels, John: Private (47729 Royal Scots [2nd]. Formerly 33624 Royal Scots Fusiliers); KIA, 02.09.18, 37 years 125 Nether Street, Kirkcaldy; Vraucourt Copse Cemetery Vaulx-Vraucourt, Pas de Calais, France. Grave I.B.22 Kirkcaldy War Memorial; *Soldiers Died* Part 6; *FA* 05.10.18; *FFP* 05.10.18; *FFP* (BMD) 05.10.18; *FA* (RoH) 19.10.18; *FA* 26.10.18; *FA* (FRoH) 14.12.18

Lessels, Thomas: Private (Machine Gun Corps); Died of pneumonia Steppinghill Hospital, Stockport, 11.07.18, 27 years; 205/7 St Clair Street, Kirkcaldy; Barony Church Plaque; Not identified on CWGC web site; Kirkcaldy War Memorial; *FA* 20.07.18; *FFP* (BMD) 20.07.18; *FA* (RoH) 14.09.18; *FFP* (RoH) 14.09.18; *FA* (FRoH) 14.12.18

Lessels, William: Trooper (345220 Black Watch [14th] [F & F Yeo Bn]. Formerly 2104 F & F Yeo); KIA, 22.09.18; 88 Links Street, Kirkcaldy; Abbotshall Parish Church Memorial Plaque; Templeux-Le-Guerard British Cemetery, Somme, France. Grave II.C.38; Kirkcaldy War Memorial; *FA* 12.10.18; *Soldiers Died* Part 46; *FA* 05.10.18; *FFP* (BMD) 12.10.18; *FA* (RoH) 19.10.18; *FA* (FRoH) 14.12.18; *FA* 19.11.21; Wauchope Vol 3; Ogilvie

Lewis, Frederick G. L., MM: Sergeant (761 RFA (129th Btt'y) [42nd Bde]); Killed in an enemy air raid at Cambrai, 24.10.18, 23 years; 86 Miller Street/86 Nether Street, Kirkcaldy; Pathhead Parish Church Memorial Plaques & Windows; Solesmes Communal Cemetery, Nord, France. Grave A.9; Kirkcaldy War Memorial; *FA* 16.11.18; *Soldiers Died* Part 2; *FA* 09.11.18; *FA* 16.11.18; *FA* (RoH) 16.11.18; *FFP* 16.11.18; *FFP* (RoH) 16.11.18; *FA* (FRoH) 14.12.18; *FA* 20.12.19; *FFP* 21.06.24

Lile, Arthur: Private (SAEF; South African Scottish); Drowned when the *Galway Castle* was sunk, 27 years; Abbotshall House, Nicol Street, Kirkcaldy; Not identified on CWGC web site; Kirkcaldy War Memorial; *FA* 21.09.18; *FA* (BMD) 21.09.18; *FFP* (BMD) 21.09.18; *FA* (RoH) 19.10.18; *FA* (FRoH) 14.12.18

Lironi, Paul D. T.: Corporal (3/1300 Black Watch [2nd] Meerut Div, Indian Expeditionary Force); On CWGC as P. Lirone; KIA Flanders, 09.05.15, 24 years; 3 Cross Street, Kirkcaldy; St Michael's Church Memorial Plaque; Le Touret Memorial, Pas de Calais, France. Panels 24-26; Kirkcaldy War Memorial; *FA* 12.06.15; *FFP* 12.06.15; *Soldiers Died* Part 46; War Album 15; *FA* 05.06.15 (2 entries); *FA* (BMD) 05.06.15; *FFP* (BMD) 05.06.15; *Dundee Advertiser* 05.06.15; *Scotsman* 05.06.15; *FA* 12.06.15; *FFP* 12.06.15; *FA* (BMD) 19.06.15; *FFP* (CasList) 03.07.15; *FFP* 05.08.16 Roll of the Brave; *FA* (Service List) 24.02.17; *FA* (FRoH) 16.11.18; Wauchope Vol 1

Livingstone, John McDonald: Private (40188 Royal Scots [11th]. Formerly 2482 F & F Yeo & 26785 KOSB); KIA, 22.10.16, 19 years; 30 Bridgeton, Kirkcaldy; Dunnikier Church Roll of Honour; Thiepval Memorial, Somme, France. Pier & Face 6D & 7D; Kirkcaldy War Memorial; *Soldiers Died* Part 6; *FA* 18.11.16; *FA* (BMD) 18.11.16; *FFP* (BMD) 18.11.16; *FFP* 25.11.16; *FFP* (CasList) 02.12.16; *FA* (RoH) 16.12.16; *FFP* (RoH) 30.12.16; *FA* (Service List) 24.02.17; *FA* (FRoH) 30.11.18; *FA* 26.04.19

Lockhart, George Barclay: Captain (RFC. Formerly HCB); Cousin of John Sutherland Lockhart; KIA, 14.04.17, 24 years; Milton Villa, Milton Road, Kirkcaldy; St Brycedale Church Plaque. Kirkcaldy High School War Memorial; La Chaudiere Military Cemetery, Vimy, Pas de Calais, France. Grave VI.D.17; Kirkcaldy War Memorial; *FA* 02.10.15; *FA* 21.04.17; *Officers Died*; *Cross of Sacrifice Vol 1*; *FA* 21.04.17; *FA* (BMD) 21.04.17; *FFP* 21.04.17; *FFP* (BMD) 21.04.17; *FFP* 05.05.17; *FA* (RoH) 19.05.17; *FFP* (RoH) 19.05.17; *FA* 14.07.17 (KHS War Honours); *FFP* (Memorial List) 05.01.18; *FA* (FRoH) 30.11.18; *FA* (KHS RoH) 29.03.19; RFC/RAF RoH

Lockhart, James Herbert: 2nd Lieutenant (Black Watch [1/7th]); KIA, 30.07.16, 33 years; The Elms, Nicol Street, Kirkcaldy; Gravestone in Abbotshall Churchyard. Abbotshall Parish Church Memorial Plaque. Kirkcaldy High School War Memorial; Combles Communal Cemtery Extension, Somme, France. Grave 4.A.11; Kirkcaldy War Memorial; *Officers Died*; *Cross of Sacrifice Vol 1*; *FA* 12.08.16 (3 entries); *FA* (BMD) 12.08.16; *FFP* 12.08.16; *FFP* (BMD) 12.08.16; *FA* (RoH) 16.09.16; *FFP* (RoH) 16.09.16; *FA* (Service List) 18.11.16; *FFP* (RoH) 30.12.16; *FA* 14.07.17 (KHS War Honours); *FA* (FRoH) 23.11.18; *FA* (KHS RoH) 29.03.19; *FA* 19.11.21; Wauchope Vol 2

Lockhart, John Sutherland: Lieutenant (Royal Scots [2nd]); Cousin of George Lockhart; KIA, 10.05.16, 23 years; Allanbank, West Albert Road, Kirkcaldy; Gravestone in Bennochy Cemetery. St Brycedale Church Plaque. Kirkcaldy High School War Memorial; La Clytte Military Cemetery, Heuvelland, West Vlaanderen, Belgium. Grave I.B.27; Kirkcaldy War Memorial; *FA* 04.09.15; *FA* 20.05.16; *FFP* 20.05.16; *Officers Died*; *Cross of Sacrifice Vol 1*; *FA* 07.08.15; *FA* 20.05.16; *FA* (BMD) 20.05.16; *FFP* 20.05.16; *FFP* (BMD) 20.05.16; *FA* 27.05.16 (3 entries); *FFP* 27.05.16 (2 entries); *FA* 17.06.16; *FA* (RoH) 17.06.16; *FFP* (RoH) 17.06.16; *FA* 24.06.16; *FFP* 05.08.16 Roll of the Brave; *FA* (Service List) 30.12.16; *FA* (Memorial Service) 06.01.17; *FA* (BMD) 11.05.18; *FFP* (BMD) 11.05.18; *FA* (FRoH) 23.11.18; *FA* (KHS RoH) 29.03.19; *FA* (BMD) 10.05.19

Lornie, Alexander Pratt: Private (12/2167; NZEF; Auckland Infantry Regt); KIA Gallipoli, 05.06.15, 24 years; 40 Lady Helen Street, Kirkcaldy; Lone Pine Memorial, Turkey. Panel 72; Kirkcaldy War Memorial; NZEF Roll of Honour; *FFP* 14.08.15; *FA* 21.08.15; *FA* (RoH) 18.09.15; *FFP* 05.08.16 Roll of the Brave; *FA* (Service List) 13.01.17; *FA* (FRoH) 16.11.18

Louden, David: Private (106369; CEF; Canadian Mounted Rifles [2nd]); KIA France, 1917, 19 years; Park Road, Kirkcaldy; Not identified on CWGC web site; Kirkcaldy War Memorial; *CBoR* Page 277; *FFP* 14.04.17; *FA* 21.04.17; *FA* (RoH) 19.05.17; *FFP* (RoH) 19.05.17; *FA* (FRoH) 30.11.18; Kirkcaldy Council Memorial Scroll

Louden, George: Corporal (S/11358 Black Watch [8th]); DOW, 03.05.17, 31 years; 75 Commercial Street, Kirkcaldy; Pathhead Parish Church Memorial Plaques & Windows; Duisans British Cemetery, Etrun, Pas de Calais, France. Grave IV.D.19; Kirkcaldy War Memorial; *Soldiers Died* Part 46; *FA* 19.05.17; *FFP* 26.05.17; *FA* (RoH) 16.06.17; *FFP* (RoH) 16.06.17; *FA* (FRoH) 30.11.18; *FFP* 21.06.24; Wauchope Vol 3

Louden, John: Corporal (S/3240 Black Watch [8th]); 25.09.15; Pathhead Parish Church Memorial Plaques & Windows; Loos Memorial, Pas de Calais, France. Panels 78-83; Kirkcaldy War Memorial; *Soldiers Died* Part 46; *FFP* 21.06.24; Wauchope Vol 3

Louden, Robert L.: Private (S/40703 Black Watch [8th]. Formerly 2655 F & F Yeo); KIA Passchendaele, 12.10.17, 21 years; 14 Cowan Street, Kirkcaldy; Gravestone in Bennochy Cemetery. West End Congregational Church Memorial Plaque; Tyne Cot Memorial, Zonnebeke, West Vlaanderen, Belgium. Panels 94-96; Kirkcaldy War Memorial; *FA* 03.11.17; *Soldiers Died* Part 46; *FA* 27.10.17; *FA* (BMD) 27.10.17; *FFP* 27.10.17; *FFP* (BMD) 27.10.17; *FA* 03.11.17; *FA* (RoH) 17.11.17; *FFP* (CasList) 17.11.17; *FFP* (RoH) 17.11.17; *FA* (BMD) 12.10.18; *FFP* (BMD) 12.10.18; *FA* (FRoH) 07.12.18; *FA* (BMD) 18.10.19; Wauchope Vol 3

Love, Charles Goode Landels: Private (201961; CEF; Canadian Infantry [4th] 1st Div 1st Bde. [Central Ontario Regt]); Died of trench nethritis in Military Hospital, Endell Street, London, 02.09.17, 31 years; 4 Bennochy Terrace, Kirkcaldy/White House, Dunshelt, Auchtermuchty; Whytescauseway Baptist Church Memorial Plaque. Kirkcaldy High School War Memorial; Bennochy Cemetery, Kirkcaldy. Grave FF89; Kirkcaldy War Memorial; *CBoR* Page 277; *FA* 08.09.17; *FA* (BMD) 08.09.17; *FFP* 08.09.17; *FFP* (BMD) 08.09.17; *FA* 15.09.17; *FFP* 15.09.17; *FA* 13.07.18; *FA* (KHS RoH) 29.03.19

Low, Herbert George Andrew: Private (632663 London Regt [1/20th] [County of London]. Formerly 81674 RAMC); KIA, 23.03.18, 23 years; 36 Nelson Street, Kirkcaldy; Gravestone in Bennochy Cemetery. Old Parish Church Memorial Panel; Arras Memorial, Pas de Calais, France. Bays 9 & 10; Kirkcaldy War Memorial; *Soldiers Died* Part 76

Low, John: Gunner (6078 RFA [48th Bde] "B" Batt'y); DOW, 12.05.17; 7 St Mary's Place, Kirkcaldy; Duisans British Cemetery, Etrun, Pas de Calais, France. Grave III.M.28; Kirkcaldy War Memorial; *Soldiers Died* Part 2; *FA* (FRoH) 07.12.18

Lumsden, James Christie: Private (S/7584 Gordon Hldrs [1st] "D" Coy); KIA, 18.06.15, 19 years; 88 Overton Road, Kirkcaldy; Pathhead Parish Church Memorial Plaques & Windows; Ypres (Menin Gate) Memorial, Ieper, West Vlaanderen, Belgium. Panel 38; Kirkcaldy War Memorial; *FA* 07.08.15; *Soldiers Died* Part 65; War Album 15; *FA* 03.07.15; *FFP* 03.07.15; *FFP* (CasList) 03.07.15; *FA* (BMD) 10.07.15; *FA* (RoH) 17.07.15; *FA* 20.11.15; *FFP* (BMD) 17.06.16; *FFP* 05.08.16 Roll of the Brave; *FA* (Service List) 18.11.16; *FFP* (BMD) 16.06.17; *FFP* (BMD) 22.06.18; *FA* (FRoH) 16.11.18; *FFP* 21.06.24

Lundy, Arthur G.: Private (17183 KOSB [7/8th]); KIA Soissons, 23.07.18, 23 years; 160 Overton Road, Kirkcaldy; Buzancy Military Cemetery, Aisne, France. Grave II.B.3; Kirkcaldy War Memorial; *Soldiers Died* Part 30; *FA* 20.09.19

Lynch, George: Private (2697 Black Watch [8th]); KIA, 27.09.15, 21 years; 68 Overton Road, Kirkcaldy; Loos Memorial, Pas de Calais, France. Panels 78-83; Kirkcaldy War Memorial; *FA* 13.11.15; *Soldiers Died* Part 46; War Album 15/16; *FA* 06.11.15; *Scotsman* 08.11.15; *FA* (RoH) 13.11.15; *FFP* 05.08.16 Roll of the Brave; *FA* (Service List) 18.11.16; *FA* (FRoH) 16.11.18; Wauchope Vol 3

Lynch, James M.: Private (622 Black Watch [2nd]); KIA Mesopotamia, 07.01.16; 75 Commercial Street, Kirkcaldy; Union Church Plaque; Amara War Cemetery, Iraq. Grave XX.H.19; Kirkcaldy War Memorial; *Soldiers Died* Part 46; *FA* 19.02.16; *FFP* 19.02.16; *FFP* (BMD) 19.02.16; *Evening News* 19.02.16; *Scotsman* 21.02.16; *FFP* 05.08.16 Roll of the Brave; *FA* (Service List) 16.12.16; *FFP* (BMD) 20.01.17; *FA* (FRoH) 23.11.18; Wauchope Vol 1

MacDonald, James Black: Private (43049 HLI [16th]. Formerly 2025 HCB [1/1st]); DOW Beaumont-Hamel, 18.11.16, 20 years; 3 Balfour Place, Kirkcaldy; Gravestone in Bennochy Cemetery (Photo). Old Parish Church Memorial Panel; Warloy-Baillon Communal Cemetery Extension, Somme, France. Grave IV.D.17; Kirkcaldy War Memorial; *FA* 11.11.16; *FA* 16.12.16; *Soldiers Died* Part 63; *FA* 02.12.16; *FA* (BMD) 02.12.16; *FFP* 02.12.16; *FA* 09.12.16; *FA* (RoH) 16.12.16; *FA* (CasList) 23.12.16; *FFP* (CasList) 23.12.16; *FFP* (RoH) 30.12.16; *FA* (Service List) 20.01.17; *FA* (BMD) 17.11.17; *FFP* (BMD) 17.11.17; *FFP* (BMD) 16.11.18; *FA* (FRoH) 30.11.18

Mackie, Robert Cunningham: Lance Corporal (S/17818 Black Watch [1/6th]); KIA, 21.03.18, 20 years; 3 Bethelfield Place, Kirkcaldy; Queant Road Cemetery, Buissy, Pas de Calais, France. Pronville German Cemetery, No 4 Mem. 6; Kirkcaldy War Memorial; *Soldiers Died* Part 46; *FA* 20.04.18; *FFP* 27.04.18; *FA* (BMD) 10.05.19; Wauchope Vol 2

Mackie, Walter: Private (4566 Black Watch [1/7th]); KIA, 03.06.16, 21 years; 119 East Smeaton Street, Kirkcaldy; Maroeuil British Cemetery, Pas de Calais, France. Grave I.G.9; Kirkcaldy War Memorial; *Soldiers Died* Part 46; *FA* 24.06.16; *FFP* 24.06.16; *FA* (CasList) 08.07.16; *FA* (RoH) 15.07.16; *FFP* 05.08.16 Roll of the Brave; *FA* (Service List) 17.02.17; *FA* (FRoH) 23.11.18; Wauchope Vol 2

Mackie, William: Private (202105 Black Watch [4/5th]); MIA France, 26.09.17, 20 years; 37 Dunnikier Road, Kirkcaldy; Tyne Cot Memorial, Zonnebeke, West Vlaanderen, Belgium. Panels 94-96; Kirkcaldy War Memorial; *Soldiers Died* Part 46; *FA* 27.10.17; *FA* 04.05.18; *FFP* (RoH) 04.05.18; *FA* (RoH) 18.05.18; *FFP* (RoH) 18.05.18; *FA* (FRoH) 07.12.18; Wauchope Vol 2

Mair, Andrew: Gunner (276686 RGA [25th Anti-Aircraft Coy]); Died of pneumonia, 2nd General Hospital, Edinburgh; 13.02.19, 54 years; Gravestone in Bennochy Cemetery; Bennochy Cemetery, Kirkcaldy. Grave EE.272; Kirkcaldy War Memorial; *FFP* (BMD) 22.02.19

Malone, Patrick: Private (S/2703 Gordon Hldrs [2nd]); KIA, 25.09.15; 51 Overton Road, Kirkcaldy; Loos Memorial, Pas de Calais, France. Panels 115-119; Kirkcaldy War Memorial; *Soldiers Died* Part 65; *FA* 09.09.16; *FA* 16.09.16; *FFP* 16.09.16; *FA* (RoH) 14.10.16; *FFP* 14.10.16; *FFP* (RoH) 14.10.16; *FA* (Service List) 18.11.16; *FFP* (RoH) 30.12.16; *FA* (FRoH) 23.11.18; RoH Dunnikier Colliery; Kirkcaldy Council Memorial Scroll

Mann, Alexander: Private (S/22532 Cameron Hldrs [1st]); 03.09.16, 25 years; 29 Meldrum Road/84 Balfour Street, Kirkcaldy; Caterpillar Valley Cemetery, Longueval, Somme, France. Grave IX.J.28; Kirkcaldy War Memorial; ‡; *Soldiers Died* Part 66

Manson, Robert Rose: Private (13162 KOSB [7th] "D" Coy); Brother-in-law of David Alexander & James Alexander; KIA Loos, 25.09.15; 272 St Clair Street, Kirkcaldy; Loos Memorial, Pas de Calais, France. Panels 53-56; Kirkcaldy War Memorial; *FA* 22.01.16; *FA* 18.03.16; *Soldiers Died* Part 30; *FA* 22.01.16; *FFP* 29.01.16; *FA* 18.03.16; *FFP* 25.03.16; *FA* (RoH) 15.04.16; *FFP* (CasList) 15.04.16; *FA* 27.05.16; *FFP* 27.05.16; *FA* 15.07.16; *FFP* 05.08.16 Roll of the Brave; *FA* (Service List) 25.11.16; *FA* (FRoH) 23.11.18

Mark, George Pearson: Gunner (192573 RFA); DOW CCS, 23.03.18, 22 years; 72 Lorne Street, Kirkcaldy; Gravestone in Dysart Cemetery. Sinclairtown Parish Church War Memorial Chair; Ennemain Communal Cemetery Extension, Somme, France. Grave I.E.7; Kirkcaldy War Memorial; *Soldiers Died* Part 2; *FFP* (BMD) 06.04.18; *FA* (RoH) 13.04.18; *FA* (FRoH) 07.12.18

Marnock, David: Gunner (344204 RGA [261st Siege Batt'y] [Forth]); Brother of John Marnock; KIA France, 10.08.17, 19 years; 76 Dunnikier Road, Kirkcaldy; Forth RGA Plaque. St Andrew's Church Memorial Plaque; Essex Farm Cemetery, Boezinge, Ieper, West Vlaanderen, Belgium. Grave I.Q.26; Kirkcaldy War Memorial; *Soldiers Died* Part 3; *FFP* 25.08.17; *FA* 01.09.17; *FA* (BMD) 08.09.17; *FFP* (BMD) 08.09.17; *FA* 15.09.17; *FFP* (RoH) 15.09.17; *FFP* (CasList) 22.09.17

Marnock, John: Sergeant (2355 Black Watch [7th]); Brother of David Marnock;KIA. Originally buried Courcelette Communal Cemetery German Extension, 25.09.15, 25 years; 76 Dunnikier Road, Kirkcaldy; St Andrew's Church Memorial Plaque; Delville Wood Cemetery, Longueval, Somme, France. Sp. Mem. 2; Kirkcaldy War Memorial; *FA* 27.11.15; *Soldiers Died* Part 46; *FA* 27.11.15 (2 entries); *FA* 08.04.16 (2 entries); *FA* (Service List) 16.12.16; *FFP* 25.08.17; *FA* 01.09.17; Wauchope Vol 2

Marr, James: Private (29290 Royal Scots [1st Garrison Bn]); 06.04.20, 35 years; 214 Links Street, Kirkcaldy; Bennochy Cemetery, Kirkcaldy. Grave O.460; Kirkcaldy War Memorial

Marshall, George Fairholm: Lance Corporal (351438 Royal Scots [9th] [Lewis Gun Section]); Brother-in-law of William N. Aitken; DOW 61 CCS, France, 23.09.17, 21 years; 8 Whytehouse Mansions, Kirkcaldy; Kirkcaldy High School War Memorial; Dozinghem Military Cemetery, Westvleteren, Poperinge, West Vlaanderen, Belgium. Grave VIII.C.19; Kirkcaldy War Memorial; *FA* 06.10.17; *Soldiers Died* Part 6; *FA* 06.10.17; *FA* (BMD) 06.10.17; *FFP* 06.10.17; *FFP* (CasList) 06.10.17; *FA* 13.10.17; *FFP* 13.10.17; *FFP* (RoH) 13.10.17; *FA* 13.07.18; *FFP* (BMD) 28.09.18; *FA* (FRoH) 07.12.18; *FA* (KHS RoH) 29.03.19

Marshall, Peter: Private (S/15067 Cameron Hldrs [1st]); MIA, 13.10.15, 21 years; 4a Bell Wynd, Kirkcaldy; Loos Memorial, Pas de Calais, France. Panels 119-124; Kirkcaldy War Memorial; *FA* 22.01.16; *Soldiers Died* Part 66; *FFP* 23.10.15; *FFP* 30.10.15; *FA* 27.11.15; *FA* 29.01.16; *FA* (Service List) 04.11.16; *FFP* (BMD) 23.12.16; *FA* (Service List) 30.12.16; *FA* (BMD) 13.10.17; *FA* (BMD) 12.10.18

Marshall, Thomas James Webster: Staff Sergeant (426 Kings Own Yorkshire Light Infantry [6th]); DOW 11th General Hospital, Rouen, 12.06.16, 46 years; 93 Mid Street, Kirkcaldy/23 Short Row, Jarrow-on-Tyne; St Sever Cemetery, Rouen, Seine-Maritime, France. Grave A.18.44; Kirkcaldy War Memorial; *Soldiers Died* Part 54; *FFP* 17.06.16; *FFP* (BMD) 17.06.16; *FA* 24.06.16; *FFP* 24.06.16; *FA* (RoH) 15.07.16; *FFP* 05.08.16 Roll of the Brave; *FA* (Service List) 28.10.16; *FA* (Service List) 23.12.16; *FFP* (BMD) 16.06.17; *FFP* (BMD) 15.06.18; *FA* (FRoH) 23.11.18; Kirkcaldy Council Memorial Scroll

Marshall, William: Private (17248 KOSB [6th]); Died in a German hospital from wounds sustained at Loos 25.09.15; Garnock's Lane, Kirkcaldy; Pathhead Parish Church Memorial Plaques & Windows; Loos Memorial Pas de Calais, France. Panels 53-56; Kirkcaldy War Memorial; *FA* 27.11.15; *FA* 13.05.16; *Soldiers Died* Part 30; *FFP* 30.10.15; *FA* 13.05.16; *FA* (BMD) 13.05.16; *FFP* 13.05.16; *FFP* (BMD) 13.05.16; *FA* (CasList) 27.05.16 *FA* (RoH) 17.06.16; *FFP* (RoH) 17.06.16; *FFP* 05.08.16 Roll of the Brave; *FA* (BMD) 30.09.16; *FFP* (BMD) 30.09.16; *FA* (Service List) 31.03.17; *FFP* (BMD) 29.09.17; *FFP* (BMD) 28.09.18; *FA* (FRoH) 23.11.18 *FFP* 21.06.24

Martin, Alexander: Private (S/3104 Black Watch [9th]); MIA Loos, 25.09.15; 58 East Smeaton Street, Kirkcaldy; Loos Memorial, Pas de Calais, France. Panels 78-83; Kirkcaldy War Memorial; *Soldiers Died* Part 46; *FFP* 30.10.15; *FFP* 07.10.16; *FA* 14.10.16; *FA* (RoH) 14.10.16; *FFP* (RoH) 14.10.16; *FFP* (RoH) 30.12.16; *FA* 10.02.17; *FFP* 10.02.17; *FA* (Service List) 17.02.17; *FA* (FRoH) 23.11.18; Wauchope Vol 3

Martin, George: Private (43177 HLI [16th]. Formerly 1327 HCB); KIA, 12.09.16, 33 years; 126 Overton Road Kirkcaldy; Cambrin Churchyard Extension, Pas de Calais, France. Grave R.14; Kirkcaldy War Memorial; *FA* 30.09.16; *Soldiers Died* Part 63; *FA* 23.09.16; *FFP* 30.09.16; *FA* (RoH) 14.10.16; *FFP* (CasList) 14.10.16 *FA* (Service List) 18.11.16; *FFP* (RoH) 30.12.16; *FA* (FRoH) 23.11.18

Mason, Alexander: Corporal (S/2961 Black Watch [8th]) Also known as Harry Mason;KIA Loos, 25.09.15, 3 years; 10 Flesh Wynd, Kirkcaldy; Pathhead Parish Church Memorial Plaques & Windows; Loos Memorial Pas de Calais, France. Panels 78-83; Kirkcaldy War Memorial; *FA* 09.10.15; *FFP* 09.10.15; *FA* 27.10.17 *Soldiers Died* Part 46; War Album 15/16; *FA* 09.10.15 *FFP* 09.10.15; *Scotsman* (CasList) 11.10.15; *FA* (RoH 16.10.15; *FFP* (RoH) 16.10.15; *FFP* (BMD) 29.03.16 (2 entries); *FFP* 05.08.16 Roll of the Brave; *FA* (Service List) 28.10.16; *FA* (Service List) 06.01.17; *FFP* (BMD 22.09.17; *FA* 27.10.17; *FFP* (BMD) 28.09.18; *FA* (FRoH 16.11.18; *FFP* 21.06.24; Wauchope Vol 3

Mason, James: Private (20610 HLI [3rd] [Labour Corps] att'd Royal Engineers); KIA, 30.10.17; 23 Nile Street, Kirkcaldy; Solferino Farm Cemetery, Brielen, Ieper, West Vlaanderen, Belgium. Grave I.D.12; Kirkcaldy War Memorial; *FA* 10.11.17; *FFP* 10.11.17; *FFP* (BMD) 10.11.17; *FA* (RoH) 17.11.17; *FFP* 17.11.17; *FFP* (RoH) 17.11.17; *FA* (FRoH) 07.12.18

Mathers, John Dunlop: Corporal (S/6758 Gordon Hldrs [9th]); Listed on Kirkcaldy War Memorial as Royal Engineers; Accidentally killed by motor car in London, 20.12.16; 4 Oswald Road, Kirkcaldy; Dalziel (Arbles) Cemetery, Sp. Mem; Dalziel (Old Manse Road) Burial Ground. Dalziel (Airbles) Cemetery, Lanarkshire. Sp. Mem.; Kirkcaldy War Memorial; *Soldiers Died* Part 65; *FA* 30.12.16; *FA* (RoH) 13.01.17; *FFP* (RoH) 13.01.17; *FA* (FRoH) 30.11.18

Matthews, Frederick James: Lance Sergeant (S/10089 Cameron Hldrs [5th] [Depot]); Died at Military Hospital, York, 30.07.16, 31 years; 20 Miller Street, Kirkcaldy; Gravestone in Dysart Cemetery. Sinclairtown Parish Church War Memorial Chair; Dysart Cemetery, Kirkcaldy. Grave 4.14.Middle; Kirkcaldy War Memorial; *FA* 12.08.16; *Soldiers Died* Part 66; *FA* 05.08.16; *FA* (RoH) 05.08.16; *FA* (BMD) 05.08.16; *FFP* 05.08.16; *FFP* 05.08.16 Roll of the Brave; *FA* (RoH) 16.09.16; *FFP* (RoH) 16.09.16; *FA* (CasList) 18.11.16; *FFP* (CasList) 18.11.16; *FFP* (RoH) 30.12.16; *FA* (Service List) 31.03.17; *FA* (FRoH) 23.11.18

Mavor, George: Private (42013 RAMC); His brother was also killed; Drowned when *Glenart Castle* hospital ship was sunk, 26.02.18, 32 years; 25 West March Street, Kirkcaldy/59 High Street, Dysart; E.U. Congregational Church Memorial Plaque; Hollybrook Memorial, Hollybrook Cemetery, Southhampton; Kirkcaldy War Memorial; *Soldiers Died* Part 79; *FA* 09.03.18; *FFP* (RoH) 09.03.18; *FA* (RoH) 16.03.18; *FFP* (RoH) 16.03.18; *FFP* 06.07.18; *FFP* (BMD) 06.07.18; *FA* 13.07.18; *FA* (RoH) 13.07.18; *FA* (BMD) 13.07.18; *FA* (FRoH) 07.12.18; *FA* (FRoH) 14.12.18

Mavor, Robert: Guardsman (5163 Scots Guards [1st] Right Flank Coy); KIA, 25.01.15, 30 years; 37 Rosabelle Street, Kirkcaldy; Gravestone in Barony Churchyard. Barony Church Plaque; Le Touret Memorial, Pas de Calais, France. Panels 3-4; Kirkcaldy War Memorial; *Soldiers Died* Part 5; *FFP* 13.02.15; *FA* 20.02.15; *FA* (CasList) 20.02.15; *FA* 03.04.15; *FFP* 03.04.15; *FFP* 12.08.16 Roll of The Brave; *FA* (RoH) 16.09.16; *FFP* (RoH) 16.09.16; *FFP* (RoH) 30.12.16; *FA* (Service List) 17.03.17; *FA* (FRoH) 23.11.18

Mayer, Thomas Aitken: Private (43006 HLI [16th]. Formerly 1003 HCB); KIA, 18.11.16, 20 years; West Mills, Kirkcaldy; Gravestone in Bennochy Cemetery. Bethelfield Church Plaque; New Munich Trench British Cemetery, Beaumont-Hamel, Somme, France. Grave C.18; Kirkcaldy War Memorial; ‡; *Soldiers Died* Part 63; *FA* 09.12.16; *FFP* 09.12.16; *FFP* (BMD) 09.12.16; *FA* (RoH) 16.12.16; *FFP* (RoH) 30.12.16; *FA* 06.01.17; *FFP* (CasList) 06.01.17; *FA* (Service List) 13.01.17; *FA* (FRoH) 30.11.18

McAra, David: Private (31956 Cameron Hldrs [3rd] [Labour Corps]); DOW CCS, 17.09.18, 21 years; 34a St Clair Place, Bridgeton, Kirkcaldy; St Columba's Church Memorial Plaque; Varennes Military Cemetery, Somme, France. Grave IV.A.16; Kirkcaldy War Memorial; *FA* 28.09.18; *FFP* 28.09.18; *FA* (FRoH) 14.12.18

McArthur, John: Private (S/10077 Cameron Hldrs [5th] "C" Coy, 11th Platoon); MIA Loos, 25.09.15, 25 years; 30/57 West Smeaton Street/42 Hill Street, Kirkcaldy; Loos Memorial, Pas de Calais, France. Panels 119-124; Kirkcaldy War Memorial; *FA* 13.11.15; *FFP* 15.01.16; *FA* 27.01.17; *Soldiers Died* Part 66; *FA* 30.10.15; *FA* 27.11.15; *FA* 27.01.17; *FFP* 27.01.17; *FA* (RoH) 17.02.17; *FFP* (RoH) 17.02.17; *FA* (BMD) 29.09.17; *FA* (FRoH) 30.11.18

McCaig, William George: 2nd Lieutenant (RAF; 13th Squadron. Formerly RGA); 01.10.18, 22 years; Myrtlebank, Pottery Street, Gallatown, Kirkcaldy; Whytescauseway Baptist Church Memorial Plaque. Pathhead Baptist Church War Memorial Roll of Honour; Anneux British Cemetery, Nord, France. Grave I.H.19; Kirkcaldy War Memorial; RFC/RAF RoH; *Cross of Sacrifice Vol 2*; *FA* 12.10.18; *FFP* 12.10.18; *FA* (BMD) 03.05.19 (2 entries)

McCormac, James: Private (3/2382 Black Watch [2nd]); On War Memorial as Charles McCormac; MIA, 25.09.15, 22 years; 128 Den Road, Kirkcaldy; Loos Memorial, Pas de Calais, France. Panels 78-83; Kirkcaldy War Memorial; *Soldiers Died* Part 46; *FA* 02.12.16; *FFP* 02.12.16; *FFP* (BMD) 02.12.16; *FA* (RoH) 16.12.16; *FFP* (RoH) 30.12.16; *FA* (FRoH) 30.11.18; Wauchope Vol 1

McDade, Hugh: Private (31696 RAMC [44th Fld Amb]); Brother-in-law of William Laverance; KIA, 16.09.16, 44 years; 47 Overton Road, Kirkcaldy; Bernafay Wood British Cemetery, Montauban, Somme, France. Grave 0.61; Kirkcaldy War Memorial; *FA* 30.09.16; *Soldiers Died* Part 79; *FA* 23.09.16; *FA* 30.09.16; *FA* (BMD) 30.09.16; *FFP* 30.09.16; *FA* (RoH) 14.10.16; *FFP* (RoH) 14.10.16; *FA* (Service List) 18.11.16; *FFP* (RoH) 30.12.16; *FA* 02.06.17; *FFP* (BMD) 22.09.17; *FA* 16.11.18; *FA* (FRoH) 23.11.18

McDermid, James: Private (34782 RAMC [58th Fld Amb]); KIA France, 14.04.18, 29 years; 14 Factory Road, Kirkcaldy; Gravestone in Dysart Cemetery; La Clytte Military Cemetery, Heuvelland, West Vlaanderen, Belgium. Sp. Mem. between plots IV & V, Row A; Kirkcaldy War Memorial; *Soldiers Died* Part 79; *FFP* (RoH) 04.05.18; *FFP* (Memorial Service) 04.05.18; *FFP* (BMD) 04.05.18; *FA* 11.05.18; *FA* (BMD) 11.05.18; *FA* (RoH) 18.05.18; *FFP* (RoH) 18.05.18; *FA* (FRoH) 14.12.18; *FA* 26.04.19

McDermott, John: Private (S/40056 Black Watch [7th]); KIA, 26.03.18, 21 years; 23 Nairn Street, Kirkcaldy; Arras Memorial, Pas de Calais, France. Bay 6; Kirkcaldy War Memorial; *FA* 04.11.16; *FA* 18.05.18; *Soldiers Died* Part 46; *FFP* (BMD) 27.04.18; *FA* (BMD) 04.05.18; *FFP* (CasList) 11.05.18; *FA* 18.05.18; *FA* (RoH) 15.06.18; *FFP* (RoH) 15.06.18; *FA* (FRoH) 14.12.18; Wauchope Vol 2

McDonald, Charles: Private (292256 Black Watch [7th]); 21.03.18; 20 Quality Street, Kirkcaldy; Queant Road Cemetery, Buissy, Pas de Calais, France. 4 Mem. 16. Pronville German Cemetery; Kirkcaldy War Memorial; *Soldiers Died* Part 46; *FA* 05.10.18; *FA* 12.04.19

McDonald, James: Private (S/11519 Black Watch [6th]); KIA, 21.03.18, 21 years; St Clair Street, Kirkcaldy; Gravestone in Dysart Cemetery; Arras Memorial, Pas de Calais, France. Bay 6; Kirkcaldy War Memorial; *Soldiers Died* Part 46; War Album 15/16; *Scotsman* 08.11.15; *FFP* 05.08.16; *FA* (Service List) 02.12.16; *FFP* (RoH) 14.09.18; *FA* (FRoH) 16.11.18; Wauchope Vol 2

McDonald, James McL.: Private (292538 Black Watch [7th]); DOW, 23.04.17; Brown's Copse Cemetery, Rouex, Pas de Calais, France. Grave VIII.F.4; Kirkcaldy War Memorial; *Soldiers Died* Part 46; Wauchope Vol 2

McDowall, Harry: Lance Corporal (2732 Black Watch [1st]); Brother of James McDowall; MIA High Wood, 03.09.16, 19 years; 121 East Smeaton Street, Kirkcaldy Old Parish Church Memorial Panel; Thiepval Memorial, Somme, France. Pier & Face 10A; Kirkcaldy War Memorial; *Soldiers Died* Part 46; *FA* (CasList) 09.12.16; *FFP* (CasList) 09.12.16; *FFP* 14.04.17; *FFP* 11.08.17; *FFP* (BMD) 11.08.17; *FA* 18.08.17; *FA* (BMD) 18.08.17; *FA* 15.09.17; *FFP* (RoH) 15.09.17; *FA* 14.09.18; Wauchope Vol 1

McDowall, James: Sapper (18977 Royal Engineers [59th Coy]); Brother of Harry McDowall; KIA, 21.08.18, 2? years; 121 East Smeaton Street, Kirkcaldy; Old Parish Church Memorial Panel; Vis-en-Artois Memorial, Haucourt, Pas de Calais, France. Panel 3; Kirkcaldy War Memorial; *Soldiers Died* Part 4; *FFP* (BMD) 07.09.18; *FA* 14.09.18; *FFP* 14.09.18; *FA* (RoH) 16.11.18; *FFP* (RoH) 16.11.18; *FA* (FRoH) 14.12.18

McDowell, William: Private (27754 KOSB [7/8th]) Formerly 2484 F & F Yeo); DOW, 10.05.18; 2 Buchanan Street, Kirkcaldy; Raith Church Memorial Plaque Faubourg D'Amiens Cemetery, Arras, Pas de Calais, France. Grave VII.D.5; Kirkcaldy War Memorial; *Soldiers Died* Part 30; *FA* 18.05.18; *FFP* 18.05.18; *FFP* (BMD) 25.05.18; *FA* (BMD) 01.06.18; F*FA* (RoH) 15.06.18; *FFP* (RoH) 14.12.18; *FA* (BMD) 10.05.19

McEwan, Thomas: Private (345354 Black Watch [14th] [F & F Yeo Bn]. Formerly 2525 F & F Yeo); DOW Sheria, Egypt, 08.11.17, 30 years; 25 Sutherland Street, Kirkcaldy; Pathhead Parish Church Memorial Plaques & Windows; Beersheba War Cemetery, Israel. Grave P.34; Kirkcaldy War Memorial; *Soldiers Died* Part 46; *FA* 17.11.17; *FFP* 17.11.17; *FFP* 01.12.17; *FFP* (CasList) 01.12.17; *FFP* (BMD) 01.12.17; *FA* (RoH) 15.12.17; *FFP* (RoH) 15.12.17; *FA* (FRoH) 07.12.18; *FFP* 21.06.24; Wauchope Vol 3; Ogilvie

McFadyen, Walter, MID: Captain (Royal Scots); KIA, 07.05.17, 22 years; St Margarets, Balwearie Road, Kirkcaldy; Kirkcaldy High School War Memorial; Faubourg D'Amiens Cemetery, Arras, Pas de Calais, France. Grave IV.G.24; Kirkcaldy War Memorial; *FFP* 19.05.17; *Officers Died*; *Cross of Sacrifice Vol 1*; *FA* 12.05.17; *FFP* 12.05.17; *FA* (RoH) 19.05.17; *FFP* 19.05.17; *FFP* (RoH) 19.05.17; *FA* 14.07.17 (KHS War Honours); *FA* (FRoH) 30.11.18; *FA* (KHS RoH) 29.03.19

McFarlane, Duncan: Private (S/8325 Black Watch [9th]); Brother of James McFarlane; KIA Arras, 26.04.17, 26 years; 10 Salisbury Street, Kirkcaldy; E.U. Congregational Church Memorial Plaque; Jemappe British Cemetery, Wancourt, Pas de Calais, France. Grave I.D.18; Kirkcaldy War Memorial; *Soldiers Died* Part 46; *FA* 19.05.17; *FFP* 19.05.17; *FA* (RoH) 16.06.17; *FFP* (RoH) 16.06.17; *FA* 03.11.17; *FFP* 03.11.17; *FFP* (BMD) 27.04.18; *FA* (FRoH) 30.11.18; Wauchope Vol 3

McFarlane, James Neil: Sergeant (7314 Black Watch [8th]); Brother of Duncan McFarlane; KIA Passchendaele, 12.10.17, 37 years; 10 Salisbury Street, Kirkcaldy/Post Office, Kilbirnie, Ayrshire; E.U. Congregational Church Memorial Plaque; Tyne Cot Memorial, Zonnebeke, West Vlaanderen, Belgium. Panels 94-96; Kirkcaldy War Memorial; *Soldiers Died* Part 46; *FA* 03.11.17; *FFP* 03.11.17; *FFP* (BMD) 12.10.18; Wauchope Vol 3

McFeat, Alexander, MM: Corporal (460578; CEF; Royal Canadian Regt); KIA, 22.12.16, 23 years; 43 Alexandra Street, Kirkcaldy/56 Juno Street, Winnipeg, Canada; Ecoivres Military Cemetery, Mont-St Eloi, Pas de Calais, France. Grave IV.A.8; Kirkcaldy War Memorial; *FA* 24.02.17; *CBoR* Page125; *FA* 10.02.17; *FA* (BMD) 10.02.17; *FFP* 10.02.17; *FFP* 24.02.17; *FA* 03.03.17; *FFP* 03.03.17; *FA* (RoH) 17.03.17; *FA* 02.02.18; *FA* (FRoH) 30.11.18

McGillivray, Donald: Private (4569 Black Watch [1/7th]); KIA, 30.07.16, 24 years; 58 Commercial Street, Pathhead, Kirkcaldy; Serre Road Cemetery No. 2, Somme, France. Grave V.G.28; Kirkcaldy War Memorial; *Soldiers Died* Part 46; *FA* (BMD) 02.09.16; *FFP* 02.09.16; *FFP* (BMD) 02.09.16; *FA* (CasList) 09.09.16; *FA* (BMD) 09.09.16; *FFP* (CasList) 09.09.16; *FA* (RoH) 16.09.16; *FFP* (RoH) 16.09.16; *FA* (Service List) 04.11.16; *FA* (Service List) 16.12.16; *FFP* (RoH) 30.12.16; *FA* (FRoH) 23.11.18; Wauchope Vol 2

McGlashan, William S.: Private (S/42246 Gordon Hldrs [1st]); MIA, 15.06.18, 18 years; 68 Harriet Street, Kirkcaldy; Pathhead Baptist Church War Memorial Roll of Honour; Loos Memorial, Pas de Calais, France. Panels 115-119; Kirkcaldy War Memorial; *Soldiers Died* Part 65; *FA* 10.08.18; *FFP* 10.08.18; *FA* (BMD) 26.07.19; *FA* (RoH) 13.09.19

McGregor, Alexander: Private (16181 KOSB [1st]); Drowned when the *Royal Edward* was sunk in the Aegean, 13.08.15, 29 years; 10 Buchanan Street, Kirkcaldy; Helles Memorial, Gallipoli, Turkey. Panels 84-92 or 220-222; Kirkcaldy War Memorial; *FFP* 04.09.15; *FA* 04.09.15; *Soldiers Died* Part 30; War Album 15/16; *FA* 04.09.15; *FFP* 04.09.15; *FA* 11.09.15; *FA* (RoH) 18.09.15; *FA* (BMD) 18.09.15; *FFP* 05.08.16 Roll of the Brave; *FFP* (BMD) 12.08.16; *FA* (Service List) 30.12.16; *FA* (FRoH) 16.11.18

McGregor, Charles James: Private (43252 HLI [2nd]. Formerly 1447 HCB); KIA, 28.03.18, 20 years; 6 Nicol Street, Kirkcaldy; Abbotshall Parish Church Memorial Plaque; Arras Memorial, Pas de Calais, France. Bay 8; Kirkcaldy War Memorial; *Soldiers Died* Part 63; *FA* 13.04.18; *FFP* 20.04.18; *FA* (RoH) 18.05.18; *FFP* (RoH) 18.05.18; *FA* (FRoH) 07.12.18; *FA* 19.11.21; Telfer-Smollett

McGregor, Thomas Baxter: Private (241234 Black Watch (4/5th]. Formerly F & F Yeo); KIA France, 09.07.17, 27 years; 99 High Street, Kirkcaldy; Brandhoek Military Cemetery, Vlamertinghe, Ieper, West Vlaanderen, Belgium. Grave I.M.5; Kirkcaldy War Memorial; *Soldiers Died* Part 46; *FA* (BMD) 28.07.17; *FFP* 28.07.17; *FFP* (BMD) 28.07.17; *FA* 15.09.17; *FFP* (RoH) 15.09.17; Wauchope Vol 2

McInnes, Alexander: Lance Corporal (46819 Royal Engineers [2nd Fld Coy]); KIA, 09.11.16; 56 Bridgeton, Kirkcaldy; Invertiel Parish Church Memorial Table; Guards' Cemetery, Lesboeufs, Somme, France. Grave XII.D.10; Kirkcaldy War Memorial; *Soldiers Died* Part 4; *FFP* (BMD) 02.12.16; *FFP* 09.12.16; *FA* (RoH) 16.12.16; *FFP* (RoH) 30.12.16

McIntosh, Alexander: Private (33354 Royal Scots [13th]); MIA France, 22.08.17, 20 years; 110 Mid Street, Kirkcaldy; Tyne Cot Memorial, Zonnebeke, West Vlaanderen, Belgium. Panels 11-14 & 162; Kirkcaldy War Memorial; *Soldiers Died* Part 6; *FFP* 27.04.18; *FA* 27.07.18; *FFP* 27.07.18; *FFP* (BMD) 24.08.18; *FA* (RoH) 14.09.18; *FFP* (RoH) 14.09.18; *FA* (FRoH) 14.12.18

McIntosh, Alexander Henry: Private (1963 London Regt [14th] [County of London] [London Scottish]); Wounded at Ypres. DOW Boulogne, France, 22.11.14, 21 years; Victoria House, Victoria Road, Kirkcaldy/London; St Andrew's Church Memorial Plaque; Bennochy Cemetery, Kirkcaldy. Grave Q.102; Kirkcaldy War Memorial; *Soldiers Died* Part 76; *FA* 28.11.14; *FA* (BMD) 28.11.14; *FFP* 28.11.14; *FFP* (BMD) 28.11.14; *StAC* (BMD) 28.11.14; *FA* 05.12.14; *FFP* 05.12.14; *StAC* (BMD) 05.12.14; *FA* (CasList) 19.12.14; *FA* 02.01.15; *FFP* 02.01.15; *FA* (CasList) 20.02.15; *FFP* 05.08.16 Roll of the Brave; *FA* (Service List) 02.12.16; *FA* (FRoH) 16.11.18

McIntosh, Allan: Private (S/3097 Black Watch [8th]); DOW CCS, 10.04.17, 23 years; 162 Rosslyn Street, Kirkcaldy; Aubigny Communal Cemetery Extension, Pas de Calais, France. Grave II.A.48; Kirkcaldy War Memorial; *Soldiers Died* Part 46; *FA* 21.04.17; *FFP* 21.04.17; *FA* (CasList) 12.05.17; *FFP* (CasList) 12.05.17; *FA* (RoH) 19.05.17; *FFP* (RoH) 19.05.17; *FFP* (BMD) 18.05.18; *FA* (FRoH) 30.11.18; Wauchope Vol 3

McIntosh, Archibald Melville St Clair: Gunner (1788; AIF; Australian Field Artillery [10th Bde]); KIA Arras, 11.04.17, 25 years; 54 Nicol Street, Kirkcaldy; Ecoust Military Cemetery, Ecoust-St Mein, Pas de Calais, France. Grave II.A.26; Australian War Memorial web site; Kirkcaldy War Memorial; *FFP* 19.05.17; *FFP* (BMD) 13.04.18

McIntosh, John R. Hugh: Sergeant (8978 Seaforth Hldrs [1st]); KIA, 09.05.15, 27 years; 141 Rosslyn Street, Kirkcaldy; Gallatown Church Roll of Honour; Le Touret Memorial, Pas de Calais, France. Panels 38-39; Kirkcaldy War Memorial; *Soldiers Died* Part 64; War Album 15; *FFP* (BMD) 05.06.15; *FA* 12.06.15; *FFP* 12.06.15; *FFP* (BMD) 12.06.15; *FFP* (CasList) 03.07.15; *FA* (RoH) 17.07.15; *FFP* (BMD) 13.05.16; *FFP* 05.08.16 Roll of the Brave; *FA* (Service List) 09.12.16; *FA* (FRoH) 16.11.18

McIntosh, Robert: Corporal (23766 Royal Scots [11th]. Formerly 56023 RAMC); KIA, 19.12.16, 25 years; 101 Mid Street Kirkcaldy; Faubourg D'Amiens Cemetery, Arras, Pas de Calais, France. Grave III.A.3; Kirkcaldy War Memorial; *Soldiers Died* Part 6; *FFP* 30.12.16; *FA* 06.01.17; *FA* (RoH) 13.01.17; *FFP* (RoH) 13.01.17; *FFP* (BMD) 13.01.17; *FA* (CasList) 27.01.17; *FFP* 27.01.17; *FFP* (CasList) 27.01.17; *FFP* (BMD) 22.12.17; *FFP* (BMD) 21.12.18; *FA* (FRoH) 30.11.18

McIntyre, William: Private (201142 Royal Scots [4th]. Queen's Edinburgh Rifles"A" Coy); KIA Palestine, 02.11.17, 21 years; 179 St Clair Street, Kirkcaldy; Gravestone in Dysart Cemetery. Barony Church Plaque; Jerusalem Memorial, Israel. Panel 10;Kirkcaldy War Memorial; *Soldiers Died* Part 6; *FA* 24.11.17; *FFP* 01.12.17; *FFP* (BMD) 01.12.17; *FA* (RoH) 15.12.17; *FFP* (RoH) 15.12.17; *FA* (FRoH) 07.12.18

McKaig, James Bennett: Private (S/10309 Black Watch [8th]. Formerly 8859 Reserve Cavalry Regt [5th]); DOW, 21.10.15, 22 years; 12 Thistle Street, Kirkcaldy; St Andrew's Church Memorial Plaque; Railway Dugouts Burial Ground, Zillebeke, Ieper, West Vlaanderen, Belgium. Grave I.F.15; Kirkcaldy War Memorial; *FA* 18.12.15; *Soldiers Died* Part 46; War Album 15/16; *FA* 13.11.15; *Scotsman* 15.11.15; *FA* (RoH) 18.12.15; *FFP* 05.08.16 Roll of the Brave; *FFP* (BMD) 21.10.16; *FA* (Service List) 03.02.17; *FA* (FRoH) 16.11.18; Wauchope Vol 3

McKay, Duncan: Lance Corporal (53115 Royal Engineers [104th Fld Coy]. Formerly HCB); KIA Loos, 25.09.15; 8 St Clair Street/69 Sutherland Street, Kirkcaldy; Sinclairtown Parish Church War Memorial Chair; Dud Corner Cemetery, Loos, Pas de Calais, France. Grave IV.G.20; Kirkcaldy War Memorial; *FFP* 30.10.15; *Soldiers Died* Part 4; War Album 15/16; *FFP* 09.10.15; *Scotsman* (CasList) 11.10.15; *FA* 16.10.15; *FA* (RoH) 16.10.15; *FFP* (RoH) 16.10.15; *FA* 30.10.15; *FFP* 30.10.15; *FFP* 05.08.16 Roll of the Brave; *FFP* (BMD) 30.09.16; *FA* (Service List) 02.12.16; *FA* (Service List) 03.03.17; *FA* (FRoH) 16.11.18

McKay, Hugh Munro: Private (43176 HLI [1st] "L" Coy. Formerly 2183 HCB); DOW Mesopotamia, 31.10.18, 28 years; 86 Mid Street, Kirkcaldy; St Serf's Church Memorial Plaque; Baghdad (North Gate) or (Jift) War Cemetery, Iraq. Grave II.A.3; Kirkcaldy War Memorial; *Soldiers Died* Part 63; *FFP* 16.11.18; *FFP* (BMD) 16.11.18; *FA* (FRoH) 14.12.18; *FFP* (RoH) 14.12.18; *FFP* 11.01.19

McKay, Norman: Private (12340 KOSB [6th]); KIA, 25.09.15; 266 Rosslyn Street, Kirkcaldy; Loos Memorial, Pas de Calais, France. Panels 53-56; Kirkcaldy War Memorial; *Soldiers Died* Part 30; *FA* (RoH) 16.09.16; *FFP* (RoH) 16.09.16; *FA* (Service List) 09.12.16; *FFP* (RoH) 30.12.16; *FA* (FRoH) 23.11.18

McKay, Robert: Private (S/4402 Black Watch [9th]); KIA, 03.09.15, 26 years; 21 Horse Wynd, Kirkcaldy; Fosse 7 Military Cemetery, Mazingarbe, Pas de Calais, France. Grave II.B.2; Kirkcaldy War Memorial; *FA* 25.09.15; *Soldiers Died* Part 46; War Album 15/16; *FA* 18.09.15; *FA* (BMD) 18.09.15; *FFP* 18.09.15; *FFP* (BMD) 18.09.15; *FA* (BMD) 25.09.15; *FA* (RoH) 16.10.15; *FFP* (RoH) 16.10.15; *FFP* 05.08.16 Roll of the Brave; *Scotsman* 15.09.16; *FA* (Service List) 28.10.16; *FA* (Service List) 06.01.17; *FA* (FRoH) 16.11.18; Wauchope Vol 3

McKenzie, Edward James: Private (S/11305 Seaforth Hldrs [8th]); KIA near Ypres, 20.07.17, 39 years; 31 Abbotshall Road, Kirkcaldy; Brandhoek Military Cemetery, Vlamertinghe, Ieper, West Vlaanderen, Belgium. Grave II.N.9; Kirkcaldy War Memorial; *Soldiers Died* Part 64; *FFP* 04.08.17; *FFP* (BMD) 04.08.17; *FA* 11.08.17; *FA* (BMD) 11.08.17; *FFP* (BMD) 20.07.18

McKinnon, Hugh: Private (42395 Norfolk Regt [7th]. Divisional Cyclist Corps); Brother-in-law of James Williams; DOW 6th CCS, 18.10.18; 43 Balfour Street, Kirkcaldy; Houchin British Cemetery, Pas de Calais, France. Grave III.A.20; Kirkcaldy War Memorial; *Soldiers Died* Part 14; *FA* 26.10.18; *FA* (RoH) 16.11.18; *FFP* (RoH) 16.11.18; *FA* (FRoH) 14.12.18; *FA* (BMD) 28.12.18; *FA* (BMD) 18.10.19; *FA* 25.10.19; *FA* (BMD) 25.10.19 (2 entries)

McKinnon, Hugh: Lance Corporal (S/8001 Seaforth Hldrs [9th] [Pioneer Bn]); PC 19, Kirkcaldy Burgh Police; DOW France, 02.03.16, 29 years; High Street, Kirkcaldy; Gravestone in Bennochy Cemetery. Police Memorial Plaque; Tancrez Farm Cemetery, Comines-Warneton, Hainaut, Belgium. Grave I.A.9; Kirkcaldy War Memorial. Auchterderran War Memorial; *FA* 18.03.16; *Soldiers Died* Part 64; *FA* 11.03.16; *FA* 18.03.16; *FA* 01.04.16; *FFP* 05.08.16 Roll of the Brave; *FA* 18.05.18; *FA* (FRoH) 23.11.18; Pictorial History of Fife Constabulary

McLaren, David: Private (Royal Scots); Not identified on CWGC web site; Kirkcaldy War Memorial

McLaren, James: Private (14655 KOSB [8th]); KIA Loos, 25.09.15, 22 years; 7 Garnock's Lane, Kirkcaldy; Gallatown Church Roll of Honour; Loos Memorial, Pas de Calais, France. Panels 53-56; Kirkcaldy War Memorial; *Soldiers Died* Part 30; *FA* 30.10.15; *FFP* 30.10.15; *FFP* (BMD) 18.12.15; *FFP* (BMD) 25.12.15; *FA* (RoH) 15.01.16; *FFP* 05.08.16 Roll of the Brave; *FFP* (BMD) 23.09.16; *FA* (Service List) 31.03.17; *FFP* (BMD) 29.09.17; *FFP* (BMD) 28.09.18; *FA* (FRoH) 16.11.18

McLaren, Lawrence: Private (S/10218 Cameron Hldrs [5th]); KIA France, 21.09.17; 146A Rosslyn Street, Kirkcaldy; Tyne Cot Memorial, Zonnebeke, West Vlaanderen, Belgium. Panels 136-138; Kirkcaldy War Memorial; *Soldiers Died* Part 66; *FA* 20.10.17; *FFP* 20.10.17; *FA* 27.10.17; *FFP* (BMD) 10.11.17; *FA* (RoH) 17.11.17; *FA* (BMD) 17.11.17; *FFP* (RoH) 17.11.17; *FA* (FRoH) 07.12.18

McLaren, Robert: Gunner (344397 RGA (221st Siege Batt'y] [Forth]); KIA, 01.11.17; Smeaton Road, Kirkcaldy; Forth RGA Plaque; Ypres Reservoir Cemetery, Ieper, West Vlaanderen, Belgium. Grave I.I.74; Kirkcaldy War Memorial; *Soldiers Died* Part 2; *FA* 17.11.17; *FA* (BMD) 17.11.17; *FFP* 17.11.17; *FFP* (CasList) 08.12.17; *FA* (RoH) 15.12.17; *FFP* (CasList) 15.12.17; *FFP* (RoH) 15.12.17; *FFP* (BMD) 16.11.18; *FA* (FRoH) 07.12.18

McLauchlan, John: Lance Corporal (S/7616 Black Watch [2nd]); KIA Persian Gulf, 21.01.16, 28 years; Basra Memorial, Iraq. Panels 25 & 63; Kirkcaldy War Memorial; *Soldiers Died* Part 46; Wauchope Vol 1

McLeod, Frederick James, MM: Private (12/1746; NZEF; Auckland Infantry Regt [16th] Waikato Regt); In *FA* (FRoH) 16.11.18 as H. J. McLeod. Brother of Henry Orlando McLeod; KIA Gallipoli, 08.05.15; 78 Harcourt Road, Kirkcaldy; Old Parish Church Memorial Panel; Twelve Tree Copse (New Zealand) Memorial, Krithia, Helles, Turkey. Grave 12.1.10; Kirkcaldy War Memorial; NZEF Roll of Honour; War Album 15/16; *FA* 20.11.15; *FA* (RoH) 18.12.15; *FA* 01.04.16; *FFP* 01.04.16; *FFP* (BMD) 08.04.16; *FA* (RoH) 15.04.16; *FFP* (CasList) 15.04.16; *FFP* 05.08.16 Roll of the Brave; *FFP* (BMD) 05.08.16; *FA* (Service List) 03.03.17; *FA* (FRoH) 16.11.18; *FA* (FRoH) 23.11.18

McLeod, George Munro: Private (S/12961 Black Watch [1st]); KIA, 08.09.16, 36 years; 41 Loughborough Road, Kirkcaldy; St Brycedale Church Plaque; Thiepval Memorial, Somme, France. Pier & Face 10A; Kirkcaldy War Memorial; *Soldiers Died* Part 46; *FA* 23.09.16; *FFP* 23.09.16; *FA* (CasList) 30.09.16; *FFP* 30.09.16; *FFP* (CasList) 30.09.16; *FA* (RoH) 14.10.16; *FFP* (RoH) 14.10.16; *FFP* (RoH) 30.12.16; *FA* (Memorial Service) 06.01.17; *FA* (Service List) 17.02.17; *FA* (FRoH) 23.11.18; Wauchope Vol 1

McLeod, Henry Orlando: Private (3252 London Regt [14th] [County of London] [London Scottish]); Brother of Frederick J. McLeod; DOW, 22.12.14, 31 years; 78 Harcourt Road, Kirkcaldy; Old Parish Church Memorial Panel; Le Touret Memorial, Pas de Calais, France. Panel 45; Kirkcaldy War Memorial; *Soldiers Died* Part 76; War Album 14/15; *FA* 16.01.15; *FA* (BMD) 16.01.15; *FFP* 16.01.15; *FFP* (BMD) 16.01.15; *FFP* 23.01.15; *FFP* (RoH) 30.01.15; *FA* (CasList) 20.02.15; *FA* 20.11.15; *FFP* (BMD) 18.12.15; *FA* 01.04.16; *FFP* 01.04.16; *FFP* 05.8.16 Roll of the Brave; *FA* (Service List) 03.03.17; *FA* (FRoH) 16.11.18

McLeod, William: Private (S/10755 Gordon Hldrs [8/10th]); DOW, 29.07.16, 43 years; 99 Harcourt Road, Kirkcaldy; St Sever Cemetery, Rouen, Seine-Maritime, France. Grave A.39.S; Kirkcaldy War Memorial; *Soldiers Died* Part 65; *FFP* 05.08.16; *FA* 12.08.16; *FA* (CasList) 12.08.16; *FA* (BMD) 12.08.16; *FA* (RoH) 16.09.16; *FFP* (RoH) 16.09.16; *FFP* (RoH) 30.12.16; *FA* (Service List) 03.03.17; *FA* (FRoH) 16.11.18; *FA* (FRoH) 23.11.18

McLonney, William: Private (CEF; Canadian Army Medical Corps [3rd Fld Amb]); KIA, 29.08.18, 26 years; 30 St Clair Place, Bridgeton, Kirkcaldy; Invertiel Parish Church Memorial Table. Gravestone in Dysart Cemetery; Faubourg D'Amiens Cemetery, Arras, Pas de Calais, France. Grave VII.E.33; Kirkcaldy War Memorial; *CBoR* Page 463; *FA* (BMD) 14.09.18; *FFP* (BMD) 14.09.18; *FA* 16.11.18; *FFP* (RoH) 16.11.18; *FA* (FRoH) 14.12.18

McLure, Joseph: Private (S/3656 Black Watch [9th]); DOW received at Arras, 21.04.17, 25 years; 17 Mid Street, Kirkcaldy; Duisans British Cemetery, Etrun, Pas de Calais, France. Grave IV.A.16; Kirkcaldy War Memorial; *Soldiers Died* Part 46; *FFP* (BMD) 05.05.17; *FA* 12.05.17; *FA* (BMD) 12.05.17; *FFP* 12.05.17; *FA* (RoH) 19.05.17; *FFP* 19.05.17; *FFP* (RoH) 19.05.17; *FFP* (CasList) 02.06.17; *FFP* (BMD) 20.04.18; *FA* (FRoH) 30.11.18; Wauchope Vol 3

McLusky: Private (Gordon Hldrs [1st]); 00.11.14; Pathhead, Kirkcaldy; Not identified on CWGC web site; Kirkcaldy War Memorial; War Album 14/15; *FFP* 21.11.14; *Despatch* 23.11.14; *FA* 28.11.14; *FA* (CasList) 19.12.14; *FA* 02.01.15; *FA* (CasList) 20.02.15; *FFP* 05.08.16 Roll of the Brave; *FA* (FRoH) 16.11.18

McMahon, Samuel: Private (201062 Black Watch [7th]); Brother of Walter McMahon; KIA Cambrai, 26.03.18, 25 years; 3 Forth Avenue South, Kirkcaldy; Abbotshall Parish Church Memorial Plaque; Queant Road Cemetery, Buissy, Pas de Calais, France. 4.Mem.12. Pronville German Cemetery; Kirkcaldy War Memorial; *Soldiers Died* Part 46; *FA* 20.04.18; *FFP* 20.04.18; *FFP* (BMD) 20.04.18; *FA* (BMD) 27.04.18; *FFP* (RoH) 27.04.18; *FFP* (CasList) 11.05.18; *FA* (RoH) 18.05.18; *FFP* (RoH) 18.05.18; *FA* 25.05.18; *FA* (FRoH) 07.12.18; *FA* 21.06.19; *FA* 19.11.21; Wauchope Vol 2

McMahon, Walter: Private (S/40576 Black Watch [6th]); Brother of Samuel McMahon; KIA, 10.04.18, 20 years; 3 Forth Avenue South, Kirkcaldy; Abbotshall Parish Church Memorial Plaque; Loos Memorial, Pas de Calais, France. Panels 78-83; Kirkcaldy War Memorial; *Soldiers Died* Part 46; *FFP* 20.04.18; *FA* 25.05.18; *FA* 21.06.19; *FA* 19.11.21; Wauchope Vol 2

McPhee, Robert: Corporal (5252 Scots Guards [1st]); PC 21, Kirkcaldy Burgh Police. Wounded in the neck at Aisne and died in hospital at Namur, Belgium, 01.10.14; 96 Meldrum Road, Kirkcaldy; St Peter's Church Memorial Plaque. Police Memorial Plaque; Vendresse Churchyard, Aisne, France. Sp. Mem. 22; Kirkcaldy War Memorial; *FA* 17.10.14; *Soldiers Died* Part 5; War Album 14/15; *FA* 17.10.14; *FFP* 17.10.14; *FA* 31.10.14; *FFP* 31.10.14; *FA* 07.11.14; *FA* (RoH) 07.11.14; *FA* (CasList) 21.11.14; *FA* 02.01.15; *FA* 16.01.15; *FA* (CasList) 20.02.15; *FFP* 05.08.16 Roll of the Brave; *FA* (Service List) 17.03.17; *FA* (FRoH) 16.11.18; Pictorial History of Fife Constabulary

McPherson, John: Private (6636 KOSB [2nd]); KIA Hill 60, Ypres, 23.04.15, 34 years; Hendry Road/51 East Smeaton Street, Kirkcaldy; Raith Church Memorial Plaque; Ypres (Menin Gate) Memorial, Ieper, West Vlaanderen, Belgium. Panel 22; Kirkcaldy War Memorial; *Soldiers Died* Part 30; War Album 15; *FA* 08.05.15; *FFP* (CasList) 05.06.15; *FFP* 05.08.16; *FA* (Service List) 06.01.17; *FA* (Service List) 17.02.17; *FA* (FRoH) 16.11.18

McQuattie, Robert: Lance Corporal (2453 Black Watch [1st]); 15.09.14; Wemyss Close, 19 Mid Street, Kirkcaldy; La Ferte-Sous-Jouarre Memorial, Seine-et-Marne, France; Kirkcaldy War Memorial; *Soldiers Died* Part 46; War Album 14/15; *Scotsman* (CasList) 19.11.14; *FA* 28.11.14; *FA* (CasList) 19.12.14; *FA* 02.01.15; *FA* (CasList) 20.02.15; *FFP* 05.08.16 Roll of the Brave; *FA* (Service List) 28.10.16; *FA* (Service List) 06.01.17; *FFP* (BMD) 15.09.17; *FA* (FRoH) 16.11.18; Wauchope Vol 1

McWilliams, Edward: Private (15754 Royal Scots [13th]); MIA Loos, 26.09.15, 24 years; 4 Ann Place/187 Links Street, Kirkcaldy; Loos Memorial, Pas de Calais, France. Panels 10-13; Kirkcaldy War Memorial; *Soldiers Died* Part 6; *FFP* 21.10.16; *FA* 28.10.16; *FA* (RoH) 18.11.16; *FFP* (RoH) 18.11.16; *FFP* (RoH) 30.12.16; *FA* (FRoH) 30.11.18

Meldrum, Archibald McLaughlan: Air Mechanic 1st Class (123679; RAF); Died at Lewisham Military Hospital as the result of an accident, 19.08.18, 39 years; 15 Harriet Street, Kirkcaldy; Edinburgh Eastern Cemetery. Grave E.124; Kirkcaldy War Memorial; *Cross of Sacrifice Vol 4*; *FA* 24.08.18; *FFP* (BMD) 24.08.18; *FA* (BMD) 31.08.18; *FFP* (RoH) 16.11.18; *FA* (FRoH) 14.12.18

Mellor, Haydn: Corporal (S/23078 Gordon Hlds [8/10th]); KIA, 20.04.18, 19 years; 127 Dunnikier Road, Kirkcaldy; Gravestone in Bennochy Cemetery. Kirkcaldy High School War Memorial; Tilloy British Cemetery, Tilloy-Les-Mofflaines, Pas de Calais, France. Grave IV.H.9; Kirkcaldy War Memorial; *Soldiers Died* Part 65; *FA* 11.05.18; *FFP* (RoH) 11.05.18; *FA* (RoH) 18.05.18; *FFP* (RoH) 18.05.18; *FFP* (CasList) 22.06.18; *FA* 13.07.18; *FA* (FRoH) 14.12.18; *FA* (KHS RoH) 29.03.19

Melville, James: Private (3/1619 Black Watch [1st]); KIA, 09.05.15; 42 Links Street/2 Coal Wynd, Kirkcaldy; Le Touret Memorial, Pas de Calais, France. Panels 24-26; Kirkcaldy War Memorial; *FA* 01.05.15; *FA* 22.01.16; *Soldiers Died* Part 46; *War Album* 15; *FA* 22.05.15; *Dundee Advertiser* (CasList) 24.05.15; *FFP* (CasList) 05.06.15; *FA* (RoH) 17.07.15; *FA* 22.01.16; *FFP* 22.01.16; *FFP* (BMD) 13.05.16; *FFP* 05.08.16 Roll of the Brave; *FA* (Service List) 04.11.16; *FA* (Service List) 02.12.16; *FA* (Service List) 03.02.17; *FFP* (BMD) 12.05.17; *FA* (FRoH) 16.11.18 (2 entries); Wauchope Vol 1

Melville, John M.: Trooper (345411 Black Watch [14th] [F & F Yeo Bn]. Formerly 2613 F & F Yeo); Died of dysentery, Cairo, 12.11.17, 23 years; 19 Ava Street, Kirkcaldy; Kirkcaldy High School War Memorial; Cairo War Memorial Cemetery, Egypt. Grave F.3338; Kirkcaldy War Memorial; *Soldiers Died* Part 46; *FA* 24.11.17; *FA* (RoH) 15.12.17; *FFP* 15.12.17; *FFP* (RoH) 15.12.17; *FFP* (BMD) 15.12.17; *FFP* (BMD) 16.11.18; *FA* (FRoH) 07.12.18; *FA* (KHS RoH) 29.03.19; Wauchope Vol 3; Ogilvie

Melvin, John William Peter, MID: Sergeant Major (166838 CEF [2nd Pioneer Bn]); KIA, 07.04.17, 23 years; 11 High Street, Kirkcaldy; St Brycedale Church Plaque; Ecoivres Military Cemetery, Mont-St Eloi, Pas de Calais, France. Grave VI.B.8; Kirkcaldy War Memorial; *CBoR* Page 293; *FFP* (BMD) 21.04.17; *FA* 28.04.17; *FA* (RoH) 19.05.17; *FFP* (RoH) 19.05.17; *FFP* (Memorial List) 05.01.18; *FA* (FRoH) 30.11.18

Menzies, George: Private (6308 Gordon Hldrs [1/7th]); Body found on the battlefield by his brother, James; KIA Ancre, Beaumont-Hamel, 13.11.16, 31 years; Ashdean, Swan Road, Kirkcaldy; Gravestone in Bennochy Cemetery (Photo). Kirkcaldy High School War Memorial. West End Congregational Church Memorial Plaque; Serre Road Cemetery No. 1, Pas de Calais, France. Grave II.D.25; Kirkcaldy War Memorial; ‡; *FA* 25.11.16; *Soldiers Died* Part 65; *FA* 25.11.16; *FA* (BMD) 25.11.16; *FFP* 25.11.16; *FFP* (BMD) 25.11.16; *FA* 02.12.16; *FA* (RoH) 16.12.16; *FA* (CasList) 23.12.16; *FFP* (CasList) 23.12.16; *FFP* (RoH) 30.12.16; *FA* (Service List) 10.02.17; *FA* 06.04.18; *FFP* (RoH) 06.04.18; *FA* 03.08.18; *FA* (FRoH) 30.11.18; *FA* (KHS RoH) 29.03.19

Having learned that his brother, George, had been seen wounded on the battlefield, Lieutenant James **Menzies** set off to enquire about him. He could find no trace of him in casualty clearing stations or hospitals, so he searched the battlefield. Under heavy fire, he continued his search until he found his brother's body close to the German lines. He recovered the body and saw it buried by the Rev. J. M. Hunter, minister of Abbotshall Church, Kirkcaldy who was serving as chaplain to the forces.

Metcalf, William: Private (S/17621 Cameron Hldrs [1st]); KIA, 03.09.16; 111 Overton Road, Kirkcaldy; Thiepval Memorial, Somme, France. Pier & Face 15B; Kirkcaldy War Memorial; *FA* 28.10.16; *Soldiers Died* Part 66; *FA* 28.10.16; *FA* (Service List) 18.11.16; *FFP* 07.04.17; *FA* 15.09.17; *FFP* (RoH) 15.09.17

Methven, David: Private (351252 Royal Scots [9th]); DOW 53rd CCS, 18.04.18; 1 Anderson Street, Kirkcaldy; Pathhead Parish Church Memorial Plaques & Windows; Roye New British Cemetery, Somme, France. Grave IV.C.15; Kirkcaldy War Memorial; *Soldiers Died* Part 6; *FA* 27.04.18; *FFP* (RoH) 27.04.18; *FA* (RoH) 18.05.18; *FFP* (RoH) 18.05.18; *FA* (FRoH) 14.12.18

Methven, David George: Captain (Seaforth Hldrs [2nd]); KIA near Frelinghien, 20.10.14, 35 years; Wemyss Park, Wemyssfield, Kirkcaldy; Gravestone in Abbotshall Churchyard (Photo). Abbotshall Parish Church Memorial Plaque. Personal plaque in Abbotshall Church. Kirkcaldy High School War Memorial; Houplines Communal Cemetery Extension, Nord, France. Grave II.D.19; Kirkcaldy War Memorial; *FA* 31.10.14; *FFP* 31.10.14; *Officers Died*; *Cross of Sacrifice Vol 1*; War Album 14/15; *FA* 31.10.14; *FA* (BMD) 31.10.14; *FFP* 31.10.14; *FFP* (BMD) 31.10.14; *StAC* 31.10.14; *StAC* (BMD) 31.10.14; *FA* (RoH) 07.11.14; *FA* (CasList) 21.11.14; *FFP* 21.11.14; *FA* 02.01.15; *FA* (CasList) 20.02.15; *FFP* (CasList) 20.02.15; *FFP* 26.06.15; *FFP* 05.08.16 Roll of the Brave; *FA* (Service List) 06.01.17; *FA* (FRoH) 16.11.18; *FA* (KHS RoH) 29.03.19; *FA* 19.11.21

Methven, James: Corporal (28736 KOSB [2nd]. Formerly 2833 F & F Yeo); KIA, 08.05.17, 23 years; 73 Market Street, Kirkcaldy; Whytescauseway Baptist Church Memorial Plaque; Arras Memorial, Pas de Calais, France. Bay 6; Kirkcaldy War Memorial; *FA* 02.06.17; *Soldiers Died* Part 30; *FFP* 05.08.16 Roll of the Brave; *FA* 26.05.17; *FA* (BMD) 26.05.17; *FFP* 26.05.17; *FA* (RoH) 16.06.17; *FA* (BMD) 16.06.17; *FFP* (CasList) 16.06.17; *FFP* (RoH) 16.06.17; *FFP* (BMD) 11.05.18; *FA* (FRoH) 30.11.18

Michie, David: Lance Corporal (377057 Royal Scots [2/10th]. Formerly 3162 HCB); KIA Borock, North Russia, 07.10.18, 26 years; East Lynne, Whytehouse Avenue, Kirkcaldy; Gravestone in Abbotshall Churchyard. Abbotshall Parish Church Memorial Plaque. Kirkcaldy High School War Memorial; Archangel Memorial, Russia; Kirkcaldy War Memorial; *Soldiers Died* Part 6; *FA* 09.11.18; *FA* (RoH) 16.11.18; *FFP* (RoH) 16.11.18; *FA* (FRoH) 14.12.18; *FA* 19.11.21

Michie, John (James): Sapper (79463 Royal Engineers [173rd Tunnelling Coy]. Formerly S/8467 Black Watch); KIA, 16.12.15; 130 Links Street, Kirkcaldy; Aubers Ridge British Cemetery, Aubers, Nord, France. Grave VIII.B.II; Kirkcaldy War Memorial; *Soldiers Died* Part 4; *FFP* 15.01.16; *Scotsman* 17.01.16; *FFP* 05.08.16 Roll of the Brave; *FA* (FRoH) 16.11.18

Millar, Archibald MacDonald: Lance Corporal (350442 Black Watch [1/6th]. Formerly 2093 HCB); DOW, 21.07.18, 20 years; 3 Watery Wynd, Kirkcaldy; St Columba's Church Memorial Plaque; Sezanne Communal Cemetery, Haulte-Marne, France. Grave C.36; Kirkcaldy War Memorial; *FA* 17.08.18; *Soldiers Died* Part 46; *FA* 17.08.18; *FFP* 17.08.18; *FA* (RoH) 16.11.18; *FFP* (RoH) 16.11.18; *FA* (FRoH) 14.12.18; Wauchope Vol 2

Millar, James: Private (S/13454 Black Watch [9th]); Died of diabetes at Rouen General Hospital, 15.10.17, 23 years; 49 Bridgeton, Kirkcaldy; St Sever Cemetery Extension, Rouen, Seine-Maritime, France. Grave P.III.H.13B; Kirkcaldy War Memorial; *FA* 16.12.16; *Soldiers Died* Part 46; *FFP* 20.10.17; *FFP* (BMD) 20.10.17; *FFP* (CasList) 17.11.17; *FA* (RoH) 17.11.17; *FFP* (RoH) 17.11.17; *FA* (FRoH) 07.12.18; Wauchope Vol 3

Millar, Robert: Trooper (12312 Dragoon Guards [5th]); KIA, 08.08.18; 23 High Street, Kirkcaldy; Vis-en-Artois Memorial, Haucourt, Pas de Calais, France. Panel 2; Kirkcaldy War Memorial; *Soldiers Died* Part 1; *FA* (RoH) 16.11.18; *FFP* (RoH) 16.11.18; *FA* (FRoH) 14.12.18

Millar, Thomas: Private (12584 KOSB [6th]); KIA Loos, 25.09.15, 37 years; 32/38/49 Bridgeton, Kirkcaldy; St Michael's Church Memorial Plaque; Loos Memorial, Pas de Calais, France. Panels 53-56; Kirkcaldy War Memorial; *FA* 04.09.15; *FA* 30.10.15; *Soldiers Died* Part 30; War Album 15/16; *FA* 30.10.15; *FA* (BMD) 06.11.15; *FA* (RoH) 13.11.15; *FFP* 05.08.16 Roll of the Brave; *FA* (BMD) 23.09.16; *FFP* (BMD) 23.09.16; *FA* (Service List) 28.10.16; *FA* (Service List) 24.02.17; *FA* (FRoH) 16.11.18

Millar, Thomas: Lance Corporal (51288 Royal Scots Fusiliers [1st]); KIA, 22.08.18, 25 years; 12 Ann Place, Links Street, Kirkcaldy; Vis-en-Artois Memorial, Haucourt, Pas de Calais, France. Panel 6; Kirkcaldy War Memorial; *Soldiers Died* Part 26; *FFP* 12.05.17; *FA* 19.05.17; *FA* (RoH) 19.05.17; *FFP* (RoH) 19.05.17; *FA* (RoH) 16.06.17; *FFP* (RoH) 16.06.17; *FA* (FRoH) 30.11.18

Millar, Thomas Nixon McIntyre: Private (12256 KOSB [1st]); Drowned when *Royal Edward* was sunk in the Aegean, 13.08.15, 33 years; 1 Cairns Street, Kirkcaldy; Helles Memorial, Gallipoli, Turkey. Panels 84-92 or 220-222; Kirkcaldy War Memorial; *FA* 04.09.15; *Soldiers Died* Part 30; War Album 15/16; *FA* 21.08.15; *FFP* 28.08.15; *FA* 04.09.15; *FFP* 04.09.15; *FA* (RoH) 18.09.15; *FA* 19.08.16; *FA* (BMD) 18.08.17; *FFP* (BMD) 24.08.18; *FA* (FRoH) 16.11.18

Miller, John Fern Hackney: Private (251210 Royal Scots [1/4th]); KIA Gaza, 02.11.17, 40 years; 59 Ramsay Road, Kirkcaldy; Abbotshall Parish Church Memorial Plaque. Gravestone in Bennochy Cemetery; Gaza War Cemetery, Israel. Grave VIII.A.14; Kirkcaldy War Memorial; *Soldiers Died* Part 6; *FA* 24.11.17; *FFP* 01.12.17; *FA* (RoH) 15.12.17; *FFP* 15.12.17; *FFP* (RoH) 15.12.17; *FA* (FRoH) 07.12.18; *FA* 19.11.21

Miller, Matthew Kidd: Sapper (58065 Royal Engineers [106th Fld Coy]); Brother of Walter Miller; MIA, 17.02.17, 20 years; 32 Union Street, Kirkcaldy; Gallatown Church Roll of Honour; Ploegsteert Memorial, Comines-Warneton, Hainaut, Belgium. Panel 1; Kirkcaldy War Memorial; *Soldiers Died* Part 4; *FA* 26.05.17

Miller, Robert G.: Pioneer (418166 Royal Engineers [55th Div Signals Coy]); DOW 22nd CCS, 09.05.18, 29 years; 29 Harriet Street, Kirkcaldy; Gallatown Church Roll of Honour; Lapugnoy Military Cemetery, Pas de Calais, France. Grave VIII.F.1; Kirkcaldy War Memorial; *Soldiers Died* Part 4; *FFP* 18.05.18; *FFP* (BMD) 18.05.18; *FA* 25.05.18; *FA* (BMD) 25.05.18; *FA* (RoH) 15.06.18; *FFP* (RoH) 15.06.18; *FA* (FRoH) 14.12.18

Miller, Walter: Private (12349 HLI [2nd] "C" Coy); Brother of Matthew Miller; KIA, 28.04.17, 24 years; 32 Union Street, Kirkcaldy; Gallatown Church Roll of Honour; Arras Memorial, Pas de Calais, France. Bay 8; Kirkcaldy War Memorial; *Soldiers Died* Part 63; *FA* 26.05.17; *FFP* 26.05.17; *FFP* (BMD) 02.06.17; *FA* (BMD) 09.06.17; *FFP* (CasList) 09.06.17; *FA* (RoH) 16.06.17; *FFP* (RoH) 16.06.17; *FA* (FRoH) 30.11.18; Telfer-Smollett

Miller, William Sinclair: Sergeant (841086; CEF; Canadian Infantry [14th] [Quebec Regt]); 09.10.17; Kirkcaldy High School War Memorial; Barlin Communal Cemetery Extension, Pas de Calais, France. Grave II.D.42; Kirkcaldy War Memorial; *CBoR* Page 294; *FA* 17.11.17

Millie, Hugh: Private (A & S Hldrs [3rd]); Dunnikier Church Roll of Honour; Not identified on CWGC web site; Kirkcaldy War Memorial

Millie, John: Private (Labour Corps); Barony Church Plaque; Not identified on CWGC web site; Kirkcaldy War Memorial

Milliken, Robert Dale: Private (HCB [1/1]); Died in Edinburgh Royal Infirmary, 20.03.17, 22 years; 20 Douglas Street, Kirkcaldy; Old Parish Church Memorial Panel. Kirkcaldy High School War Memorial; Not identified on CWGC web site; Kirkcaldy War Memorial; *FA* (RoH) 14.04.17; *FFP* 14.04.17; *FA* (BMD) 23.03.18; *FFP* (BMD) 23.03.18; *FA* (FRoH) 30.11.18; *FA* (BMD) 22.03.19; *FA* (KHS RoH) 29.03.19

Mitchell, Robert: Private (S/25309 Seaforth Hldrs [9th]. Formerly TR/1/13952 TR Bn); KIA, 23.07.18, 19 years; 5 Rosebank, Victoria Road, Kirkcaldy; Barony Church Plaque; Caestre Military Cemetery, France. Grave I.E.3; Kirkcaldy War Memorial; *Soldiers Died* Part 64; *FA* 10.08.18; *FA* (BMD) 10.08.18; *FFP* (BMD) 10.08.18; *FFP* (BMD) 17.08.18; *FA* (RoH) 14.09.18; *FFP* (RoH) 14.09.18; *FA* (FRoH) 14.12.18

Mitchell, William: Private (291464 Black Watch [7th]); KIA, 09.04.18, 20 years; 52 Meldrum Road, Kirkcaldy; Dunnikier Church Roll of Honour; Loos Memorial, Pas de Calais, France. Panels 78-83; Kirkcaldy War Memorial; *Soldiers Died* Part 46; *FA* 25.05.18; *FA* 26.04.19; Wauchope Vol 2

Mitchelston, John Birrell: Able Seaman (Clyde Z/7202; Royal Navy; RNVR [RND] [Hawke Bn]); On CWGC as Mitchelson; KIA France whilst serving as a stretcher bearer, 26.10.17, 29 years; 71 Overton Road, Kirkcaldy; Poelkapelle British Cemetery, Langemark-Poelkapelle, West Vlaanderen, Belgium. Grave XL.A.17; Kirkcaldy War Memorial; *Cross of Sacrifice Vol 4*; *FFP* 17.11.17; *FA* (BMD) 01.12.17; *FA* (RoH) 15.12.17; *FFP* (RoH) 15.12.17; *FA* (BMD) 26.10.18; *FA* (FRoH) 07.12.18

Mitchelston, Robert: Corporal (S/3242 Black Watch [9th]); Brother-in-law of William Wilson & David Wilson; KIA Flanders. Buried in Belgium, 11.03.16; 7 West Wynd, Pathhead, Kirkcaldy; St Michael's Church Memorial Plaque; Dud Corner Cemetery, Loos, Pas de Calais, France. Grave IV.G.7; Kirkcaldy War Memorial; *FA* 25.03.16; *Soldiers Died* Part 46; *FFP* 01.04.16; *FA* (RoH) 15.04.16; *FFP* (CasList)15.04.16; *FFP* 05.08.16 Roll of the Brave; *FA* (Service List) 04.11.16; *FA* (Service List) 06.01.17; *FFP* (BMD) 10.03.17; *FA* 27.10.17; *FFP* 24.11.17; *FA* (BMD) 09.03.18; *FA* (RoH) 16.03.18; *FA* 04.05.18; *FA* (FRoH) 23.11.18; Wauchope Vol 3

Monaghan, John: Private (17235 Cameronians [Scottish Rifles] [10th]); DOW, 02.09.16; 16 Patterson Street, Kirkcaldy; Flat Iron Copse Cemetery, Mametz, Somme, France. Grave I.A.21; Kirkcaldy War Memorial; *Soldiers Died* Part 31; *FA* 05.08.16; *FFP* 09.09.16; *FA* 16.09.16; *FA* (RoH) 16.09.16; *FFP* (RoH) 16.09.16; *FFP* 23.09.16; *FFP* (CasList) 02.12.16; *FFP* 30.12.16; *FA* (Service List) 24.03.17; *FA* (FRoH) 23.11.18

Monro, John: Wireless Operator (F/21840; Royal Navy; RNAS (HM Airship C/7]); Airship shot down off the North Foreland, 21.04.17, 19 years; 108 Meldrum Road, Kirkcaldy; Kirkcaldy High School War Memorial; Chatham Memorial, Kent. Panel 25; Kirkcaldy War Memorial; *FFP* 28.04.17; *FFP* (BMD) 28.04.17; *FFP* (RoH) 19.05.17; *FA* 14.07.17 (KHS War Honours); *FA* (FRoH) 30.11.18; *FA* (KHS RoH) 29.03.19

Moodie, Alexander: Private (43388 HLI [17th]. Formerly 2245 HCB); Brother of David Moodie; MIA, 18.11.16, 21 years; 162 Rosslyn Sreet, Kirkcaldy; New Munich Trench British Cemetery, Beaumont-Hamel, Somme, France. Grave E.17; Kirkcaldy War Memorial; *Soldiers Died* Part 63; *FA* 10.03.17; *FFP* 10.03.17; *FA* (BMD) 02.02.18; *FFP* (BMD) 02.02.18

Moodie, Charles Watson, MM: Sergeant (Royal Engineers); Brother of Harry M. Moodie; 21.07.19, 32 years; 13 Balsusney Road, Kirkcaldy/20A Cross Street, Peebles; St Brycedale Church Plaque; Not identified on CWGC web site; Kirkcaldy War Memorial; *FA* (BMD) 26.07.19; *FA* 02.08.19; *FA* (RoH) 13.09.19

Moodie, Harry M.: 2nd Lieutenant (RAF; 211 Squadron. Formerly Black Watch [1/7th] & Seaforth Hldrs [9th]); Brother of Charles Watson Moodie; DOW Belgium, 16.09.18, 20 years; 13 Balsusney Road, Kirkcaldy; St Brycedale Church Plaque. Kirkcaldy High School War Memorial; Dunkerque Town Cemetery, Dunkerque, Nord, France. Grave IV.C.18; *FA* 28.09.18; Kirkcaldy War Memorial; RFC/RAF RoH; *Cross of Sacrifice Vol 2*; *FA* 21.09.18; *FA* (BMD) 21.09.18; *FFP* 21.09.18; *FFP* (BMD) 21.09.18; *FFP* 12.10.18; *FA* (RoH) 19.10.18; *FA* (FRoH) 14.12.18; *FA* (KHS RoH) 29.03.19; *FA* (KHS RoH) 19.07.19; *FA* (BMD) 26.07.19; *FA* (BMD) 06.09.19

Moodie, John: Private (27911 Royal Scots [16th]); Brother of Alexander Moodie; KIA, 01.07.16, 21 years; 4 Windmill Road, Kirkcaldy; Thiepval Memorial, Somme, France. Pier & Face 6D & 7D; Kirkcaldy War Memorial; *FA* 19.08.16; *FA* 10.03.17; *Soldiers Died* Part 6; *FA* 12.08.16; *FFP* (CasList) 26.08.16; *FA* (BMD) 10.03.17; *FFP* 10.03.17; *FA* (RoH) 17.03.17; *FA* (FRoH) 30.11.18

More, George C.: Private (263010 Gloucestershire Regt [1/5th]. Formerly 1989 HCB & Royal Warwickshire Regt); KIA, 04.11.18, 24 years; 1 Matthew Street, Kirkcaldy; Landrecies British Cemetery, Nord, France. Grave A.57; Kirkcaldy War Memorial; *Soldiers Died* Part 33; *FFP* (BMD) 30.11.18; *FA* 14.12.18; *FA* (FRoH) 14.12.18; *FFP* 14.12.18; *FFP* (RoH) 14.12.18

Morgan, Andrew, MM: Private (S/20567 Gordon Hldrs [6/7th]); KIA, 25.10.18, 20 years; 41 Anderson Street, Kirkcaldy; Vis-en-Artois Memorial, Pas de Calais, France. Panel 10; Kirkcaldy War Memorial; *Soldiers Died* Part 65; *FFP* (BMD) 07.12.18; *FA* 14.12.18; *FFP* 14.12.18; *FA* (FRoH) 21.12.18; *FA* (RoH) 18.01.19

Morgan, Andrew: Private (30144 HLI [18th] "X" Coy); Died 107th Fld Amb, 08.07.17, 34 years; 14 Thistle Street, Kirkcaldy; Old Parish Church Memorial Panel; Villers-Faucon Communal Cemetery, France. Grave C.22; Kirkcaldy War Memorial; *Soldiers Died* Part 63; *FA* 14.07.17; *FFP* 14.07.17; *FFP* (BMD) 21.07.17; *FA* (BMD) 28.07.17; *FA* 15.09.17; *FFP* (RoH) 15.09.17

Morgan, David: Private (20546 Royal Scots [1st]); KIA Salonika, 04.10.16, 39 years; 17 South Row, West Gallatown, Kirkcaldy; Sinclairtown Parish Church War Memorial Chair; Struma Military Cemetery, Kalocastron, Greece. Grave IV.J.15; Kirkcaldy War Memorial; *Soldiers Died* Part 6; *FA* 28.10.16; *FA* (BMD) 28.10.16; *FFP* 28.10.16; *FFP* (BMD) 28.10.16; *FFP* (CasList) 04.11.16; *FA* (RoH) 18.11.16; *FFP* 18.11.16; *FFP* (RoH) 18.11.16; *FFP* (RoH) 30.12.16; *FA* (Service List) 24.03.17; *FA* (FRoH) 30.11.18

Morris, Alexander: Private (43169 HLI [16th]. Formerly 1738 HCB); KIA, 19.11.16, 23 years; 5 Balfour Place, Kirkcaldy; Invertiel Parish Church Memorial Table; Thiepval Memorial, Somme, France. Pier & Face 15C; Kirkcaldy War Memorial; *FA* 09.12.16; *Soldiers Died* Part 63; *FA* 02.12.16; *FA* (BMD) 02.12.16; *FFP* 02.12.16; *FFP* 09.12.16; *FA* (RoH) 16.12.16; *FFP* (RoH) 30.12.16; *FA* (CasList) 13.01.17; *FFP* (CasList) 13.01.17; *FA* (Service List) 20.01.17; *FA* (FRoH) 30.11.18

Morris, John: Trooper (2486 F & F Yeo); DOW dressing station, Suvla, 21.10.15, 24 years; 5 Watery Wynd, Kirkcaldy; Invertiel Parish Church Memorial Table; Lala Baba Cemetery, Turkey. Grave I.A.11; Kirkcaldy War Memorial; *Soldiers Died* Part 1; War Album 15/16; *FA* 06.11.15; *FA* (RoH) 13.11.15; *FA* 05.02.16; *FFP* 05.08.16 Roll of the Brave; *FFP* (BMD) 21.10.16; *FA* (Service List) 04.11.16; *FA* (Service List) 13.01.17; *FFP* (BMD) 20.10.17; *FA* (FRoH) 16.11.18; *FFP* (BMD) 23.10.20; Ogilvie

Morrison, Duncan: Private (3/2573 Black Watch [1st]); DOW, 22.08.16, 21 years; 16 Steedman's Square/126 Links Street, Kirkcaldy; St Sever Cemetery, Rouen, Seine-Maritime, France. Grave B.30.10; Kirkcaldy War Memorial; *FA* 02.09.16; *Soldiers Died* Part 46; *FA* 26.08.16; *FA* 02.09.16; *FFP* 02.09.16; *FA* (RoH) 16.09.16; *FFP* (RoH) 16.09.16; *FA* (CasList) 23.09.16; *FFP* (CasList) 23.09.16; *FA* (Service List) 25.11.16; *FA* (Service List) 02.12.16; *FA* (Service List) 23.12.16; *FFP* (RoH) 30.12.16; *FA* (FRoH) 23.11.18; Wauchope Vol 1

Morrison, George Butters: Private (345305 Black Watch [14th] [F & F Yeo Bn] att'd Royal Engineers. Formerly 2432 F & F Yeo); Died of pneumonia at Nasrich Hospital, Cairo, 14.04.18, 23 years; 160 High Street, Kirkcaldy; Gravestone in Bennochy Cemetery. West End Congregational Church Memorial Plaque; Cairo War Memorial Cemetery, Egypt. Grave O.148; Kirkcaldy War Memorial; *FA* 27.04.18; *Soldiers Died* Part 46; *FA* 20.04.18; *FA* (BMD) 20.04.18; *FFP* (RoH) 20.04.18; *FFP* (BMD) 20.04.18; *FFP* 27.04.18; *FA* (RoH) 18.05.18; *FFP* (RoH) 18.05.18; *FA* (FRoH) 07.12.18; *FA* (BMD) 19.04.19; Wauchope Vol 3; Ogilvie

Morrison, William: Lance Corporal (S/7440 Black Watch [1st] "D"Coy); KIA, 09.05.15; 67 Overton Road, Kirkcaldy/25 Dovecot Crescent, Dysart; Le Touret Memorial, Pas de Calais, France. Panels 24-26; Kirkcaldy War Memorial; *Soldiers Died* Part 46; *FA* 19.06.15; *FFP* 19.06.15; *FA* 02.10.15; *Scotsman* 00.03.16; *FA* 04.03.16; *FA* (BMD) 04.03.16; *FFP* 04.03.16; *FFP* 05.08.16 Roll of the Brave; *FA* (FRoH) 16.11.18; *FA* 26.04.19; Wauchope Vol 1

Morrison, William: Private (S/13791 Gordon Hldrs [2nd]); KIA Mametz, 01.07.16, 23 years; St Kilda, Beveridge Road, Kirkcaldy; Gravestone in Bennochy Cemetery; Gordon Cemetery, Mametz, Somme, France. Sp. Mem. C.12; Kirkcaldy War Memorial; *FFP* 22.07.16; *FA* 29.07.16; *Soldiers Died* Part 65; *FA* 22.07.16; *FA* (BMD) 22.07.16; *FFP* 22.07.16; *FFP* (BMD) 22.07.16; *FFP* 05.08.16; *FA* 16.09.16; *FFP* (RoH) 16.09.16; *FA* 11.11.16; *FFP* 11.11.16; *FFP* (RoH) 30.12.16; *FA* 14.07.17 (KHS War Honours); *FA* (FRoH) 23.11.18; *FA* (KHS RoH) 29.03.19

Morrison, William: Private (292467 Gordon Hldrs [7th]); Number changed from 6311; KIA, 23.04.17, 34 years; 15 Buchanan Street/2 Hendry's Wynd, Kirkcaldy; Arras Memorial, Pas de Calais, France. Bays 8 & 9; Kirkcaldy War Memorial; *Soldiers Died* Part 65; *FA* 02.06.17; *FA* 23.06.17; *FA* 30.06.17; *FA* 14.07.17; *FFP* 14.07.17; *FA* 09.03.18; *FA* (BMD) 09.03.18; *FA* (RoH) 16.03.18; *FA* (FRoH) 07.12.18

Morton, Thomas: Private (IO/5916; CEF; Canadian Infantry [72nd] 4th Div 12th Bde. [British Columbia Regt]); Brother-in-law of Thomas Younger; KIA, 27.09.18, 33 years; 21 Bridgeton, Kirkcaldy/539 Burnard Street, Vancouver; Quarry Wood Cemetery, Sains-les-Marquion, Pas de Calais, France. Grave III.C.7; Kirkcaldy War Memorial; *CBoR* Page 474; *FA* (BMD) 26.10.18; *FA* (RoH) 16.11.18; *FFP* (RoH) 16.11.18; *FFP* (BMD) 23.11.18; *FA* (FRoH) 14.12.18

Moyes, Andrew Millar: Private (3322747; CEF; Canadian Infantry [2nd] 6th Reserve Bn [Eastern Ontario Regt]); Brother of Robert Moyes; Died suddenly of pneumonia 1st Western Hospital, Liverpool, 15.08.18; 66 Hill Street, Kirkcaldy; Liverpool (Kirkdale) Cemetery, Liverpool. Grave VI.C.E.100; Kirkcaldy War Memorial; *CBoR* Page 475; *FA* 05.10.18; *FFP* 05.10.18; *FFP* (BMD) 05.10.18; *FA* (BMD) 12.10.18; *FA* (RoH) 19.10.18; *FA* (FRoH) 14.12.18

Moyes, Henry: Private (108409 Machine Gun Corps [21st]. Formerly 268642 Black Watch); KIA, 24.03.18; 49 Pratt Street, Kirkcaldy; Gravestone in Kinghorn Cemetery. Abbotshall Parish Church Memorial Plaque; Pozieres Memorial, Somme, France. Panels 90-93; Kirkcaldy War Memorial; *Soldiers Died* Part 75; *FA* 04.05.18; *FA* 19.11.21

Moyes, Robert: Private (246605; CEF; Canadian Infantry [2nd] 1st Div 1st Bde. [Eastern Ontario Regt]); Brother of Andrew Moyes; KIA, 30.08.18, 30 years; 66 Hill Street, Kirkcaldy/126 Spruce Street, Ottawa; Vimy Memorial, Pas de Calais, France; Kirkcaldy War Memorial; *CBoR* Page 475; *FA* 05.10.18; *FFP* 05.10.18; *FFP* (BMD) 05.10.18; *FA* (BMD) 12.10.18; *FA* (RoH) 19.10.18; *FA* (FRoH) 14.12.18

Muir, David: Private (352340 Royal Scots [9th] "A" Coy, 3rd Platoon); KIA, 23.04.17, 30 years; 63 Nether Street, Pathhead, Kirkcaldy; Gravestone in Dysart Cemetery; Arras Memorial, Pas de Calais, France. Bays 1 & 2; Kirkcaldy War Memorial; *FA* 16.06.17; *Soldiers Died* Part 6; *FA* 16.06.17

Muir, James Keddie: Private (345350 Black Watch [14th] [F & F Yeo Bn]. Formerly 2517 F & F Yeo); KIA Sheria, Egypt, 06.11.17, 31 years; 66 Mid Street, Kirkcaldy; E.U. Congregational Church Memorial Plaque. Gravestone in Dysart Cemetery; Jerusalem Memorial, Israel. Panel 33; Kirkcaldy War Memorial; *Soldiers Died* Part 46; *FA* 01.12.17; *FFP* 01.12.17; *FFP* (BMD) 01.12.17; *FA* (RoH) 15.12.17; *FFP* (RoH) 15.12.17; *FA* (FRoH) 07.12.18; Wauchope Vol 3; Ogilvie

Muir, Robert: Stoker 2nd Class (K/53692; Royal Navy; HMS *Pembroke*); Died of pneumonia at Sailors Hospital, Chatham, 27.10.18; 335 High Street, Kirkcaldy; Dysart Cemetery, Kirkcaldy. Grave 53.10.South; Kirkcaldy War Memorial; *Cross of Sacrifice Vol 4*; *FA* (RoH) 16.11.18; *FA* (BMD) 16.11.18; *FFP* (RoH) 16.11.18; *FA* (FRoH) 14.12.18

Mulvaney, William: Stoker 1st Class (K/26511; Royal Navy; HMS *Black Prince*); Presumed drowned at Battle of Jutland, 31.05.16, 30 years; 25 Millie Street, Kirkcaldy; Portsmouth Naval Memorial, Hampshire. Plate 19; Kirkcaldy War Memorial; Jutland Roll of Honour; *Cross of Sacrifice Vol 4*; *FFP* 10.06.16; *FA* (RoH) 17.06.16; *FFP* (RoH) 17.06.16; *FFP* 05.08.16 Roll of the Brave; *FA* (Service List) 13.01.17; *FFP* (BMD) 02.06.17; *FA* (FRoH) 23.11.18

Murray, Charles Thomson: Private (34083 Royal Scots [15th]); KIA France, 22.10.17, 23 years; Avondale, Falloden Crescent, Kirkcaldy; Tyne Cot Memorial, Zonnebeke, West Vlaanderen, Belgium. Panels 11-14 & 162; Kirkcaldy War Memorial; *Soldiers Died* Part 6; *FA* 24.11.17; *FFP* (CasList) 01.12.17; *FA* (RoH) 15.12.17; *FFP* (RoH) 15.12.17; *FA* (FRoH) 07.12.18

Murray, Frederick Charles: Private (A/22118; CEF; Canadian Infantry [8th] [Manitoba Regt] "B" Coy. 1st Div 2nd Bde. [The Black Devils/90th Winnipeg Rifles]); KIA, 19.12.15; 14 Thistle Street, Kirkcaldy; Berks Cemetery Extension, Comines-Warneton, Hainaut, Belgium. Grave III.B.42; Kirkcaldy War Memorial; *CBoR* Page 30; *FFP* 08.01.16; *FFP* 22.01.16; *FA* 29.01.16; *FFP* 05.08.16 Roll of the Brave; *FA* (Service List) 03.02.17; Wauchope Vol 1

Musgrove, John William: 2nd Lieutenant (Black Watch [4th]); MIA Meteren, 19.07.18, 21 years; 93 Victoria Road, Kirkcaldy; Old Parish Church Memorial Panel. Kirkcaldy High School War Memorial; Meteren Military Cemetery, Nord, France. Grave II.J.247; Kirkcaldy War Memorial; *Officers Died*; *Cross of Sacrifice Vol 1*; *FA* 03.08.18; *FA* 10.08.18; *FA* (BMD) 10.08.18; *FFP* 10.08.18; *FFP* (BMD) 10.08.18; *FA* (RoH) 14.09.18; *FFP* (RoH) 14.09.18; *FA* (FRoH) 14.12.18; *FA* (KHS RoH) 29.03.19; *FA* (KHS RoH) 19.07.19; *FA* (BMD) 19.07.19; Wauchope Vol 2

Mustard, Charles Wright: Gunner (129075 RGA [274th Siege Batt'y]); KIA France, 28.10.17, 31 years; 60 Alexandra Street, Kirkcaldy; Gravestone in Bennochy Cemetery; Potijze Chateau Grounds Cemetery, Ieper, West Vlaanderen, Belgium. Grave I.C.1; Kirkcaldy War Memorial; *Soldiers Died* Part 3; *FA* 10.11.17; *FFP* 10.11.17; *FA* 17.11.17; *FA* (RoH) 17.11.17; *FFP* (RoH) 17.11.17; *FFP* (CasList) 08.12.17; *FFP* (CasList) 15.12.17; *FA* (FRoH) 07.12.18; *FFP* (BMD) 23.10.20

Myner, Thomas: Private (14148 KOSB [7/8th]); KIA Ypres, 31.07.17, 29 years; 239 Links Street, Kirkcaldy; Ypres (Menin Gate) Memorial, Ieper, West Vlaanderen, Belgium. Panel 22; Kirkcaldy War Memorial; *Soldiers Died* Part 30; *FFP* (CasList) 18.08.17; *FA* 25.08.17; *FFP* (CasList) 08.09.17; *FA* 15.09.17; *FFP* (RoH) 15.09.17

Nairn, Andrew: Lance Corporal (8020 Black Watch [2nd]); Died station hospital, Colaba, Bombay, of wounds suffered in Persian Gulf, 04.02.16; Links Street, Kirkcaldy; Kirkee 1914-1918 Memorial, Poona, India. Face D; Kirkcaldy War Memorial; *Soldiers Died* Part 46; *FFP* 26.02.16; *FFP* 05.08.16 Roll of the Brave; *FA* (FRoH) 23.11.18; Wauchope Vol 1

Nairn, Ian Couper, MC & Bar: Captain (Black Watch [14th] [F & F Yeo Bn]); KIA Moislains, 02.09.18, 25 years; Forth Park, Kirkcaldy; Gravestone in Bennochy Cemetery. St Brycedale Church Plaque. Kirkcaldy High School War Memorial; Peronne Communal Cemetery Extension, Ste. Radegonde, Somme, France. Grave III.B.35; Kirkcaldy War Memorial; *FFP* 14.09.18; *Officers Died*; *Cross of Sacrifice Vol 1*; *FFP* 09.03.18; *FA* 14.09.18; *FA* (CasList) 14.09.18; *FA* (BMD) 14.09.18; *FFP* 14.09.18; *FFP* (RoH) 14.09.18; *FFP* (BMD) 14.09.18; *FA* (FRoH) 14.12.18; *FA* (KHS RoH) 29.03.19; *FA* (KHS RoH) 19.07.19; Wauchope Vol 3; Ogilvie

---

Captain Ian Couper **Nairn**, MC and Bar, was killed in action in France, 2nd September 1918 aged 25.

His father, John Nairn of the linoleum family, donated the Museum and Library to the burgh of Kirkcaldy as part of the memorial to those who gave their lives in the Great War.

Neil, William: Sapper (63434 Royal Engineers [154th Fld Coy]); KIA, 01.07.16, 19 years; 4 Salisbury Street, Kirkcaldy; Bienvillers Military Cemetery, Pas de Calais, France. Grave VIII.B.5; Kirkcaldy War Memorial; *FA* 15.07.16; *Soldiers Died* Part 4; *FA* 08.07.16; *FA* 15.07.16; *FA* (RoH) 15.07.16; *FFP* 15.07.16; *FFP* (BMD) 15.07.16; *FA* (CasList) 22.07.16; *FA* (BMD) 22.07.16; *FFP* 05.08.16 Roll of the Brave; *FA* (Service List) 23.12.16; *FA* (FRoH) 23.11.18

Ness, Andrew: Private (291445 Black Watch [4/5th]); KIA, 26.09.17, 17 years; 8 Flesh Wynd, Kirkcaldy; Tyne Cot Memorial, Zonnebeke, West Vlaanderen, Belgium. Panels 94-96; Kirkcaldy War Memorial; *Soldiers Died* Part 46; *FFP* (RoH) 23.03.18; *FA* 30.03.18; Wauchope Vol 2

Ness, Andrew: Private (267281 Royal Warwickshire Regt [2/7th]. Formerly 2285 HCB); KIA, 18.08.18; 142 Den Road, Kirkcaldy; Tannay British Cemetery, Thiennes, Nord, France. Grave 5.D.12; Kirkcaldy War Memorial; *Soldiers Died* Part 11; *FA* (RoH) 14.09.18; *FFP* (RoH) 14.09.18; *FA* 05.10.18; *FA* (RoH) 19.10.18; FF] [RoH) 19.10.18; *FA* (FRoH) 14.12.18

Ness, George: Private (3/2506 Black Watch [2nd]); DOW in hospital, Nottingham. Buried in Bennochy Cemetery, 13.06.15, 19 years; 41 East Smeaton Street, Kirkcaldy; Gravestone in Bennochy Cemetery; Bennochy Cemetery, Kirkcaldy. Grave M.805; Kirkcaldy War Memorial; *Soldiers Died* Part 46; War Album 15; *FA* 15.05.15; *FA* 19.06.15; *FA* (BMD) 19.06.15; *FFP* 19.06.15; *FFP* (BMD) 19.06.15; *FFP* (CasList) 03.07.15; *FA* (RoH) 17.07.15; *FFP* 05.08.16 Roll of the Brave; *FA* (Service List) 17.02.17; *FA* (FRoH) 16.11.18; Wauchope Vol 1

Nicholson, Benjamin M.: Private (291798 Black Watch [7th]); Died of dysentery, Military Hospital, Sedan, whilst a PoW, 14.07.18, 23 years; Old Parish Church Memorial Panel; Sedan (St Charles) Communal Cemetery, Ardennes, France. Grave 502; Kirkcaldy War Memorial; *Soldiers Died* Part 46; *FFP* (BMD) 07.12.18; Wauchope Vol 2

Nicholson, David: Private (41040 KOSB [6th]. Formerly 2333 F & F Yeo); KIA France, 12.10.17, 21 years; 182 Den Road, Kirkcaldy; Tyne Cot Memorial, Zonnebeke, West Vlaanderen, Belgium. Panels 66-68; Kirkcaldy War Memorial; *Soldiers Died* Part 30; *FFP* 27.10.17; *FFP* (BMD) 27.10.17; *FA* 03.11.17; *FA* (RoH) 17.11.17; *FFP* (RoH) 17.11.17; *FFP* (CasList) 24.11.17; *FFP* (BMD) 12.10.18; *FA* (FRoH) 07.12.18

Nicol, Alexander: Guardsman (11780 Scots Guards [1st]); PC 175, Fife Constabulary; KIA, 10.06.15, 22 years; 17/29 Rose Street, Kirkcaldy; Gravestone in Bennochy Cemetery. Old Parish Church Memorial Panel. Police Memorial Plaque; Woburn Abbey Cemetery, Cuinchy, Pas de Calais, France. Grave III.C.8; Kirkcaldy War Memorial; *FA* 14.08.15; *Soldiers Died* Part 5; War Album 15; *FA* 19.06.15; *FFP* (BMD) 19.06.15; *Scotsman* 19.06.15; *FA* (BMD) 26.06.15; *FFP* (CasList) 03.07.15; *FFP* 10.07.15; *FA* (RoH) 17.07.15; *FFP* 19.05.16; *FFP* 05.08.16 Roll of the Brave; *FA* (Service List) 27.01.17; *FFP* 14.04.17; *FA* (FRoH) 16.11.18; Pictorial History of Fife Constabulary

Nicol, James: Private (345115 Black Watch [14th] [F & F Yeo Bn]. Formerly 1832 F & F Yeo); Brother of William Nicol; KIA Sheria, Egypt, 06.11.17, 23 years; 80 Institution Street, Kirkcaldy; Beersheba War Cemetery, Israel. Grave L.34; Kirkcaldy War Memorial; *Soldiers Died* Part 46; *FA* 24.11.17; *FFP* 24.11.17; *FFP* (BMD) 08.12.17; *FA* (RoH) 15.12.17; *FA* (BMD) 15.12.17; *FFP* (RoH) 15.12.17; *FA* (FRoH) 07.12.18; *FA* 14.12.18; *FFP* 14.12.18; Wauchope Vol 3; Ogilvie

Nicol, Magnus: Private (1445 Black Watch [2nd]); KIA, 27.11.14, 22 years; 87 Institution Street/8 Bute Wynd, Kirkcaldy; Sinclairtown Parish Church War Memorial Chair; Le Touret Memorial, Pas de Calais, France. Panels 24-26; Kirkcaldy War Memorial; *FFP* 12.12.14; *Soldiers Died* Part 46; War Album 14/15; *Daily Telegraph* 00.12.14; *FA* 12.12.14; *FFP* 12.12.14; *FFP* (BMD) 12.12.14; *FA* (CasList) 19.12.14; *FA* 02.01.15; *FA* (CasList) 20.02.15; *FFP* 05.08.16 Roll of the Brave; *FA* (Service List) 24.02.17; *FA* (FRoH) 16.11.18; Wauchope Vol 1

Nicol, William: Private (56913 RAMC att'd Sanitary Section [41st]); Brother of James Nicol; Died of cerebral malaria at No 1 British General Hospital, Hamadan, 21.11.18, 20 years; 90 Institution Street, Kirkcaldy; Tehran War Cemetery, Iran. Grave IV.G.13; Kirkcaldy War Memorial; *FFP* (BMD) 07.12.18; *FA* 14.12.18; *FFP* 14.12.18; *FA* (FRoH) 21.12.18; *FA* (RoH) 18.01.19

Nicolson, Alexander: Private (RAMC); Spelt Nicholson in *FFP* 21.06.24; Pathhead Parish Church Memorial Plaques & Windows; Not identified on CWGC web site; Kirkcaldy War Memorial; *FFP* 21.06.24

Niven, Robert: Private (27852 KOSB [1st]. Formerly 3211 F & F Yeo); KIA, 23.04.17, 23 years; 11 Glasswork Street, Kirkcaldy. Formerly Kelty; Arras Memorial, Pas de Calais, France. Bay 6; Kirkcaldy War Memorial; *Soldiers Died* Part 30; *FFP* 12.05.17; *FFP* (BMD) 12.05.17; *FA* 19.05.17; *FA* (RoH) 19.05.17; *FA* (BMD) 19.05.17; *FFP* (RoH) 19.05.17; *FA* (CasList) 26.05.17; *FFP* (CasList) 26.05.17; *FFP* (RoH) 16.06.17; *FFP* (BMD) 27.04.18; *FA* (FRoH) 30.11.18

Noble, George: Private (40216 Royal Scots [11th]. Formerly 3336 F & F Yeo & 27523 KOSB); DOW, 22.05.17, 28 years; 6 Russell Place, Kirkcaldy; Union Church Plaque. Gravestone in Bennochy Cemetery; St Sever Cemetery Extension, Rouen, Seine-Maritime, France. Grave P.II.M.6B; Kirkcaldy War Memorial; *Soldiers Died* Part 6; *FA* 26.05.17; *FFP* 26.05.17; *FFP* (BMD) 26.05.17; *FA* (RoH) 16.06.17; *FFP* (RoH) 16.06.17; *FFP* (CasList) 23.06.17; *FFP* (BMD) 25.05.18; *FA* (FRoH) 30.11.18

Noble, Thomas Hart: Private (291805 Black Watch [8th]); Also listed as Duncan Noble; KIA, 21.03.18, 26 years; 21 Octavia Street, Kirkcaldy; Pozieres Memorial, Somme, France. Panels 49-50; Kirkcaldy War Memorial; *Soldiers Died* Part 46; *FA* 27.04.18; *FFP* (BMD) 27.04.18; *FA* (BMD) 04.05.18; *FA* (RoH) 18.05.18; *FFP* (RoH) 18.05.18; *FA* (FRoH) 07.12.18; Wauchope Vol 3

Oates, William: Private (16568 KOSB [7th]); DOW, 26.09.15, 27 years; 253 Rosslyn Street, Kirkcaldy; Loos Memorial, Pas de Calais, France. Panels 53-56; Kirkcaldy War Memorial. East Wemyss War Memorial; *FFP* 30.10.15; *Soldiers Died* Part 30; War Album 15/16; *FFP* 02.10.15; *FFP* 23.10.15; *Scotsman* (CasList) 25.10.15; *FA* 30.10.15; *FFP* 30.10.15; *FA* (RoH) 13.11.15; *FFP* 05.08.16 Roll of the Brave; *FFP* (BMD) 30.09.16; *FA* (Service List) 09.12.16; *FFP* (BMD) 29.09.17; *FA* (FRoH) 16.11.18

O'Brien, Bernard: Lance Corporal (1524 Black Watch [1/7th] [Sniper Section]); KIA High Wood, 20.07.16, 23 years; 210 St Clair Street, Kirkcaldy; Pathhead Baptist Church War Memorial Roll of Honour; Thiepval Memorial, Somme, France. Pier & Face 10A; Kirkcaldy War Memorial; *FA* 19.08.16; *Soldiers Died* Part 46; *FA* 12.08.16 (2 entries); *FA* 19.08.16; *FFP* 19.08.16; *FFP* 26.08.16; *FA* (CasList) 09.09.16; *FFP* (CasList) 09.09.16; *FA* (RoH) 16.09.16; *FFP* (RoH) 16.09.16; *FFP* (RoH) 30.12.16; *FFP* (BMD) 28.07.17; *FFP* (BMD) 03.08.18; *FA* (FRoH) 23.11.18; Wauchope Vol 2

O'Donnell, James: Private (3/2584 Black Watch [2nd]); KIA Persian Gulf, 21.04.17; Steedman's Square, 126 Links Street, Kirkcaldy; Basra Memorial, Iraq. Panels 25 & 63; Kirkcaldy War Memorial; *Soldiers Died* Part 46; *FFP* 12.05.17; *FA* 19.05.17; *FA* (RoH) 19.05.17; *FFP* (RoH) 19.05.17; *FA* (CasList) 26.05.17; *FFP* (CasList) 26.05.17; *FA* (BMD) 11.05.18; *FA* (FRoH) 30.11.18; Wauchope Vol 1

Ogilvie, Charles Taylor: Sapper (499560 Royal Engineers [92nd Fld Coy]); DOW 4th CCS, 22.01.18, 35 years; 22 Harriet Street, Kirkcaldy; Pathhead Parish Church Memorial Plaques & Windows; Dozinghem Military Cemetery, Westvleteren, Poperinge, West Vlaanderen, Belgium. Grave XIII.G.7; Kirkcaldy War Memorial; *Soldiers Died* Part 4; *FFP* (RoH) 02.02.18; *FFP* (BMD) 02.02.18; *FFP* (RoH) 09.02.18; *FA* 16.02.18; *FA* (RoH) 16.02.18; *FFP* (RoH) 16.02.18; *FA* (FRoH) 07.12.18; *FFP* (BMD) 25.01.19; *FFP* 21.06.24

Oliver, Richard Ferris: Sergeant (345009 Black Watch [14th] [F & F Yeo Bn]); KIA Beitania, Palestine & buried there, 28.12.17, 26 years; 349 High Street, Kirkcaldy; Gravestones in Bennochy Cemetery (Photo) & Abbotshall Churchyard. Kirkcaldy High School War Memorial; Jerusalem War Cemetery, Israel. Grave Y.82; Kirkcaldy War Memorial; *FA* 19.01.18; *FFP* 19.01.18; *Soldiers Died* Part 46; *FA* 19.01.18; *FA* (BMD) 19.01.18; *FFP* (RoH) 19.01.18; *FFP* (BMD) 19.01.18; *FA* (RoH) 16.02.18; *FFP* (RoH) 16.02.18; *FA* 13.07.18; *FA* (FRoH) 07.12.18; *FFP* (BMD) 28.12.18; *FA* (KHS RoH) 29.03.19; Wauchope Vol 3; Ogilvie

Page, David Kinghorn: Private (S/21253 Gordon Hldrs [6/7th]); KIA, 14.10.18, 19 years; 242 High Street, Kirkcaldy; Avesnes-Le-Sec Communal Cemetery Extension, Nord, France. Grave A.16; Kirkcaldy War Memorial. Strathmiglo War Memorial; *Soldiers Died* Part 65; *FA* 02.11.18; *FA* (RoH) 16.11.18; *FFP* (RoH) 16.11.18; *FA* (FRoH) 14.12.18

Page, James Stark: Private (5978 KOSB [2nd]); KIA Hill 60, France, 23.04.15, 29 years; 7 St Clair Street, Kirkcaldy; E.U. Congregational Church Memorial Plaque; Not identified on CWGC web site; Kirkcaldy War Memorial; *FA* 15.04.16; *Soldiers Died* Part 30; *FA* 22.05.15; *FA* 11.03.16; *FFP* (BMD) 11.03.16; *FFP* (BMD) 18.03.16; *FFP* (BMD) 23.04.16; *FFP* 05.08.16 Roll of the Brave; *FA* (Service List) 02.12.16; *FFP* (BMD) 28.04.17; *FFP* (BMD) 20.04.18; *FA* (FRoH) 23.11.18

Page, John: Private (30140 HLI [16th]); KIA France, 28.11.17, 36 years; 14 Barnet Crescent, Kirkcaldy; Passchendaele New Military Cemetery, Belgium. Grave VIII.A.R; Kirkcaldy War Memorial; *FA* 22.12.17; *Soldiers Died* Part 63; *FA* 22.12.17; *FA* (BMD) 22.12.17; *FFP* 22.12.17; *FFP* (CasList) 12.01.18; *FA* (RoH) 19.01.18; *FFP* (BMD) 30.11.18; *FA* (FRoH) 07.12.18

Page, John: Gunner (107607 RGA [256th Siege Batt'y]); DOW No 10 CCS, France, 08.10.17, 26 years; 4 Bell Wynd, Links Street, Kirkcaldy; Lijssenthoek Military Cemetery, Poperinge, West Vlaanderen, Belgium. Grave XXI.B.4; Kirkcaldy War Memorial; *FA* 31.03.17; *Soldiers Died* Part 3; *FA* 20.10.17; *FA* (BMD) 20.10.17; *FFP* 20.10.17; *FFP* (BMD) 20.10.17; *FA* (RoH) 17.11.17; *FFP* (RoH) 17.11.17; *FA* (BMD) 05.10.18; *FFP* (BMD) 05.10.18; *FA* (FRoH) 07.12.18

Page, William: Private (3/3507 Black Watch [2nd]); 25.09.15, 18 years; 58 Balfour Street, Kirkcaldy; St Brycedale Church Plaque; Loos Memorial, Pas de Calais, France. Panels 78-83; Kirkcaldy War Memorial; *Soldiers Died* Part 46; *FA* (Service List) 18.11.16; *FA* 30.12.16; *FFP* 30.12.16; *FA* (Memorial Service) 06.01.17; Wauchope Vol 1

Page, William Summers: Lance Corporal (S/9794 Seaforth Hldrs [7th]); DOW France, 15.10.16, 25 years; 294 High Street, Kirkcaldy; Not identified on CWGC web site; Kirkcaldy War Memorial; *FA* 11.11.16; *Soldiers Died* Part 64; *FA* 04.11.16; *FFP* (BMD) 04.11.16; *FA* (BMD) 11.11.16; *FFP* (BMD) 11.11.16; *FA* (RoH) 18.11.16; *FFP* (CasList) 18.11.16; *FFP* (RoH) 18.11.16; *FFP* (RoH) 30.12.16; *FFP* (BMD) 12.10.18; *FA* (FRoH) 30.11.18

Pake, John: Private (345394 Black Watch [14th] [F & F Yeo Bn]. Formerly 2586 F & F Yeo); KIA Sheria, Egypt, 06.11.17, 22 years; 56 Bank Street, Kirkcaldy; Dunnikier Church Roll of Honour; Beersheba War Cemetery, Israel. Grave L.43; Kirkcaldy War Memorial; *Soldiers Died* Part 46; *FA* 24.11.17; *FFP* 24.11.17; *FFP* (BMD) 24.11.17; *FA* (RoH) 15.12.17; *FFP* (RoH) 15.12.17; *FA* (FRoH) 07.12.18; *FA* 26.04.19; Wauchope Vol 3; Ogilvie

Palmer, Reginald: Rifleman (592753 London Regt [18th] [London Irish Rifles]. Formerly G/12771 Middlesex Regt); DOW France, 27.02.17, 24 years; 2 Whyte Melville Road, Kirkcaldy; Gravestone in Bennochy Cemetery. St Peter's Church Memorial Plaque; Lijssenthoek Military Cemetery, Poperinge, West Vlaanderen, Belgium. Grave XI.B.8A; Kirkcaldy War Memorial; *Soldiers Died* Part 76; *FA* 03.03.17; *FA* (BMD) 03.03.17; *FFP* 03.03.17; *FFP* 10.03.17; *FFP* (BMD) 10.03.17; *FA* (RoH) 17.03.17; *FA* (CasList) 31.03.17; *FFP* 31.03.17; *FA* (FRoH) 30.11.18

Parker, John: Private (292229 Gordon Hldrs [6th]); Died at home, 16.06.18, 23 years; 102 Hospital Hill, Dunfermline; Brighton (Bear Road) Borough Cemetery, Brighton, Sussex. Grave ZGV.61; Kirkcaldy War Memorial; *Soldiers Died* Part 65; Captain D. MacKenzie

Paterson, Alfred N.: Private (S/19822 Black Watch [2nd]); Drowned, Egypt. Buried British Cemetery El Jalil, near Jaffa, 21.06.18, 24 years; 15 Aitken Street, Kirkcaldy; Pathhead Parish Church Memorial Plaques & Windows; Ramleh War Cemetery, Israel. Grave R.53; Kirkcaldy War Memorial; *Soldiers Died* Part 46; *FFP* 06.07.18; *FA* 13.07.18; *FA* (RoH) 13.07.18; *FFP* 03.08.18; *FA* 10.08.18; *FA* (FRoH) 14.12.18; *FFP* 21.06.24; Wauchope Vol 1

Paterson, James: Corporal (350428 Black Watch [6th]. Formerly 2036 HCB); KIA, 20.07.18, 29 years; 9 Gas Wynd, Kirkcaldy; La Neuville-Aux-Larris Military Cemetery, Marne, France. Grave A.1; Kirkcaldy War Memorial; *FA* 17.08.18; *Soldiers Died* Part 46; *FA* 03.08.18; *FA* 10.08.18; *FFP* 10.08.18; *FFP* (BMD) 10.08.18; *FA* (BMD) 17.08.18; *FFP* 31.08.18; *FA* (RoH) 14.09.18; *FFP* (RoH) 14.09.18; *FA* (FRoH) 14.12.18; Wauchope Vol 2

Paterson, Peter: Private (S/32210 Cameron Hldrs [6th]. Formerly Lovat Scouts); KIA, 23.07.18; 132 Park Road, Kirkcaldy; Soissons Memorial, Aisne, France; Kirkcaldy War Memorial; *FA* 14.09.18; *Soldiers Died* Part 66; *FA* 07.09.18; *FA* (RoH) 13.09.19

Paterson, Robert: Private (S/11296 Black Watch [1st]); KIA, 22.09.16, 38 years; Thiepval Memorial, Somme, France. Pier & Face 10A; Kirkcaldy War Memorial; *Soldiers Died* Part 46; *FFP* (BMD) 22.09.17; Wauchope Vol 2

Paterson, Thomas: Sergeant (29494 KOSB [6th]. Formerly 2413 F & F Yeo); DOW CCS, 21.09.17, 23 years; 3 Hill Place, Kirkcaldy; Gravestone in Bennochy Cemetery. Abbotshall Parish Church Memorial Plaque; Nine Elms British Cemetery, Poperinge, West Vlaanderen, Belgium; Grave 1.D.3; Kirkcaldy War Memorial; *Soldiers Died* Part 30; *FA* 29.09.17; *FFP* 29.09.17; *FFP* 06.10.17; *FFP* (BMD) 06.10.17; *FA* 13.10.17; *FA* (BMD) 13.10.17; *FFP* (RoH) 13.10.17; *FFP* (BMD) 13.10.17; *FA* (BMD) 21.09.18; *FFP* (BMD) 21.09.18 (2entries); *FA* (FRoH) 07.12.18

Paton, James Hart: Private (1380; AIF; Australian Infantry [16th]); KIA Dardanelles, 02.05.15, 25 years; 34 Dunnikier Road, Kirkcaldy; Lone Pine Memorial, Gallipoli, Turkey. Panel 56; Kirkcaldy War Memorial; Australian War Memorial RoH Database; *FA* 19.06.15; *FFP* 19.06.15; *FA* 20.05.16; *FFP* 20.05.16; *FFP* 27.05.16; *FA* (RoH) 17.06.16; *FFP* (RoH) 17.06.16; *FFP* 05.08.16 Roll of the Brave; *FA* (Service List) 16.12.16; *FFP* (BMD) 04.05.18; *FA* (FRoH) 23.11.18

Paton, Peter: Private (7516 A & S Hldrs [2nd]); KIA, 21.10.14; 3 Victoria Road, Kirkcaldy; Abbotshall Parish Church Memorial Plaque; Ploegsteert Memorial, Comines-Warneton, Hainaut, Belgium. Panels 9 & 10; Kirkcaldy War Memorial; *Soldiers Died* Part 70; *FFP* 04.09.15; *FA* 12.02.16; *FFP* 12.02.16; *FFP* 05.08.16 Roll of the Brave; *FA* (FRoH) 16.11.18; *FA* 19.11.21

Patterson, George: Private (138089 Machine Gun Corps [18th]. Formerly 30513 Cameron Hldrs); KIA, 18.09.18, 19 years; 34 Rose Street, Kirkcaldy; Gravestone in Bennochy Cemetery. Bethelfield Church Plaque; Saulcourt Cemetery Extension, Guyencourt-Saulcourt, Somme, France. Grave B.II; Kirkcaldy War Memorial; *Soldiers Died* Part 75; *FFP* (BMD) 12.10.18; *FA* (RoH) 19.10.18; *FA* (FRoH) 14.12.18

Patterson, James: Corporal (S/4507 Gordon Hldrs [10th]); KIA, 25.09.15, 23 years; 4 Horse Wynd, Kirkcaldy; Whytescauseway Baptist Church Memorial Plaque; Loos Memorial, Pas de Calais, France. Panels 115-119; Kirkcaldy War Memorial; *FA* 30.10.15; *FA* 13.11.15; *FA* 30.09.16; *Soldiers Died* Part 65; *FFP* 30.10.15; *FFP* 20.11.15; *FA* 30.09.16; *FA* (BMD) 30.09.16; *FA* (RoH) 14.10.16; *FFP* (RoH) 14.10.16; *FA* (Service List) 28.10.16; *FFP* (RoH) 30.12.16; *FA* (Service List) 06.01.17; *FA* (BMD) 29.09.17; *FA* (FRoH) 23.11.18

Patterson, Norman L.: Lance Corporal (S/40086 Black Watch [1st]); MIA Somme, 25.09.16, 24 years; 94 Cumming's Terrace/84 Harriet Street/162 Dunnikier Road, Kirkcaldy; Gravestone in Dysart Cemetery. Dunnikier Church Roll of Honour; Thiepval Memorial, Somme, France. Pier & Face 10A; Kirkcaldy War Memorial; *Soldiers Died* Part 46; *FA* 07.10.16; *FFP* (CasList) 07.10.16; *FA* (RoH) 14.10.16; *FFP* (RoH) 14.10.16; *FA* 04.11.16; *FFP* 04.11.16; *FFP* (RoH) 30.12.16; *FA* (Service List) 20.01.17; *FA* 17.02.17; *FA* (BMD) 17.02.17; *FFP* 17.02.17; *FFP* 24.02.17; *FFP* (CasList) 10.03.17; *FA* (BMD) 21.09.18; *FFP* (BMD) 21.09.18; *FA* (FRoH) 23.11.18; *FA* 26.04.19; *FA* (BMD) 27.09.19; Wauchope Vol 1

Pattinson, James: Trooper (1730 F & F Yeo); KIA Suvla, 18.10.15, 18 years; 38 Loughborough Road, Kirkcaldy; Green Hill Cemetery, Turkey. Grave 1.E.12; Kirkcaldy War Memorial; *Soldiers Died* Part 1; War Album 15/16; *FA* (RoH) 13.11.15; *FA* 27.11.15; *FA* (CasList) 15.01.16; *FFP* 05.08.16 Roll of the Brave; *FA* (Service List) 17.02.17; *FA* (FRoH) 16.11.18; Ogilvie

Patullo, Alexander: Private (3/3776 Black Watch [1st]); DOW, 06.10.15; Loos Memorial, Pas de Calais, France. Panels 78-83; Kirkcaldy War Memorial; *Soldiers Died* Part 46; Wauchope Vol 1

Paul, Joseph: Private (26434 KOSB [1st]); KIA France, 24.08.17, 37 years; 37 High Street/29 Hill Street, Kirkcaldy; Old Parish Church Memorial Panel; Tyne Cot Memorial, Zonnebeke, West Vlaanderen, Belgium. Panels 66-68; Kirkcaldy War Memorial; *Soldiers Died* Part 30; *FA* 15.09.17; *FFP* 15.09.17; *FFP* (BMD) 15.09.17; *FA* (BMD) 06.10.17; *FFP* (BMD) 06.10.17; *FA* 13.10.17; *FFP* (RoH) 13.10.17; *FA* (BMD) 24.08.18; *FFP* (BMD) 24.08.18; *FA* (FRoH) 07.12.18

Peebles, Thomas B.: Private (43009 HLI [16th]. Formerly 1337 HCB); Killed the same day as his cousin, Alexander Pheely; MIA, 18.11.16, 22 years; 105 Rosslyn Street, Kirkcaldy; New Munich Trench British Cemetery, Beaumont-Hamel, Somme, France. Grave F.5; Kirkcaldy War Memorial; ‡; *Soldiers Died* Part 63; *FA* 09.12.16; *FA* 16.12.16; *FA* (CasList) 13.01.17; *FA* 21.04.17; *FA* 14.07.17; *FFP* 14.07.17; *FA* 21.07.17; *FFP* (CasList) 21.07.17; *FFP* (BMD) 17.11.17; *FA* (FRoH) 07.12.18

Penman, Andrew Palace: Able Seaman (Z/22468; Royal Navy; RNVR (HMS *Crescent*). Formerly Royal Scots & HCB); Different number in *Cross of Sacrifice*; Died of pneumonia aboard HM Hospital Ship *Garth Castle*, 10.11.18, 42 years; 4 Heggie's Square, Kirkcaldy; Gravestone in Abbotshall Churchyard; Abbotshall Parish Churchyard, Kirkcaldy. Grave Old. (N.) 125; Kirkcaldy War Memorial; *FA* 23.11.18; *Cross of Sacrifice Vol 4*; *FFP* (BMD) 16.11.18; *FA* 23.11.18; *FA* 30.11.18; *FFP* 07.12.18; *FA* (FRoH) 14.12.18; *FFP* (RoH) 14.12.18

Penny, James: Private (14295 Royal Scots [11th]); KIA, 21.03.17; Kelty; Arras Memorial, Pas de Calais, France. Bays 1 & 2; Kirkcaldy War Memorial. Kelty War Memorial; *Soldiers Died* Part 6; *FA* 07.04.17; *FA* (RoH) 14.04.17; *FA* (FRoH) 30.11.18

Petrie, Alexander: Private (203151 Black Watch [4/5th]. Transferred to Military Police); Relative of John Innes; KIA, 23.07.18, 39 years; 1 Church Lane, Kirkcaldy; Bethelfield Church Plaque; Vauxbuin French National Cemetery, Aisne, France. Grave II.B.9; Kirkcaldy War Memorial; *Soldiers Died* Part 46; *FA* 03.08.18; *FFP* 10.08.18; *FA* (CasList) 14.09.18; *FFP* (RoH) 14.09.18; *FA* (FRoH) 14.12.18; Wauchope Vol 2

Petrie, Alexander: Corporal (4079 RGA [Forth] 5th Coy); Died Craigleith Hospital as the result of an accident, 04.10.15, 31 years; 295 High Street, Kirkcaldy; Gravestone in Bennochy Cemetery. Dunnikier Church RoH. Forth RGA Plaque; Bennochy Cemetery, Kirkcaldy. Grave O.243; Kirkcaldy War Memorial; *Soldiers Died* Part 3; War Album 15/16; *FFP* (BMD) 09.10.15; *FA* 16.10.15; *FA* (RoH) 16.10.15; *FFP* (RoH) 16.10.15; *FFP* 05.08.16 Roll of the Brave; *FFP* (BMD) 07.10.16; *FA* (Service List) 28.10.16; *FA* (Service List) 09.12.16; *FA* (FRoH) 16.11.18; *FA* 26.04.19

Cousins, Thomas **Peebles** and Alexander **Pheely**, both served with the 16th HLI, having formerly been with the HCB. They were killed on the same day, 18th November, 1916 and are both buried in New Munich Trench Cemetery, Beaumont-Hamel on the Somme.

Petrie, Charles: Driver (7245 RFA [90th Batt'y]); Brother-in-law of James Fisher; Died of malarial fever at Peshawar, 04.11.16; 14 Flesh Wynd, Kirkcaldy; Peshawar British Cemetery, India (Right) B.C.XLIV.16. Delhi Memorial (India Gate), Delhi, India. Face 1; Kirkcaldy War Memorial; *FA* 06.11.15; *FA* 18.11.16; *Soldiers Died* Part 2; *FFP* (BMD) 18.11.16; *FA* (RoH) 16.12.16; *FFP* (RoH) 30.12.16; *FA* (Service List) 06.01.17; *FFP* (BMD) 03.11.17; *FA* (FRoH) 30.11.18

Phair, James: Private (3/3024 Black Watch [1st]); Spelt Fair in some sources; KIA, 09.05.15, 33 years; 27 Links Street, Kirkcaldy; Le Touret Memorial, Pas de Calais, France. Panels 24-26; Kirkcaldy War Memorial; *FA* 19.06.15; *Soldiers Died* Part 46; War Album 15; *FA* 05.06.15; *Dundee Advertiser* 09.06.15; *FA* (BMD) 12.06.15; *FFP* 12.06.15; *FFP* (CasList) 03.07.15; *FFP* (BMD) 13.05.16; *FFP* 05.08.16 Roll of the Brave; *FA* (Service List) 02.12.16; *FA* (FRoH) 16.11.18; Wauchope Vol 1

Pheely, Alexander D.: Private (43046 HLI [16th]. Formerly 2321 HCB); Killed the same day as his cousin, Thomas B. Peebles; MIA, 18.11.16, 20 years; 465 High Street, Kirkcaldy; New Munich Trench British Cemetery, Beaumont-Hamel, Somme, France. Grave B.4; Kirkcaldy War Memorial; *Soldiers Died* Part 63; *FA* 16.12.16; *FA* (CasList) 13.01.17; *FA* 20.01.17; *FA* 21.07.17; *FFP* 21.07.17; *FFP* (BMD) 28.07.17; *FA* 04.08.17; *FFP* (CasList) 04.08.17; *FA* 15.09.17; *FFP* (RoH) 15.09.17

Philp, Alexander: Private (291802 Black Watch [7th]); KIA, 28.10.18; Barony Church Plaque; Poznan Old Garrison Cemetery, Poland. Grave IV.C.2; Kirkcaldy War Memorial. Dysart War Memorial; *Soldiers Died* Part 46; Wauchope Vol 2

Philp, Andrew: Lieutenant Surgeon (RAMC); Died of accidental injuries at Royal Infirmary, Hull, 30.05.15, 49 years; Victoria Road, Kirkcaldy; Gravestone in Bennochy Cemetery; Bennochy Cemetery, Kirkcaldy. Grave O.345; Kirkcaldy War Memorial; *Officers Died*; *Cross of Sacrifice Vol 1*; War Album 15; *FA* (BMD) 05.06.15; *FFP* (BMD) 05.06.15; *FFP* (CasList) 03.07.15; *FFP* 5.08.16 Roll of the Brave; *FA* (FRoH) 16.11.18

Philp, David Brown: Private (S/8844 Gordon Hldrs [1st]); Died 8th CCS, 06.05.17, 22 years; 17 Mitchell Place, Kirkcaldy; Duisans British Cemetery, Etrun, Pas de Calais, France. Grave IV.K.51; Kirkcaldy War Memorial; *Soldiers Died* Part 65; *FFP* 12.05.17; *FA* 19.05.17; *FA* (RoH) 19.05.17; *FA* (BMD) 19.05.17; *FFP* 19.05.17; *FFP* (RoH) 19.05.17; *FFP* (BMD) 19.05.17; *FFP* (BMD) 04.05.18; *FA* (FRoH) 30.11.18

Pirie, Roy Spears: Signaller (12/3785; NZEF; Auckland Infantry Regt [2nd] 16th Waikato Coy); KIA Somme, 21.09.16, 21 years; Townsend Villa, Townsend Crescent, Kirkcaldy; St Brycedale Church Plaque. Kirkcaldy High School War Memorial; Caterpillar Valley (New Zealand Memorial), Longueval, Somme, France; ‡; *FA* 14.10.16; Kirkcaldy War Memorial; NZEF Roll of Honour; *FA* 12.02.16; *FA* 07.10.16; *FA* (BMD) 07.10.16; *FFP* (CasList) 07.10.16; *FFP* (BMD) 07.10.16; *FA* 14.10.16; *FA* (RoH) 14.10.16; *FFP* 14.10.16; *FFP* (RoH) 14.10.16; *FFP* 21.10.16; *FA* 04.11.16; *FA* 11.11.16; *FFP* (RoH) 30.12.16; *FA* (Memorial Service) 06.01.17; *FA* (Service List) 13.01.17; *FA* 20.01.17; *FA* 14.07.17 (KHS War Honours); *FFP* (BMD) 22.09.17; *FFP* (Memorial List) 05.01.18; *FA* (BMD) 21.09.18; *FFP* (BMD) 21.09.18; *FA* (FRoH) 23.11.18; *FA* (KHS RoH) 29.03.19

Platt, Charles Edward Marlow: Petty Officer/Stoker (189300; Royal Navy; HMS *Broke*); KIA, 31.05.16; 11 Birrell Street Wynd, Pathhead, Kirkcaldy; Plymouth Memorial, Devon. Plate 14; Kirkcaldy War Memorial; *FA* 17.06.16; *Cross of Sacrifice Vol 4*; *FA* 10.06.16; *FFP* 10.06.16; *FFP* (BMD) 10.06.16; *FA* (RoH) 17.06.16; *FFP* (RoH) 17.06.16; *FFP* 05.08.16 Roll of the Brave; *FA* (Service List) 06.01.17; *FA* (FRoH) 23.11.18; Jutland Roll of Honour

Ponton, James V.: Sergeant (21006 Royal Scots [2nd]); Died PoW in hospital Wurttemberg, Germany, 15.01.17; 13 Bridgeton, Links Street, Kirkcaldy; Aubencheul-au-Bac Churchyard, Nord, France; Kirkcaldy War Memorial; *FA* 24.02.17; *FA* 16.06.17; *Soldiers Died* Part 6; *FA* 02.12.16; *FFP* 02.12.16; *FA* 09.12.16; *FA* (RoH) 16.12.16; *FA* (CasList) 23.12.16; *FA* 24.02.17; *FA* (Service List) 24.02.17; *FA* 16.06.17; *FFP* 16.06.17; *FA* 14.07.17; *FFP* 14.07.17; *FFP* (CasList) 28.07.17; *FA* (FRoH) 30.11.18; *FA* (FRoH) 07.12.18

Porter, John: Rifleman (24/2075; NZEF; 3rd New Zealand Rifle Bde [1st Bn]); KIA, 15.09.16, 29 years; 35 Balfour Street, Kirkcaldy; Caterpillar Valley (New Zealand Memorial), Longueval, Somme, France; Kirkcaldy War Memorial; ‡; NZEF Roll of Honour; *FA* (Service List) 18.11.16; *FA* (BMD) 12.05.17; *FA* (RoH) 19.05.17; *FFP* (RoH) 19.05.17; *FFP* (RoH) 16.03.18; *FA* (FRoH) 30.11.18; *FA* (FRoH) 07.12.18

Pratt, James: Private (39396 Royal Scots [15th]. Formerly 6866 Black Watch); DOW, 09.04.17, 33 years; 86 Mid Street, Kirkcaldy; St Nicolas Cemetery, Arras, Pas de Calais, France. Grave I.A.7; Kirkcaldy War Memorial; *Soldiers Died* Part 6; *FA* 05.05.17; *FFP* 05.05.17; *FA* (BMD) 12.05.17; *FFP* (BMD) 12.05.17; *FA* (RoH) 19.05.17; *FFP* (RoH) 19.05.17; *FFP* (CasList) 19.05.17; *FFP* (BMD) 13.04.18; *FA* (FRoH) 30.11.18

Pratt, Robert: Corporal (672 Black Watch [2nd]); KIA Persian Gulf, 07.01.16; 4 Invertiel Road, Kirkcaldy; Amara War Cemetery, Iraq. Grave XXX.J.16; Kirkcaldy War Memorial; *Soldiers Died* Part 46; *Evening News* 19.02.16; *Scotsman* 21.02.16; *FA* 26.02.16; *FFP* 18.03.16; *FFP* 05.08.16 Roll of the Brave; *FA* (Service List) 03.03.17; *FA* (FRoH) 23.11.18; Wauchope Vol 1

Proctor, Julien Russell: Corporal (20640; RAF; 15th Squadron); Accidentally killed, 26.09.18, 31 years; 14 Nether Street/High Street, Kirkcaldy; Gravestone in Dysart Cemetery; Varennes Military Cemetery, Somme, France. Grave V.A.9; Kirkcaldy War Memorial; RFC/RAF RoH; *Cross of Sacrifice Vol 4*; *FA* 05.10.18; *FFP* 05.10.18; *FFP* (BMD) 12.10.18; *FA* (RoH) 19.10.18; *FA* (FRoH) 14.12.18

Proudfoot, James Turner: Private (267452 Seaforth Hldrs [6th]); KIA France, 22.09.17, 20 years; 23 Quality Street, Kirkcaldy; Abbotshall Parish Church Memorial Plaque; Tyne Cot Memorial, Zonnebeke, West Vlaanderen, Belgium. Panels 132-135 & 162A; Kirkcaldy War Memorial; *Soldiers Died* Part 64; *FA* 06.10.17; *FFP* 13.10.17; *FA* 20.10.17; *FA* (BMD) 20.10.17; *FFP* 27.10.17; *FFP* (BMD) 27.10.17; *FA* (RoH) 17.11.17; *FFP* (RoH) 17.11.17; *FFP* (BMD) 21.09.18; *FA* (FRoH) 07.12.18; *FA* 19.11.21

Rae, Alexander: Private (1987 Black Watch [1/7th] "B" Coy); KIA Battle of the Ancre, 13.11.16, 23 years; 66 Nether Street, Kirkcaldy; Gravestone in Dysart Cemetery; Y Ravine Cemetery, Beaumont-Hamel, Somme, France. Grave E.I; Kirkcaldy War Memorial; *FA* 25.11.16; *Soldiers Died* Part 46; *FA* 25.11.16; *FA* (BMD) 25.11.16; *FFP* (CasList) 02.12.16; *FFP* (BMD) 02.12.16; *FA* (CasList) 16.12.16; *FA* (RoH) 16.12.16; *FFP* (CasList) 16.12.16; *FFP* 30.12.16; *FFP* (RoH) 30.12.16; *FFP* (BMD) 10.11.17; *FFP* (BMD) 16.11.18; *FA* (FRoH) 30.11.18; Wauchope Vol 2

Rae, Charles, DCM: Sergeant (242044 Royal Warwickshire Regt [2/6th]. Formerly 1852 HCB). On *Soldiers Died* as Rac; KIA, 21.03.18, 19 years; 6 Flesh Wynd, Kirkcaldy; Pozieres Memorial, Somme, France. Panels 18-19; Kirkcaldy War Memorial; *Soldiers Died* Part 11; *FFP* 02.02.18; *FFP* (RoH) 20.04.18; *FA* 27.04.18; *FFP* (RoH) 27.04.18; *FA* (RoH) 18.05.18; *FFP* (RoH) 18.05.18; *FA* (FRoH) 07.12.18; *FA* 26.04.19

Sergeant Charles **Rae** enlisted when he was sixteen years old. He transferred from the HCB to the Royal Warwickshire Regiment and refused to take the usual home leave before going to the front in case his parents tried to stop him going. Rae was wounded three times and awarded the DCM in 1917. He was killed in 1918, aged 19.

Rae, George: Private (11595 Royal Army Ordnance Corps); Died of dysentery at Voi Hospital, British East Africa, 26.11.16, 33 years; 25 Stewart's Place, Coal Wynd, Kirkcaldy; Voi Cemetery, Kenya. Grave III.B.7; Kirkcaldy War Memorial; *Soldiers Died* Part 80; *FFP* 06.01.16; *FA* 02.12.16; *FFP* 02.12.16; *FA* (RoH) 16.12.16; *FFP* (RoH) 30.12.16; *FA* (Service List) 03.02.17; *FFP* (BMD) 24.11.17; *FFP* (BMD) 23.11.18; *FA* (FRoH) 30.11.18

Rae, James Hoy: Private (15973 Royal Scots [12th]); MIA, 28.09.15, 29 years; 148 Institution Street, Kirkcaldy; Loos Memorial, Pas de Calais, France. Panels 10-13; Kirkcaldy War Memorial; *Soldiers Died* Part 6; *FA* (BMD) 07.10.16; *FFP* (BMD) 07.10.16; *FA* (RoH) 14.10.16; *FFP* (RoH) 14.10.16; *FFP* (RoH) 30.12.16; *FA* (Service List) 24.02.17; *FFP* (BMD) 22.09.17; *FFP* (BMD) 28.09.18; *FA* (FRoH) 23.11.18

Ramsay, Andrew: Private (S/3480 A & S Hldrs [11th]); KIA Somme, 16.09.16, 23 yearss; 4 Russell Place/47 Ava Street, Kirkcaldy; Thiepval Memorial, Somme, France. Pier & Face 15A & 16C; Kirkcaldy War Memorial; *FA* 07.10.16; *Soldiers Died* Part 70; *FA* 30.09.16; *FA* (RoH) 14.10.16; *FFP* (RoH) 14.10.16; *FFP* (CasList) 28.10.16; *FFP* (RoH) 30.12.16; *FA* (Service List) 13.01.17; *FFP* (BMD) 15.09.17; *FFP* (BMD) 14.09.18; *FFP* (BMD) 21.09.18; *FA* (FRoH) 23.11.18

Ramsay, James: Lance Corporal (760293; CEF; Canadian Infantry [7th] 1st Div 2nd Bde. [1st British Columbia Regt]); KIA. Buried near the Lens-Arras road, 09.04.17, 35 years; 92 Dunnikier Road, Kirkcaldy; Arras Road Cemetery, Roclincourt, Pas de Calais, France. Grave I.B.10; Kirkcaldy War Memorial; *CBoR* Page 313; *FFP* 28.04.17; *FFP* (BMD) 28.04.17; *FA* 05.05.17; *FA* (BMD) 05.05.17; *FFP* 05.05.17; *FA* (RoH) 19.05.17; *FFP* (RoH) 19.05.17; *FA* (FRoH) 30.11.18

Ramsay, John L.: Lance Corporal (35171 HLI [2nd]. Formerly S/15490 A & S Hldrs [13th]); Brother of David H. Ramsay. Black Watch; KIA, 03.05.17; Mitchell Street, Kirkcaldy; Gravestone in Newburgh Cemetery. Dunnikier Church Roll of Honour; Roclincourt Valley Cemetery, Pas de Calais, France. Grave IV.B.19; Kirkcaldy War Memorial. Newburgh War Memorial; *Soldiers Died* Part 63; *FFP* 23.06.17; *FA* 14.07.17; *FFP* 14.07.17; *FA* (FRoH) 07.12.18; *FA* 26.04.19; Telfer-Smollett

Ramsay, John Nicol: Private (1626 Black Watch [7th]); KIA Somme, 31.10.16, 20 years; 71 Links Street, Kirkcaldy; Auchonvillers Military Cemetery, Somme, France. Grave II.E.48; Kirkcaldy War Memorial; *FA* 18.11.16; *Soldiers Died* Part 46; *FA* 11.11.16 (2 entries); *FFP* 11.11.16; *FA* (RoH) 18.11.16; *FFP* (RoH) 18.11.16; *FFP* (CasList) 02.12.16; *FFP* (RoH) 30.12.16; *FFP* 14.04.17; *FFP* (BMD) 27.10.17; *FA* (FRoH) 30.11.18; Wauchope Vol 2

Ramsay, Robert: Private (S/4587 Black Watch [9th] "B" Coy); KIA, 25.09.15, 24 years; Hunter's Buildings, Sands Road, Kirkcaldy; Raith Church Memorial Plaque; Loos Memorial, Pas de Calais, France. Panels 78-83; Kirkcaldy War Memorial; *FA* 30.10.15; *Soldiers Died* Part 46; War Album 15/16; *Scotsman* 27.10.15; *FA* 30.10.15; *FFP* 30.10.15; *FA* (RoH) 13.11.15; *FFP* 05.08.16 Roll of the Brave; *FA* (Service List) 28.10.16; *FA* (Service List) 06.01.17; *FA* (FRoH) 16.11.18; Wauchope Vol 3

Ramsay, Robert: Private (950 Guards Machine Gun Regt [4th]. Formerly 13612 Scots Guards); On *Soldiers Died* as Ramsey; KIA, 03.12.17; 23 Balsusney Road/134 Dunnikier Road, Kirkcaldy; Cambrai Memorial, Louverval, Nord, France. Panel 3; Kirkcaldy War Memorial; *Soldiers Died* Part 5; *FFP* 15.12.17; *FFP* (BMD) 15.12.17; *FA* 22.12.17; *FA* (BMD) 22.12.17; *FFP* (CasList) 12.01.18; *FA* (RoH) 19.01.18; *FFP* (BMD) 30.11.18; *FA* (FRoH) 07.12.18; *FFP* (BMD) 07.12.18

Ramsay, William: Private (131629 RAMC [55th General Hospital]); Died of pneumonia Boulogne General Hospital, 22.04.18, 30 years; Links Street, Kirkcaldy; Old Parish Church Memorial Panel; Wimereux Communal Cemetery, Pas de Calais, France. Grave XI.F.7; Kirkcaldy War Memorial; *Soldiers Died* Part 79; *FA* 04.05.18; *FFP* (BMD) 04.05.18

Reekie, David (Simon) K.: Gunner (6732 RFA [108 Bde] "C" Batt'y); On CWGC website as Simon; 30.10.19, 37 years; 4 Park Road, Kirkcaldy; Gravestone in Dysart Cemetery; Dysart Cemetery, Kirkcaldy. Grave 3.I.Middle; Kirkcaldy War Memorial; *FA* 26.04.19

Reekie, John: Private (1460 HCB [1st]); Accidentally shot, Fortrose, 31.08.16, 34 years; 3 Meldrum Place/24 Quality Street, Kirkcaldy; Gravestone in Bennochy Cemetery. Bethelfield Church Plaque; Bennochy Cemetery, Kirkcaldy. Grave O.67; Kirkcaldy War Memorial; *Soldiers Died* Part 77; *FA* 02.09.16; *FA* 09.09.16; *FA* (BMD) 09.09.16; *FFP* (BMD) 09.09.16; *FA* (RoH) 16.09.16; *FFP* (RoH) 16.09.16; *FA* (Service List) 25.11.16; *FFP* (RoH) 30.12.16; *FA* (Service List) 20.01.17; *FFP* (BMD) 01.09.17; *FFP* (BMD) 31.08.18; *FA* (FRoH) 23.11.18

Reid, Alexander Kennedy: Private (S/15966 Cameron Hldrs [7th]); KIA, 25.09.15; 100 Sutherland Street, Kirkcaldy; Gallatown Church Roll of Honour; Loos Memorial, Pas de Calais, France. Panels 119-124; Kirkcaldy War Memorial; *FA* 18.12.15; *Soldiers Died* Part 66; *FA* 04.12.15; *FFP* 11.12.15; *FA* (RoH) 16.09.16; *FFP* (RoH) 16.09.16; *FFP* (RoH) 30.12.16; *FA* (Service List) 03.03.17; *FA* (FRoH) 23.11.18

Reid, Alexander T.: Private (HCB); Bethelfield Church Plaque; Not identified on CWGC web site; Kirkcaldy War Memorial

Reid, Anderson J.: Private (241241 Black Watch [4/5th]); KIA, 09.07.17; 84 Balfour Street/49 Meldrum Road, Kirkcaldy; Brandhoek Military Cemetery, Vlamertinghe, Ieper, West Vlaanderen, Belgium. Grave I.M.4; Kirkcaldy War Memorial; *Soldiers Died* Part 46; *FA* 04.08.17; *FFP* (BMD) 13.07.18; Wauchope Vol 2

Reid, Arthur Stanley: Sergeant (17213 Royal Scots [15th] "A" Coy); KIA Somme, 01.07.16, 31 years; 4 Swan Road, Kirkcaldy; Gravestone in Bennochy Cemetery. Bethelfield Church Plaque. Kirkcaldy High School War Memorial; Thiepval Memorial, Somme, France. Pier & Face 6D & 7D; Kirkcaldy War Memorial; *FA* 12.08.16; *Soldiers Died* Part 6; *FA* 12.08.16; *FFP* 12.08.16; *FA* (CasList) 26.08.16; *FFP* (CasList) 26.08.16; *FA* (RoH) 16.09.16; *FFP* (RoH) 16.09.16; *FFP* (RoH) 30.12.16; *FA* (Service List) 10.02.17; *FA* 14.07.17 (KHS War Honours); *FA* (BMD) 18.08.17; *FA* (FRoH) 23.11.18; *FA* (KHS RoH) 29.03.19

Reid, Henry Kidd: Private (31885 Machine Gun Corps [133rd]. Formerly 992 HCB); MIA Mesopotamia, 25.03.17, 22 years; 43 Viceroy Street, Kirkcaldy; Gravestone in Bennochy Cemetery. St Andrew's Church Memorial Plaque; Basra Memorial, Iraq. Panel 41; Kirkcaldy War Memorial; *Soldiers Died* Part 75; *FFP* 25.05.18; *FFP* (BMD) 25.05.18; *FA* 01.06.18; *FA* (BMD) 01.06.18; *FA* (RoH) 15.06.18; *FFP* (RoH) 15.06.18; *FA* (FRoH) 14.12.18

Reid, John: Private (345311 Black Watch [14th] [F & F Yeo Bn]. Formerly 2446 F & F Yeo); KIA Beitania, Palestine, 28.12.17, 19 years; 47 Cowan Street, Kirkcaldy; Gravestone in Bennochy Cemetery. Whytescauseway Baptist Church Memorial Plaque; Jerusalem War Cemetery, Israel. Grave D.41; Kirkcaldy War Memorial; *Soldiers Died* Part 46; *FA* 19.01.18; *FFP* (RoH) 19.01.18; *FFP* (BMD) 19.01.18; *FA* (BMD) 26.01.18; *FA* (RoH) 16.02.18; *FFP* (RoH) 16.02.18; *FA* (FRoH) 07.12.18; *FFP* (BMD) 28.12.18; Wauchope Vol 3; Ogilvie

Reid, John W.: Private (13516 KOSB [2nd] "C" Coy); KIA, 05.05.15, 22 years; Pringles Buildings,153 Overton Road/9 Cowan Street, Kirkcaldy; Bethelfield Church Plaque; Ypres (Menin Gate) Memorial, Ieper, West Vlaanderen, Belgium. Panel 22; Kirkcaldy War Memorial; *Soldiers Died* Part 30; War Album 15; *FA* 15.05.15; *FA* 22.05.15; *FFP* (CasList) 05.06.15; *FFP* 05.08.16 Roll of the Brave; *FA* (Service List) 18.11.16; *FA* (Service List) 03.02.17; *FA* (FRoH) 16.11.18; Kirkcaldy Council Memorial Scroll

Reid, Robert: Private (2842 Black Watch [1/7th] "B"Coy); Twin brother of Walter Reid; KIA, 16.06.15, 19 years; 37 Victoria Road, Kirkcaldy; Gravestone in Bennochy Cemetery. Bethelfield Church Plaque; Le Touret Memorial, Pas de Calais, France. Panels 24-26; Kirkcaldy War Memorial; *FFP* 09.06.17; *Soldiers Died* Part 46; War Album 15; *Scotsman* 07.06.15; *FA* 26.06.15; *FFP* 26.06.15; *FFP* (BMD) 26.06.15; *FFP* (CasList) 03.07.15; *FA* (RoH) 17.07.15; *FA* (CasList) 17.07.15; *FFP* (BMD) 17.06.16; *FFP* 05.08.16 Roll of the Brave; *FA* 19.05.17; *FFP* 19.05.17; *FFP* (BMD) 16.06.17; *FA* (FRoH) 16.11.18; *FA* (FRoH) 07.12.18; Wauchope Vol 2

Reid, Walter: Private (S/40586 Black Watch [8th]); Twin brother of Robert Reid; KIA, 03.05.17, 21 years; 37 Victoria Road, Kirkcaldy; Gravestone in Bennochy Cemetery. Bethelfield Church Plaque; Arras Memorial, Pas de Calais, France. Bay 6; Kirkcaldy War Memorial; *Soldiers Died* Part 46; *FFP* (BMD) 19.07.15; *FA* 19.05.17; *FFP* 19.05.17; *FA* (RoH) 16.06.17; *FFP* (RoH) 16.06.17; *FFP* (CasList) 16.06.17; *FFP* (BMD) 16.06.17; *FFP* (BMD) 15.06.18; *FA* (FRoH) 30.11.18; *FA* (FRoH) 07.12.18; Wauchope Vol 3

Reilly, James: Private (1342 HLI [2nd] "A" Coy); KIA Loos, 25.09.15, 40 years; 132 Den Road, Kirkcaldy; Loos Memorial, Pas de Calais, France. Panels 108-112; Kirkcaldy War Memorial; *FFP* 23.10.15; *Soldiers Died* Part 63; War Album 15/16; *FFP* 16.10.15; *FA* 23.10.15; *FA* (RoH) 13.11.15; *FFP* 05.08.16 Roll of the Brave; *FA* (Service List) 10.02.17; *FA* (FRoH) 16.11.18; Telfer-Smollett

Reilly, James Miller F.: 2nd Lieutenant (Royal Scots [12th]); KIA, 20.09.17, 20 years; 6 Rosebery Terrace, Kirkcaldy; Kirkcaldy High School War Memorial; Tyne Cot Memorial, Zonnebeke, West Vlaanderen, Belgium. Panels 11-14 & 162; Kirkcaldy War Memorial; *Officers Died*; *Cross of Sacrifice Vol 1*; *FA* 04.12.15; *FA* 29.09.17; *FA* (BMD) 29.09.17; *FFP* 29.09.17; *FFP* (BMD) 29.09.17; *FFP* 06.10.17; *FA* 13.10.17; *FFP* (RoH) 13.10.17; *FA* 13.07.18; *FA* (BMD) 21.09.18; *FFP* (BMD) 21.09.18 (2 entries); *FA* (FRoH) 07.12.18; *FA* (KHS RoH) 29.03.19

Richmond, William: Private (4495 Black Watch [1/7th]); KIA, 30.07.16, 19 years; 113 East Smeaton Street, Kirkcaldy; St Peter's Church Memorial Plaque; Thiepval Memorial, Somme, France. Pier & Face 10A; Kirkcaldy War Memorial; *FA* 09.09.16; *Soldiers Died* Part 46; *FA* 12.08.16; *FA* 02.09.16; *FA* 09.09.16; *FA* (CasList) 09.09.16; *FFP* 09.09.16; *FFP* (CasList) 09.09.16; *FA* (RoH) 16.09.16; *FFP* (RoH) 16.09.16; *FFP* (RoH) 30.12.16; *FA* (Service List) 17.02.17; *FA* (FRoH) 23.11.18; Wauchope Vol 2

Rigging, Hugh: Private (19448 Cheshire Regt [15th] Bantam Bn); Also spelt Riggans & Riggins; DOW, 18.07.16; 105 Overton Road, Kirkcaldy; Peronne Road Cemetery, Maricourt, Somme, France. Grave I.D.15; Kirkcaldy War Memorial; *FFP* 12.08.16; *Soldiers Died* Part 27; *FFP* 05.08.16; *FFP* 05.08.16 Roll of the Brave; *FFP* 12.08.16; *FA* (RoH) 16.09.16; *FFP* (RoH) 16.09.16; *FA* (Service List) 18.11.16; *FFP* (RoH) 30.12.16; *FA* (FRoH) 23.11.18

Ritchie, David: Private (24564 Machine Gun Corps Infantry [26th Coy]. Formerly 1724 HCB); KIA, 12.05.17, 21 years; 18 Strathearn Road, Kirkcaldy; Gravestone in Dysart Cemetery. St Andrew's Church Memorial Plaque; Arras Memorial, Pas de Calais, France. Bay 10; Kirkcaldy War Memorial; *Soldiers Died* Part 75; *FA* 26.05.17; *FA* (BMD) 26.05.17; *FFP* 26.05.17; *FFP* (BMD) 26.05.17; *FA* (RoH) 16.06.17; *FFP* (RoH) 16.06.17; *FFP* (CasList) 23.06.17; *FFP* (BMD) 11.05.18; *FA* (FRoH) 30.11.18

Ritchie, John B.: Lance Corporal (203122 Black Watch [1/7th]); DOW, 24.11.17; Orival Wood Cemetery, Flesquieres, Nord, France. Grave I.A.11; Kirkcaldy War Memorial; *Soldiers Died* Part 46; Wauchope Vol 2

Ritchie, John Christie: Sergeant (S/1827 Gordon Hldrs [1st]); DOW 23rd General Hospital, Etaples, 06.04.16, 25 years; 81 Victoria Road, Kirkcaldy; Etaples Military Cemetery, Pas de Calais, France. Grave V.A.5; Kirkcaldy War Memorial; *FA* 15.04.16; *Soldiers Died* Part 65; *FA* 15.04.16; *FA* (BMD) 15.04.16; *FFP* 15.04.16; *FFP* (BMD) 15.04.16; *FA* (RoH) 13.05.16; *FFP* 05.08.16 Roll of the Brave; *FA* (BMD) 07.04.17; *FFP* (BMD) 07.04.17; *FFP* (BMD) 06.04.18; *FA* (FRoH) 23.11.18

Ritchie, Robert Lyall: Lance Corporal (S/18735 Black Watch [4/5th]); KIA, 01.08.18, 20 years; 50 Rosabelle Street, Kirkcaldy; Pathhead Parish Church Memorial Plaques & Windows; Raperie British Cemetery, Villemontoire, Aisne, France. Grave IV.D.7; Kirkcaldy War Memorial; *Soldiers Died* Part 46; *FFP* 24.08.18; *FFP* (BMD) 24.08.18; *FA* 31.08.18; *FA* (BMD) 31.08.18; *FA* (RoH) 14.09.18; *FFP* (RoH) 14.09.18; *FA* (FRoH) 14.12.18; *FA* (KHS RoH) 29.03.19; Wauchope Vol 2

Robb, George: Private (99125 Machine Gun Corps [247th Coy]. Formerly 19472 Black Watch); KIA France, 10.10.17, 26 years; 42 Alexandra Street, Kirkcaldy; St Andrew's Church Memorial Plaque; Tyne Cot Memorial, Zonnebeke, West Vlaanderen, Belgium. Panels 154-159 & 163A; Kirkcaldy War Memorial; *Soldiers Died* Part 75; *FA* 20.10.17; *FFP* 20.10.17; *FFP* (BMD) 20.10.17; *FA* (RoH) 17.11.17; *FFP* (CasList) 17.11.17; *FFP* (RoH) 17.11.17; *FA* 20.07.18; *FA* (FRoH) 07.12.18

Robb, Peter: Private (S/18767 Black Watch [1/7th] 9th Platoon); KIA, 26.05.18, 20 years; Battery Place, Glasswork Street, Kirkcaldy; Bethelfield Church Plaque; Roclincourt Military Cemetery, Pas de Calais, France. Grave VI.D.7; Kirkcaldy War Memorial; *Soldiers Died* Part 46; *FFP* 08.06.18; *FFP* (BMD) 15.06.18; *FA* (BMD) 22.06.18; *FFP* (BMD) 22.06.18; *FA* 13.07.18; *FA* (FRoH) 14.12.18; Wauchope Vol 2

Robb, Samuel Wardlaw: Private (S/41761 Seaforth Hldrs [4th]. Formerly TR/1/18113 TR Bn); DOW, 13.04.18, 19 years; 207 St Clair Street, Kirkcaldy; Pernes British Cemetery, Pas de Calais, France. Grave I.B.39; Kirkcaldy War Memorial; *FFP* 04.05.18; *Soldiers Died* Part 64; *FA* 27.04.18; *FA* (BMD) 04.05.18; *FFP* 04.05.18; *FFP* (BMD) 04.05.18; *FA* (RoH) 18.05.18; *FFP* (RoH) 18.05.18; *FFP* (CasList) 22.06.18; *FA* (FRoH) 14.12.18

Robb, Thomas: Driver (46822 Royal Engineers [23rd Fld Coy]); KIA, 12.11.17, 25 years; 33 Nicol Street, Kirkcaldy; Abbotshall Parish Church Memorial Plaque; Hospital Farm Cemetery, Ieper, West Vlaanderen, Belgium. Grave D.5; Kirkcaldy War Memorial; *Soldiers Died* Part 4; *FA* 24.11.17; *FFP* 24.11.17; *FA* (RoH) 15.12.17; *FFP* (RoH) 15.12.17; *FA* (FRoH) 07.12.18; *FA* 19.11.21

Roberts, James Stratton: Private (S/17810 Black Watch [9th]); KIA Ypres, 31.07.17, 20 years; Sinclairtown Station Hotel, Kirkcaldy; Gravestone in Dysart Cemetery. Pathhead Parish Church Memorial Plaques & Windows. Kirkcaldy High School War Memorial; Ypres (Menin Gate) Memorial, Ieper, West Vlaanderen, Belgium. Panel 37; Kirkcaldy War Memorial; *Soldiers Died* Part 46; *FA* 11.08.17; *FFP* 11.08.17; *FFP* (BMD) 08.09.17; *FA* 15.09.17; *FFP* (RoH) 15.09.17; *FA* 13.07.18; *FFP* (BMD) 03.08.18; *FA* (KHS RoH) 29.03.19; *FFP* 21.06.24; Wauchope Vol 3

Robertson, Albert John; Sub-Lieutenant (Royal Navy; RNVR [RND] [*Nelson* Bn]. Formerly Royal Scots); KIA, 04.01.18, 20 years; 19 Sang Road, Kirkcaldy/Royal Crescent, Edinburgh; St Brycedale Church Plaque. Kirkcaldy High School War Memorial; Thiepval Memorial, Somme, France. Pier & Face 1A; Kirkcaldy War Memorial; *Cross of Sacrifice Vol 2*; *FA* 12.01.18; *FA* (BMD) 12.01.18; *FFP* 12.01.18; *FFP* (BMD) 12.01.18; *FA* (RoH) 19.01.18; *FA* (BMD) 19.01.18; *FA* 13.07.18; *FA* (FRoH) 07.12.18; *FA* (KHS RoH) 29.03.19

Robertson, Duncan: Private (9220 A & S Hldrs [2nd]); KIA, 25.09.15, 37 years; 21 Carson Square, Kirkcaldy; Cambrin Churchyard Extension, Pas de Calais, France. Grave C.5; Kirkcaldy War Memorial; *Soldiers Died* Part 70; *FA* (Service List) 31.03.17

Robertson, George: Lance Corporal (14273 HLI [16th]); Brother of James B. Robertson; KIA, 01.07.16, 36 years; 62 Balfour Street, Kirkcaldy; Lonsdale Cemetery, Authuile, Somme, France. Grave VI.N.9; Kirkcaldy War Memorial; *Soldiers Died* Part 63; *FA* (Service List) 18.11.16; *FFP* (BMD) 28.04.17; *FA* (BMD) 05.05.17; *FFP* 31.08.18

Robertson, Henry: Private (S/21614 Black Watch [4/5th]); KIA, 22.02.18; Mid Street, Kirkcaldy; E.U. Congregational Church Memorial Plaque; Fins New British Cemetery, Sorel-Le-Grand, Somme, France. Grave IV.C.1; Kirkcaldy War Memorial; *Soldiers Died* Part 46; *FA* 09.03.18; *FA* (BMD) 09.03.18; *FFP* (RoH) 09.03.18; *FFP* (BMD) 09.03.18; *FA* (RoH) 16.03.18; *FFP* (RoH) 16.03.18; *FA* (FRoH) 07.12.18; *FFP* (BMD) 22.02.19; Wauchope Vol 2

Robertson, James Begg: Private (34124 Royal Warwickshire Regt [14th]. Formerly 8325 Dragoon Guards [16th]); Brother of George Robertson; MIA, 26.10.17, 33 years; 62 Balfour Street, Kirkcaldy/Lower Oakfield, Kelty; Hooge Crater Cemetery, Ieper, West Vlaanderen, Belgium. Grave IX.J.2; Kirkcaldy War Memorial; *Soldiers Died* Part 11; *FA* 31.08.18; *FA* (BMD) 31.08.18; *FFP* 31.08.18; *FFP* (BMD) 31.08.18; *FA* (RoH) 14.09.18; *FFP* 14.09.18; *FFP* (RoH) 14.09.18; *FA* (FRoH) 14.12.18

Robertson, John: Private (S/1720 Gordon Hldrs [1st]); MIA, 29.03.18, 25 years; 24 Forth Avenue South, Kirkcaldy; Wancourt British Cemetery, Pas de Calais, France. Sp. Mem. 2; Kirkcaldy War Memorial; *FA* 22.01.16; *Soldiers Died* Part 65; *FFP* 20.04.18; *FA* 01.06.18; *FFP* 12.10.18; *FA* 19.10.18; *FA* (RoH) 19.10.18; *FA* (BMD) 26.10.18; *FA* (FRoH) 14.12.18

Robertson, John: Able Seaman (J/40121; Royal Navy; HMS *Marmion*); Drowned in a collision in North Sea, 21.10.17, 21 years; 37/39 Anderson Street, Kirkcaldy; Pathhead Parish Church Memorial Plaques & Windows; Plymouth Memorial, Devon. Plate 21; Kirkcaldy War Memorial; *Cross of Sacrifice Vol 4*; *FA* 27.10.17; *FFP* 27.10.17; *FA* (BMD) 03.11.17; *FFP* (BMD) 03.11.17; *FFP* (RoH) 17.11.17; *FA* 16.02.18; *FA* 03.08.18; *FFP* 03.08.18; *FA* (BMD) 19.10.18; *FA* (FRoH) 07.12.18; *FFP* 21.06.24

Robertson, Robert: Private (13717 KOSB [2nd] "D" Coy); KIA, 18.04.15, 28 years; 29 Lorne Street, Kirkcaldy; Ypres (Menin Gate) Memorial, Ieper, West Vlaanderen, Belgium. Panel 22; Kirkcaldy War Memorial; *Soldiers Died* Part 30; *FA* 05.06.15; *FFP* 12.06.15; *FA* 19.06.15; *FA* (RoH) 15.07.16; *FFP* 05.08.16 Roll of the Brave; *FA* (Service List) 03.02.17; *FA* (FRoH) 23.11.18

Robertson, Thomas Cousin: AM2 (57731; RFC; 52nd Squadron. Formerly Scottish Horse); MIA, 21.10.17, 36 years; 80 Dunnikier Road, Kirkcaldy; St Brycedale Church Plaque; Arras Flying Services Memorial, Arras, Pas de Calais, France; Kirkcaldy War Memorial; RFC/RAF RoH; *Cross of Sacrifice Vol 4*; *FA* 03.11.17; *FFP* (Memorial List) 05.01.18; *FFP* (BMD) 25.05.18; *FA* (BMD) 01.06.18; *FA* (RoH) 15.06.18; *FFP* (RoH) 15.06.18; *FA* 13.07.18; *FFP* 20.07.18; *FA* (FRoH) 14.12.18

Robertson, William: Private (S/10824 Black Watch [11th]); Died at home, 06.07.16; Gravestone in Abbotshall Churchyard; Abbotshall Parish Churchyard, Kirkcaldy. Grave New. (C.) 251; Kirkcaldy War Memorial; *Soldiers Died* Part 46; Wauchope Vol 3

Robson, Archibald: Private (27738 KOSB [7/8th]. Formerly 2274 F & F Yeo); Brother of Peter Robson; KIA, 23.07.18, 27 years; 92 Mid Street/3 Junction Road, Kirkcaldy; St Michael's Church Memorial Plaque; Buzancy Military Cemetery, Aisne, France. Grave II.A.7; Kirkcaldy War Memorial; *Soldiers Died* Part 30; *FA* 17.08.18; *FA* (BMD) 17.08.18; *FFP* 17.08.18; *FFP* (BMD) 17.08.18; *FA* (RoH) 14.09.18; *FFP* (RoH) 14.09.18; *FA* (FRoH) 14.12.18

Rodger, David: Sapper (144817 Royal Engineers [175th Tunnelling Coy]); DOW, 13.10.18, 24 years; 70 Kidd Street/29 Macindoe Crescent, Kirkcaldy; Honnechy British Cemetery, Nord, France. Grave I.A.6; Kirkcaldy War Memorial; *Soldiers Died* Part 4; *FA* 02.11.18; *FA* (RoH) 16.11.18; *FFP* (RoH) 16.11.18; *FA* (FRoH) 14.12.18

Rodger, James: Private (S/15914 Black Watch [8th]); KIA, 19.10.18, 39 years; 15 Page's Pend, Heggie's Wynd, Kirkcaldy; Harlebeke New British Cemetery, Harlebeke, West Vlaanderen, Belgium. Grave II.C.7; Kirkcaldy War Memorial; *Soldiers Died* Part 46; *FA* 09.11.18; *FA* 16.11.18; *FA* (RoH) 16.11.18; *FA* (BMD) 16.11.18; *FFP* (RoH) 16.11.18; *FFP* 30.11.18; *FA* (FRoH) 14.12.18

Rodger, John Marshall: Lance Corporal (200502 Royal Tank Corps [3rd Bn]. Formerly 2379 Machine Gun Corps); DOW Aisne. Buried at Larrier Cemetery, 06.10.18, 25 years; Fife Arms, 250 St Clair Street, Kirkcaldy; Gravestone in Barony Churchyard. Kirkcaldy High School War Memorial; Bellicourt British Cemetery, Aisne, France. Grave LI.P.4; Kirkcaldy War Memorial; *Soldiers Died* Part 75; *FA* 26.10.18; *FA* (BMD) 26.10.18; *FA* (RoH) 16.11.18; *FFP* (RoH) 16.11.18; *FA* (FRoH) 14.12.18; *FA* (KHS RoH) 29.03.19; *FA* (KHS RoH) 19.07.19; *FA* (BMD) 04.10.19

Rodger, William: Private (345239 Black Watch [14th] [F & F Yeo Bn]); KIA Gaza, 06.11.17, 25 years; 14 Viceroy Street, Kirkcaldy; Union Church Plaque. Gravestone Dysart Cemetery; Beersheba War Cemetery, Israel. Grave L.27; Kirkcaldy War Memorial; *Soldiers Died* Part 46; *FA* 24.11.17; *FA* 01.12.17; *FFP* 01.12.17; *FA* (RoH) 15.12.17; *FFP* (RoH) 15.12.17; *FA* (FRoH) 07.12.18; Wauchope Vol 3; Ogilvie

Rolland, James: Artificer Engineer (M/12027; Royal Navy; HMS/ME6); Killed by a mine explosion North Sea, 26.12.15, 22 years; 63 Salisbury Street, Kirkcaldy; Gravestone in Dysart Cemetery. St Andrew's Church Memorial Plaque; Portsmouth Naval Memorial, Hampshire. Plate 8; Kirkcaldy War Memorial; *Cross of Sacrifice Vol 4*; *FFP* 01.01.16; *FFP* (BMD) 01.01.16; *FA* 08.01.16; *FA* (RoH) 15.01.16; *FFP* 05.08.16 Roll of the Brave; *FFP* (BMD) 23.12.16; *FFP* (BMD) 29.12.17; *FA* (FRoH) 16.11.18; *FFP* (BMD) 28.12.18

Ronaldson, John: Private (412849; CEF; Canadian Infantry [20th] 2nd Div 4th Bde. [1st Central Ontario Regt]); DOW West Bridgeforth Military Hospital, Notts. Interred Kirkcaldy Cemetery, 12.06.16, 25 years; 7 Rideau Avenue, Toronto/41 Pratt Street, Kirkcaldy; Bennochy Cemetery, Kirkcaldy. Grave N.393; Kirkcaldy War Memorial; *CBoR* Page 156; *FA* 06.05.16; *FFP* 17.06.16; *FA* 24.06.16; *FA* (RoH) 15.07.16; *FFP* 05.08.16 Roll of the Brave; *FA* (Service List) 16.12.16; *FFP* (BMD) 09.06.17; *FFP* 08.06.18; *FA* (FRoH) 23.11.18

Rose, David Yule: Stoker 1st Class (173595; Royal Navy; HMS *Natal*); KIA, 30.12.15, 41 years; 33 Nicol Street, Kirkcaldy; Plymouth Memorial, Devon. Plate 7; Kirkcaldy War Memorial; *FA* (Service List) 18.11.16;

Rose; John Allan: Piper (290539 Black Watch [7th]); In *FFP* 21.06.24 as Ross; KIA, 08.01.17, 24 years; 7 Harriet Street, Kirkcaldy; Pathhead Parish Church Memorial Plaques & Windows; Thiepval Memorial, Somme, France. Pier & Face 10A; Kirkcaldy War Memorial; *FFP* 21.04.17; *Soldiers Died* Part 46; *FA* 27.01.17; *FFP* 27.01.17; *FFP* 10.02.17; *FA* (RoH) 17.02.17; *FFP* (RoH) 17.02.17; *FFP* 14.04.17; *FA* 21.04.17; *FA* (BMD) 21.04.17; *FFP* 21.04.17; *FFP* (BMD) 21.04.17; *FFP* (BMD) 12.01.18; *FA* (FRoH) 30.11.18; *FFP* 21.06.24 Wauchope Vol 2

Ross, Charles: Private (291072 Black Watch [7th]); KIA 30.07.16, 19 years; 23 Forth Avenue South, Kirkcaldy; Caterpillar Valley Cemetery, Longueval, Somme, France. Grave XVI.K.I; Kirkcaldy War Memorial; *FA* 30.06.17; *Soldiers Died* Part 46; *FA* 26.08.16; *FA* (CasList) 02.09.16; *FFP* 09.09.16; *FA* (Service List) 17.02.17; *FA* 23.06.17; *FA* (BMD) 23.06.17; *FFP* 30.06.17; *FA* 29.06.18; *FA* 06.07.18; *FA* (BMD) 27.07.18; Wauchope Vol 2

Ross, Charles: Private (S/42025 Black Watch [8th]. Formerly 1/1914 38th TR Bn); Brother of Donald Ross; KIA, 19.07.18, 19 years; 203½ St Clair Street, Kirkcaldy; Ploegsteert Memorial, Comines-Warneton, Hainaut, Belgium. Panel 7; Kirkcaldy War Memorial; *FA* 24.08.18; *Soldiers Died* Part 46; *FA* 17.08.18; *FFP* 17.08.18; *FA* (RoH) 14.09.18; *FFP* (RoH) 14.09.18; *FA* (FRoH) 14.12.18; Wauchope Vol 3

Ross, Charles Gardner: Gunner (193257 RFA [33rd Batt'y, 33rd Bde]); DOW No 10 CCS, 11.07.17, 20 years; 66 Bank Street, Kirkcaldy; Pathhead Parish Church Memorial Plaques & Windows; Lijssenthoek Military Cemetery, Poperinge, West Vlaanderen, Belgium. Grave XV.B.2;Kirkcaldy War Memorial; *Soldiers Died* Part 2; *FA* 21.07.17; *FFP* 21.07.17; *FFP* (BMD) 28.07.17; *FA* 04.08.17; *FFP* (CasList) 18.08.17; *FA* 15.09.17; *FFP* (RoH) 15.09.17; *FFP* (BMD) 13.07.18; *FFP* 21.06.24

Ross, Donald: Private (267923 Black Watch [1/6th]); Brother of Charles Ross; KIA, 20.07.18; 54 Overton Road, Kirkcaldy; Soissons Memorial, Aisne, France; Kirkcaldy War Memorial; *FA* 24.08.18; *Soldiers Died* Part 46; *FA* 17.08.18; *FA* (RoH) 14.09.18; Wauchope Vol 2

Ross, William: Sapper (134681 Royal Engineers [83rd Coy]); DOW Somme, 12.04.17, 20 years; 8 Greenhill Place, Horse Wynd, Kirkcaldy; Invertiel Parish Church Memorial Table; Bray Military Cemetery, Somme, France. Grave II.E.30; Kirkcaldy War Memorial; *FA* 28.04.17; *Soldiers Died* Part 4; *FA* 21.04.17; *FFP* 28.04.17; *FA* (RoH) 19.05.17; *FFP* (RoH) 19.05.17; *FFP* (CasList) 19.05.17; *FFP* (BMD) 13.04.18; *FA* (FRoH) 30.11.18; *FA* (BMD) 12.04.19

Russell, George: Private (43035 HLI [16th]. Formerly 2009 HCB); MIA, 18.11.16; 62 Ramsay Road, Kirkcaldy; Thiepval Memorial, Somme, France. Pier & Face 15C; Kirkcaldy War Memorial; *FA* 11.11.16; *FA* 16.12.16; *Soldiers Died* Part 63; *FA* 09.12.16 (2 entries); *FFP* 09.12.16; *FA* 16.12.16; *FA* (Service List) 16.12.16; *FA* (CasList) 13.01.17; *FA* 03.03.17; *FA* 29.12.17; *FA* (BMD) 29.12.17; *FFP* (BMD) 29.12.17; *FFP* 05.01.18; *FFP* (RoH) 05.01.18; *FA* (RoH) 19.01.18; *FA* (FRoH) 07.12.18

Russell, John: Private (1729 HLI [10th]); KIA Loos, 25.09.15, 19 years; 83 Institution Street, Kirkcaldy; Barony Church Plaque; Loos Memorial, Pas de Calais, France. Panels 108-112; Kirkcaldy War Memorial; *FA* 30.10.15; *FFP* 11.05.18; *Soldiers Died* Part 63; War Album 15/16; *FA* 30.10.15; *FFP* 30.10.15; *FFP* (BMD) 30.10.15; *FA* (BMD) 06.11.15; *FA* (RoH) 13.11.15; *FFP* 05.08.16 Roll of the Brave; *FA* (Service List) 24.02.17; *FFP* (BMD) 22.09.17; *FFP* (RoH) 04.05.18; *FFP* 11.05.18; *FFP* (BMD) 28.09.18; *FA* (FRoH) 16.11.18

Russell, Thomas: Private (2013; AIF; Australian Infantry [50th]); 02.04.17; St Clair Place, Bridgeton, Kirkcaldy; Villers-Bretonneux Memorial, Somme, France. Panel 26; Australian War Memorial web site; Kirkcaldy War Memorial; *FA* (BMD) 26.05.17; *FA* (RoH) 16.06.17; *FFP* (RoH) 16.06.17; *FA* (FRoH) 30.11.18

Salt, Ernest St Clair: Corporal (9595 Black Watch [1st]); DOW Aisne No 5 Amb Train, 18.10.14, 30 years; 29 Bank Street, Kirkcaldy; St Sever Cemetery, Rouen, Seine-Maritime, France. Grave A.1.3; Kirkcaldy War Memorial; *Soldiers Died* Part 46; War Album 14/15; *FA* 21.11.14; *FA* (CasList) 21.11.14; *FFP* (BMD) 21.11.14; *FA* 05.12.14; *FFP* 05.12.14; *FA* (CasList) 19.12.14; *FA* 23.01.15; *FA* (CasList) 20.02.15; *FA* 05.06.15; *FFP* (BMD) 02.10.15; *FFP* 05.08.16 Roll of the Brave; *FFP* (BMD) 21.10.16; *FA* (Service List) 25.11.16; *FFP* (BMD) 20.10.17; *FA* (FRoH) 16.11.18; Wauchope Vol 1

Sandilands, Archibald: Private (S/41010 Seaforth Hldrs [1/6th]. Formerly S/18333 Black Watch); DOW CCS, France, 31.07.17, 21 years; 5a Anderson Street, Kirkcaldy; Brandhoek New Military Cemetery, Vlamertinghe, Ieper, West Vlaanderen, Belgium. Grave II.C.12; Kirkcaldy War Memorial; *Soldiers Died* Part 64; *FA* 11.08.17; *FFP* 11.08.17; *FA* 15.09.17; *FFP* (RoH) 15.09.17

Sands, George Rattray: Sergeant (3/766 Black Watch [3rd] att'd [1st]); KIA Ypres, 09.11.14, 23 years; 20 Charlotte Street, Kirkcaldy; Ypres (Menin Gate) Memorial, Ieper, West Vlaanderen, Belgium. Panel 37; Kirkcaldy War Memorial; *Soldiers Died* Part 46; War Album 14/15; *FA* 12.12.14; *FFP* 12.12.14; *FFP* (BMD) 12.12.14; *FA* (CasList) 19.12.14; *Scotsman* (CasList) 00.01.15; *FA* 02.01.15; *FA* (CasList) 20.02.15; *FFP* 05.08.16 Roll of the Brave; *FA* (Service List) 27.01.17; *FA* (FRoH) 16.11.18; Wauchope Vol 1

Sang, William Alastair: Sapper (88; CEF; Canadian Overseas Railway Construction Corps [1st]); KIA, 25.03.16, 28 years; Kirkcaldy; Gravestone in Abbotshall Churchyard. Kirkcaldy High School War Memorial; Lijssenthoek Military Cemetery, Poperinge, West Vlaanderen, Belgium. Grave V.D.17; Kirkcaldy War Memorial; *CBoR* Page 158; *FA* 08.04.16; *FA* (BMD) 08.04.16; *FFP* 08.04.16; *FFP* (BMD) 08.04.16; *FA* 15.04.16; *FA* (RoH) 15.04.16; *FFP* (CasList) 15.04.16; *FFP* 05.08.16 Roll of the Brave; *FA* (FRoH) 23.11.18

Saunders, Adam Melrose: Sergeant (345334 Black Watch [14th] [F & F Yeo Bn]. Formerly 2584 F & F Yeo); Brother of John Saunders; DOW El Arish, Cairo, 18.11.17, 25 years; 21 Alexandra Street, Kirkcaldy; Kantara War Memorial Cemetery, Egypt. Grave F.431; Kirkcaldy War Memorial; *FFP* 26.01.18; *Soldiers Died* Part 46; *FA* 24.11.17; *FFP* 24.11.17; *FFP* 01.12.17; *FA* (RoH) 15.12.17; *FFP* (RoH) 15.12.17; *FFP* (CasList) 22.12.17; *FFP* (RoH) 26.01.18; *FA* 23.11.18; *FA* (FRoH) 07.12.18; *FFP* 07.12.18; Wauchope Vol 3; Ogilvie

Saunders, David: Ordinary Seaman (Clyde Z/8952; Royal Navy; RNVR [RN Depot] [*Crystal Palace*]); Brother of James Saunders; Died of pneumonia at Base Hospital, Malden, Essex, 04.11.18, 19 years; 5 Marion Street, Kirkcaldy; Whytescauseway Baptist Church Memorial Plaque; Abbotshall Parish Churchyard, Kirkcaldy. Grave New. (S.) 428; Kirkcaldy War Memorial; *FA* 16.11.18; *Cross of Sacrifice Vol 4*; *FA* 16.11.18; *FA* (RoH) 16.11.18; *FA* (BMD) 16.11.18; *FFP* (RoH) 16.11.18; *FFP* 23.11.18; *FA* (FRoH) 14.12.18; *FA* (BMD) 08.11.19

Saunders, James Blair: Private (5689 Black Watch [6th] "C" Coy); Brother of David Saunders; KIA Beaumont-Hamel, 13.11.16, 22 years; 5 Marion Street, Kirkcaldy; Gravestone in Abbotshall Churchyard. Whytescauseway Baptist Church Memorial Plaque; Hunter's Cemetery, Newfoundland Park, Beaumont-Hamel, Somme, France. Grave 4; Kirkcaldy War Memorial; ‡; *FA* 25.11.16; *Soldiers Died* Part 46; *FA* 25.11.16; *FFP* 25.11.16; *FA* (BMD) 02.12.16; *FFP* (BMD) 02.12.16; *FA* (RoH) 16.12.16; *FA* (CasList) 23.12.16; *FFP* (CasList) 23.12.16; *FFP* (RoH) 30.12.16; *FFP* 27.01.17; *FFP* (BMD) 17.11.17; *FA* (BMD) 16.11.18; *FA* (FRoH) 30.11.18; *FA* (BMD) 08.11.19; Wauchope Vol 2

Saunders, John: Corporal (USEF; 309th Infantry, American Expeditionary Forces); Brother of Adam Saunders; KIA France, 20.10.18, 28 years; 21 Alexandra Street, Kirkcaldy; Kirkcaldy War Memorial; *FA* 30.11.18; *FFP* (BMD) 30.11.18; *FFP* 07.12.18; *FA* (FRoH) 14.12.18; *FFP* (RoH) 14.12.18

Saunders, John: Private (99126 Machine Gun Corps [37th Bn]. Formerly 19471 Black Watch); Died of pneumonia 56th CCS, 14.07.18, 26 years; 16 Alexandra Street, Kirkcaldy; Gravestone in Abbotshall Churchyard; Bagneux British Cemetery, Gezaincourt, Somme, France. Grave III.D.4; Kirkcaldy War Memorial; *FA* 20.07.18; *Soldiers Died* Part 75; *FA* 20.07.18; *FA* (BMD) 20.07.18; *FA* (BMD) 27.07.18; *FFP* 27.07.18; *FA* (RoH) 14.09.18; *FFP* (RoH) 14.09.18; *FA* (FRoH) 14.12.18

Saunders, Peter: Driver (6401 RFA [35th Batt'y]); Brother of William G. Saunders; KIA Flanders, 21.06.15, 30 years; 9 Horse Wynd/Foulford, Raith by Kirkcaldy; Bethelfield Church Plaque; Cabaret-Rouge British Cemetery, Souchez, Pas de Calais, France. Grave XVII.E.15; Kirkcaldy War Memorial; *Soldiers Died* Part 2; War Album 15; *FA* 03.07.15; *FFP* (CasList) 03.07.15; *FFP* (BMD) 03.07.15; *FA* (RoH) 17.07.15; *FA* (Service List) 06.01.17; *FA* (Service List) 20.01.17; *FFP* 17.11.17; *FA* 24.11.17

Saunders, Thomas: Private (25272 HLI [2nd] "A" Coy); KIA, 24.03.18, 30 years; 5 Horse Wynd, Kirkcaldy; Arras Memorial, Pas de Calais, France. Bay 8; Kirkcaldy War Memorial; *Soldiers Died* Part 63; *FFP* 08.02.19; *FA* (BMD) 12.07.19; Telfer-Smollett

Saunders, William G.: Private (S/20984 A & S Hldrs [10th]); Brother of Peter Saunders; KIA France, 12.10.17, 32 years; Carwhinny Cottage, 284 Rosslyn Street, Kirkcaldy; Bethelfield Church Plaque; Tyne Cot Memorial, Zonnebeke, West Vlaanderen, Belgium. Panels 141-143 & 162; Kirkcaldy War Memorial; *Soldiers Died* Part 70; *FFP* 17.11.17; *FFP* (BMD) 17.11.17; *FA* 24.11.17; *FA* (BMD) 24.11.17; *FFP* (CasList) 01.12.17; *FFP* (BMD) 12.10.18

Scott, Alexander: Private (2112 Royal Scots [2nd]); KIA, 26.04.15, 22 years; 48 Links Street, Kirkcaldy; Kemmel Chateau Military Cemetery, Heuvelland, West Vlaanderen, Belgium. Grave A.50; Kirkcaldy War Memorial; *Soldiers Died* Part 6; War Album 15; *FA* 22.05.15; *Dundee Advertiser* 24.05.15; *FFP* 05.08.16 Roll of the Brave; *FA* (Service List) 02.12.16; *FA* (FRoH) 16.11.18

Scott, Alexander Park Knight: Private (43081 HLI [16th] "B" Coy. Formerly 2330 HCB); MIA, 18.11.16, 19 years; 30 Caledonian Terrace, Patterson Street, Kirkcaldy; New Munich Trench British Cemetery, Beaumont-Hamel, Somme, France. Grave B.12; Kirkcaldy War Memorial; ‡; *Soldiers Died* Part 63; *FFP* 09.12.16; *FA* (CasList) 13.01.17; *FA* 07.04.17; *FA* (RoH) 14.04.17; *FFP* 14.04.17; *FA* (FRoH) 30.11.18

Scott, Arthur: Private (2562 Black Watch [1st]); DOW whilst PoW, Germany, 21.06.15, 22 years; 150 Den Road, Kirkcaldy; Le Touret Memorial, Pas de Calais, France. Panels 24-26; Kirkcaldy War Memorial; *FA* 10.07.15; *Soldiers Died* Part 46; *War Album* 15/16; *Scotsman* 08.07.15; *FA* 10.07.15; *FA* (RoH) 18.09.15; *FFP* 05.08.16 Roll of the Brave; *FA* (Service List) 10.02.17; *FFP* 24.08.18; *FA* 31.08.18; *FA* (FRoH) 16.11.18; Wauchope Vol 1; Army Returns 1914-1918 (SRO)

Scott, George: Private (43024 HLI [16th]. Formerly 1848 HCB); KIA, 18.11.16, 21 years; Patterson Street, Kirkcaldy; Old Parish Church Memorial Panel; Thiepval Memorial, Somme, France. Pier & Face 15C; Kirkcaldy War Memorial; *Soldiers Died* Part 63; *FA* 09.12.16; *FA* (CasList) 13.01.17; *FFP* 14.04.17

Scott, Inglis: Private (6326; AIF; Australian Infantry [11th]); KIA. Buried five miles east of Ypres, 20.09.17; 6 Harriet Street, Kirkcaldy; Ypres (Menin Gate) Memorial, Ieper, West Vlaanderen, Belgium. Panel 64; Australian War Memorial web site; Kirkcaldy War Memorial; St Andrew's War Memorial; *FA* 10.11.17; *FA* (BMD) 10.11.17; *FFP* 10.11.17; *FFP* (BMD) 10.11.17; *FA* (RoH) 17.11.17; *FFP* (RoH) 17.11.17

Scott, John: Private (S/9089 Black Watch [9th]); DOW, 15.07.16, 31 years; 15 Harriet Street/The Laurels, Kirkcaldy; Pathhead Parish Church Memorial Plaques & Windows; Bethune Town Cemetery, Pas de Calais, France. Grave V.F.90; Kirkcaldy War Memorial; *Soldiers Died* Part 46; *FA* 22.07.16; *FA* (BMD) 22.07.16; *FFP* 22.07.16; *FFP* (BMD) 22.07.16; *FA* 29.07.16; *FFP* 05.08.16 Roll of the Brave; *FFP* (CasList) 26.08.16; *FA* (RoH) 16.09.16; *FFP* (RoH) 16.09.16; *FFP* (RoH) 30.12.16; *FA* (Service List) 20.01.17; *FA* (BMD) 14.07.17; *FFP* 14.07.17; *FFP* (BMD) 13.07.18; *FA* (FRoH) 23.11.18; *FFP* 21.06.24; Wauchope Vol 3

Scott, John: Private (S/5784 Gordon Hldrs [1st]); KIA, 25.09.15, 22 years; 11 Page's Pend, Heggie's Wynd, Kirkcaldy; Raith Church Memorial Plaque; Ypres (Menin Gate) Memorial, Ieper, West Vlaanderen, Belgium. Panel 38; Kirkcaldy War Memorial; *Soldiers Died* Part 65; *War Album* 15/16; *FA* 09.10.15; *FFP* 09.10.15; *Scotsman* (CasList) 11.10.15; *FA* (RoH) 16.10.15; *FFP* (RoH) 16.10.15; *FFP* 05.08.16 Roll of the Brave; *FA* (Service List) 04.11.16; *FA* (Service List) 30.12.16; *FA* (FRoH) 16.11.18

Scott, John: Sapper (79473 Royal Engineers [173rd Tunnelling Coy]. Formerly S/15310 Cameron Hldrs); KIA Loos, 08.03.16, 24 years; 118 Den Road, Kirkcaldy; Noeux-Les-Mines Communal Cemetery & Extension, Pas de Calais, France. Grave I.H.8; Kirkcaldy War Memorial; *FA* 25.03.16; *Soldiers Died* Part 4; *FA* 18.03.16; *FFP* 25.03.16; *FA* (RoH) 15.04.16; *FFP* (CasList) 15.04.16; *FFP* 05.08.16 Roll of the Brave; *FA* (Service List) 10.02.17; *FFP* (BMD) 10.03.17; *FFP* (BMD) 09.03.18; *FA* (FRoH) 23.11.18

Scott, William: 2nd Lieutenant (South Wales Borderers att'd Welsh Regt [13th]. Formerly Royal Scots [9th]); DOW, 08.10.18, 26 years; 73 Pratt Street, Kirkcaldy; Invertiel Parish Church Memorial Table; Bellicourt British Cemetery, Aisne, France. Grave V.A.9; Kirkcaldy War Memorial; *FA* 26.10.18; *Officers Died*; *Cross of Sacrifice Vol 1*; *FA* 26.10.18; *FA* (BMD) 26.10.18

Selkirk, Daniel McGregor: Pioneer (49449 Royal Engineers [92nd Fld Coy]); Brother of John Selkirk & Arthur Selkirk. CWGC gives his number as 49559; KIA Delville Wood, 14.07.16, 37 years; 403 High Street, Kirkcaldy; Old Parish Church Memorial Panel; Thiepval Memorial, Somme, France. Pier & Face 8A & 8D; Kirkcaldy War Memorial; *Soldiers Died* Part 4; *FA* (CasList) 30.09.16; *FFP* (CasList) 30.09.16; *FA* 11.11.16; *FFP* 11.11.16; *FA* (Service List) 09.12.16; *FFP* (BMD) 10.03.17; *FA* (BMD) 17.03.17; *FFP* 17.03.17; *FA* (RoH) 14.04.17; *FA* 06.10.17; *FFP* (BMD) 28.09.18; *FA* (FRoH) 30.11.18

Selkirk, John: Private (31042 Royal Scots [13th]); Brother of Daniel Selkirk & Arthur Selkirk. CWGC gives date of death as 27.08.17; DOW CCS, 27.09.17, 27 years; 403 High Street, Kirkcaldy; Old Parish Church Memorial Panel; Dozinghem Military Cemetery, Westvleteren, Poperinge, West Vlaanderen, Belgium. Grave V.F.8; Kirkcaldy War Memorial; *Soldiers Died* Part 6; *FA* (Service List) 09.12.16; *FA* 06.10.17; *FA* (BMD) 06.10.17; *FFP* 06.10.17; *FFP* 13.10.17; *FFP* (RoH) 13.10.17; *FFP* (CasList) 03.11.17; *FFP* (BMD) 28.09.18; *FA* (FRoH) 07.12.18

Shannon, James Swinton: Private (25934 Cameronians [Scottish Rifles] [2nd]. Formerly 133805 Black Watch & RFA); KIA, 25.03.18, 29 years; 6 Hendry's Wynd, Kirkcaldy; Gravestone in Bennochy Cemetery. Invertiel Parish Church Memorial Table; Pozieres Memorial, Somme, France. Panels 37-38; Kirkcaldy War Memorial; *Soldiers Died* Part 31

Sharp, Alexander L.: Private (290255 Black Watch [7th]); KIA France, 19.09.17, 22 years; 82 Commercial Street, Kirkcaldy; Pathhead Parish Church Memorial Plaques & Windows; Cement House Cemetery, Langemarck-Poelkapelle, West Vlaanderen, Belgium. Grave XI.D.15; Kirkcaldy War Memorial; *Soldiers Died* Part 46; *FA* 06.10.17; *FFP* 06.10.17; *FA* 13.10.17; *FFP* (RoH) 13.10.17; *FFP* (CasList) 27.10.17; *FA* (FRoH) 07.12.18; *FFP* 21.06.24; Wauchope Vol 2

Sharp, David: Private (8149 Cameron Hldrs [5th]); DOW 64th CCS, 15.10.17, 28 years; 74 Links Street, Kirkcaldy; Mendinghem Military Cemetery, Poperinge, West Vlaanderen, Belgium. Grave VI.E.43; Kirkcaldy War Memorial; *Soldiers Died* Part 66; *FA* 24.11.17; *FA* (BMD) 24.11.17; *FA* 01.12.17; *FFP* 01.12.17; *FA* (RoH) 15.12.17; *FFP* (RoH) 15.12.17; *FA* (BMD) 12.10.18; *FA* (FRoH) 07.12.18

Sheach, Thomas: Lance Corporal (9356 Black Watch [2nd] "A" Coy); DOW, 09.11.14, 30 years; 48/52 Links Street, Kirkcaldy; St Columba's Church Memorial Plaque; Gorre British & Indian Cemetery, Pas de Calais, France. Grave I.A.2; Kirkcaldy War Memorial; *Soldiers Died* Part 46; War Album 14/15; *Scotsman* 24.11.14; *FA* 28.11.14; *FFP* 28.11.14; *FA* 02.01.15; *FA* (CasList) 20.02.15; *FFP* 05.08.16 Roll of the Brave; *FFP* (BMD) 11.11.16; *FA* (Service List) 02.12.16; *FA* (FRoH) 16.11.18; Wauchope Vol 1

Shepherd, Robert: Private (118434 RAMC (43rd General Hospital]); Died of smallpox at 43rd General Hospital, Kalamaria, 09.05.19, 39 years; 136 Overton Road, Kirkcaldy; Mikra British Cemetery, Kalamaria, Greece. Grave 1411; Kirkcaldy War Memorial; *FA* (BMD) 31.05.19

Shevlin, John: Private (3/4221 Black Watch [2nd]); KIA, 25.09.15, 44 years; 37/67 East Smeaton Street, Kirkcaldy; Rue-Du-Bacquerot No 1 Military Cemetery, Laventie, Nord, France. Grave II.C.12; Kirkcaldy War Memorial; *Soldiers Died* Part 46; War Album 15/16; *FA* 16.10.15; *FA* (RoH) 13.11.15; *FFP* 05.08.16 Roll of the Brave; *FA* (Service List) 17.02.17; Wauchope Vol 1

Shields, David: Lance Sergeant (3/8336 Yorkshire Regt [6th]); KIA Gallipoli, 22.08.15; 27 Pottery Street, Pathhead, Kirkcaldy; Helles Memorial, Gallipoli, Turkey. Panels 55-58; Kirkcaldy War Memorial; *Soldiers Died* Part 24; *FFP* (BMD) 13.01.17; *FA* 20.01.17; *FFP* 20.01.17; *FA* (RoH) 17.02.17; *FFP* (RoH) 17.02.17; *FA* (FRoH) 30.11.18

Shields, George Gordon: Private (700171; CEF; Canadian Infantry [43rd] [Manitoba Regt]); DOW, 06.10.16; 15 Millie Street, Kirkcaldy; Contay British Cemetery, Contay, Somme, France. Grave III.A.25; Kirkcaldy War Memorial; *CBoR* Page 161; *FFP* (BMD) 21.10.16; *FA* 28.10.16; *FFP* 04.11.16; *FA* (RoH) 18.11.16; *FFP* (RoH) 18.11.16; *FFP* (RoH) 30.12.16; *FA* (Service List) 13.01.17; *FA* 27.01.17; *FA* (BMD) 27.01.17; *FA* (FRoH) 30.11.18

Simond, Forgan A.: Lance Corporal (S/23204 Seaforth Hldrs [6th] "A" Coy. Formerly TR/1/4918 TR Bn); KIA, 22.09.17, 19 years; Tyne Cot Memorial, Zonnebeke, West Vlaanderen, Belgium. Panels 132-135 & 162A; Kirkcaldy War Memorial; *Soldiers Died* Part 64

Simpson, David: Corporal (267298 Royal Warwickshire Regt [2/7th]. Formerly 711 HCB); MIA, 19.07.16, 20 years; 23 Mitchell Place, Pathhead, Kirkcaldy; Pathhead Parish Church Memorial Plaques & Windows; Loos Memorial, Pas de Calais, France. Panels 22-25; Kirkcaldy War Memorial; *Soldiers Died* Part 11; *FA* 19.08.16; *FA* (Service List) 06.01.17; *FA* 20.01.17; *FFP* 30.06.17; *FFP* (BMD) 30.06.17; *FA* 14.07.17; *FFP* 14.07.17; *FA* 19.01.18; *FFP* (BMD) 20.07.18; *FA* (FRoH) 07.12.18; *FFP* 21.06.24; Wauchope Vol 1

Simpson, Gilbert Archer: Private (15499 Somerset Light Infantry [8th]); KIA, 25.09.15; 7 Buchanan Street, Kirkcaldy; Loos Memorial, Pas de Calais, France. Panels 38-39; Kirkcaldy War Memorial; *FA* 30.10.15; *Soldiers Died* Part 18; *FA* 30.10.15; *FFP* 30.10.15; *FA* (Service List) 04.11.16; *FA* (Service List) 30.12.16

Simpson, Hardie: Private 2nd Class (294700; RAF; 83rd Wing); Died of pneumonia at No 8 Canadian Hospital, 23.10.18, 33 years; 8 Thistle Street, Kirkcaldy; Abbotshall Parish Church Memorial Plaque; Charmes Military Cemetery, Essegney, Vosges, France. Grave I.C.20; Kirkcaldy War Memorial; *Cross of Sacrifice Vol 4*; *FA* 02.11.18; *FA* (BMD) 09.11.18; *FA* (RoH) 16.11.18; *FFP* (RoH) 16.11.18; *FA* (FRoH) 14.12.18; *FFP* (BMD) 23.10.20; *FA* 19.11.21

Simpson, John: Private (27746 KOSB [6th]. Formerly 2364 F & F Yeo); KIA, 12.10.17, 20 years; 29 Mitchell Street, Kirkcaldy; Tyne Cot Memorial, Zonnebeke, West Vlaanderen, Belgium. Panels 66-68; Kirkcaldy War Memorial; *FA* 30.11.18; *Soldiers Died* Part 30; *FA* 09.11.18; *FA* (RoH) 16.11.18; *FFP* (RoH) 16.11.18; *FA* (BMD) 23.11.18; *FA* (FRoH) 14.12.18

Simpson, William: Stoker 2nd Class (K/35254; Royal Navy; HMS *Derwent*); Killed by a mine explosion in English Channel, 02.05.17, 18 years; 167 Links Street, Kirkcaldy; Portsmouth Naval Memorial, Hampshire. Plate 26; Kirkcaldy War Memorial; *FA* 12.05.17; *Cross of Sacrifice Vol 4*; *FA* 05.05.17; *FA* 14.07.17; *FFP* 14.07.17; *FA* (BMD) 10.11.17; *FA* (FRoH) 07.12.18

Simpson, William: Private (43320 Royal Scots Fusiliers [2nd]); KIA, 23.03.18, 27 years; 29 York Place, Kirkcaldy; Pozieres Memorial, Somme, France. Panels 34-35; Kirkcaldy War Memorial; *Soldiers Died* Part 26

Sinclair, Francis: Private (S/2182 Seaforth Hldrs [7th]); MIA, 12.10.16, 29 years; 6 Pottery Street, Gallatown, Kirkcaldy; Thiepval Memorial, Somme, France. Pier & Face 15C; Kirkcaldy War Memorial; *Soldiers Died* Part 64; *FFP* 28.07.17; *FA* 04.08.17; *FFP* (CasList) 04.08.17; *FA* 15.09.17; *FFP* (RoH) 15.09.17; *FFP* (BMD) 13.10.17

Small, James A.: Private (350536 Black Watch [4/5th]. Formerly 2425 HCB); KIA, 01.08.18, 31 years; 88 Pratt Street, Kirkcaldy; Invertiel Parish Church Memorial Table; Raperie British Cemetery, Villemontoire, Aisne, France. Grave III.E.2; Kirkcaldy War Memorial; *Soldiers Died* Part 46; *FA* 24.08.18; *FA* (BMD) 24.08.18; *FFP* 31.08.18; *FFP* (BMD) 31.08.18; *FA* (RoH) 14.09.18; *FFP* (RoH) 14.09.18; *FA* (FRoH) 14.12.18; Wauchope Vol 2

Small, John: Private (755 Black Watch [2nd]); Brother of Thomas Small; KIA, 09.05.15; Le Touret Memorial, Pas de Calais, France. Panels 24-26; Kirkcaldy War Memorial; *FA* 18.09.15; *Soldiers Died* Part 46; *FA* 19.06.15; *FA* (BMD) 19.06.15; *FFP* 26.06.15; *FFP* (CasList) 03.07.15; Wauchope Vol 1

Small, Thomas: Private (7524 Black Watch [1st]); Brother of John Small; KIA, 11.11.14; Ypres (Menin Gate) Memorial, Ieper, West Vlaanderen, Belgium. Panel 37; Kirkcaldy War Memorial; *FA* 18.09.15; *Soldiers Died* Part 46; Wauchope Vol 1

Smart, James: Private (43145 Cameronians [Scottish Rifles] [1st]. Formerly 22352 KOSB); KIA Somme, 29.10.16, 29 years; Rosslyn Street/165 Park Road, Kirkcaldy; Sinclairtown Parish Church War Memorial Chair; AIF Burial Ground, Flers, Somme, France. Grave V.E.2; Kirkcaldy War Memorial; *FA* 02.12.16; *Soldiers Died* Part 31; *FA* 18.11.16; *FA* (BMD) 18.11.16; *FA* (Service List) 24.03.17; *FA* (BMD) 27.10.17; *FA* (FRoH) 16.11.18

Smith, Archibald: Private (43157 HLI [16th]. Formerly 2114 HCB); Brother of James Smith, Black Watch. Cousin of John Knott; KIA near Albert, 18.11.16, 22 years; 119 Commercial Street, Kirkcaldy; Old Parish Church Memorial Panel; Waggon Road Cemetery, Beaumont-Hamel, Somme, France. Grave C.26; Kirkcaldy War Memorial; *Soldiers Died* Part 63; *FA* 09.12.16; *FA* (CasList) 13.01.17; *FFP* 14.04.17; *FA* 12.05.17; *FFP* 11.08.17; *FFP* (BMD) 11.08.17; *FA* 18.08.17; *FA* (BMD) 18.08.17; *FA* 15.09.17; *FFP* (RoH) 15.09.17; *FFP* (BMD) 17.11.17; *FFP* (BMD) 16.11.18

Smith, David Gourlay: Lance Corporal (2402 Black Watch [1st]. Formerly HCB); KIA, 16.09.14, 20 years; 22 Cloanden Place, Kirkcaldy; La Ferte-Sous-Jouarre Memorial, Seine-et-Marne, France; Kirkcaldy War Memorial; *FA* 10.10.14; *FA* 30.09.16; *Soldiers Died* Part 46; *FFP* 17.10.14; *FA* (CasList) 20.02.15; *FA* 30.09.16; *FFP* 30.09.16; *FA* (RoH) 14.10.16; *FFP* (RoH) 14.10.16; *FFP* (RoH) 30.12.16; *FA* (Service List) 20.01.17; *FA* (FRoH) 23.11.18; Wauchope Vol 1

Smith, James: Private (5152 Black Watch [6th] [Lewis Gun Section]. Formerly Scottish Horse); KIA Beaumont-Hamel, 13.11.16, 24 years; 134 St Clair Street, Kirkcaldy; Hunter's Cemetery, Newfoundland Park, Beaumont-Hamel, Somme, France. Grave 40; Kirkcaldy War Memorial; *Soldiers Died* Part 46; *FA* (RoH) 16.12.16; *FA* 23.12.16; *FA* (CasList) 23.12.16; *FFP* 30.12.16; *FFP* (RoH) 30.12.16; *FFP* (BMD) 13.01.17; *FA* (FRoH) 30.11.18; Wauchope Vol 2

Smith, James: Lance Corporal (S/2836 Black Watch [8th]); Brother of Archibald Smith. Cousin of John Knott; KIA Loos, 27.09.15, 27 years; 119 Commercial Street, Kirkcaldy; Loos Memorial, Pas de Calais, France. Panels 78-83; Kirkcaldy War Memorial; *FFP* 09.10.15; *Soldiers Died* Part 46; War Album 15/16; *FA* 09.10.15; *FFP* 09.10.15; *FA* (RoH) 13.11.15; *FFP* 18.12.15 Pathhead Church Memorial; *FFP* 05.08.16 Roll of the Brave; *FFP* (BMD) 23.09.16; *FA* (Service List) 04.11.16; *FA* (Service List) 16.12.16; *FFP* 14.04.17; *FA* 12.05.17; *FFP* 11.08.17; *FFP* (BMD) 17.11.17; *FFP* (BMD) 28.09.18; *FFP* (BMD) 12.10.18; *FA* (FRoH) 16.11.18; Wauchope Vol 3

Smith, James: Private (Cameron Hldrs); Not identified on CWGC web site; Kirkcaldy War Memorial

Smith, John P.: Sergeant (SAEF; East African Ordnance Corps); Died in hospital at Devonport. Buried in Bennochy Cemetery, Kirkcaldy, 20.07.16, 52 years; 4 Munro Street, Kirkcaldy; Gravestone in Bennochy Cemetery, Kirkcaldy; Not identified on CWGC web site; Kirkcaldy War Memorial; *FA* 29.07.16; *FA* (BMD) 29.07.16; *FFP* 29.07.16; *FA* (RoH) 05.08.16; *FFP* 05.08.16 Roll of the Brave; *FA* (RoH) 16.09.16; *FFP* (RoH) 16.09.16; *FFP* (RoH) 30.12.16; *FA* (FRoH) 23.11.18

Smith, Oswald W.: Private (S/6425 Black Watch [8th] "B" Coy); DOW, 25.03.18, 22 years; 242 Links Street, Kirkcaldy; St Pierre Cemetery, Amiens, France. Grave VIII.F.9; Kirkcaldy War Memorial; *Soldiers Died* Part 46; *FA* 13.04.17; *FFP* (RoH) 13.04.18; *FFP* (BMD) 13.04.18; *FA* (BMD) 20.04.18; *FFP* (CasList) 11.05.18; *FA* (RoH) 18.05.18; *FFP* (RoH) 18.05.18; *FA* (FRoH) 07.12.18; Wauchope Vol 3

Smith, Percy Kirk: 2nd Lieutenant (Royal Engineers [212nd Fld Coy]. Formerly Cameron Hldrs & HLI); KIA near Ypres, 12.09.17, 28 years; Westerlea, Swan Road, Kirkcaldy; Gravestone in Bennochy Cemetery (Photo). St Brycedale Church Plaque. Kirkcaldy High School War Memorial; Ridge Wood Military Cemetery, Voormezeele, Heuvelland, West Vlaanderen, Belgium. Grave III.R.5; Kirkcaldy War Memorial; *Officers Died*; *Cross of Sacrifice Vol 1*; *FA* 22.09.17; *FFP* 22.09.17; *FFP* (BMD) 22.09.17; *FA* (BMD) 29.09.17; *FA* 13.10.17; *FFP* (RoH) 13.10.17; *FFP* (Memorial List) 05.01.18; *FA* 13.07.18; *FA* (FRoH) 07.12.18; *FA* (KHS RoH) 29.03.19

Smith, Thomas: Lance Corporal (16677 Royal Scots [12th]); KIA, 15.07.16, 36 years; Muttonhall Cottages, Kirkcaldy; Thiepval Memorial, Somme, France. Pier & Face 6D & 7D; Kirkcaldy War Memorial; *Soldiers Died* Part 6; *FA* 26.08.16; *FFP* 26.08.16; *FFP* (CasList) 09.09.16

Smith, Thomas (Toss): Acting Sergeant (46810 Royal Engineers [1st Fld Survey Coy] [9th Observation Group]); Died from gas and wounds at No 6 CCS, 15.04.18, 24 years; Manuel Cottage, Dunnikier Road, Kirkcaldy; Union Church Plaque. Gravestone in Bennochy Cemetery (Photo). Kirkcaldy High School War Memorial; Houchin British Cemetery, Pas de Calais, France. Grave I.F.20; Kirkcaldy War Memorial; *FA* 27.04.18; *Soldiers Died* Part 4; *FA* 27.04.18; *FA* (BMD) 27.04.18; *FFP* (RoH) 27.04.18; *FFP* (BMD) 27.04.18; *FA* (RoH) 18.05.18; *FFP* (RoH) 18.05.18; *FA* 13.07.18; *FA* (FRoH) 14.12.18; *FA* (KHS RoH) 29.03.19

Smith, Thomas Gordon, MM: Private (S/10073 Cameron Hldrs [5th] "C" Coy); KIA France, 12.10.17, 30 years; 68 Nairn Street, Kirkcaldy; Tyne Cot Memorial, Zonnebeke, West Vlaanderen, Belgium. Panels 136-138; Kirkcaldy War Memorial; *Soldiers Died* Part 66; *FFP* 10.11.17; *FA* (RoH) 17.11.17; *FFP* (RoH) 17.11.17; *FFP* (CasList) 24.11.17; *FA* (FRoH) 07.12.18; Kirkcaldy Council Memorial Scroll

Somerville, Alexander: Private KOSB [7th]); KIA Loos; 65 East March Street, Kirkcaldy; Not identified on CWGC web site; Kirkcaldy War Memorial; War Album 15/16; *FA* 16.10.15; *FA* (RoH) 13.11.15; *FFP* 05.08.16 Roll of the Brave; *FA* (Service List) 27.01.17; *FA* (FRoH) 16.11.18

Somerville, Robert Simpson: Private (27032 Royal Scots [13th]); KIA Somme, 15.09.16, 20 years; 27 Glasswork Street, Kirkcaldy; Gravestone in Bennochy Cemetery; Thiepval Memorial, Somme, France. Pier & Face 6D & 7D; Kirkcaldy War Memorial; *FA* 30.09.16; *Soldiers Died* Part 6; *FA* 30.09.16; *FFP* 30.09.16; *FFP* (BMD) 30.09.16; *FFP* 07.10.16; *FA* (RoH) 14.10.16; *FFP* (RoH) 14.10.16; *FA* 02.12.16; *FA* (BMD) 02.12.16; *FFP* (BMD) 02.12.16; *FFP* (BMD) 09.12.16; *FFP* (CasList) 16.12.16; *FFP* (RoH) 30.12.16; *FA* (Service List) 27.01.17; *FFP* (BMD) 15.09.17; *FFP* (BMD) 14.09.18; *FA* 19.10.18; *FA* (FRoH) 23.11.18

Soutar, Andrew: Private (16772 Royal Scots [11th]); KIA, 03.05.17, 28 years; 11 Birrell Street Wynd, Pathhead, Kirkcaldy; Arras Memorial, Pas de Calais, France. Bays 1 & 2; Kirkcaldy War Memorial; *Soldiers Died* Part 6; *FA* 19.05.17; *FFP* 19.05.17; *FA* (CasList) 02.06.17; *FFP* (CasList) 02.06.17; *FA* (RoH) 16.06.17; *FFP* (RoH) 16.06.17; *FA* (FRoH) 30.11.18

Soutar, John: Private (122960 Machine Gun Corps [21st]. Formerly T2/13030 RASC); KIA, 11.04.18, 33 years; 66 Oswald's Wynd, Kirkcaldy; Loos Memorial, Pas de Calais, France. Panel 136; Kirkcaldy War Memorial; *Soldiers Died* Part 75; *FA* 18.05.18; *FA* (BMD) 18.05.18; *FFP* 18.05.18; *FA* (RoH) 15.06.18; *FFP* (RoH) 15.06.18; *FA* (FRoH) 14.12.18

Spalding, Robert Johnston: Private (DM2/166252 RASC (781st MT Coy)); DOW Salonika, 05.01.17, 23 years; Glebe Park, Kirkcaldy; Lahana Military Cemetery, Greece. Grave II.C.I; Kirkcaldy War Memorial; *Soldiers Died* Part 78; *FFP* 24.02.17; *FA* 03.03.17; *FA* (RoH) 17.03.17; *FFP* (BMD) 05.01.18; Kirkcaldy Council Memorial Scroll

Spears, John: Private (29598; CEF; Canadian Infantry [16th] 1st Div 3rd Bde. [Manitoba Regt] 2nd Coy [Canadian Scottish]); DOW, 19.05.15, 26 years; 40 Lady Helen Street, Kirkcaldy; Bethelfield Church Plaque. Kirkcaldy High School War Memorial; Bethune Town Cemetery, Pas de Calais, France. Grave III.D.50; *FFP* 12.06.15; *FA* 19.06.15; Kirkcaldy War Memorial; *CBoR* Page 37; War Album 15; *FA* 05.06.15; *FFP* (BMD) 05.06.15; *FFP* 12.06.15; *FFP* (CasList) 03.07.15; *FFP* 05.08.16 Roll of the Brave; *FA* (Service List) 13.01.17; *FA* (FRoH) 16.11.18; *FA* (KHS RoH) 29.03.19; Urquhart

Speed, Alexander: Private (888223; CEF; Canadian Infantry [28th] 2nd Div 6th Bde. [Saskatchewan Regt]); Died Ampton Hall Hospital, England. Buried Abbotshall Churchyard 23.11.17, 23 years; 13 Mitchell Place, Kirkcaldy; Gravestone in Abbotshall Churchyard. Abbotshall Parish Church Memorial Plaque; Abbotshall Parish Churchyard, Kirkcaldy. Grave New. (N.) 383; Kirkcaldy War Memorial; *CBoR* Page 330; *FA* 24.11.17; *FFP* 24.11.17; *FFP* 01.12.17; *FFP* (BMD) 01.12.17; *FA* (RoH) 15.12.17; *FFP* (RoH) 15.12.17; *FFP* (RoH) 23.02.18; *FA* 02.03.18; *FA* (FRoH) 07.12.18; *FA* 19.11.21

Speed, Andrew: Private (S/3602 Gordon Hldrs [1st] "C" Coy); MIA, 19.07.16, 27 years; 357 High Street, Kirkcaldy; Thiepval Memorial, Somme, France. Pier & Face 15B & 15C; Kirkcaldy War Memorial; *Soldiers Died* Part 65; *FA* 09.09.16; *FFP* (CasList) 09.09.16; *FA* 19.05.17; *FFP* 19.05.17; *FFP* (BMD) 19.05.17; *FA* (BMD) 26.05.17; *FA* (RoH) 16.06.17; *FFP* (RoH) 16.06.17; *FA* (FRoH) 30.11.18

Speed, William: Pioneer (46236 Royal Engineers [98th Fld Coy]); DOW base hospital, Boulogne, 22.07.16, 39 years; 234 Links Street, Kirkcaldy; Boulogne Eastern Cemetery, Pas de Calais, France. Grave VIII.A.136; Kirkcaldy War Memorial; *Soldiers Died* Part 4; *FA* 29.07.16; *FFP* 29.07.16; *FFP* (BMD) 29.07.16; *FA* (BMD) 05.08.16; *FFP* 05.08.16 Roll of the Brave; *FFP* (BMD) 05.08.16; *FFP* (CasList) 26.08.16; *FA* (RoH) 16.09.16; *FFP* (RoH) 16.09.16; *FA* (Service List) 25.11.16; *FA* (Service List) 02.12.16; *FFP* (RoH) 30.12.16; *FA* (FRoH) 23.11.18

Speedie, David: Lance Corporal (27747 KOSB [7/8th]. Formerly 2384 F & F Yeo); DOW CCS, 20.08.17, 25 years; 27 Loughborough Road, Kirkcaldy; Dunnikier Church Roll of Honour; Brandhoek New Military Cemetery No. 3. Vlamertinghe, Ieper, Belgium. Grave I.B.4; Kirkcaldy War Memorial; *Soldiers Died* Part 30; *FA* 01.09.17; *FFP* 01.09.17; *FA* 15.09.17; *FFP* (RoH) 15.09.17; *FA* 26.04.19

Spence, Peter Watson: Private (S/3769 Black Watch [1st]); KIA, 09.05.15; Le Touret Memorial, Pas de Calais, France. Panels 24-26; Kirkcaldy War Memorial; *Soldiers Died* Part 46; *FFP* (BMD) 17.07.15; Wauchope Vol 1

Spence, Thomas Duncan: Private (1727 HLI [10th] "B" Coy); MIA Loos, 25.09.15, 19 years; 66 Nether Street, Kirkcaldy; Loos Memorial, Pas de Calais, France. Panels 108-112; Kirkcaldy War Memorial; *FA* 11.03.16; *FA* 30.09.16; *Soldiers Died* Part 63; *FA* 11.03.16; *FA* 03.06.16; *FFP* 03.06.16; *FA* (RoH) 17.06.16; *FFP* (RoH) 17.06.16; *FFP* 05.08.16 Roll of the Brave; *FA* 30.09.16; *FFP* 30.09.16; *FA* (Service List) 30.12.16; *FFP* 13.07.18; *FA* 31.08.18; *FA* (FRoH) 23.11.18

Stanners, Thomas Williamson: Corporal (345381 Black Watch [1st]. Formerly 2571 F & F Yeo); KIA, 19.09.18, 31 years; High Street, Kirkcaldy/Hopetoun Terrace, Bo'ness; Bellicourt British Cemetery, Aisne, France. Grave Lothian.IV.O.5; Kirkcaldy War Memorial; *Soldiers Died* Part 46; *FA* 19.10.18; *FA* (BMD) 26.10.18; *FA* (RoH) 16.11.18; *FFP* (RoH) 16.11.18; *FA* (FRoH) 14.12.18; Wauchope Vol 1

Stark, James: Private (33150 HLI [17th]); In *Fifeshire Advertiser* as Thomas Stark; KIA, 01.04.17, 37 years; Hunter's Buildings, Sands Road, Kirkcaldy; Savy British Cemetery, Aisne, France. Grave I.B.21; Kirkcaldy War Memorial; *Soldiers Died* Part 63; *FA* 21.04.17; *FFP* 21.04.17; *FFP* (BMD) 28.04.17; *FA* (BMD) 05.05.17; *FA* (RoH) 19.05.17; *FFP* (RoH) 19.05.17; *FFP* (BMD) 06.04.18; *FA* (FRoH) 30.11.18

Steedman, Richard M.: Sergeant (739 Royal Engineers [54th Fld Coy]); KIA, 13.05.15, 35 years; 94 Nicol Street, Kirkcaldy/North Shields; Post Office Rifles Cemetery, Festubert, Pas de Calais, France. Grave I.D.6; Kirkcaldy War Memorial; *Soldiers Died* Part 4; War Album 15; *FA* 05.06.15; *FFP* (CasList) 05.06.15; *FFP* (BMD) 05.06.15; *FA* 12.06.15; *FFP* (CasList) 03.07.15; *FFP* 05.08.16 Roll of the Brave; *FA* (Service List) 18.11.16; *FA* (FRoH) 16.11.18

Steel, John: Private (S/42038 Black Watch [6th]. Formerly 1/2235 38th TR Bn); KIA, 04.08.18, 19 years; 16 Rosebery Terrace, Kirkcaldy; La Kreule Military Cemetery, Hazebrouck, Nord, France. Grave III.B.II; Kirkcaldy War Memorial; *Soldiers Died* Part 46; *FFP* 17.08.18; *FA* 24.08.18; *FA* (BMD) 24.08.18; *FFP* (BMD) 24.08.18; *FA* (RoH) 14.09.18; *FFP* (RoH) 14.09.18; *FA* (FRoH) 14.12.18; Wauchope Vol 2

Stein, Adam: Private (23463 Durham Light Infantry [14th]. Formerly 10/6823 Northumberland Fusiliers); Real name Steven. On CWGC web site and *Soldiers Died* name is given as Steen; 18.09.16; 109 Rosslyn Street, Kirkcaldy; Thiepval Memorial, Somme, France. Pier & Face 14A & 15C; Kirkcaldy War Memorial; *Soldiers Died* Part 62; *FA* 04.11.16; *FA* (Service List) 09.12.16; *FA* (BMD) 07.04.17; *FA* (RoH) 14.04.17; *FA* (FRoH) 30.11.18

Stenhouse, Daniel: Private (126095 RAMC [27th CCS]); Died of bronchial pneumonia at 50th General Hospital, Salonika, 24.12.18, 21 years; 147 Rosslyn Street, Kirkcaldy; Gallatown Church Roll of Honour; Mikra British Cemetery, Kalamaria, Greece. Grave 1078; Kirkcaldy War Memorial; *FA* (BMD) 08.02.19; *FFP* (BMD) 08.02.19; *FA* (RoH) 15.02.19

Stenhouse, John Smith: Private (2448; AIF; Australian Infantry [47th]); KIA, 11.04.17, 30 years; 411 High Street, Kirkcaldy; Gravestone in Bennochy Cemetery; Kirkcaldy High School War Memorial; Villers-Bretonneux Memorial, Somme, France. Panel 26; Australian War Memorial web site; Kirkcaldy War Memorial; *FA* 12.05.17; *FA* (BMD) 12.05.17; *FFP* 12.05.17; *FA* (RoH) 19.05.17; *FFP* (RoH) 19.05.17; *FA* (RoH) 16.06.17; *FFP* (RoH) 16.06.17; *FA* (FRoH) 30.11.18

Stevens, Peter Melville: Private (A/22682; CEF; Canadian Infantry [8th] 1st Div 2nd Bde. [Manitoba Regt]); KIA Ypres, 03.06.16, 27 years; 11 Anderson Street, Kirkcaldy; Pathhead Parish Church Memorial Plaques & Windows; Woods Cemetery, Zillebeke, Ieper, West Vlaanderen, Belgium. Grave V.A.1; Kirkcaldy War Memorial; *FA* 17.06.16; *CBoR* Page 167; *FA* 10.06.16; *FA* (BMD) 10.06.16; *FFP* 10.06.16; *FA* (RoH) 17.06.16; *FFP* (RoH) 17.06.16; *FFP* 05.08.16 Roll of the Brave; *FA* (Service List) 13.01.17; *FA* (FRoH) 23.11.18; *FFP* 21.06.24

Stevenson, Alexander: Private (14631 Cameronians [Scottish Rifles] [11th]); KIA Salonika, 28.04.17, 37 years; 60 Kidd Street, Kirkcaldy; Doiran Memorial, Greece; Kirkcaldy War Memorial; *Soldiers Died* Part 31; *FA* (CasList) 26.05.17; *FFP* 26.05.17; *FFP* (CasList) 26.05.17; *FA* 02.06.17; *FA* (RoH) 16.06.17; *FFP* (RoH) 16.06.17; *FA* (BMD) 20.04.18; *FA* (FRoH) 30.11.18; *FA* (BMD) 03.05.19; *FA* 10.05.19

Stevenson, George: Private (3/2674 Black Watch [2nd] Meerut Div, Indian Expeditionary Force); KIA Sheik Saadh, Mesopotamia, 07.01.16, 20 years; 142 Den Road, Kirkcaldy; Amara War Cemetery, Iraq. Grave XXX.J.10; Kirkcaldy War Memorial; *FA* 12.02.16; *Soldiers Died* Part 46; *FA* 12.02.16; *FFP* 12.02.16; *FA* (BMD) 19.02.16; *FA* 04.03.16; *FFP* 11.03.16; *FA* 10.06.16; *FFP* 05.08.16 Roll of the Brave; *FA* 02.09.16; *FA* (BMD) 06.01.17; *FA* (Service List) 10.02.17; *FA* (BMD12.01.18; *FA* (FRoH) 16.11.18; *FA* (BMD) 11.01.19; Wauchope Vol 1

Stevenson, George: Private (7665 Labour Corps [13th Coy]. Formerly S/18581/19247 Seaforth Hldrs [1st Labour Coy]); DOW France, 23.01.18, 39 years; 13 Page's Pend, Heggie's Wynd, Kirkcaldy; Raith Church Memorial Plaque; Mendinghem Military Cemetery, Poperinge, West Vlaanderen, Belgium. Grave IX.C.35; Kirkcaldy War Memorial; *Soldiers Died* Part 80; *FFP* (RoH) 02.02.18; *FA* 09.02.18; *FA* (RoH) 16.02.18; *FFP* (RoH) 16.02.18; *FA* (FRoH) 07.12.18

Stewart, Charles: Private (2755 Black Watch [1st]); DOW Glasgow Royal Infirmary, 05.08.16, 22 years; 36 Nicol Street, Kirkcaldy; Glasgow Western Necropolis. Grave H.1324A; Kirkcaldy War Memorial; *Soldiers Died* Part 46; *FFP* 12.08.16; *FA* 19.08.16; *FA* (CasList) 16.09.16; *FA* (RoH) 16.09.16; *FFP* (CasList) 16.09.16; *FFP* (RoH) 16.09.16; *FA* (Service List) 18.11.16; *FFP* (RoH) 30.12.16; *FA* (FRoH) 23.11.18; Wauchope Vol 1

Stewart, Charles G.: Private (S/10281 Cameron Hldrs [5th]);Brother of Robert Stewart; KIA, 28.08.15, 24 years; 39 Market Street, Kirkcaldy; Le Touret Memorial, Pas de Calais, France. Panels 41-42; Kirkcaldy War Memorial; *Soldiers Died* Part 66; *FA* 30.10.15

Stewart, Charles Lamb: Private (S/20442 A & S Hldrs [1/5th]); KIA, 30.12.17, 27 years; Garnock's Lane, Kirkcaldy; Abbotshall Parish Church Memorial Plaque; Chatby Memorial, Egypt; Kirkcaldy War Memorial; *Soldiers Died* Part 70; *FFP* 19.08.16; *FA* 19.11.21

Stewart, John: Lance Corporal (1858 Black Watch [1/7th]); DOW. Buried Corbie Cemetery, 29.07.16, 30 years; 3 Garnock's Lane, Kirkcaldy; Heilly Station Cemetery, Mericourt-L'Abbe, Somme, France. Grave II.E.45; Kirkcaldy War Memorial; *Soldiers Died* Part 46; *FA* 12.08.16; *FFP* 12.08.16; *FA* 19.08.16; *FFP* 19.08.16; *FFP* (BMD) 19.08.16; *FA* (BMD) 26.08.16; *FA* (CasList) 02.09.16; *FFP* 02.09.16; *FFP* (CasList) 02.09.16; *FA* (RoH) 16.09.16; *FFP* (RoH) 16.09.16; *FFP* (RoH) 30.12.16; *FA* (Service List) 31.03.17; *FFP* (BMD) 04.08.17; *FFP* (BMD) 03.08.18; *FA* (FRoH) 23.11.18; Wauchope Vol 2

Stewart, John M.: Trooper (2440 F & F Yeo [1st]); DOW Suvla, 03.12.15, 28 years; 29/39 Loughborough Road, Kirkcaldy; Lala Baba Cemetery, Turkey. Grave I.D.14; *FA* 26.02.16; Kirkcaldy War Memorial; *Soldiers Died* Part 1; *FA* 01.01.16; *FFP* 01.01.16; *FA* (BMD) 08.01.16; *FFP* (BMD) 08.01.16; *FA* (CasList) 15.01.16; *FA* (RoH) 15.01.16; *FFP* 05.08.16 Roll of the Brave; *FA* (Service List) 17.02.17; *FA* (FRoH) 16.11.18; Ogilvie

Stewart, Robert: Corporal (4769 Cameron Hldrs [1st]); Brother of Charles Stewart; KIA Loos, 13.10.15; 39 Market Street, Kirkcaldy; Loos Memorial, Pas de Calais, France. Panels 119-124; Kirkcaldy War Memorial; *Soldiers Died* Part 66; War Album 15/16; *FA* 30.10.15; *FA* (RoH) 13.11.15; *FFP* 05.08.16 Roll of the Brave; *FFP* 14.10.16; *FFP* (BMD) 14.10.16; *FA* (Service List) 27.01.17; *FA* (FRoH) 16.11.18

Stewart, William: Private (S/1722 Gordon Hldrs [8th]); MIA Loos, 25.9.15, 32 years; 46 Nairn Street/50 Balsusney Road, Kirkcaldy; Loos Memorial, Pas de Calais, France. Panels 115-119; Kirkcaldy War Memorial; *FFP* 21.04.17; *Soldiers Died* Part 65; *FA* 24.03.17; *FFP* 24.03.17; *FA* (RoH) 14.04.17; *FFP* 21.04.17; *FA* (FRoH) 30.11.18

Stocks, Andrew C.: Private (S/8543 A & S Hldrs [2nd]); KIA, 15.07.16, 21 years; 53 Sutherland Street, Kirkcaldy; Gravestone in Dysart Cemetery. Gallatown Church Roll of Honour; Flatiron Copse Cemetery, Mametz, Somme, France. Grave IV.B.3; Kirkcaldy War Memorial; *Soldiers Died* Part 70; *FA* 12.08.16 (2 entries); *FFP* 12.08.16; *FFP* (BMD) 12.08.16; *FA* (CasList) 26.08.16; *FFP* (CasList) 26.08.16; *FA* (RoH) 16.09.16; *FFP* (RoH) 16.09.16; *FFP* (RoH) 30.12.16; *FA* (Service List) 03.03.17; *FFP* (BMD) 14.07.17; *FFP* (BMD) 13.07.18; *FA* (FRoH) 23.11.18

Stocks, Harris Lawrence, DSO: Major (Royal Scots [15th]); KIA Somme, 01.07.16, 45 years; St Katherine's, Townsend Crescent, Kirkcaldy; Gravestone in Bennochy Cemetery. St Brycedale Church Plaque. Kirkcaldy High School War Memorial; Bouzincourt Communal Cemetery Extension, Somme, France. Grave III.D.11; Kirkcaldy War Memorial; ‡; *FA* 08.07.16; *FA* 17.02.17; *FFP* 24.02.17; *Officers Died*; *Cross of Sacrifice Vol 1*; *FA* 08.07.16; *FA* 15.07.16; *FFP* 15.07.16; *FFP* 22.07.16; *FA* 05.08.16; *FA* 12.08.16; *FA* 19.08.16; *FA* 25.11.16; *FFP* 25.11.16; *FA* 06.01.17; *FA* (Memorial Service) 06.01.17; *FA* (Service List) 13.01.17; *FA* 17.02.17; *FA* (BMD) 17.02.17; *FFP* 17.02.17; *FFP* (BMD) 17.02.17; *FA* 24.02.17 (2 entries); *FFP* 24.02.17; *FA* 03.03.17 (2 entries); *FA* (RoH) 17.03.17; *FA* 14.07.17 (KHS War Honours); *FA* 15.03.18; *FA* (FRoH) 30.11.18; *FA* (KHS RoH) 29.03.19

Stoddart, William: Lance Corporal (35336 HLI [17th]. Formerly 25329 Royal Scots); PC 25, Kirkcaldy Burgh Police; KIA, 11.02.17, 30 years; 54 Harcourt Road, Kirkcaldy; E.U. Congregational Church Memorial Plaque. Police Memorial Plaque; Thiepval Memorial, Somme, France. Pier & Face 15C; Kirkcaldy War Memorial; *FA* 25.11.16; *FA* 03.03.17; *Soldiers Died* Part 63; *FA* 03.03.17; *FA* (Service List) 03.03.17; *FFP* 03.03.17; *FA* (RoH) 17.03.17; *FFP* (CasList) 24.03.17; *FFP* (BMD) 16.02.18; *FA* (FRoH) 30.11.18; Pictorial History of Fife Constabulary

Stuart, George: Gunner (135867 RGA (303rd Siege Batt'y]); KIA France, 01.05.17, 20 years; 160 Institution Street, Kirkcaldy; Dranoutre Military Cemetery, Heuvelland, West Vlaanderen, Belgium. Grave II.H.6; Kirkcaldy War Memorial; *Soldiers Died* Part 3; *FA* 19.05.17; *FA* (RoH) 19.05.17; *FFP* (RoH) 19.05.17; *FFP* (BMD) 19.05.17; *FFP* 26.05.17; *FFP* (BMD) 04.05.18; *FA* (FRoH) 30.11.18 (2 entries)

Stuart, John F.: Private (28769 KOSB [2nd]. Formerly 3520 F & F Yeo); KIA, 04.10.17; West End Congregational Church Memorial Plaque; Tyne Cot Cemetery, Zonnebeke, West Vlaanderen, Belgium. Grave LVI.A.10; Kirkcaldy War Memorial; *Soldiers Died* Part 30

Sutherland, Kenneth: Private (S/21913 Black Watch [3rd]); Died of appendicitis en route to Military Hospital, Cromarty, 08.09.17, 28 years; 32 Milton Road, Kirkcaldy; Gravestone in Abbotshall Churchyard; Abbotshall Parish Churchyard, Kirkcaldy. Grave Old. (C.) 589; Kirkcaldy War Memorial; *Soldiers Died* Part 46; *FA* 15.09.17; *FA* (BMD) 15.09.17; *FFP* 15.09.17; *FA* 13.10.17; *FFP* (RoH) 13.10.17; *FA* (FRoH) 07.12.18; Wauchope Vol 1

Sutherland, William: Pioneer (Royal Engineers); Died Longmore Hospital, Edinburgh as the result of an accident, 03.09.17, 25 years; 76A St Clair Street, Kirkcaldy; Pathhead Parish Church Memorial Plaques & Windows. Gravestone in Dysart Cemetery; Not identified on CWGC web site; Kirkcaldy War Memorial; *FA* 08.09.17; *FFP* 08.09.17; *FA* 15.09.17; *FFP* 27.10.17; *FFP* (BMD) 07.09.18; *FFP* 21.06.24

Swan, David McD.: Lance Corporal (3/6525 Gordon Hldrs [3rd]); Buried by a shell at Ypres. Died in Aberdeen after contracting bronchitis, 02.03.15; 119 Links Street, Kirkcaldy; Aberdeen (Allenvale) Cemetery, Aberdeen. Grave S/180; Kirkcaldy War Memorial; *FFP* 13.03.15; *Soldiers Died* Part 65; *FFP* 06.03.15; *FA* 13.03.15; *FFP* 13.03.15; *FFP* (BMD) 13.03.15; *FFP* (CasList) 27.03.15; *FA* (Service List) 26.11.16; *FA* (Service List) 02.12.16; *FA* (FRoH) 16.11.18

Lance Corporal David **Swan** was a time served regular who re-enlisted at the outbreak of war. Swan was buried by a shell explosion at Ypres on 23rd December 1914. When he was dug out, he was found to be paralysed on his left side. The ship taking him home hit bad seas and Swan was thrown from his bunk and knocked out. On regaining consciousness, he discovered the fall had somehow cured his paralysis. He made a good recovery and enjoyed home furlough. Back at Regimental Barracks in Aberdeen, he caught a cold that developed into bronchitis. He died on 2nd March, 1915, probably due to a combination of bronchitis and internal injuries resulting from his experiences.

Swan, George Grieve: Lieutenant (Manchester Regt [4th] att'd [22nd]); Cousin of George Harry Swan; KIA, 01.07.16, 27 years; Annfield, Milton Road, Kirkcaldy; Kirkcaldy High School War Memorial. West End Congregational Church Memorial Plaque; Thiepval Memorial, Somme, France. Pier & Face 13A & 14C; Kirkcaldy War Memorial; *FA* 15.07.16; *Officers Died*; *Cross of Sacrifice Vol 1*; *FA* 08.07.16; *FA* (BMD) 08.07.16; *FFP* 08.07.16; *FFP* (BMD) 08.07.16; *FA* 15.07.16; *FA* (RoH) 15.07.16; *FFP* 15.07.16; *FA* 22.07.16; *FFP* 29.07.16; *FFP* 05.08.16 Roll of the Brave; *FA* (FRoH) 23.11.18; *FA* (KHS RoH) 29.03.19

Swan, George Harry: 2nd Lieutenant (Royal Scots Fusiliers [1st]. Formerly HCB); Cousin of George Grieve Swan; KIA Montauban, 14.07.16, 21 years; 12 West Albert Road, Kirkcaldy; Gravestone in Bennochy Cemetery (Photo). Kirkcaldy High School War Memorial. West End Congregational Church Memorial Plaque; Flatiron Copse Cemetery, Mametz, Somme, France. Sp. Mem.7; Kirkcaldy War Memorial; *FA* 05.08.16; *Officers Died*; *Cross of Sacrifice Vol 1*; *FA* 22.07.16; *FA* (BMD) 22.07.16; *FFP* 22.07.16; *FFP* (BMD) 22.07.16; *FA* 29.07.16; *FA* 05.08.16; *FFP* 05.08.16; *FFP* 05.08.16 Roll of the Brave; *FA* (RoH) 16.09.16; *FFP* (RoH) 16.09.16; *FA* (Service List) 30.12.16; *FFP* (RoH) 30.12.16; *FA* 14.07.17 (KHS War Honours); *FA* (FRoH) 23.11.18; *FA* (KHS RoH) 29.03.19; *FA* (BMD) 19.07.19

Swan, Walter: Air Mechanic 3rd Class (265541 RAF); Died at Shrewsbury Camp, 11.02.19, 30 years; 22 Alexandra Street, Kirkcaldy; UK Memorial, UK; Kirkcaldy War Memorial; *FFP* (BMD) 15.02.19

Sweeney, James: Private (Northumberland Fusiliers); Not identified on CWGC web site; Kirkcaldy War Memorial

Sweeney, John: Private (7349 Connaught Rangers [6th]); MIA, 03.09.16; 246 Links Street, Kirkcaldy; Thiepval Memorial, Somme, France. Pier & Face 15A; Kirkcaldy War Memorial; *Soldiers Died* Part 69; *FA* (CasList) 31.03.17; *FFP* 31.03.17; *FFP* 10.11.17; *FA* 17.11.17; *FA* (RoH) 17.11.17; *FFP* (RoH) 17.11.17; *FA* (FRoH) 07.12.18

Swinley, David Inglis: Private (Black Watch); Brother of George Inglis Swinley; 142 Overton Road, Kirkcaldy; Not identified on CWGC web site; Kirkcaldy War Memorial; *FA* (RoH) 15.02.19

Swinley, George Inglis: Private (S/2945 Black Watch [8th] "A" Coy); Brother of David Inglis Swinley; DOW, 14.10.17, 23 years; 142 Overton Road, Kirkcaldy; Mendinghem Military Cemetery, Poperinge, West Vlaanderen, Belgium. Grave VI.E.42; Kirkcaldy War Memorial; *Soldiers Died* Part 46; *FFP* 27.10.17; *FA* 03.11.17 (2 entries); *FA* (RoH) 17.11.17; *FFP* (RoH) 17.11.17; *FFP* (CasList) 24.11.17; *FA* (FRoH) 07.12.18; Wauchope Vol 3

Swinley, Renwick: Private (S/4584 Black Watch [8th] "A" Coy); Accidentally killed, 23.07.15, 25 years; 17 Edington Place, Dysart; Barony Church Plaque; Gorre British & Indian Cemetery, Pas de Calais, France. Grave I.A.II; Kirkcaldy War Memorial. Dysart War Memorial; *Soldiers Died* Part 46; *FA* 22.05.15; *Scotsman* 28.07.15; *FA* 31.07.15; *FFP* 31.07.15; *FFP* (BMD) 22.07.16; *FFP* 05.08.16 Roll of the Brave; *FFP* (BMD) 28.07.17; *FFP* (BMD) 27.07.18; Wauchope Vol 3

Syme, Thomas Braid: Private (41049 KOSB [6th]. Formerly 2697 F & F Yeo); Wounded at Arras, 14.04.17, 19 years; 8 Sutherland Street, Kirkcaldy; Gravestone in Dysart Cemetery; Aubigny Communal Cemetery Extension, Pas de Calais, France. Grave II.E.8; Kirkcaldy War Memorial; *Soldiers Died* Part 30; *FA* 21.04.17; *FFP* 21.04.17; *FFP* (BMD) 21.04.17; *FA* (BMD) 28.04.17; *FFP* 05.05.17; *FA* (RoH) 19.05.17; *FFP* (CasList) 19.05.17; *FFP* (RoH) 19.05.17; *FFP* (BMD) 20.04.18; *FA* (FRoH) 30.11.18; *FA* 26.04.19

Tasker, William: Private (7671 Seaforth Hldrs Labour Corps [13th Coy]. Formerly S/19253 Seaforth Hldrs [2nd Infantry Labour Coy]); Died of accidental injuries, 26.11.17, 32 years; 142 Den Road, Kirkcaldy; E.U. Congregational Church Memorial Plaque; Dozinghem Military Cemetery, Westvleteren, Poperinge, West Vlaanderen, Belgium. Grave XIV.E.8; Kirkcaldy War Memorial; *Soldiers Died* Part 80; *FA* 08.12.17; *FA* (BMD) 08.12.17; *FFP* (BMD) 08.12.17; *FA* (RoH) 15.12.17; *FFP* 15.12.17; *FFP* (RoH) 15.12.17; *FFP* (BMD) 23.11.18; *FA* (FRoH) 07.12.18

Taylor, Alexander: Private (2561 Black Watch [1st]); KIA, 13.10.15; 42 Links Street, Kirkcaldy; Loos Memorial, Pas de Calais, France. Panels 78-83; Kirkcaldy War Memorial; *FA* 16.09.16; *FFP* 23.09.16; *Soldiers Died* Part 46; *FFP* 23.09.16; *FA* (Service List) 02.12.16; Wauchope Vol 1

Taylor, Alexander: Private (SAEF; South African Scottish); Brother of Andrew Taylor & John Taylor. Paper reports Andrew & Alexander were killed on the same day; 21.09.17; 54 Harriet Street, Kirkcaldy; Not identified on CWGC web site; Kirkcaldy War Memorial; *FA* 11.05.18; *FA* (FRoH) 30.11.18

The **Taylor** family suffered the loss of three sons during the Great War. Andrew, John and Alexander were all serving with the South African forces when they were killed. Andrew and Alexander were killed on the same day, 21st September, 1917.

Taylor, Alexander Nicholson: Private (16951 KOSB [6th]); MIA Loos, 25.09.15, 41 years; 32 Institution Street, Kirkcaldy; Pathhead Parish Church Memorial Plaques & Windows; Loos Memorial, Pas de Calais, France. Panels 53-56; Kirkcaldy War Memorial; *FA* 23.09.16; *Soldiers Died* Part 30; *FA* 30.10.15; *FFP* 30.10.15; *FFP* 14.10.16; *FFP* (BMD) 14.10.16; *FA* (RoH) 18.11.16; *FFP* (RoH) 18.11.16; *FFP* (RoH) 30.12.16; *FA* (Service List) 24.02.17; *FA* (FRoH) 30.11.18; *FFP* 21.06.24

Taylor, Andrew: Sapper (79577 Royal Engineers [179th Tunnelling Coy]. Formerly 6918 Seaforth Hldrs); KIA, 21.10.15; 8 Invertiel Road, Kirkcaldy; Invertiel Parish Church Memorial Table; Albert Communal Cemetery Extension, Albert, Somme, France. Grave I.A.16; Kirkcaldy War Memorial; *FA* 18.12.15; *Soldiers Died* Part 4; *FA* 23.10.15; *FFP* 23.10.15; *Scotsman* (CasList) 25.10.15; *FA* 11.12.15; *FFP* 18.12.15; *FA* (RoH) 15.01.16; *FA* 19.02.16; *FFP* 05.08.16 Roll of the Brave; *FA* (Service List) 28.10.16; *FA* (Service List) 03.03.17; *FA* (FRoH) 16.11.18; *FFP* (BMD) 23.11.18

Taylor, Andrew: Corporal (3785; SAEF; South African Scottish [4th Infantry Regt]); Brother of Alexander Taylor & John Taylor. Paper reports Andrew & Alexander were killed on the same day. KIA France, 21.09.17; 54 Harriet Street, Kirkcaldy; Ypres (Menin Gate) Memorial, Ieper, West Vlaanderen, Belgium. Panels 15-16 & 16A; Kirkcaldy War Memorial; *FFP* 17.11.17; *FA* 24.11.17; *FA* (RoH) 15.12.17; *FFP* (RoH) 15.12.17; *FA* 11.05.18; *FA* (FRoH) 30.11.18; *FA* (FRoH) 07.12.18

Taylor, Charles: Private (S/10123 Cameron Hldrs [5th]); Brother of George Taylor; KIA Loos, 25.09.15; 245 Links Street/56 Nicol Street, Kirkcaldy; St Columba's Church Memorial Plaque; Loos Memorial, Pas de Calais, France. Panels 119-124; Kirkcaldy War Memorial; *Soldiers Died* Part 66; *FA* 04.12.15; *FFP* 08.01.16; *FA* 15.01.16; *FFP* 29.04.16; *FA* 06.05.16 (2 entries); *FA* (RoH) 13.05.16; *FA* 20.05.16; *FFP* 05.08.16 Roll of the Brave; *FA* (CasList) 19.08.16; *FA* (Service List) 18.11.16; *FA* (Service List) 02.12.16; *FFP* 29.12.17; *FA* 05.01.18; *FFP* (BMD) 28.09.18 (2 entries); *FA* (FRoH) 23.11.18; *FA* (FRoH) 07.12.18

Taylor, George: Private (TR/1/9401 Gordon Hldrs [52nd]); Brother of Charles Taylor; Died Canterbury Military Hospital of pneumonia & meningitis, 20.12.17, 19 years; 38/56 Nicol Street, Kirkcaldy; Gravestone in Dysart Cemetery; Dysart Cemetery, Kirkcaldy. Grave 30.L.South; Kirkcaldy War Memorial; *Soldiers Died* Part 65; *FA* 06.05.16; *FFP* 29.12.17; *FFP* (BMD) 29.12.17; *FA* 05.01.18; *FA* (RoH) 19.01.18; *FFP* (BMD) 21.12.18

Taylor, John: Lance Corporal (290254 Black Watch [7th]); KIA, 30.07.16; 11 St Clair Street, Kirkcaldy; Pathhead Parish Church Memorial Plaques & Windows; Thiepval Memorial, Somme, France. Pier & Face 10A; Kirkcaldy War Memorial; *FA* 02.09.16; *Soldiers Died* Part 46; *FA* 26.08.16; *FA* 02.09.16; *FA* (CasList) 02.09.16; *FFP* 02.09.16; *FA* 09.09.16; *FA* (Service List) 02.12.16; *FFP* 10.02.17; *FFP* 14.04.17; *FA* 21.04.17; *FA* (RoH) 19.05.17; *FFP* (RoH) 19.05.17; *FA* (FRoH) 30.11.18; *FFP* 21.06.24; Wauchope Vol 2

Taylor, Robert: Private (Black Watch [7th]); KIA; 11 St Clair Street, Kirkcaldy; Not identified on CWGC web site; Kirkcaldy War Memorial; *FA* 27.01.17; *FFP* 27.01.17; *FA* (RoH) 17.02.17; *FFP* (RoH) 17.02.17; *FA* (FRoH) 30.11.18

Taylor, William Burgess: Private (40998 KOSB [6th] Formerly 2418 HLI); DOW 1st Australian CCS, 19.06.18, 28 years; 155a St Clair Street, Kirkcaldy; Union Church Plaque; Longuenesse (St Omer) Souvenir Cemetery, France. Grave V.B.72; Kirkcaldy War Memorial; *Soldiers Died* Part 30; *FA* 06.07.18; *FA* (BMD) 06.07.18; *FA* (RoH) 13.07.18

Tester, George: Private (T2/10816; RFC; 20 Squadron. Formerly RASC); MIA, 28.09.17, 27 years; 95 East Smeaton Street, Kirkcaldy; Pont-du-Hem Military Cemetery, La Gorgue, Nord, France. Grave IV.G.26; Kirkcaldy War Memorial; *Cross of Sacrifice Vol 4*; *FA* 13.10.17; *FFP* 20.10.17; *FA* 16.03.18; *FFP* 16.03.18; *FFP* (RoH) 16.03.18; *FA* 13.04.18; *FA* (FRoH) 07.12.18

Thain, William Longmuir: Private (S/40203 Black Watch [1st]. Formerly HCB); Brother-in-law of Thomas Ferguson & William Adams; KIA, 25.09.16, 27 years; 9 Balfour Place, Kirkcaldy; St Brycedale Church Plaque; Thiepval Memorial, Somme, France. Pier & Face 10A; *Soldiers Died* Part 46; Kirkcaldy War Memorial; *FA* 14.10.16; *FA* (BMD) 14.10.16; *FFP* 14.10.16; *FFP* (BMD) 14.10.16; *FA* (CasList) 04.11.16; *FA* (Service List) 04.11.16; *FFP* (CasList) 04.11.16; *FA* (RoH) 18.11.16; *FFP* (RoH) 18.11.16; *FFP* 02.12.16; *FFP* (RoH) 30.12.16; *FA* (Memorial Service) 06.01.17; *FA* 15.09.17; *FFP* 15.09.17; *FA* (FRoH) 30.11.18; *FA* (BMD) 27.09.19; Wauchope Vol 1

Thomas, George W.: Private (G/555 Royal Scots Fusiliers [9th]); KIA, 07.07.16, 25 years; 95c St Clair Street, Kirkcaldy; St Michael's Church Memorial Plaque; Ovillers Military Cemetery, Somme, France. Grave XIV.T.1; Kirkcaldy War Memorial; *Soldiers Died* Part 26; *FFP* (CasList) 19.08.16; *FA* 23.09.16; *FFP* 23.09.16; *FFP* (BMD) 23.09.16; *FA* (CasList) 30.09.16; *FFP* (CasList) 30.09.16; *FA* (RoH) 14.10.16; *FFP* 14.10.16; *FFP* (RoH) 14.10.16; *FA* (Service List) 25.11.16; *FA* (Service List) 02.12.16; *FFP* (RoH) 30.12.16; *FFP* (BMD) 07.07.17; *FFP* (BMD) 06.07.18; *FA* (FRoH) 23.11.18

Thomson, Adam: Private (3/1213 Black Watch [1st]); DOW, 25.09.15, 24 years; 45 Nicol Street, Kirkcaldy; Abbotshall Parish Church Memorial Plaque; Dud Corner Cemetery, Loos, Pas de Calais, France. Grave VI.A.1; Kirkcaldy War Memorial; *Soldiers Died* Part 46; *FFP* 15.01.16; *FA* 22.01.16; *FFP* 25.11.16; *FA* 02.12.16; *FA* (RoH) 16.12.16; *FFP* (RoH) 30.12.16; *FA* (FRoH) 30.11.18; *FA* 19.11.21; Wauchope Vol 1

Thomson, David: Private (18437 Royal Scots [13th]); KIA, 11.05.16; Loos Memorial, Pas de Calais, France. Panels 10-13; Kirkcaldy War Memorial; *Soldiers Died* Part 6; *FA* (CasList) 17.06.16

Thomson, George: Private (39658 Royal Scots [13th]. Formerly S/13344 Black Watch); Brother of James Thomson. On CWGC date of death is 25.04.16. MIA, 25.04.18; 111 Victoria Road, Kirkcaldy; Arras Memorial, Pas de Calais, France. Bays 1 & 2; Kirkcaldy War Memorial; *Soldiers Died* Part 6; *FFP* 10.08.18; *FA* 17.08.18; *FA* 26.04.19; *FA* (RoH) 13.09.19

Thomson, George Miller: Petty Officer Class 1 (153945; Royal Navy; HMS *Clan McNaughton*); Drowned when the *Clan McNaughton* was sunk, 03.02.15, 40 years; Buchanan Street, Kirkcaldy/33 Eaton Road, Stockton on Tees; Chatham Memorial, Kent. Panel 9; Kirkcaldy War Memorial; *War Album 15*; *FA* (BMD) 27.02.15; *FFP* 27.02.15; *FFP* (BMD) 27.02.15; *FFP* (BMD) 05.02.16; *FFP* 05.08.16 Roll of the Brave; *FA* (FRoH) 16.11.18

Thomson, Hugh Philip: Private (S/10080 Cameron Hldrs [5th]); KIA Loos, 25.09.15, 24 years; 71 West Smeaton Street, Kirkcaldy; Loos Memorial, Pas de Calais, France. Panels 119-124; Kirkcaldy War Memorial; *FA* 30.10.15; *Soldiers Died* Part 66; *FA* 30.10.15; *FFP* 30.10.15; *FFP* (BMD) 30.10.15; *FA* (BMD) 06.11.15; *FA* (RoH) 13.11.15; *FFP* 05.08.16 Roll of the Brave; *FFP* (BMD) 23.09.16 (2 entries); *FA* (Service List) 24.02.17; *FFP* (BMD) 22.09.17; *FFP* (BMD) 29.09.17; *FFP* (BMD) 28.09.18 (2 entries); *FA* (FRoH) 16.11.18

Thomson, James: Private (3/3064 Black Watch [8th]); KIA, 13.07.16, 38 years; 5 Pratt Street, Kirkcaldy; Thiepval Memorial, Somme, France. Pier & Face 10A; Kirkcaldy War Memorial; *FA* 19.08.16; *Soldiers Died* Part 46; *FA* 19.08.16; *FFP* 19.08.16; *FFP* 02.09.16; *FFP* (CasList) 02.09.16; *FA* (RoH) 16.09.16; *FFP* (RoH) 16.09.16; *FFP* (RoH) 30.12.16; *FA* (BMD) 14.07.17; *FA* (FRoH) 23.11.18; Wauchope Vol 3

Thomson, James: Lance Corporal (20317 Cheshire Regt [15th] Bantam Bn); Listed as George Thomson in *FA* (RoH) 16.09.16 & *FA* 23.11.18; KIA, 21.08.16, 20 years; 82 Institution Street, Kirkcaldy; Quarry Cemetery, Montauban, Somme, France. Grave IV.J.7; Kirkcaldy War Memorial; *Soldiers Died* Part 27; *FA* 16.09.16; *FA* (RoH) 16.09.16; *FFP* (BMD) 23.09.16; *FA* (RoH) 16.12.16; *FFP* (RoH) 30.12.16; *FA* (Service List) 24.02.17; *FFP* (BMD) 25.08.17; *FFP* (BMD) 24.08.18; *FA* (FRoH) 23.11.18; *FA* (FRoH) 30.11.18

Thomson, James: Guardsman (Scots Guards [1st]); KIA, 23.10.14; 23 East Smeaton Street, Kirkcaldy; Not identified on CWGC web site; Kirkcaldy War Memorial; *FA* 15.05.15; *FFP* (CasList) 05.06.15; *FFP* 05.08.16 Roll of the Brave; *FA* (RoH) 16.09.16; *FFP* (RoH) 16.09.16; *FFP* (RoH) 30.12.16; *FA* (Service List) 17.02.17; *FA* (FRoH) 23.11.18

Thomson, James: Private (S/22957 Seaforth Hldrs [8th]. Formerly TR/1/13283 TR Bn); Brother of George Thomson; MIA, 22.08.17, 19 years; 116 Victoria Road/ 317 High Street, Kirkcaldy; Tyne Cot Memorial, Zonnebeke, West Vlaanderen, Belgium. Panels 132-135 & 162A; Kirkcaldy War Memorial; *Soldiers Died* Part 64; *FFP* 10.08.18; *FA* 17.08.18; *FA* (RoH) 14.09.18; *FFP* (RoH) 14.09.18; *FA* (FRoH) 14.12.18; *FA* 26.04.19

Thomson, John, MM: Sergeant (2238 Black Watch [1st]); 23.02.19; Cologne Southern Cemetery, Cologne, Nordrhein-Westfal, Germany. Grave XII.C.5; Kirkcaldy War Memorial

Thomson, John: Private (16268 KOSB [1st] "C" Coy); Drowned when the *Royal Edward* was sunk in the Aegean, 13.08.15; 94 Nicol Street, Kirkcaldy; West End Congregational Church Memorial Plaque; Helles Memorial, Gallipoli, Turkey. Panels 84-92 or 220-222; Kirkcaldy War Memorial; *FA* 04.09.15; *FFP* 04.09.15; *Soldiers Died* Part 30; War Album 15/16; *FA* 21.08.15; *FFP* 28.08.15; *FA* 04.09.15; *FFP* 04.09.15; *FA* 11.09.15; *FA* (BMD) 11.09.15; *FA* (RoH) 18.09.15; *FFP* 05.08.16 Roll of the Brave; *FA* (Service List) 18.11.16; *FA* (FRoH) 16.11.18

Thomson, Robert W.: Private (Black Watch); Not identified on CWGC web site; Kirkcaldy War Memorial

Thomson, William: Private (M2/227869 RASC [59th Div MT Coy]); General Canadian Hospital, Orpington, Kent, 24.02.19, 27 years; 149 Overton Rd, Kirkcaldy; Gravestone in Dysart Cemetery. Gallatown Church Roll of Honour; Dysart Cemetery, Kirkcaldy. Grave 4.J.South; Kirkcaldy War Memorial; *FA* (BMD) 08.03.19 (2 entries)

Thomson, William: Gunner (3904 RGA); Died war hospital, Norwich, 06.07.16, 52 years; 23 East Smeaton Street, Kirkcaldy; Gravestone in Abbotshall Churchyard; Abbotshall Parish Churchyard, Kirkcaldy. Grave New. (C.) 337; Kirkcaldy War Memorial; *FA* 08.07.16; *FFP* (BMD) 08.07.16; *FA* (RoH) 15.07.16; *FFP* 15.07.16; *FFP* 05.08.16 Roll of the Brave; *FA* (Service List) 17.02.17; *FA* (FRoH) 23.11.18

Thomson, William: Leading Seaman (Clyde Z/7230; RNVR; RNVR [RND] [*Nelson* Bn]); KIA, 31.12.17, 31 years; 5c Institution Street, Kirkcaldy; Gravestone in Barony Churchyard; Thiepval Memorial, Somme, France. Pier & Face 1A; Kirkcaldy War Memorial; *FA* 24.02.17; *Cross of Sacrifice Vol 4*; *FFP* (RoH) 19.01.18; *FFP* (BMD) 19.01.18; *FA* 26.01.18; *FA* (BMD) 26.01.18; *FFP* (RoH) 26.01.18; *FA* (RoH) 16.02.18; *FFP* (RoH) 16.02.18; *FA* (FRoH) 07.12.18

Thomson, William: Private (22701 Royal Scots [2nd]); KIA Ypres, 16.10.15, 21 years; 48 Bank Street, Kirkcaldy; Ypres (Menin Gate) Memorial, Ieper, West Vlaanderen, Belgium. Panel 11; Kirkcaldy War Memorial; *Soldiers Died* Part 6

Todd, Bernard Douglas: Private (1828 London Regt [14th] [County of London] [London Scottish]); On *Soldiers Died* and CWGC as Tod; KIA, 23.12.14, 19 years; 7 Bennochy Terrace, Kirkcaldy; Kirkcaldy High School War Memorial. St Peter's Church Memorial Plaque; Le Touret Memorial, Pas de Calais, France. Panel 45; Kirkcaldy War Memorial; *Soldiers Died* Part 76; War Album 14/15; *FA* 02.01.15; *FFP* 02.01.15; *FA* 16.01.15; *FFP* (RoH) 30.01.15; *FA* (CasList) 20.02.15; *FFP* 05.08.16 Roll of the Brave; *FA* (Service List) 06.01.17; *FA* (FRoH) 16.11.18; *FA* (KHS RoH) 29.03.19

Todd, David: Sapper (63961 Royal Engineers [103 Fld Coy]); KIA Somme, 31.08.16, 22 years; 2 Ravenscraig Street, Kirkcaldy; Gravestone in Dysart Cemetery. Pathhead Parish Church Memorial Plaques & Windows; Quarry Cemetery, Montauban, Somme, France. Grave III.M.2; Kirkcaldy War Memorial; *FA* 16.10.15; *FA* 16.09.16; *Soldiers Died* Part 4; *FA* 16.10.15; *FA* 16.09.16; *FA* (BMD) 16.09.16; *FFP* 16.09.16; *FFP* (BMD) 16.09.16; *FA* (CasList) 30.09.16; *FFP* (CasList) 30.09.16; *FA* (RoH) 14.10.16; *FFP* (RoH) 14.10.16; *FFP* (RoH) 30.12.16; *FA* (Service List) 13.01.17; *FA* 01.09.17; *FA* (BMD) 01.09.17; *FFP* (BMD) 01.09.17; *FFP* (BMD) 15.09.17; *FFP* (BMD) 31.08.18; *FA* (FRoH) 23.11.18; *FFP* 21.06.24

Todd, Edward: Private (3/2343 Black Watch [3rd] att'd [1st]); Killed at the Aisne, 22.10.14, 19 years; 42/48 Links Street, Kirkcaldy; Ypres (Menin Gate) Memorial, Ieper, West Vlaanderen, Belgium. Panel 37; Kirkcaldy War Memorial; *Soldiers Died* Part 46; War Album 14/15; *FA* 14.11.14; *FFP* 14.11.14; *FA* 28.11.14; *FA* (CasList) 19.12.14; *FA* 02.01.15; *FA* (CasList) 20.02.15; *FFP* 05.08.16 Roll of the Brave; *FFP* (BMD) 21.10.16; *FA* (Service List) 02.12.16; *FA* (FRoH) 16.11.18; Wauchope Vol 1

Todd, John: Private (S/5255 A & S Hldrs [12th]); Died of dysentery at Salonika, 08.10.16, 33 years; 56 Factory Road, Kirkcaldy; Gravestone in Bennochy Cemetery. Pathhead Parish Church Memorial Plaques & Windows; Sarigol Military Cemetery, Kriston, Greece. Grave A.85; Kirkcaldy War Memorial; *FA* 21.10.16; *Soldiers Died* Part 70; *FA* 21.10.16; *FA* (BMD) 21.10.16; *FFP* 21.10.16; *FA* (Service List) 04.11.16; *FA* (RoH) 18.11.16; *FFP* (RoH)) 18.11.16; *FFP* (RoH) 30.12.16; *FA* (Service List) 06.01.17; *FFP* (BMD) 06.10.17; *FA* (FRoH) 30.11.18; *FFP* 21.06.24

Torrance, John: Private (43051 HLI [16th]. Formerly 1563 HCB); MIA, 18.11.16, 33 years; 19 Cairns Street/7 Anderson Street, Kirkcaldy; New Munich Trench British Cemetery, Beaumont-Hamel, Somme, France. Grave E.10; Kirkcaldy War Memorial; *FA* 16.12.16; *FA* 21.07.17; *Soldiers Died* Part 63; *FA* 02.12.16; *FA* 09.12.16; *FA* 16.12.16; *FA* 30.12.16; *FA* (CasList) 13.01.17; *FA* (Service List) 27.01.17; *FA* 21.07.17; *FA* (BMD) 21.07.17; *FFP* 21.07.17; *FFP* (CasList) 04.08.17; *FA* (BMD) 11.08.17; *FFP* (BMD) 18.08.17; *FA* 15.09.17; *FFP* (RoH) 15.09.17

Torrance, Spiers: Lance Corporal (S/13239 Cameron Hldrs [6th] "C" Coy); Believed died near Vermelles in German hands, 12.05.16, 25 years; 6 Douglas Street, Kirkcaldy; Gravestone in Bennochy Cemetery (Photo). Abbotshall Parish Church Memorial Plaque; Loos Memorial, Pas de Calais, France. Panels 119-124; Kirkcaldy War Memorial; *Soldiers Died* Part 66; *FA* (Service List) 10.02.17; *FA* (BMD) 08.03.19; *FA* 19.11.21

Turpie, Christopher: Private (14304 Cameronians [Scottish Rifles] [10th] "D" Coy); KIA Loos, 25.09.15, 36 years; 139 Park Road/2 Back Lane, Kirkcaldy; Sinclairtown Parish Church War Memorial Chair; Loos Memorial, Pas de Calais, France. Panels 57-59; Kirkcaldy War Memorial; *FA* 22.01.16; *Soldiers Died* Part 31; *FA* 06.11.15; *FA* 11.12.15; *FFP* 18.12.15; *FA* (RoH) 15.01.16; *FA* 22.01.16; *FA* (BMD) 29.01.16; *FFP* 29.01.16; *FFP* (BMD) 29.01.16; *FFP* 12.02.16; *FFP* 05.08.16 Roll of the Brave; *FA* (Service List) 24.03.17; *FA* (Service List) 31.03.17; *FA* (FRoH) 16.11.18; *FFP* (BMD) 22.09.19

Turpie, James: Private (S/1903 A & S Hldrs [2nd] "D" Coy); KIA, 25.09.15, 38 years; 23 Nicol Street, Kirkcaldy; Cambrin Churchyard Extension, Pas de Calais, France. Grave B.8; Kirkcaldy War Memorial; *Soldiers Died* Part 70; War Album 15/16; *FA* 27.11.15; *FA* (RoH) 18.12.15; *FFP* 05.08.16 Roll of the Brave; *FA* (Service List) 18.11.16; *FA* (FRoH) 16.11.18

Vaughan, Robert H.: Private (6250 Kings Shropshire Light Infantry [1st] [16th Bde]); 06.05.15; 7/12 Heggie's Wynd, Kirkcaldy; Y Farm Military Cemetery, Bois Grenier, Nord, France. Grave D.29; Kirkcaldy War Memorial; *Soldiers Died* Part 55; War Album 15; *FA* 15.05.15; *FFP* (CasList) 05.06.15; *FFP* 05.08.16 Roll of the Brave; *FA* (Service List) 04.11.16; *FA* (Service List) 30.12.16; *FA* (FRoH) 16.11.18

Veitch, David: Private (27764 KOSB [7/8th]. Formerly 2699 F & F Yeo); KIA, 31.07.17, 19 years; 238 St Clair Street, Kirkcaldy; Gravestone in Dysart Cemetery. Sinclairtown Parish Church War Memorial Chair; Ypres (Menin Gate) Memorial, Ieper, West Vlaanderen, Belgium. Panels 22; Kirkcaldy War Memorial; *FFP* 09.02.18; *Soldiers Died* Part 30; *FFP* 15.09.17; *FA* 22.09.17; *FFP* (RoH) 09.02.18; *FA* 16.02.18

Walker, Alexander Scott: Rifleman (A/202873 Kings Royal Rifle Corps [17th]); DOW whilst PoW. Buried Troissy, France by a fellow PoW; 28.03.18; 24 Forth Avenue South, Kirkcaldy; Dunnikier Church Roll of Honour; Pozieres Memorial, Somme, France. Panels 61-64; *Soldiers Died* Part 57; Kirkcaldy War Memorial; *FA* 14.12.18; *FA* (FRoH) 14.12.18; *FFP* 14.12.18; *FA* (BMD) 21.12.18; *FA* (RoH) 18.01.19; *FA* 26.04.19

Walker, David: Private (241253 Black Watch [4/5th]. Formerly F & F Yeo); MIA France, 27.09.17, 23 years; 65 Sutherland Street, Kirkcaldy; Gravestone in Dysart Cemetery. Sinclairtown Parish Church War Memorial Chair; Tyne Cot Memorial, Zonnebeke, West Vlaanderen, Belgium. Panels 94-96; Kirkcaldy War Memorial; *Soldiers Died* Part 46; *FA* 03.11.17; *FA* 03.08.18; *FFP* 03.08.18; *FA* (CasList) 14.09.18; *FFP* (RoH) 14.09.18; *FA* (FRoH) 14.12.18; Wauchope Vol 2

Walker, John: Able Seaman (Clyde Z/6921; Royal Navy; RNVR [HMS *Ceto*]); Died of pneumonia aboard HMS *Ceto* at Ramsgate, 12.11.18, 31 years; 81 Victoria Road, Kirkcaldy; Union Church Plaque; Abbotshall Parish Churchyard, Kirkcaldy. Grave Old. (N.) 320; Kirkcaldy War Memorial; *Cross of Sacrifice Vol 4*; *FFP* (BMD) 16.11.18; *FA* (FRoH) 14.12.18; *FFP* (RoH) 14.12.18

Wallace, James Millar: Lieutenant (CEF; 3rd Div 9th Bde. 43rd Infantry Bn ["A" Coy] [Manitoba Regt]); KIA, 27.08.18, 31 years; 32 Forth Avenue North, Kirkcaldy; Gravestone in Bennochy Cemetery. Raith Church Memorial Plaque. Kirkcaldy High School War Memorial; Windmill British Cemetery, Monchy-le-Preux, Pas de Calais, France. Grave II.B.28; *FA* 14.09.18; Kirkcaldy War Memorial; *CBoR* Page 518; *Cross of Sacrifice Vol 3*; *FA* 07.09.18; *FA* (BMD) 07.09.18; *FFP* 07.09.18; *FFP* (BMD) 07.09.18; *FA* 14.09.18; *FA* (RoH) 14.09.18; *FFP* (RoH) 14.09.18; *FFP* 28.09.18; *FA* (FRoH) 14.12.18; *FA* (KHS RoH) 29.03.19; *FA* (KHS RoH) 19.07.19

Wallace, Peter Yaun: Guardsman (8320 Scots Guards [2nd]); On *Soldiers Died* as Peter Young Wallace; MIA, 28.10.14, 21 years; 17 Alexandra Street, Kirkcaldy; Union Church Plaque; Ypres (Menin Gate) Memorial, Ieper, West Vlaanderen, Belgium. Panel 11; Kirkcaldy War Memorial; *FA* 03.07.15; *Soldiers Died* Part 5; *FFP* 12.08.16 Roll of The Brave; *FFP* (BMD) 28.10.16; *FA* (Service List) 25.11.16; *FFP* (BMD) 27.10.17

Wallace, Robert: Private (S/22595 Cameron Hldrs [6th]); KIA, 22.03.18, 28 years; Argyle House, 2 Pottery Street, Gallatown, Kirkcaldy; Barony Church Plaque; Faubourg D'Amiens Cemetery, Arras, Pas de Calais, France. Grave VI.C.8; Kirkcaldy War Memorial; *Soldiers Died* Part 66; *FFP* (RoH) 20.04.18; *FA* 27.04.18; *FFP* (RoH) 27.04.18; *FFP* (BMD) 27.04.18; *FA* (RoH) 18.05.18; *FFP* (RoH) 18.05.18; *FA* (FRoH) 07.12.18

Private **Robert Wallace** was acting as an officer's servant when the house in which they were quartered with six other officers and servants, was shelled. The servants were killed, but the officers in the front of the house, escaped with cuts and bruises.

Wallace, William Robert: Rifleman (330096 Hampshire Regt [1/8th]); DOW Palestine, 02.05.17, 21 years; 291 High Street, Kirkcaldy; Alexandria (Hadra) War Memorial Cemetery, Egypt. Grave D.112; Kirkcaldy War Memorial; *Soldiers Died* Part 41; *FFP* (BMD) 04.05.18

Watson, Alexander: Gunner (119061 RGA [228th Siege Btt'y]. Formerly 5282 1/6th [Forth] RGA [T]); Died of pneumonia 5th General Hospital, Rouen, 21.10.18, 28 years; 11 Forth Avenue South/7 West Wynd, Pathhead, Kirkcaldy; Forth RGA Plaque; St Sever Cemetery Extension, Rouen, Seine-Maritime, France. Grave S.11.R.8; Kirkcaldy War Memorial; *Soldiers Died* Part 3; *FA* 02.11.18; *FA* (RoH) 16.11.18; *FFP* 16.11.18; *FFP* (RoH) 16.11.18; *FA* (FRoH) 14.12.18

Watson, Andrew: Sergeant (52211 RFA [178th Bde] "A" Batt'y); KIA, 30.03.18, 28 years; 83 Institution Street, Kirkcaldy/5 Hanson Avenue, East Toronto, Ontario; Bellacourt Military Cemetery, Riviere, Pas de Calais, France. Grave I.O.3; Kirkcaldy War Memorial; *Soldiers Died* Part 2; *FA* 04.05.18; *FFP* (RoH) 04.05.18; *FFP* (BMD) 04.05.18; *FFP* (RoH) 11.05.18; *FA* (RoH) 18.05.18; *FFP* (RoH) 18.05.18; *FA* (FRoH) 07.12.18

Watson, Charles: Private (41054 KOSB [6th]. Formerly 2672 F & F Yeo); DOW Aachen Hospital, Germany whilst a PoW, 22.08.17; Bridgeton, Kirkcaldy; Cologne Southern Cemetery, Germany. Grave XIII.D.22; Kirkcaldy War Memorial; *FA* 10.11.17; *Soldiers Died* Part 30; *FA* 23.06.17; *FA* 27.10.17; *FFP* 03.11.17; *FA* 10.11.17; *FFP* 10.11.17; *FA* (RoH) 17.11.17; *FFP* (RoH) 17.11.17; *FFP* (BMD) 24.08.18; *FA* (FRoH) 07.12.18

Watson, George: Private (290839 Black Watch [7th]); Reported wounded & missing in France, 31.07.17, 27 years; 7 Harriet Street, Kirkcaldy; St Michael's Church Memorial Plaque; Ypres (Menin Gate) Memorial, Ieper, West Vlaanderen, Belgium. Panel 37; Kirkcaldy War Memorial; *FFP* 13.04.18; *Soldiers Died* Part 46; *FA* 06.10.17; *FFP* 13.04.18; *FFP* (BMD) 13.04.18; *FA* 20.04.18; *FA* (RoH) 18.05.18; *FFP* (RoH) 18.05.18; *FFP* (BMD) 03.08.18; *FFP* (BMD) 10.08.18; *FA* (FRoH) 07.12.18; Wauchope Vol 2

Watson, John: Corporal (292502 Black Watch [7th]); Brother of William C. Watson; KIA, 23.04.17, 27 years; 16 Viceroy Street, Kirkcaldy; Brown's Copse Cemetery, Roeux, Pas de Calais, France. Grave III.B.II; Kirkcaldy War Memorial; *Soldiers Died* Part 46; *FA* (Service List) 17.03.17; *FA* 09.06.17; *FA* (BMD) 09.06.17; *FFP* 09.06.17; *FFP* (BMD) 09.06.17; *FA* (RoH) 16.06.17; *FFP* (RoH) 16.06.17; *FFP* (CasList) 23.06.17; *FA* (BMD) 20.04.18; *FFP* (BMD) 20.04.18; *FA* (FRoH) 30.11.18; Wauchope Vol 2

Watson, John: Corporal (43017 HLI [16th]. Formerly HCB [11th Signals Section]); DOW 36 CCS, 31.03.17, 21 years; 183 St Clair Street, Kirkcaldy; Gravestone in Dysart Cemetery. Sinclairtown Parish Church War Memorial Chair; Cayeux Military Cemetery, Somme, France. Grave I.A.6; Kirkcaldy War Memorial; *Soldiers Died* Part 63; *FA* 07.04.17; *FFP* 07.04.17; *FA* (RoH) 14.04.17; *FFP* 14.04.17; *FFP* (BMD) 14.04.17; *FA* (BMD) 21.04.17; *FFP* (CasList) 05.05.17; *FA* (RoH) 19.05.17; *FFP* (RoH) 19.05.17; *FFP* (BMD) 16.03.18; *FA* (FRoH) 30.11.18

Watson, John: Private (86183 Machine Gun Corps [44th]. Formerly 18562 Black Watch); KIA France, 22.08.17; 14 Balfour Street, Kirkcaldy; Dochy Farm New British Cemetery, Zonnebeke, West Vlaanderen, Belgium. Grave II.B.8; Kirkcaldy War Memorial; *Soldiers Died* Part 75; *FA* 15.09.17; *FFP* 15.09.17; *FFP* (BMD) 15.09.17; *FA* (BMD) 22.09.17; *FFP* (BMD) 29.09.17; *FA* 13.10.17; *FFP* (RoH) 13.10.17; *FFP* (BMD) 24.08.18; *FFP* (BMD) 14.09.18; *FA* (FRoH) 07.12.18

Watson, Neil: Trooper (345444 Black Watch [14th] [F & F Yeo Bn]. Formerly 2709 F & F Yeo); KIA Sheria, Egypt, 06.11.17, 37 years; 60 Alexandra Street, Kirkcaldy; Beersheba War Cemetery, Israel. Grave L.5; Kirkcaldy War Memorial; *Soldiers Died* Part 46; *FA* 24.11.17; *FFP* 24.11.17; *FFP* (BMD) 24.11.17; *FA* (RoH) 15.12.17; *FFP* (RoH) 15.12.17; *FA* (FRoH) 07.12.18; Wauchope Vol 3; Ogilvie

Watson, Robert: Private (S/4530 Black Watch [9th]); KIA Loos, 25.09.15, 22 years; 4 Stein Place, Commercial Street/93 East Smeaton Street, Kirkcaldy; E.U. Congregational Church Memorial Plaque; Loos Memorial, Pas de Calais, France. Panels 78-83; Kirkcaldy War Memorial; *FA* 13/11/15; *Soldiers Died* Part 46; War Album 15/16; *FA* 06.11.15; *Scotsman* 08.11.15; *FA* (RoH) 13.11.15; *FFP* 05.08.16 Roll of the Brave; *FA* (BMD) 30.09.16; *FFP* (BMD) 30.09.16 (2 entries); *FA* (Service List) 16.12.16; *FA* (Service List) 17.02.17; *FA* (BMD) 29.09.17; *FFP* (BMD) 29.09.17; *FFP* (BMD) 28.09.18; *FFP* (BMD) 12.10.18; *FA* (FRoH) 16.11.18; Wauchope Vol 3

Watson, William Christie: Corporal (3/2162 Black Watch [3rd] "C" Coy att'd [1st]); CWGC gives his number as 312162. Brother of John Watson; KIA, 09.05.15, 20 years; 16 Viceroy Street, Kirkcaldy; Le Touret Memorial, Pas de Calais, France. Panels 24-26; Kirkcaldy War Memorial; *FA* 13.05.16; *Soldiers Died* Part 46; War Album 15; *FFP* 19.06.15; *FA* 26.06.15; *FFP* 24.07.15; *FA* 15.01.16; *FA* 13.05.16; *FA* (BMD) 13.05.16; *FFP* 13.05.16; *FFP* (BMD) 13.05.16; *FA* (RoH) 17.06.16; *FFP* (RoH) 17.06.16; *FFP* 05.08.16 Roll of the Brave; *FA* (Service List) 17.03.17; *FA* 09.06.17; *FFP* 09.06.17; *FA* (BMD) 20.04.18; *FFP* (BMD) 20.04.18; *FA* (FRoH) 23.11.18; Wauchope Vol 1

Watson, William Kirk: Private (S/4557 Gordon Hldrs [8/10th] att'd Trench Mortar Batt'y [44th]); KIA, 30.12.17, 29 years; 5 Gow's Square, Glasswork Street, Kirkcaldy; Gravestone in Bennochy Cemetery; Faubourg D'Amiens Cemetery, Arras, Pas de Calais, France. Grave VIII.A.23; Kirkcaldy War Memorial; *FFP* 09.02.18; *Soldiers Died* Part 65; *FFP* (RoH) 26.01.18; *FFP* (BMD) 02.02.18; *FFP* (RoH) 09.02.18; *FA* 16.02.18; *FA* (RoH) 16.02.18; *FFP* (RoH) 16.02.18; *FA* (FRoH) 07.12.18; *FFP* (BMD) 28.12.18

Watters, James: Lance Corporal (S/3482 A & S Hldrs [11th]); KIA, 02.09.16, 21 years; 395 High Street, Kirkcaldy; Thiepval Memorial, Somme, France. Pier & Face 15A & 15C; Kirkcaldy War Memorial; *FA* 12.02.16; *FA* 16.09.16; *Soldiers Died* Part 70; *FA* 16.09.16; *FFP* 16.09.16; *FA* 23.09.16; *FA* (BMD) 23.09.16; *FFP* 23.09.16; *FA* 30.09.16; *FA* 07.10.16; *FA* (CasList) 07.10.16; *FFP* (CasList) 07.10.16; *FA* (RoH) 14.10.16; *FFP* (RoH) 14.10.16; *FA* (Service List) 28.10.16; *FA* (Service List) 09.12.16; *FFP* (RoH) 30.12.16; *FFP* (BMD) 01.09.17; *FFP* (BMD) 07.09.18; *FA* (FRoH) 23.11.18

Watters, John Crighton: Private (93149 RAMC [45th] [15th Fld Amb]); DOW, 25.07.18, 22 years; 50 Alexandra Street, Kirkcaldy; St Brycedale Church Plaque; Buzancy Military Cemetery, Aisne, France. Grave III.F.10; Kirkcaldy War Memorial; *Soldiers Died* Part 79; *FA* 03.08.18; *FFP* 03.08.18; *FFP* (BMD) 10.08.18; *FA* (BMD) 17.08.18; *FFP* 24.08.18; *FA* (RoH) 14.09.18; *FFP* (RoH) 14.09.18; *FA* (FRoH) 14.12.18

Private Sigmund Wehrle

Watters, Richard: Private (S/9317 Gordon Hldrs [1st]); KIA, 03.03.16; 56 Nicol Street, Kirkcaldy; Ypres (Menin Gate) Memorial, Ieper, West Vlaanderen, Belgium. Panel 38; Kirkcaldy War Memorial; *Soldiers Died* Part 65; *FFP* 06.05.16; *FFP* (BMD) 06.05.16; *FA* 13.05.16; *FA* (RoH) 13.05.16; *FFP* 20.05.16; *FFP* 05.08.16 Roll of the Brave; *FA* (Service List) 18.11.16; *FA* (FRoH) 23.11.18

Weatherby, David: Lance Corporal (11038 Royal Scots [2nd]); On *Soldiers Died* as Weatherly & CWGC as Weatherley; DOW France & Flanders, 29.10.17; Links Street, Kirkcaldy; Wimereux Communal Cemetery, Pas de Calais, France. Grave VI.F.5; Kirkcaldy War Memorial; *Soldiers Died* Part 6; *FFP* 03.11.17; *FA* 10.11.17; *FA* (RoH) 17.11.17; *FFP* (RoH) 17.11.17; *FA* (FRoH) 07.12.18; Kirkcaldy Council Memorial Scroll

Webster, James: Sergeant (9471 Northumberland Fusiliers [15th]); Died Edinburgh, 11.11.15, 48 years; 23 Kidd Street, Kirkcaldy; Gravestone in Dysart Cemetery; Dysart Cemetery, Kirkcaldy. Grave 14.6. North; Kirkcaldy War Memorial; *FA* 13/11/15; *Soldiers Died* Part 10; War Album 15/16; *FA* 13.11.15; *FA* (BMD) 13.11.15; *FA* (RoH) 18.12.15; *FFP* 05.08.16 Roll of the Brave; *FA* (Service List) 27.01.17; *FA* (FRoH) 16.11.18

Weepers, Alexander: Private (47463 Lancashire Fusiliers [2/5th]); KIA, 26.04.18, 35 years; Gravestone in Dysart Cemetery; Loos Memorial, Pas de Calais, France. Panels 45-46; Kirkcaldy War Memorial; *Soldiers Died* Part 25

Wehrle, Sigmund: Private (3/3546 Black Watch [1st] "C" Coy); DOW, 30.12.14, 39 years; 15 Harriet Street, Kirkcaldy; Barony Church Plaque; Le Touret Memorial, Pas de Calais, France. Panels 24-26; Kirkcaldy War Memorial; *FA* 05.09.14; *FFP* (RoH) 30.01.15; *FA* 24.07.15; *Soldiers Died* Part 46; War Album 14/15; *FA* 05.09.14; *FFP* 16.01.15; *FA* (BMD) 23.01.15; *FFP* (RoH) 30.01.15; *FA* (CasList) 20.02.15; *FFP* 05.08.16 Roll of the Brave; *FA* (Service List) 20.01.17; *FA* (FRoH) 16.11.18; Wauchope Vol 1

Weir, Frank Renwick: Lance Corporal (26/645; NZEF; 3rd New Zealand Rifle Brigade [4th Bn]); KIA Somme, 11.09.16, 22 years; Helm Cottage, 12 Lady Helen Street, Kirkcaldy/West Park, Falkland; Old Parish Church Memorial Panel; Caterpillar Valley Cemetery, Longueval, Somme, France. Grave XI.D.27; Kirkcaldy War Memorial; ‡; *FA* 30.09.16; NZEF Roll of Honour; *FA* 23.09.16; *FA* (BMD) 23.09.16; *FFP* 23.09.16; *FFP* (BMD) 30.09.16; *FA* (RoH) 14.10.16; *FFP* (RoH) 14.10.16; *FA* 11.11.16; *FFP* 11.11.16; *FFP* (RoH) 30.12.16; *FA* (Service List) 13.01.17; *FA* (BMD) 08.09.17; *FFP* (BMD) 08.09.17; *FFP* (BMD) 14.09.18; *FA* (FRoH) 23.11.18

Weir, James: Private (2871 Black Watch [1/7th]); DOW, 03.06.16, 21 years; 165/185 High Street/41 Bridgeton, Kirkcaldy; Old Parish Church Memorial Panel; Aubigny Communal Cemetery Extension, Pas de Calais, France. Grave I.C.54; Kirkcaldy War Memorial; *FA* 17.06.16; *Soldiers Died* Part 46; *FA* 10.06.16; *FA* (BMD) 10.06.16; *FFP* 10.06.16; *FFP* (BMD) 10.06.16; *FA* (RoH) 17.06.16; *FFP* 17.06.16; *FFP* (RoH) 17.06.16; *FA* (CasList) 01.07.16; *FFP* 05.08.16 Roll of the Brave; *FA* (Service List) 09.12.16; *FFP* 14.04.17; *FA* (FRoH) 23.11.18; Wauchope Vol 2

Welsh, George B.: Private (448241; CEF; Canadian Infantry [3rd] 1st Div 1st Bde. [Central Ontario Regt]); DOW CCS, 11.07.17, 32 years; 66 Victoria Street, Boreland, Dysart/56 Viewforth Street, Kirkcaldy; Barony Church Plaque. Pathhead Parish Church Memorial Plaques & Windows; Noeux-Les-Mines Communal Cemetery & Extension, Pas de Calais, France. Grave II.E.17; Kirkcaldy War Memorial; *FFP* 09.10.15; *CBoR* Page 347; *FA* 09.10.15; *FFP* 09.10.15; *FFP* 05.08.16 Roll of the Brave; *FA* 21.07.17; *FFP* 21.07.17; *FFP* (BMD) 21.07.17; *FA* (BMD) 28.07.17; *FA* 15.09.17; *FFP* (RoH) 15.09.17

Welsh, William: Driver (307734 Royal Tank Corps [15th]. Formerly 43125 HLI & HCB); KIA, 08.08.18, 28 years; Cairnylea, Chapel/55 Cowan Street, Kirkcaldy; Heath Cemetery, Harbonnieres, Somme, France. Grave II.H.5; Kirkcaldy War Memorial; *Soldiers Died* Part 75; *FA* 24.08.18; *FFP* 24.08.18; *FFP* 31.08.18; *FA* (RoH) 14.09.18; *FFP* (RoH) 14.09.18; *FA* (FRoH) 14.12.18

Westwater, Edward M.: Private (17779 Royal Scots Fusiliers [2nd]); Died, 30.07.16; 381 High Street, Kirkcaldy; Thiepval Memorial, Somme, France. Pier & Face 3C; Kirkcaldy War Memorial; *FA* 16.09.16; *Soldiers Died* Part 26; *FA* 09.09.16; *FFP* (CasList) 16.09.16; *FA* (Service List) 09.12.16; *FA* 19.05.17; *FA* (RoH) 16.06.17; *FFP* (RoH) 16.06.17; *FA* (FRoH) 30.11.18

Westwood, David Bruce: Lance Corporal (28607 KOSB [2nd]); 16.05.19, 31 years; Dysart Cemetery, Kirkcaldy. Grave 56.24.Middle; Kirkcaldy War Memorial

Westwood, Peter T.: Corporal (443478; CEF; Canadian Infantry [2nd] 1st Div 1st Bde. [Eastern Ontario Regt] Machine Gun Corps); DOW 34 CCS, 29.04.17, 31 years; 3 Bute Wynd, Kirkcaldy; Raith Church Memorial Plaque; Aubigny Communal Cemetery Extension, Pas de Calais, France. Grave II.G.83; Kirkcaldy War Memorial; *FA* 19.05.17; *CBoR* Page 347; *FA* 12.05.17; *FFP* 12.05.17; *FFP* (BMD) 12.05.17; *FA* (RoH) 19.05.17; *FFP* (RoH) 19.05.17; *FA* (BMD) 27.04.18; *FFP* (BMD) 27.04.18; *FA* (FRoH) 30.11.18; *FA* (BMD) 26.04.19

White, William: Private (22698 KOSB [7/8th]); DOW; 03.05.17, 21 years; 33 Nicol Street, Kirkcaldy; Boulogne Eastern Cemetery, Pas de Calais, France. Grave IV.C.49; Kirkcaldy War Memorial; *Soldiers Died* Part 30; *FA* (CasList) 02.06.17; *FFP* (CasList) 02.06.17

Whitehead, James: Private (Black Watch [2nd]); KIA France. Possibly James Whitelaw on Kirkcaldy War Memorial; 00.12.15; Pathhead; Not identified on CWGC web site; Not on Kirkcaldy War Memorial. Not on Dysart War Memorial; *FA* 18.12.15; *FFP* 18.12.15; *Scotsman* 20.12.15; *FA* (RoH) 15.01.16; *FFP* 05.08.16 Roll of the Brave; *FA* (FRoH) 16.11.18

Whitelaw, James: Private (Black Watch); Not identified on CWGC web site; Kirkcaldy War Memorial

Whitton, David John: Surgeon Probationer (Royal Navy; RNVR [HMS *Cullist*]); KIA submarine attack, Dundalk Bay, Ireland, 11.02.18, 21 years; St Clair Street/22 Carlyle Road, Kirkcaldy; Gravestone in Bennochy Cemetery (Photo). St Brycedale Church Plaque. Kirkcaldy High School War Memorial; Portsmouth Naval Memorial, Hampshire. Plate 31; Kirkcaldy War Memorial; *FA* 23.02.18; *Cross of Sacrifice Vol 2*; *FFP* 16.02.18; *FA* 23.02.18 (2 entries); *FFP* (RoH) 23.02.18; *FFP* (BMD) 23.02.18; *FFP* (RoH) 09.03.18; *FA* (RoH) 16.03.18; *FA* 13.07.18; *FA* (FRoH) 07.12.18; *FA* (BMD) 08.02.19; *FFP* (BMD) 08.02.19; *FA* (KHS RoH) 29.03.19

Whyte, Peter J.: Gunner (191570 RGA [68th Anti-Aircraft Section]); Died of pneumonia in Calais General Hospital, 30.11.18, 23 years; 49 Links Street, Kirkcaldy; St Columba's Church Memorial Plaque; Les Baraques Military Cemetery, Sangatte, Pas de Calais, France. Grave VII.B.3; Kirkcaldy War Memorial; *FA* 11.12.15; *FA* (BMD) 29.11.18; *FA* 07.12.18; *FA* (FRoH) 14.12.18; *FFP* 14.12.18; *FFP* (RoH) 14.12.18

Whyte, Robert: Private (S/14637 Seaforth Hldrs [1st Garrison Bn]. Formerly S/15561 Black Watch); On *Soldiers Died* as White; Died of pneumonia at Salonika, 19.10.18; 7 Pool Lane, Gallatown, Kirkcaldy; Sarigol Military Cemetery, Kriston, Greece. Grave A.21; Kirkcaldy War Memorial; *Soldiers Died* Part 64; *FA* (BMD) 16.11.18; *FA* (FRoH) 14.12.18; *FFP* (RoH) 14.12.18

Wilkie, Norman Craig: Private (137328 RAMC [1st NG Hospital] Formerly 292273 Black Watch); Died of pneumonia at Newcastle Hospital, 11.07.18, 35 years; 63 Institution Street, Kirkcaldy; Gravestone in Dysart Cemetery. Pathhead Parish Church Memorial Plaques & Windows; Dysart Cemetery, Kirkcaldy. Grave 10.W. North; Kirkcaldy War Memorial; *Soldiers Died* Part 79; *FFP* 13.07.18; *FFP* (BMD) 13.07.18; *FA* 20.07.18; *FA* (CasList) 14.09.18; *FFP* (RoH) 14.09.18; *FA* (FRoH) 14.12.18; *FFP* 21.06.24

Willard, Robert: Sapper (Royal Engineers); Not identified on CWGC web site; Kirkcaldy War Memorial

Williams, Alfred: Private (S/18697 Black Watch [14th] [F & F Yeo Bn]); Died when Troopship *Arcadia* was sunk, 15.04.17, 38 years; 148/246 Links Street, Kirkcaldy; Gravestone in Dysart Cemetery; Mikra Memorial, Greece; Kirkcaldy War Memorial; *FA* 12.05.17; *Soldiers Died* Part 46; *FA* 05.05.17; *FA* (RoH) 19.05.17; *FFP* (RoH) 19.05.17; *FFP* (CasList) 09.06.17; *FA* (BMD) 20.04.18; *FA* (FRoH) 16.11.18; *FA* (BMD) 12.04.19; Wauchope Vol 3

Williams, James Pratt: Lance Corporal (S/21715 Black Watch [14th] [F & F Yeo Bn]); Brother-in-law of Hugh McKinnon; DOW Zeitun, Palestine, 28.12.17, 29 years; 32 Patterson Street, Kirkcaldy; Jerusalem War Cemetery, Israel. Grave D.52; Kirkcaldy War Memorial; *Soldiers Died* Part 46; *FA* 19.01.18; *FA* (BMD) 19.01.18; *FFP* 19.01.18; *FFP* (RoH) 19.01.18; *FFP* (BMD) 19.01.18; *FA* (RoH) 16.02.18; *FFP* (RoH) 16.02.18; *FA* (FRoH) 07.12.18; *FA* (BMD) 28.12.18; *FFP* (BMD) 28.12.18; Ogilvie; Wauchope Vol 3

Williamson, Barn: Pioneer (94885 Royal Engineers [155th Fld Coy]); Originally buried Marchelepot British Cemetery, Somme, 21.03.18, 22 years; 13 Rosabelle Street, Kirkcaldy; Roye New British Cemetery, Somme, France. Memorial 36; Kirkcaldy War Memorial; *Soldiers Died* Part 4; *FFP* (BMD) 06.04.18; *FA* (RoH) 13.04.18; *FA* (FRoH) 07.12.18

Williamson, George: Sapper (121327 Royal Engineers [64th Fld Coy]); Wounded at Marancourt. DOW 3rd Western General Hospital, Newport, Shropshire, 14.08.16, 36 years; 53 Hill Street, Kirkcaldy; Gravestone in Bennochy Cemetery; Bennochy Cemetery, Kirkcaldy. Grave M.851; Kirkcaldy War Memorial; ‡; *Soldiers Died* Part 4; *FA* 12.08.16; *FA* 19.08.16 (2 entries); *FA* (BMD) 19.08.16; *FFP* 19.08.16 (2 entries); *FFP* (BMD) 19.08.16; *FA* (RoH) 16.09.16; *FFP* (RoH) 16.09.16; *FA* (CasList) 30.09.16; *FFP* (CasList) 30.09.16; *FA* (Service List) 04.11.16; *FFP* (RoH) 30.12.16; *FA* (Service List) 20.01.17; *FA* (BMD) 18.08.17; *FFP* (BMD) 18.08.17; *FFP* (BMD) 10.08.18; *FA* (FRoH) 23.11.18

Williamson, Thomas: Private (14375 KOSB [7th]); KIA Hill 70, 25.09.15; 29 Tolbooth Street, Kirkcaldy; Loos Memorial, Pas de Calais, France. Panels 53-56; Kirkcaldy War Memorial; *Soldiers Died* Part 30; War Album 15/16; *FA* 23.10.15; *Scotsman* (CasList) 25.10.15; *FA* 30.10.15; *FFP* 30.10.15; *FA* (RoH) 13.11.15; *FFP* 05.08.16 Roll of the Brave; *FA* (Service List) 04.11.16; *FA* (Service List) 27.01.17; *FA* (FRoH) 16.11.18

Wilson, David Allan: Guardsman (5088 Scots Guards [2nd] "F" Coy); Brother of William Wilson & brother-in-law of Robert Michelston. In *Soldiers Died* & CWGC as David Allan; KIA Ypres, 18.12.14, 31 years; 132 Den Road/105 Links Street/36 Thistle Street, Kirkcaldy; Cabaret-Rouge British Cemetery, Souchez, Pas de Calais, France. Grave XVIII.A.11; Kirkcaldy War Memorial; *FA* 06.02.15; *FFP* 06.02.15; *Soldiers Died* Part 5; War Album 14/15; *FA* 06.02.15; *FFP* 06.02.15; *FA* (CasList) 20.02.15; *FA* 25.03.16; *FFP* 05.08.16 Roll of the Brave; *FFP* (CasList) 28.10.16; *FA* (Service List) 02.12.16; *FA* (Service List) 03.02.17; *FA* 27.10.17; *FFP* 24.11.17; *FA* 04.05.18; *FA* (FRoH) 16.11.18

Wilson, George: Private (42124 Royal Irish Fusiliers [9th]. Formerly 16975 RAVC); Brother also killed; KIA, 24.08.18, 21 years; 202/159 Links Street, Kirkcaldy/ Walkerton, Leslie; Bailleul Communal Cemetery Extension, Nord, France. Grave III.F.107; Kirkcaldy War Memorial; *Soldiers Died* Part 68; *FA* 05.10.18; *FA* (BMD) 05.10.18; *FFP* 05.10.18; *FA* (RoH) 19.10.18; *FA* 02.11.18; *FA* (FRoH) 14.12.18; *FA* (BMD) 23.08.19

Wilson, John: Private (124120 Labour Corps [196th Coy]. Formerly 5127 Black Watch [2/7th] "E" Coy); Presumed drowned, 25.01.18, 23 years; 28 Hill Place, Kirkcaldy; St Marie Cemetery, Le Havre, Seine-Maritime, France. Normandy Memorial; Kirkcaldy War Memorial; *Soldiers Died* Part 80; *FFP* 15.06.18; *FA* 22.06.18; *FFP* 22.06.18; *FA* 29.06.18; *FA* (RoH) 13.07.18; *FFP* 20.07.18; *FA* (FRoH) 14.12.18

Wilson, Robert: Private (S/18042 Cameron Hldrs [1st]); KIA, 13.10.15, 21 years; 21/147 Ramsay Road, Kirkcaldy; Abbotshall Parish Church Memorial Plaque; Loos Memorial, Pas de Calais, France. Panels 119-124; Kirkcaldy War Memorial; *FA* 29.01.16; *Soldiers Died* Part 66; War Album 15/16; *FFP* 02.10.15; *FFP* 23.10.15; *Scotsman* (CasList) 25.10.15; *FA* (RoH) 13.11.15; *FA* 27.11.15; *FA* 22.01.16; *FA* (BMD) 22.01.16; *FFP* 22.01.16; *FFP* (BMD) 22.01.16; *FFP* 29.01.16; *FFP* 05.08.16 Roll of the Brave; *FFP* (BMD) 14.10.16; *FA* (Service List) 16.12.16; *FFP* 13.10.17; *FFP* (BMD) 12.10.18; *FA* (FRoH) 16.11.18; *FA* 19.11.21

Wilson, William: Private (4765 Black Watch [2/7th]; Drowned in Grangemouth Harbour, 01.09.15, 37 years; Hendry's Wynd/76 Harriet Street, Kirkcaldy; Grangemouth (Grandsable) Cemetery. Grave 8.80; Kirkcaldy War Memorial; *Soldiers Died* Part 46; War Album 15/16; *FA* 04.09.15; *FA* (BMD) 04.09.15; *FA* 11.09.15; *FA* (BMD) 11.09.15; *FA* (RoH) 18.09.15; *FA* 16.10.15; *FFP* 05.08.16; *FFP* (BMD) 02.09.16; *FA* (Service List) 20.01.17; *FFP* (BMD) 01.09.17; *FA* (FRoH) 16.11.18; Wauchope Vol 2

Wilson, William: Private (16299 KOSB [6th]); Brother of David Wilson & brother-in-law of Robert Mitchelston; MIA, 20.09.17, 24 years; 36 Thistle Street, Kirkcaldy; Tyne Cot Memorial, Zonnebeke, West Vlaanderen, Belgium. Panels 66-68; Kirkcaldy War Memorial; *Soldiers Died* Part 30; *FA* 27.10.17; *FA* 24.11.17; *FFP* 24.11.17; *FFP* 01.12.17; *FA* 04.05.18; *FFP* (RoH) 04.05.18; *FA* (RoH) 18.05.18; *FFP* (RoH) 18.05.18; *FA* (FRoH) 14.12.18

Wilson, William Gordon: Private (285442 Seaforth Hldrs [1/6th]. Formerly 4567 Black Watch); KIA, 25.10.18, 20 years; 18 West Smeaton Street, Kirkcaldy; Gravestone in Bennochy Cemetery; Maing Communal Cemetery Extension, Nord, France. Grave A.19; Kirkcaldy War Memorial; *FA* 18.11.16; *Soldiers Died* Part 64; *FA* 09.11.18; *FA* (BMD) 09.11.18; *FA* (RoH) 16.11.18; *FFP* (RoH) 16.11.18; *FFP* (BMD) 23.11.18; *FFP* 30.11.18; *FA* (FRoH) 14.12.18; *FA* (FRoH) 21.12.18; *FA* 26.04.19

Wood, Robert C.: Private (43130 HLI [16th]. Formerly 2110 HCB); KIA, 18.11.16; 1 Fergus Wynd/Greenhill Place, Kirkcaldy; New Munich Trench British Cemetery, Beaumont-Hamel, Somme, France. Grave D.23; Kirkcaldy War Memorial; ‡; *Soldiers Died* Part 63; *FFP* 09.12.16; *FFP* (BMD) 09.12.16; *FA* 16.12.16 (2 entries); *FA* (RoH) 16.12.16; *FFP* (RoH) 30.12.16; *FA* 06.01.17; *FA* (FRoH) 30.11.18

Wotherspoon, John: Private (S/17995 Cameron Hldrs [7th]); Adopted brother of James Jones; KIA, 12.03.16; 171 Den Road, Kirkcaldy; Loos Memorial, Pas de Calais, France. Panels 119-124; Kirkcaldy War Memorial; *Soldiers Died* Part 66; *FFP* 08.07.16; *FA* 15.07.16; *FA* (RoH) 15.07.16; *FFP* 05.08.16; *FFP* 12.08.16; *FA* (Service List) 10.02.17; *FA* (FRoH) 23.11.18

Wright, David: Private (S/18769 Black Watch [6th]); DOW France, 08.08.17, 19 years; 21 Milton Road, Kirkcaldy; Bethelfield Church Plaque; Dozinghem Military Cemetery, Westvleteren, Poperinge, West Vlaanderen, Belgium. Grave II.F.7; Kirkcaldy War Memorial; *Soldiers Died* Part 46; *FA* 18.08.17; *FFP* (CasList) 18.08.17; *FA* 15.09.17; *FFP* (RoH) 15.09.17; Wauchope Vol 2

Wright, James Robb: Private (S/10091 Cameron Hldrs [5th]); MIA Loos, 25.09.15, 26 years; 19 Kidd Street, Kirkcaldy; Loos Memorial, Pas de Calais, France. Panels 119-124; Kirkcaldy War Memorial; *FA* 24.02.17; *Soldiers Died* Part 66; *FA* 27.11.15; *FA* 17.02.17; *FA* (BMD) 17.02.17; *FFP* 24.02.17; *FA* (RoH) 17.03.17; *FA* (FRoH) 30.11.18

Wright, John: Private (7037 Cameron Hldrs [1st]); Brother of Robert Wright; MIA Marne. PoW Roulers, Belgium. 25.09.14; 28 Fraser Place, Dysart/116 Mid Street, Kirkcaldy; La Ferte-Sous-Jouarre Memorial, Seine-et-Marne, France; Kirkcaldy War Memorial. Dysart War Memorial; *Soldiers Died* Part 66; *FA* 19.06.15; *FA* 27.11.15; *FFP* (BMD) 20.05.16; *FA* 03.06.16; *FFP* 10.06.16; *FA* (RoH) 17.06.16; *FFP* (RoH) 17.06.16; *FFP* 05.08.16 Roll of the Brave; *FA* 08.09.17

Wright, John: Private (17231 KOSB [6th]); KIA, 25.09.15; 50 Union Street, Kirkcaldy/Rosslyn Cottage, Pettycur Road, Kinghorn; Loos Memorial, Pas de Calais, France. Panels 53-56; Kirkcaldy War Memorial; *Soldiers Died* Part 30; War Album 15/16; *FA* 27.11.15; *FA* (RoH) 18.12.15; *FFP* 18.12.15 (Pathhead Church Memorial); *FFP* 05.08.16 Roll of the Brave; *FA* (Service List) 17.03.17; *FA* (FRoH) 16.11.18

Wright, Robert: Private (510493 RAMC [T] [2/2nd London Fld Amb]. Formerly 4566 London Regt [3/14th]); Brother of John M. Wright; KIA France, 16.08.17, 23 years; 90 Nether Street, Kirkcaldy/Stepney, London; Menin Road South Military Cemetery, Ieper, West Vlaanderen, Belgium. Grave II.F.21; Kirkcaldy War Memorial; *Soldiers Died* Part 79; *FA* 08.09.17; *FFP* (BMD) 08.09.17; *FA* 15.09.17; *FFP* (RoH) 15.09.17; *FFP* (BMD) 17.08.18

Wright, William: Private (290105 Black Watch [7th]); DOW No 1 Canadian General Hospital, Etaples, 02.06.17, 22 years; 7 Meldrum Place, Quality Street, Kirkcaldy; Gravestone in Abbotshall Churchyard. Abbotshall Parish Church Memorial Plaque; Etaples Military Cemetery, Pas de Calais, France. Grave XXV.F.4; Kirkcaldy War Memorial; *Soldiers Died* Part 46; *FA* 09.06.17; *FFP* 09.06.17; *FFP* (BMD) 09.06.17; *FA* (RoH) 16.06.17; *FA* (BMD) 16.06.17; *FFP* (RoH) 16.06.17; *FFP* (CasList) 07.07.17; *FA* (FRoH) 30.11.18; *FA* 19.11.21; Wauchope Vol 2

Young, David G.: Private (443; AIF; Australian Infantry [26th]); Died of accidental injuries, 04.06.16, 25 years; 39 Viceroy Street, Kirkcaldy; Gravestone in Bennochy Cemetery, Kirkcaldy; Ration Farm Military Cemetery, Chapelle-D'Armentieres, Nord, France. Grave I.G.4; Australian War Memorial Site; Kirkcaldy War Memorial; *FA* 01.07.16 (2 entries); *FA* (BMD) 01.07.16; *FFP* 01.07.16; *FFP* (BMD) 01.07.16; *FA* 08.07.16; *FA* (RoH) 15.07.16; *FFP* 05.08.16 Roll of the Brave; *FA* (Service List) 17.03.17; *FFP* (BMD) 09.06.17; *FA* (FRoH) 23.11.18

Young, David L.: Private (43194 HLI [16th]. Formerly 2283 HCB); KIA, 18.11.16; 62 Viewforth Street, Kirkcaldy; Thiepval Memorial, Somme, France. Pier & Face 15C; Kirkcaldy War Memorial; *Soldiers Died* Part 63; *FA* 16.12.16; *FA* (CasList) 13.01.17; *FA* 24.11.17

Young, George T.: Driver (92989 RFA [78th Bde] ["A" Batt'y]); Died Napsbury War Hospital, St Albans, 27.02.18, 21 years; Kirk Wynd, Kirkcaldy; Gravestone in Dysart Cemetery. Barony Church Plaque; Dysart Cemetery, Kirkcaldy. Grave 14.W. North; Kirkcaldy War Memorial; *Soldiers Died* Part 2; *FFP* (RoH) 02.03.18; *FFP* (BMD) 02.03.18; *FA* 09.03.18; *FA* (RoH) 16.03.18; *FFP* (RoH) 16.03.18; *FA* (FRoH) 07.12.18

Young, Magnus: Private (40258 Royal Scots [12th]. Formerly 3381 F & F Yeo & 27561 KOSB); Brother of John Young, Auchterderran; KIA, 22.04.17, 19 years; 25 Pottery Street, Kirkcaldy; Faubourg D'Amiens Cemetery, Arras, Pas de Calais, France. Grave IV.B.19; Kirkcaldy War Memorial; *Soldiers Died* Part 6; *FA* 19.05.17; *FFP* 19.05.17; *FA* (CasList) 02.06.17; *FFP* (CasList) 02.06.17; *FA* (RoH) 16.06.17; *FFP* (RoH) 16.06.17; *FFP* 10.11.17; *FA* 17.11.17; *FFP* (BMD) 12.10.18; *FA* (FRoH) 30.11.18

Younger, Alexander: Private (249 52nd Lowland Divisional Cyclist Coy. Formerly 1932 HCB); Came from Canada to enlist. Brother of James S. Younger; KIA, 04.08.16, 25 years; 7 Oliphant's Terrace, Kirkcaldy; Gravestone in Bennochy Cemetery; Kantara War Memorial Cemetery, Egypt. Grave E.354; Kirkcaldy War Memorial; *FA* 26.08.16; *Soldiers Died* Part 77; *FA* 26.08.16; *FA* (BMD) 26.08.16; *FFP* 26.08.16; *FFP* (BMD) 26.08.16; *FA* 09.09.16; *FA* (RoH) 16.09.16; *FFP* (RoH) 16.09.16; *FFP* (CasList) 23.09.16; *FA* (Service List) 04.11.16; *FFP* (RoH) 30.12.16; *FA* (Service List) 03.02.17; *FA* (FRoH) 23.11.18

Younger, James S.: Private (S/13342 Black Watch [10th]); Brother of Alexander Younger; KIA Salonika, 09.05.17, 20 years; 7 Oliphant's Terrace, Kirkcaldy; Gravestone in Bennochy Cemetery; Doiran Memorial, Greece; Kirkcaldy War Memorial; *Soldiers Died* Part 46; *FA* 16.06.17; *FA* (CasList) 16.06.17; Wauchope Vol 3

Younger, Thomas: Private (202350 A & S Hldrs [1/7th]); Brother-in-law of Thomas Morton; DOW 48th CCS, 23.11.17, 37 years; 21 Bridgeton, Kirkcaldy; Rocquigny-Equancourt Road British Cemetery, Manancourt, Somme, France. Grave II.C.5; Kirkcaldy War Memorial; *Soldiers Died* Part 70; *FFP* 01.12.17; *FA* 08.12.17; *FA* (RoH) 15.12.17; *FFP* (RoH) 15.12.17; *FFP* (CasList) 29.12.17; *FFP* (BMD) 16.03.18; *FFP* (BMD) 23.11.18; *FA* (FRoH) 07.12.18

Yule, Charles Whitehead, MC; Captain (Royal Scots [13th]); KIA, 12.05.16, 27 years; Giffen Park, Dysart; St Serf's Church Memorial Plaque. Kirkcaldy High School War Memorial; Vermelles British Cemetery, Pas de Calais, France. Grave IV.E.5; Kirkcaldy War Memorial; *Officers Died*; *Cross of Sacrifice Vol 1*; *FA* 13.11.15; *FA* 20.05.16; *FA* (BMD) 20.05.16; *FFP* 20.05.16; *FFP* (BMD) 20.05.16; *FA* 27.05.16; *FFP* 27.05.16; *FFP* Roll of the Brave 05.08.16; *FFP* 26.08.16; *FA* 02.09.16; *FA* (KHS RoH) 29.03.19

Yule, Peter: Gunner (5669; AIF; 3rd Australian Field Artillery Bde); KIA Messines Ridge, 21.06.17, 33 years; 7 Pratt Street, Kirkcaldy; West End Congregational Church Memorial Plaque; Kandahar Farm Cemetery, Neuve-Eglise, Heuvelland, Belgium. Grave II.B.38; Australian War Memorial web site; Kirkcaldy War Memorial; *FFP* (BMD) 14.07.17; *FA* (BMD) 21.07.17; *FA* 04.08.17; *FFP* 04.08.17; *FA* 15.09.17; *FFP* (RoH) 15.09.17; *FFP* (BMD) 22.06.18

DAVID BAIN
ALEX BARCLAY
ROBERT BROWN
SAMUEL BROWN
ANDREW BUCHAN
THOMAS BURNET
DAVID BURT
WILLIAM CAIRNS
FRANK CAMPBELL
JOHN CARGILL
ANDREW COOK
ANDREW COOPER
DAVID COWAN
JAMES COWIE
GEO. CUNNINGHAM
W. CUNNINGHAM
ALEX CUTHILL
THOMAS DICK
ALEXANDER DUFF
JAMES EADIE
DAVID FORREST
ROBERT FORRESTER
JAMES GOURLAY
DAVID GRUBB
GEORGE HAY
DAVID HENDERSON
HENRY HUTCHISON
W. HUTCHISON
ROBERT IMRIE
JOHN JACKSON
W. JOHNSTONE
ROBERT KERR
NEIL KIDD
JOHN LEIGHTON
GEORGE LENNOX
WILLIAM LESLIE
GEORGE LESSELS

THOMAS LESSELS
W. McGREGOR
WILLIAM McINTYRE
JAMES McKAY
JOHN McLACHLAN
ROBERT MAVOR
DAVID MAXWELL
ARTHUR MAYNE
GEORGE MENZIES
SAMUEL MENZIES
JOHN MILLIE
GEORGE MITCHELL
ROBERT MITCHELL
JOHN MORRISON
ROBERT NICOLSON
JOHN PAGE
JOHN PATTERSON
DAVID PATON
ALEXANDER PHILP
ANDREW REID
JOHN RUSSELL
GEORGE SANDS
ALEXANDER SCOTT
JOHN SINCLAIR
ROBERT SKINNER
ARCH. STODDART
RENWICK SWINLEY
W. THOMSON
ROBERT WALLACE
WILLIAM WATT
GEORGE WATTERS
FRANK WATSON
SYDNEY WATSON
SIGMUND WEHPLE
GEORGE WELSH
GEORGE YOUNG
DAVID YOUNG

Normand Road Church, Dysart, Great War Memorial panel, now bady eroded.

Dysart War Memorial

Alexander, James: Private (7297 Black Watch [1st]); KIA, 05.11.14, 32 years; 21 West Moorpark Road, Stevenston, Ayrshire. Native of Gallatown; Ypres (Menin Gate) Memorial, Ieper, West Vlaanderen, Belgium. Panel 37; Dysart War Memorial; *FFP* 21.11.14; *Soldiers Died* Part 46; *Scotsman* 18.11.14; *FA* 21.11.14; *FA* (CasList) 21.11.14; *FFP* (BMD) 26.12.14; Wauchope Vol 1

Allan, Thomas: Private (12819 Kings Own [Royal Lancaster Regt] [8th]); KIA Zonnebeke, 29.09.17; 4 Glasswork Street, Kirkcaldy; Abbotshall Parish Church Memorial Plaque; Tyne Cot Memorial, Zonnebeke, West Vlaanderen, Belgium. Panels 18-19; Dysart War Memorial; *Soldiers Died* Part 9; *FFP* (RoH) 17.01.17; *FA* 20.10.17; *FA* (BMD) 20.10.17; *FFP* (BMD) 20.10.17; *FFP* (CasList) 03.11.17; *FA* (RoH) 17.11.17; *FA* (BMD) 28.09.18; *FFP* (BMD) 28.09.18; *FA* (FRoH) 07.12.18; *FA* 19.11.21

Anderson, James: Private (791 Black Watch [2nd]); KIA Battle of Neuve Chapelle, 11.03.15, 28 years; 9 Fourth Street, Bowhill; Le Touret Memorial, Pas de Calais, France. Panels 24-26; Dysart War Memorial. Kirkcaldy War Memorial. Auchterderran War Memorial; *Soldiers Died* Part 46; *FA* 27.03.15; *FA* 03.04.15; Wauchope Vol 1

Anderson, R.; May be 2nd Lieutenant Robert Anderson, Royal Scots on Kirkcaldy War Memorial; Not identified on CWGC web site; Dysart War Memorial

Barclay, Alexander, MSM: Sergeant (137559 Royal Engineers [179th Tunnelling Coy]. Formerly 2741 Black Watch [1/9th]); KIA, 25.04.18, 28 years; 9 Front Row, Boreland, Dysart. Formerly of Bowhill; Barony Church Plaque; Foncquevillers Military Cemetery, Pas de Calais, France. Grave II.B.4; Dysart War Memorial; *Soldiers Died* Part 4; *FFP* (BMD) 11.05.18; *FA* 18.05.18; *FA* (BMD) 18.05.18; *FFP* (BMD) 25.05.18; *FFP* 22.06.18; *FA* 29.06.18; *FA* 03.08.18; *FA* 26.10.18

Barret, William: Stoker 2nd Class (K/48929; Royal Navy; HMS *Duke*); KIA in a submarine attack in the Mediterranean, 12.09.18, 18 years; 31 Fraser Place, Dysart; Chatham Memorial, Kent. Panel 29; Dysart War Memorial; *Cross of Sacrifice Vol 4*

Belford, Charles Roberts: 2nd Lieutenant (Black Watch [9th]. Formerly HCB & Royal Warwickshire Regt); Cousin of Robert Potter; KIA, 02.09.18, 27 years; 74 High Street, Dysart; St Mary's ADS Cemetery, Haisnes, Pas de Calais, France. Grave VII.F.10; Dysart War Memorial; *FFP* 21.09.18; *Officers Died*; *Cross of Sacrifice Vol 1*; *FA* (BMD) 14.09.18; *FFP* 14.09.18; *FFP* (BMD) 14.09.18; *FFP* 21.09.18; *FA* 12.10.18; *FA* 26.10.18; Wauchope Vol 3

Bennie, William: Lieutenant (Royal Defence Corps); Died in Leith War Hospital, Edinburgh, 10.10.17, 46 years; Dysart Road, Kirkcaldy; E.U. Congregational Church Memorial Plaque; Falkirk Cemetery. Grave G.127; Dysart War Memorial; *Officers Died*; *Cross of Sacrifice Vol 1*; *FA* 13.10.17; *FFP* 13.10.17; *FFP* 20.10.17; *FA* (RoH) 17.11.17; *FFP* (RoH) 17.11.17; *FA* (FRoH) 07.12.18

Black, James: Private (S/6453 Black Watch [8th] "C" Coy); KIA Loos, 25.09.15; 27 Berwick Place, Dysart; Loos Memorial, Pas de Calais, France. Panels 78-83; Dysart War Memorial; *Soldiers Died* Part 46; *FFP* 18.03.16; *FA* 25.03.16; *FFP* (BMD) 15.09.17; Wauchope Vol 3

Brown, Samuel: Private (120787 Labour Corps [202nd Employment Coy]. Formerly 9300 A & S Hldrs); Died of malarial fever, 24.09.18; 58 Edward Street, Kirkcaldy; Barony Church Plaque; Pieta Military Cemetery, Malta. Grave A.XIX.6; Dysart War Memorial; *Soldiers Died* Part 80; *FA* 26.10.18

Burnet, Thomas: Sergeant (41360 Northumberland Fusiliers [26th] [Tyneside Irish]. Formerly 20410 Yorks & Lancs Regt); DOW, 13.11.17, 35 years; 40 The Cross, Dysart; Barony Church Plaque; St Sever Cemetery Extension, Rouen, Seine-Maritime, France. Grave P.III.R.2B; Dysart War Memorial; *Soldiers Died* Part 10; *FA* 24.11.17; *FFP* (BMD) 16.11.18

Cairns, William: Private (16010 Royal Scots [12th]); KIA Loos, 26.09.15, 19 years; 7 Fitzroy Square, Dysart; Barony Church Plaque; Loos Memorial, Pas de Calais, France. Panels 10-13; Dysart War Memorial; *FFP* 09.10.15; *Soldiers Died* Part 6; *FA* 02.10.15; *FFP* 02.10.15; *FFP* 09.10.15; *FA* (BMD) 06.11.15; *FFP* 05.08.16 Roll of the Brave; *FFP* (BMD) 28.09.18

Campbell, James Penman: Private (3/3023 Black Watch [1st] "C" Coy, 9th Platoon); KIA, 09.04.15, 41 years; 10 The Braes, Dysart; St Serf's Church Memorial Plaque; Le Touret Military Cemetery, Richebourg-L'Avoue, Pas de Calais, France. Grave I.G.12; Dysart War Memorial; *Soldiers Died* Part 46; *FA* 24.04.15; *FFP* 24.04.15; *FFP* 01.05.15; *FA* 08.05.15; *FFP* 15.04.16; *FFP* 05.08.16 Roll of the Brave; *FFP* 14.04.17; *FFP* (BMD) 13.04.18; Wauchope Vol 1

Capel, Robert (Bertie), MM: Private (47914 Machine Gun Corps. Formerly 1641 F & F Yeo [17th Machine Gun Section]); Brother of William Capel; Died of malaria in Damascus Hospital, 17.10.18, 24 years; Woodbine Cottage, Normand Road, Dysart; St Michael's Church Memorial Plaque; Damascus Commonwealth War Cemetery, Syria. Grave B.93; Dysart War Memorial; *Soldiers Died* Part 75; *FA* 26.10.18; *FA* 21.12.18; *FFP* 28.12.18

Capel, William T.: Petty Officer (R/2080; Royal Navy; RNVR [RND] [Drake Bn]. Formerly HCB); Brother of Robert (Bertie) Capel; KIA, 30.12.17, 21 years; Woodbine Cottage, Normand Road, Dysart; St Michael's Church Memorial Plaque; Flesquieres Hill British Cemetery, Nord, France. Grave V.C.12; Dysart War Memorial; *FFP* 02.03.18; *Cross of Sacrifice Vol 4*; *FA* (BMD) 19.01.18; *FFP* 19.01.18; *FFP* (BMD) 19.01.18; *FA* (BMD) 26.01.18; *FA* 23.02.18; *FA* (BMD) 23.02.18; *FFP* 02.03.18; *FA* 26.10.18; Wauchope Vol 3

Cargill, Henry: Sergeant (44221 RAMC [33rd Fld Amb]); DOW CCS, 20.12.16, 36 years; 10 Orchard Lane, Dysart; Varennes Military Cemetery, Somme, France. Grave I.F.3; Dysart War Memorial; *Soldiers Died* Part 79; *FFP* 30.12.16; *FFP* (BMD) 30.12.16; *FA* 06.01.17; *FFP* (CasList) 27.01.17

Cargill, John: Private (16851 Royal Scots [11th]); KIA, 13.05.16; Edington Place, Dysart; Barony Church Plaque; Rifle House Cemetery, Comines-Warneton, Hainaut, Belgium. Grave I.B.5; Dysart War Memorial; *Soldiers Died* Part 6; *FFP* 20.05.16; *FA* 27.05.16; *FFP* 27.05.16; *FFP* (BMD) 27.05.16; *FFP* 05.08.16 Roll of the Brave; *FFP* (BMD) 12.05.17; *FFP* (BMD) 19.05.17

Chrystal, William: Sergeant (3/2475 Black Watch [2nd]); Died Persian Gulf, 19.06.16; Basra War Cemetery, Iraq. Grave VI.N.7; Dysart War Memorial; *Soldiers Died* Part 46; *FFP* (BMD) 16.06.17; Wauchope Vol 1

Clark, David McLeod: Private (9047 HLI [2nd]); KIA, 20.09.14, 31 years; 13 Watt Street, Dysart; Pathhead Parish Church Memorial Plaques & Windows; La Ferte-Sous-Jouarre Memorial, Seine-et-Marne, France; Dysart War Memorial; *Soldiers Died* Part 63; *FFP* 31.10.14; *FA* 31.10.14; *FA* (CasList) 21.11.14; *FA* 02.01.15; *FA* (CasList) 20.02.15; *FFP* 05.08.16 Roll of the Brave

Clark, James: Private (3/1572 Black Watch [3rd] "C" Coy att'd [1st]); KIA Ypres, 29.10.14, 24 years; 8 The Braes, Dysart; Gravestone in Strathmiglo Churchyard; Ypres (Menin Gate) Memorial, Ieper, West Vlaanderen, Belgium. Panel 37; Dysart War Memorial. Kirkcaldy War Memorial; *Soldiers Died* Part 46; *FA* 13.03.15; *FFP* 27.03.15; *FFP* 29.04.16; *FA* 06.05.16; *FFP* 05.08.16 Roll of the Brave; Wauchope Vol 1

Clark, William: Private (2080 Black Watch [2nd]); KIA Neuve-Chapelle, 10.03.15, 22 years; Nether Street, Dysart; Le Touret Memorial, Pas de Calais, France. Panels 24-26; Dysart War Memorial; *Soldiers Died* Part 46; *FA* 03.04.15; *FFP* 05.08.16 Roll of the Brave; Wauchope Vol 1

Cobban, James: Corporal (15975 Royal Scots [11th]); KIA, 07.07.16; Philp's Close, High Street, Dysart; Thiepval Memorial, Somme, France. Pier & Face 6D & 7D; Dysart War Memorial; *Soldiers Died* Part 6; *FFP* 12.08.16; *FA* 19.08.16; *FFP* (RoH) 30.12.16

Combe, Alexander: Private (S/32357 Cameron Hldrs [1st]); DOW, 03.10.18, 20 years; 24 The Braes, Dysart; Tincourt New British Cemetery, Somme, France. Grave VI.G.24; Dysart War Memorial; *Soldiers Died* Part 66; *FA* 26.10.18; *FA* (BMD) 09.11.18

Cook, Andrew: Sergeant (S/2830 Black Watch [1st]); MIA, 18.08.16, 34 years; 21 Nether Street, Kirkcaldy; Barony Church Plaque; Thiepval Memorial, Somme, France. Pier & Face 10A; Dysart War Memorial; *FA* 03.06.16; *FA* 02.12.16; *Soldiers Died* Part 46; *FA* 02.12.16; *FFP* 02.12.16; *FA* (CasList) 09.12.16; *FFP* (BMD) 04.08.17; *FA* 11.08.17; *FA* (BMD) 11.08.17; Wauchope Vol 1

Cooper, Andrew: Private (S/22508 Seaforth Hldrs [1st]); Died of typhoid fever at 23rd Stationary Hospital, Kantara, 21.03.18, 29 years; 49 East Quality Street, Dysart; Barony Church Plaque; Kantara War Memorial Cemetery, Egypt. Grave C.157; Dysart War Memorial; *Soldiers Died* Part 64; *FFP* (BMD) 30.03.18; *FA* 06.04.18

Coventry, David B. Scott: Private (S/20062 A & S Hldrs [12th] "A" Coy); KIA Salonika, 19.09.18, 29 years; 12 Watt Street, Dysart; Doiran Memorial, Greece; Dysart War Memorial. West Wemyss War Memorial Panel 2; *Soldiers Died* Part 70; *FA* (BMD) 01.11.19

Cowan, David: Driver (141930 RFA [XVI Corps] Ammunition Column); Died of malarial fever in Salonika, 16.09.17, 26 years; 3 Ivy Lane, Dysart; Gravestone in Dysart Cemetery. Barony Church Plaque; Mikra British Cemetery, Kalamaria, Greece. Grave 112; Dysart War Memorial; *Soldiers Died* Part 2; *FA* 06.10.17; *FA* (BMD) 06.10.17; *FFP* 06.10.17; *FFP* (BMD) 14.09.18

Cumming, William Linton: Gunner (144803 RGA [275th Siege Batt'y]); KIA, 30.09.17, 23 years; 133 High Street, Dysart; Huts Cemetery, Dickebusch, Kemmel, Belgium. Grave VIII.C.12; Dysart War Memorial; ‡; *Soldiers Died* Part 3; *FFP* 13.10.17; *FA* 20.10.17; *FFP* (BMD) 05.10.18

Cunningham, William: Private (19447 Royal Scots [16th]); MIA, 01.07.16; 27 Forth Street, Dysart; Barony Church Plaque; London Cemetery & Extension, Longueval, Somme, France. Grave 4.D.6; Dysart War Memorial; *Soldiers Died* Part 6; *FFP* (CasList) 26.08.16; *FFP* 12.05.17; *FFP* (BMD) 12.05.17

Dick, Thomas: Private (S/41336 Gordon Hldrs [9th]. Formerly A & S Hldrs); DOW 32nd CCS, France, 27.08.17, 24 years; 3 High Street, Dysart; Barony Church Plaque; Brandhoek New Military Cemetery No. 3, Ieper, West Vlaanderen, Belgium. Grave II.A.15; Dysart War Memorial; *FA* 15.09.17; *Soldiers Died* Part 65; *FA* 01.09.17; *FFP* 01.09.17; *FFP* (BMD) 08.09.17; *FFP* (BMD) 31.08.18; *FFP* (BMD) 07.09.18

Donnelly, Arthur: Private (203020 Black Watch [6th]); KIA, 10.04.18; Late of The Braes, Dysart; Pont-du-Hem Military Cemetery, La Gorgue, Nord, France. Grave V.C.22; Dysart War Memorial; *Soldiers Died* Part 46; *FA* 18.05.18; Wauchope Vol 2

Duff, Charles Ramsay: Private (905122; CEF; Canadian Infantry [10th] 2nd Bde. [Alberta Regt]); KIA, 28.04.17, 36 years; 15 Normand Road/Alexander Street, Dysart; Kirkcaldy High School War Memorial; Vimy Memorial, Pas de Calais, France; *CBoR* Page 231; Dysart War Memorial; *FFP* 12.05.17; *FFP* (BMD) 19.05.17

Eadie, James: 2nd Lieutenant (Seaforth Hldrs [5th]); KIA, 14.05.17, 24 years; 17 West Quality Street, Dysart; Barony Church Plaque; Arras Memorial, Pas de Calais, France. Bay 8; Dysart War Memorial; *FFP* 02.06.17; *Officers Died*; *Cross of Sacrifice Vol 1*; *FA* 26.05.17; *FFP* 26.05.17; *FFP* (BMD) 02.06.17; *FFP* 23.06.17; *FFP* (BMD) 18.05.18

Farquhar, James: Private (16011 Royal Scots [12th]); DOW 28th Fld Amb, 03.01.17, 23 years; 80 High Street, Dysart; Habarcq Communal Cemetery Extension, Pas de Calais, France. Grave VIII.F.8; Dysart War Memorial; *Soldiers Died* Part 6; *FFP* (BMD) 13.01.17; *FA* 20.01.17; *FFP* 20.01.17; *FFP* (CasList) 03.02.17; *FFP* 10.03.17; *FFP* (BMD) 05.01.18 (2 entries)

Fernie, Robert: Private (S/14586 Black Watch [6th] att'd Royal Warwickshire Regt); MIA, 10.04.18, 38 years; Forth Street, Dysart/Balcarres Road, Largoward; Loos Memorial, Pas de Calais, France. Panels 78-83; Dysart War Memorial; *Soldiers Died* Part 46; *FFP* 24.08.18; *FA* 31.08.18; Wauchope Vol 2

Galloway, Joseph Gordon: Private (2279 Black Watch [1/7th]); Brother of William Galloway & John Galloway; KIA, 03.06.16, 19 years; 36 Victoria Street, Boreland, Dysart; St Michael's Church Memorial Plaque; Maroeuil British Cemetery, Pas de Calais, France. Grave I.G.7; Dysart War Memorial; *FA* 17.07.15; *FA* 17.06.16; *FA* 25.11.16; *Soldiers Died* Part 46; *FFP* 17.06.16; *FFP* 24.06.16; *FFP* 05.08.16 Roll of the Brave; *FA* 25.11.16; *FFP* 25.11.16; *FFP* (BMD) 02.06.17; *FA* 11.08.17; *FFP* (BMD) 10.11.17; *FFP* (BMD) 01.06.18; *FFP* (BMD) 16.11.18; Wauchope Vol 2

Grubb, David: Lance Corporal (21631 KOSB [6th] "A" Coy); Nephew of William Watt; DOW in hospital, Abbeville, 24.07.16, 24 years; 9 South Street, Dysart; Barony Church Plaque; Abbeville Communal Cemetery, Somme, France. Grave VI.B.16; Dysart War Memorial; *Soldiers Died* Part 30; *FA* 22.07.16; *FFP* 29.07.16; *FA* 05.08.16; *FFP* 05.08.16 Roll of the Brave; *FFP* 19.08.16; *FFP* (CasList) 02.09.16

Grubb, Philip: Private (350976 A & S Hldrs [1/8th]. Formerly S/5320 Black Watch); DOW, 03.10.18, 37 years; 30 Victoria Street, Boreland, Dysart; Noeux-Les-Mines Communal Cemetery & Extension, Pas de Calais, France. Grave V.A.17; Dysart War Memorial; *FA* 13.11.15; *Soldiers Died* Part 70; *FA* 19.10.18; *FFP* (BMD) 30.11.18

Hay, George: Private (DM2/137861 Army Service Corps [24th Motor Amb Coy]); DOW, 04.08.17, 20 years; 23 Relief Street, Dysart; Barony Church Plaque; Gwalia Cemetery, Poperinge, West Vlaanderen, Belgium. Grave I.F.5; Dysart War Memorial; *Soldiers Died* Part 78; *FA* 11.08.17; *FFP* 11.08.17; *FFP* 18.08.17; *FA* 25.08.17; *FA* (BMD) 25.08.17; *FFP* (BMD) 25.08.17; *FFP* (CasList) 08.09.17; *FFP* (BMD) 10.08.18

Hutchison, Henry: Private (20319 Cheshire Regt [15th] Bantam Bn); KIA, 24.10.17, 21 years; 29 Fitzroy Street, Dysart; Barony Church Plaque; Tyne Cot Memorial, Zonnnebeke, West Vlaanderen, Belgium. Panels 61-63; Dysart War Memorial; *Soldiers Died* Part 27; *FFP* 03.11.17; *FA* 10.11.17; *FFP* (CasList) 01.12.17

Johnston, William: Driver (84359 RFA (63rd Div) Ammunition Column); Died of influenza, 28.11.18, 21 years; 13 South Street, Dysart; Gravestone in Dysart Cemetery. Barony Church Plaque; Dysart Cemetery, Kirkcaldy. Grave 50.V.Middle; Dysart War Memorial; *FA* 07.12.18; *FA* (BMD) 07.12.18; *FFP* 07.12.18

Kerr, Robert: Private (S/40562 Black Watch [8th]); 12.10.17, 20 years; East Quality Street, Dysart; Barony Church Plaque; Tyne Cot Memorial, Zonnebeke, West Vlaanderen, Belgium. Panels 94-96; Dysart War Memorial; *Soldiers Died* Part 46; *FA* 30.03.18; Wauchope Vol 3

Kidd, James: Private (21168 Bedfordshire Regt [2nd] [Lewis Gun Section]). Formerly 45460 RGA); KIA Albert, 25.06.18, 24 years; St David's, Fitzroy Street, Dysart; Gravestone in Dysart Cemetery; Warloy-Baillon Communal Cemetery Extension, Somme, France. Grave IV.G.17; Dysart War Memorial; *Soldiers Died* Part 21; *FA* 06.07.18; *FFP* 06.07.18; *FA* (BMD) 13.07.18; *FFP* (BMD) 13.07.18

Kidd, James: Private (S/43317 Black Watch [8th]); Brother of John D. Kidd, Coaltown of Wemyss. Another brother also killed; KIA France, 03.11.17, 25 years; 24 Relief Street, Dysart; Ramscapelle Road Military Cemetery, Nieuwpoort, West Vlaanderen, Belgium. Grave III.A.10; Dysart War Memorial; *Soldiers Died* Part 46; *FFP* 10.11.17; *FA* 17.11.17; *FFP* (CasList) 08.12.17; Wauchope Vol 3

King, Harry: Private (2629 Black Watch [1st] [Machine Gun Section]); KIA, 25.09.16, 21 years; 27 Victoria Street, Boreland, Dysart; St Michael's Church Memorial Plaque; Thiepval Memorial, Somme, France. Pier & Face 10A; Dysart War Memorial; *Soldiers Died* Part 46; *FA* 21.10.16; *FA* (BMD) 21.10.16; *FFP* 21.10.16; *FFP* (BMD) 21.10.16; *FA* (CasList) 04.11.16; *FFP* (BMD) 18.11.16; *FFP* (RoH) 30.12.16; *FFP* (BMD) 29.09.17; Wauchope Vol 1

Leslie, William: Private (20321 Cheshire Regt [15th] Bantam Bn); KIA, 17.07.16, 23 years; 29 Fitzroy Square, Dysart; Pathhead Parish Church Memorial Plaques & Windows; Bernafay Wood British Cemetery, Montauban, Somme, France. Grave G.39; Dysart War Memorial; *Soldiers Died* Part 27; *FFP* 29.07.16; *FFP* 05.08.16; *FFP* 05.08.16 Roll of the Brave; *FFP* (BMD) 05.08.16; *FFP* 12.08.16; *FFP* (CasList) 09.09.16; *FFP* (BMD) 21.07.17; *FFP* (BMD) 20.07.18

Lessels, George: Private (S/19585 Black Watch [1/6th] "B" Coy, 6th Platoon); MIA, 10.04.18, 21 years; 3 West Quality Street, Dysart; Barony Church Plaque; Loos Memorial, Pas de Calais, France. Panels 78-83; Dysart War Memorial; *Soldiers Died* Part 46; *FA* 25.05.18; *FFP* 17.08.18; *FA* 24.08.18; *FFP* 11.01.19; *FA* (BMD) 19.07.19; *FA* 26.07.19; Wauchope Vol 2

Lessels, T.; May be Thomas Lessels, Machine Gun Corps on Kirkcaldy War Memorial; Not identified on CWGC web site; Dysart War Memorial

Lindsay, Walter Gibb: Private (2752 Black Watch [1st]); KIA, 25.09.15, 19 years; 64 High Street, Dysart; Loos Memorial, Pas de Calais, France. Panels 78-83; Dysart War Memorial; *Soldiers Died* Part 46; *FA* 30.10.15; *FFP* 05.08.16 Roll of the Brave; Wauchope Vol 1

Low, Peter: Private (14234 Cameronians [Scottish Rifles] [10th]); Brother of John Low; KIA Loos, 25.09.15, 29 years; 28 Quality Street, Dysart; Loos Memorial, Pas de Calais, France. Panels 57-59; Dysart War Memorial; *Soldiers Died* Part 31; *FFP* 22.01.16; *FFP* (BMD) 22.01.16; *FA* 29.01.16; *FFP* 05.08.16 Roll of the Brave; *FFP* 15.12.17; *FA* 22.12.17

Low, Robert: Private (S/2050 Seaforth Hldrs [2nd] "A" Coy); KIA, 01.09.18, 34 years; 1 Anderson Street, Dysart; Dury Crucifix Cemetery, Pas de Calais, France. Grave III.C.17; Dysart War Memorial; *Soldiers Died* Part 64; *FFP* (BMD) 14.09.18; *FA* 21.09.18; *FFP* 21.09.18; *FA* 28.09.18; *FFP* 05.10.18

Lowrie, Alexander: Sergeant (7967 Cameron Hldrs [5th] "C" Coy. Formerly 280 Black Watch); On CWGC as Allan Lawrie; KIA Loos, 25.09.15, 27 years; Factory Road/23 Nairn Street/44 Links Street, Kirkcaldy; Ypres (Menin Gate) Memorial, Ieper, West Vlaanderen, Belgium. Panels 38-40; Dysart War Memorial; *FA* 30.10.15; *FA* 22.01.16; *FA* 12.02.16; *Soldiers Died* Part 66; *FA* 30.10.15; *FA* 13.11.15; *FA* 18.12.15; *FFP* 25.12.15; *FA* 22.01.16; *FA* 29.01.16; *FFP* 29.01.16; *FA* 12.02.16; *FA* (RoH) 15.04.16; *FFP* (CasList) 15.04.16; *FFP* 05.08.16 Roll of the Brave; *FA* (Service List) 02.12.16; *FA* (Service List) 13.01.17; *FFP* (BMD) 06.10.17; *FFP* (BMD) 28.09.18 (2 entries); *FA* (FRoH) 23.11.18

MacKay, James McFarlane: Private (28761 KOSB [2nd]. Formerly 2887 F & F Yeo); KIA, 12.04.18, 20 years; 33 Normand Road, Dysart; Barony Church Plaque; Le Grand Hasard Military Cemetery, Morbecque, Nord, France. Grave IV.D.1; Dysart War Memorial; *Soldiers Died* Part 30; *FFP* 11.05.18; *FA* 18.05.18; *FFP* (CasList) 22.06.18

Mavor, John: Private (13729 KOSB [1st]); Died in hospital, 03.11.15, 23 years; 12 Alexander Street, Dysart; Gibraltar (North Front) Cemetery, Gibraltar. Grave D.3169; Dysart War Memorial; *Soldiers Died* Part 30; *FFP* 09.10.15; *FA* 13.11.15; *FA* 20.11.15; *FFP* 05.08.16 Roll of the Brave

Maxwell, David: Private (20251 Royal Scots [1st]); KIA Salonika, 02.10.16, 20 years; 12 Dovecot Crescent, Dysart; Barony Church Plaque; Doiran Memorial, Greece; Dysart War Memorial; *Soldiers Died* Part 6; *FFP* 22.12.17; *FA* 29.12.17

Mayne, Arthur: Private (27916 Royal Scots [16th] [Depot]); In *FA* (CasList) 16.09.16 as Main; DOW military hospital, Foulford, Yorkshire, 16.07.16, 22 years; 4 Bell Place, Watt Street, Dysart; Gravestone in Dysart Cemetery. Barony Church Plaque; Dysart Cemetery, Kirkcaldy. Grave 52.8.South; Dysart War Memorial; *Soldiers Died* Part 6; *FA* 22.07.16; *FA* (BMD) 22.07.16; *FFP* 22.07.16; *FFP* (BMD) 22.07.16; *FFP* 05.08.16 Roll of the Brave; *FA* 16.09.16; *FA* (CasList) 16.09.16; *FFP* (CasList) 16.09.16; *FA* 23.09.16; *FFP* (BMD) 20.07.18

McGregor, William: Private (267266 Royal Warwickshire Regt [2/7th]. Formerly 928 HCB); DOW 48th CCS, 04.12.17, 22 years; 77 Normand Road, Dysart; Barony Church Plaque; Rocquigny-Equancourt Road British Cemetery, Manancourt, Somme, France. Grave VI.B.30; Dysart War Memorial; *Soldiers Died* Part 11; *FFP* 15.12.17; *FA* 22.12.17; *FFP* (BMD) 22.12.17; *FFP* (BMD) 07.12.18

McKenzie, John Sydney: Private (268077 Black Watch [1/6th] "C" Coy. Formerly 6506 Scottish Horse); KIA Ypres, 02.07.17, 20 years; Stewartville, 2 Berwick Place, Dysart; Gravestone in Dysart Cemetery. Kirkcaldy High School War Memorial; Vlamertinghe New Military Cemetery, Ieper, West Vlaanderen, Belgium. Grave I.E.3; Dysart War Memorial; ‡; *Soldiers Died* Part 46; *FA* 14.07.17; *FFP* 14.07.17; *FFP* (BMD) 14.07.17; *FA* (BMD) 21.07.17; *FFP* (CasList) 04.08.17; Wauchope Vol 2

McKinlay, David: Private (7509 Cameron Hldrs [1st]); KIA, 06.03.15, 26 years; 19 Nether Street, Dysart; Le Touret Military Cemetery, Richebourg-L'Avoue, Pas de Calais, France. Grave II.A.12; Dysart War Memorial; *Soldiers Died* Part 66; *FA* 20.03.15; *FFP* 05.08.16 Roll of the Brave

McLachlan, John Duncan: Lance Corporal (S/7545 Black Watch [2nd]); KIA, 09.05.15, 26 years; Bracklinn, Normand Road, Dysart; Barony Church Plaque; Le Touret Memorial, Pas de Calais, France. Panels 24-26; Dysart War Memorial; *Soldiers Died* Part 46; *FA* 12.06.15; *FA* 19.06.15 (2 entries); Wauchope Vol 1

McLeod, James Charles: Driver (120169 RFA [155th] "D" Batt'y. Formerly 8366 Horsekeeper RAVC); Son of Provost McLeod; KIA, 03.11.18, 26 years; Gravestone in Dysart Cemetery; Romeries Communal Cemetery Extension, Nord, France. Grave V.E.I; Dysart War Memorial; *Soldiers Died* Part 2; *FA* 23.11.18; *FA* 07.12.18; *FFP* 07.12.18

McMillan, Joseph: Private (345680 Black Watch [14th] [F & F Yeo Bn]); DOW Palestine, 06.11.17, 26 years; 56 Edington Place, Dysart; Beersheba War Cemetery, Israel. Grave L.36; Dysart War Memorial; *Soldiers Died* Part 46; *FA* (BMD) 29.12.17; *FFP* 29.12.17; *FFP* (BMD) 29.12.17; *FFP* (CasList) 05.01.18; Wauchope Vol 3; Ogilvie

Menzies, Andrew: Private (20959 Cameronians [Scottish Rifles] [10th]); Brother of Samuel Menzies & George Menzies; KIA, 23.02.16; Loos Memorial, Pas de Calais, France. Panels 57-59; Dysart War Memorial; *Soldiers Died* Part 31; *FFP* 12.05.17; *FA* 19.05.17; *FFP* (BMD) 26.01.18

Menzies, George: Private (3/2696 Black Watch [1st] "C" Coy); Brother of Samuel Menzies & Andrew Menzies; KIA Belgium, 25.01.15, 43 years; 12 Forth Street, Dysart; Barony Church Plaque; Le Touret Memorial, Pas de Calais, France. Panels 24-26; Dysart War Memorial; *Soldiers Died* Part 46; *FA* 21.11.14; *Scotsman* 00.01.15; *Dundee Advertiser* 06.02.15; *Dundee Courier* 06.02.15; *FA* 13.02.15; *FA* (CasList) 20.02.15; *FA* 22.05.15; *FFP* (CasList) 05.06.15; *FFP* (BMD) 29.01.16; *FFP* 05.08.16 Roll of the Brave; *FFP* (BMD) 27.01.17; *FFP* 12.05.17; *FA* 19.05.17; *FA* 14.07.17 (KHS War Honours); *FFP* (BMD) 26.01.18; Wauchope Vol 1

Menzies, Samuel: Gunner (347473 RGA [Forth Batt'y]); Brother of George Menzies & Andrew Menzies; DOW CCS, 03.05.17, 37 years; Barony Church Plaque; Noeux-Les-Mines Communal Cemetery, Pas de Calais, France. Grave I.Q.19; Dysart War Memorial; *Soldiers Died* Part 3; *FFP* 12.05.17; *FFP* (BMD) 12.05.17; *FA* 19.05.17; *FA* (BMD) 19.05.17; *FA* (CasList) 02.06.17; *FFP* (CasList) 02.06.17; *FFP* (BMD) 26.01.18

Mitchell, George: Private (27917 Royal Scots [13th]); KIA, 28.08.16, 23 years; 67 Edington Place, Dysart; Barony Church Plaque; Thiepval Memorial, Somme, France. Pier & Face 6D & 7D; Dysart War Memorial; *Soldiers Died* Part 6; *FA* 09.09.16; *FA* 16.09.16; *FFP* 16.09.16; *FA* (CasList) 30.09.16; *FFP* (CasList) 30.09.16; *FFP* 07.10.16; *FFP* (RoH) 30.12.16; *FFP* (BMD) 25.08.17; *FFP* (BMD) 31.08.18

Mitchell, Robert: Private (S/21751 Black Watch [7th]); KIA, 21.03.18; Arras Memorial, Pas de Calais, France. Bay 6; Dysart War Memorial; *Soldiers Died* Part 46; Wauchope Vol 2

Morrison, John: Private (290809 Black Watch [7th]); Died of influenza at Craigleith Hospital, Edinburgh, 04.11.18; 24 Relief Street, Dysart; Gravestone in Dysart Cemetery. Barony Church Plaque; Dysart Cemetery, Kirkcaldy. Grave 5.22.Middle; Dysart War Memorial; *Soldiers Died* Part 46; *FFP* 16.11.18; *FA* 23.11.18; *FFP* (BMD) 07.12.18; Wauchope Vol 2

Nicholson, Robert: Private (16574 Royal Scots [13th]); KIA, 28.05.16, 25 years; 21 Forth Street, Dysart; Barony Church Plaque; Vermelles British Cemetery, Pas de Calais, France. Grave IV.C.28; Dysart War Memorial; *FA* 17.06.16; *Soldiers Died* Part 6; *FA* 10.06.16; *FFP* 10.06.16; *FA* 17.06.16; *FFP* 05.08.16 Roll of the Brave

O'Connor, Harry, French Croix-de-Guerre with Palms, Mons Star: Sergeant (14778 Royal Engineers [6th Reserve Bn]); Died of pneumonia at Bogside Auxiliary Hospital, 16.11.18, 31 years; 13 Ivy Lane, Dysart; Kilbowie Cemetery, Dunbartonshire. Grave E.35; Dysart War Memorial; *FA* 30.11.18; *FA* 07.12.18; *FFP* 07.12.18

Sergeant Harry **O'Connor** went to France with the original British Expeditionary Force. He served through fierce fighting gaining the Mons Star and the Croix de Guerre with Palms from the French government for conspicuous gallantry. He was sent home after four years of fighting where he unfortunately contracted influenza and died during the epidemic. He was buried with full military honours.

Paton, David: Pioneer (317080 Royal Engineers [Signals Depot, Bedford]); Died at Kempston Military Hospital, Bedford, 01.11.18, 24 years; 47 High Street, Dysart. Gravestone in Dysart Cemetery. Barony Church Plaque; Dysart Cemetery, Kirkcaldy. Grave 3.E.South; Dysart War Memorial; *Soldiers Died* Part 4; *FA* 16.11.18; *FA* (BMD) 16.11.18

Patterson, John, DCM: Sergeant (122032 RFA [156th Bde] "C" Batt'y); KIA, 25.04.18, 33 years; 23 Fraser Place, Dysart; Barony Church Plaque; Tyne Cot Memorial, Zonnebeke, West Vlaanderen, Belgium. Panels 4-6 & 162; Dysart War Memorial; *FA* 01.04.16; *Soldiers Died* Part 2; *FA* 01.04.16; *FA* 18.05,18; *FFP* (BMD) 01.06.18; *FA* (BMD) 08.06.18

Philp, Alexander: Private (291802 Black Watch [7th]); KIA, 28.10.18; Barony Church Plaque; Poznan Old Garrison Cemetery, Poland. Grave IV.C.2; Dysart War Memorial; Kirkcaldy War Memorial; *Soldiers Died* Part 46; Wauchope Vol 2

Potter, Robert, MC: 2nd Lieutenant (Black Watch [8th]); Cousin of Charles Belford; KIA, 14.10.18, 27 years; 64 High Street, Dysart; Aeroplane Cemetery, Ieper, West Vlaanderen, Belgium. Grave VIII.A.15; Dysart War Memorial; *Officers Died*; *Cross of Sacrifice Vol 1*; *FA* 26.10.18; *FA* 23.11.18; *FFP* 23.11.18; Wauchope Vol 3

Pratt, Alexander: Private (S/2959 Black Watch [8th]); KIA Loos, 25.09.15, 35 years; 1 Fitzroy Square, Dysart; Loos Memorial, Pas de Calais, France. Panels 78-83; *FFP* 09.10.15; *Soldiers Died* Part 46; Dysart War Memorial; *FA* 09.10.15; *FFP* 09.10.15; *FFP* 05.08.16 Roll of the Brave; *FFP* (BMD) 29.09.17; *FFP* (BMD) 05.10.18; Wauchope Vol 3

Ramsay, John Wilkie Black: Private (345313 Black Watch [14th] [F & F Yeo Bn]. Formerly 2450 F & F Yeo); KIA, 10.09.18, 33 years; 29 High Street, Dysart; Vis-En-Artois Memorial, Haucourt, Pas de Calais, France. Panel 7; Dysart War Memorial; *Soldiers Died* Part 46; Wauchope Vol 3; Ogilvie

Reid, Andrew: Private (3442 Black Watch [7th]); KIA, 30.07.16, 27 years; 33 Watt Street, Dysart; Barony Church Plaque; Thiepval Memorial, Somme, France. Pier & Face 10A; Dysart War Memorial; *Soldiers Died* Part 46; *FFP* 12.08.16; *FFP* 19.08.16; *FA* (BMD) 02.09.16; *FA* (CasList) 09.09.16; *FFP* (RoH) 30.12.16; Wauchope Vol 2

Riley, William: Corporal (11602 Durham Light Infantry [2nd]); *Soldiers Died* gives date of death as 23.04.18; KIA Ypres, 09.08.15, 22 years; 16 Dovecot Crescent, Dysart/87 Lorne Street, Kirkcaldy; Ypres (Menin Gate) Memorial, Ieper, West Vlaanderen, Belgium. Panels 36 & 38; Dysart War Memorial; *Soldiers Died* Part 62; *FA* 01.01.16; *FFP* 01.01.16; *FFP* 05.08.16 Roll of the Brave; *FFP* (BMD) 19.08.16

Robb, Angus: Trooper (4161 Life Guards [1st]); KIA, 19.05.18, 23 years; Dysart House Gardens, Dysart/ Miltonbank, Auchtertool; Gravestone in Dysart Cemetery; Etaples Military Cemetery, Pas de Calais, France. Grave LXVI.C.34; Dysart War Memorial; *Soldiers Died* Part 1; *FA* 01.06.18; *FFP* 01.06.18

Robertson, Alexander: Lieutenant (RFA att'd RFC [34 Squadron]); DOW CCS, 16.08.17, 21 years; Seaview, Dysart; Gravestone in Dysart Cemetery. St Serf's Church Memorial Plaque. Kirkcaldy High School War Memorial; Zuydcoote Military Cemetery, Nord, France. Grave I.A.4; Dysart War Memorial; *Officers Died*; *Cross of Sacrifice Vol 1*; *FA* 25.08.17; *FFP* 25.08.17; *FA* 13.07.18; *FA* (KHS RoH) 29.03.19; RFC/RAF RoH

Rodger, William T.: Private (S/2942 Seaforth Hldrs [2nd]); DOW, 14.04.17, 20 years; Hill Street, Dysart; Aubigny Communal Cemetery Extension, Pas de Calais, France. Grave II.C.61; Dysart War Memorial; *Soldiers Died* Part 64; *FFP* 05.05.17; *FFP* (BMD) 05.05.17; *FA* 12.05.17; *FA* (BMD) 12.05.17; *FFP* 12.05.17; *FFP* (CasList) 26.05.17

Scott, Alexander: Private (16936 KOSB [6th]); MIA Loos, 25.09.15; High Street, Dysart; Barony Church Plaque; Loos Memorial, Pas de Calais, France. Panels 53-56; Dysart War Memorial; *FFP* 23.10.15; *Soldiers Died* Part 30; *FA* 23.10.15; *FFP* 23.10.15; *FFP* 05.08.16 Roll of the Brave; *FFP* (BMD) 07.10.16; *FFP* (BMD) 22.09.17; *FFP* 02.03.18

Scott, Matthew Munroe: Private (16814; CEF; Canadian Infantry [7th] 1st Div 2nd Bde. [1st British Columbia Regt]); KIA, 24.04.15, 34 years; 20 Cross Street, Dysart; Gravestone in Dysart Cemetery; Ypres (Menin Gate) Memorial, Ieper, West Vlaanderen, Belgium. Panels 18-28-30; Dysart War Memorial; *CBoR Page 35*; *FA* 22.05.15; *FFP* 26.02.16; *FFP* 05.08.16 Roll of the Brave; *FFP* (BMD) 16.02.18

Sinclair, John Pearson: Lance Corporal (19640 Royal Scots [16th]); KIA, 31.07.16, 27 years; 27 Forth Street, Dysart/ 1402 Fifth Avenue West, Vancouver, B.C.; Barony Church Plaque; Thiepval Memorial, Somme, France. Pier & Face 6D & 7D; Dysart War Memorial; *Soldiers Died* Part 6; *FFP* 26.08.16; *FA* 02.09.16; *FFP* (CasList) 16.09.16; *FFP* (BMD) 24.02.17; *FFP* 17.03.17

Skinner, Robert Ramsey: Private (CH.21403; Royal Navy; Royal Marine Light Infantry [3rd Bn]); Died of influenza at Royal Naval Hospital, Mudros, 03.12.18, 18 years; 1 Howard Place, Dysart; Barony Church Plaque; Portianos Military Cemetery, Greece. Grave III.C.326; Dysart War Memorial; *Cross of Sacrifice Vol 4*; *FFP* (BMD) 14.12.18; *FA* (BMD) 21.12.18; *FFP* 04.01.19

Smith, Charles: Lance Corporal (16125 Royal Scots Fusiliers [6th]); Died, 26.09.15; Shore Road, Dysart; Loos Memorial, Pas de Calais, France. Panels 46-49; Dysart War Memorial; *Soldiers Died* Part 26; *FA* 13.11.15

Steele, Alexander: Private (1705 Black Watch [1st]); KIA, 22.09.16, 24 years; 14 Dovecot, Dysart; Thiepval Memorial, Somme, France. Pier & Face 10A; Dysart War Memorial; *FA* 14.10.16; *Soldiers Died* Part 46; *FA* 14.10.16; *FFP* 14.10.16; *FFP* 21.10.16; *FFP* (CasList) 28.10.16; *FFP* (RoH) 30.12.16; *FFP* (BMD) 21.09.18; Wauchope Vol 1

Stewart, John: Private (43100 HLI [15th]); 01.10.18; 46 Fitzroy Street, Dysart; Vis-en-Artois Memorial Pas de Calais, France. Panels 9-10; Dysart War Memorial; *Soldiers Died* Part 63; *FA* 09.11.18

Stoddart, Archibald C.: Gunner (152357 RGA); Died of pneumonia at No. 2 General Hospital, 24.03.18, 19 years; 23 Cross Street, Dysart; Barony Church Plaque; Ste. Marie Cemetery, Le Havre, Seine-Maritime, France. Grave Div.62.III.A.1; Dysart War Memorial; *FFP* 06.04.18; *Soldiers Died* Part 3; *FFP* (BMD) 30.03.18; *FA* 06.04.18; *FFP* (RoH) 06.04.18

Storrar, David: Private (5711 Royal Warwickshire Regt [2/7th]. Formerly 704 HCB); KIA Lavantie, 20.09.16, 20 years; 106 High Street, Dysart; Gravestone in Dysart Cemetery; Laventie Military Cemetery, La Gorgue, Nord, France. Grave III.A.1; Dysart War Memorial; *Soldiers Died* Part 11; *FA* 30.09.16; *FFP* 30.09.16; *FFP* 07.10.16; *FFP* (RoH) 30.12.16; *FFP* (BMD) 22.09.17; *FFP* (BMD) 21.09.18

Swinley, Renwick: Private (S/4584 Black Watch [8th] "A" Coy); Accidentally killed, 23.07.15, 25 years; 17 Edington Place, Dysart; Barony Church Plaque; Gorre British & Indian Cemetery, Pas de Calais, France. Grave I.A.II; Dysart War Memorial. Kirkcaldy War Memorial; *Soldiers Died* Part 46; *FA* 22.05.15; *Scotsman* 28.07.15; *FA* 31.07.15; *FFP* 31.07.15; *FFP* (BMD) 22.07.16; *FFP* 05.08.16 Roll of the Brave; *FFP* (BMD) 28.07.17; *FFP* (BMD) 27.07.18; Wauchope Vol 3

Thomson, William: Barony Church Plaque; Not identified on CWGC web site; Dysart War Memorial

Turpie, John Brodie: Private (16230 KOSB [1st]); DOW Dardanelles, 06.01.16, 29 years; 10 Orchard Lane Dysart; Gravestone in Dysart Cemetery; Lancashire Landing Cemetery, Turkey. Grave J.123; Dysart War Memorial; *FA* 04.03.16; *Soldiers Died* Part 30; *FA* 05.02.16; *FA* (BMD) 05.02.16; *FFP* 05.02.16; *FFP* (BMD) 05.02.16; *FFP* 12.02.16; *FFP* 05.08.16 Roll of the Brave *FFP* (BMD) 06.01.17; *FFP* (BMD) 05.01.18

Walton, Robert: Drummer (2862 Black Watch [7th] "B" Coy); KIA, 31.10.16, 24 years; 4 Front Row, Boreland Dysart; Gravestone in Dysart Cemetery; Auchonvillers Military Cemetery, Somme, France. Grave II.E.47 Dysart War Memorial; *FA* 20.11.15; *Soldiers Died* Part 46; *FA* 11.11.16; *FA* (CasList) 18.11.16; *FFP* 18.11.16 *FFP* (CasList) 18.11.16; *FFP* (CasList) 02.12.16; *FFP* 09.12.16; *FFP* (RoH) 30.12.16; *FA* (BMD) 27.10.17 Wauchope Vol 2

Watson, Alexander B.: Private (S/5044 A & S Hldrs [14th]) KIA, 24.04.17, 22 years; Rectory Lane, Dysart; Thiepval Memorial, Somme, France. Pier & Face 15A & 16C Dysart War Memorial; *Soldiers Died* Part 70; *FA* 05.05.17; *FA* 12.05.17; *FA* (CasList) 02.06.17; *FA* (CasList) 02.06.17; *FFP* (BMD) 27.04.18

Watson, Frank Fairweather: 2nd Lieutenant (Royal Scots [14th] att'd [15th]); Brother of Sidney F. Watson; KL by a bomb, 08.08.16, 23 years; Thornliebank, Fort Street, Dysart; Barony Church Plaque. Kirkcaldy High School War Memorial; Caterpillar Valley Cemetery Longueval, Somme, France. Grave XVI.D.20; Dysart War Memorial; *FA* 19.08.16; *Officers Died*; *Cross of Sacrifice Vol 1*; *FA* 12.08.16; *FFP* 12.08.16; *FA* (BMD) 19.08.16 *FFP* 19.08.16; *FA* 26.08.16; *FA* 16.09.16; *FFP* 16.09.16 *FFP* (RoH) 30.12.16; *FA* 14.07.17 (KHS War Honours) *FFP* (BMD) 04.08.17; *FA* (BMD) 18.08.17; *FFP* (BMD) 10.08.18; *FA* (KHS RoH) 29.03.19

Watson, Sidney Fairweather: 2nd Lieutenant (Gordon Hldrs [2nd]); Brother of Frank Fairweather Watson; KIA, 06.09.16, 20 years; Thornliebank, Dysart; Barony Church Plaque. Kirkcaldy High School War Memorial; Thiepval Memorial, Somme, France. Pier & Face 15B & 15C; Dysart War Memorial; *FA* 19.08.16; *FA* 16.09.16; *Officers Died*; *Cross of Sacrifice Vol 1*; *FA* 16.09.16; *FFP* 16.09.16; *FA* 07.10.16; *FFP* (RoH) 30.12.16; *FA* 14.07.17 (KHS War Honours); *FFP* (BMD) 04.08.17; *FFP* (BMD) 10.08.18; *FA* (KHS RoH) 29.03.19

Watt, William: Private (18735 KOSB [1st]); Uncle of David Grubb; DOW in hospital, 06.07.16, 31 years; 9 South Street, Dysart; Barony Church Plaque; Beauval Communal Cemetery, Somme, France. Grave F.10; Dysart War Memorial; *Soldiers Died* Part 30; *FA* 15.07.16; *FFP* 15.07.16; *FA* 22.07.16; *FA* 05.08.16; *FFP* 05.08.16 Roll of The Brave; *FFP* (BMD) 05.08.16

Watters, George Young: Private (4379; AIF; Australian Infantry [15th]); On Australian War Memorial as Waters; KIA France, 01.07.17, 33 years; West Quality Street, Dysart; Barony Church Plaque; Messines Ridge British Cemetery, Mesen, West Vlaanderen, Belgium. Grave IV.D.49; Australian War Memorial web site; Dysart War Memorial; *FFP* 15.09.17; *FFP* 28.07.17; *FFP* (BMD) 28.07.17; *FA* 04.08.17

Wright, John: Private (7037 Cameron Hldrs [1st]); Brother of Robert Wright; MIA Marne. PoW Roulers, Belgium, 25.09.14; 28 Fraser Place, Dysart/116 Mid Street, Kirkcaldy; La Ferte-Sous-Jouarre Memorial, Seine-et-Marne, France; Dysart War Memorial. Kirkcaldy War Memorial; *Soldiers Died* Part 66; *FA* 19.06.15; *FA* 27.11.15; *FFP* (BMD) 20.05.16; *FA* 03.06.16; *FFP* 10.06.16; *FA* (RoH) 17.06.16; *FFP* (RoH) 17.06.16; *FFP* 05.08.16 Roll of the Brave; *FA* 08.09.17

Young, David Wilkie: Private (180719; CEF; Canadian Infantry [7th] [British Columbia Regt]); DOW, 23.03.17, 31 years; 8 Station Road, Dysart; Barony Church Plaque; Ecoivres Military Cemetery, Mont-St Eloi, Pas de Calais, France. Grave III.K.17; Dysart War Memorial; *CBoR* Page 354; *FA* 31.03.17; *FFP* 31.03.17; *FFP* (BMD) 28.04.17; *FA* (BMD) 05.05.17

Young, George: May be George Young (92989 RFA); on Kirkcaldy War Memorial; Not identified on CWGC web site; Dysart War Memorial

Yule, Charles Whitehead: Captain (Royal Scots [13th]); 11.05.16, 27 years; Giffen Park, Dysart; Vermelles British Cemetery, Pas de Calais, France. Grave IV.E.5; Dysart War Memorial; *Officers Died*